THE
CHINESE
HUMAN
RIGHTS
READER

THE
CHINESE
HUMAN
RIGHTS
READER

DOCUMENTS
AND COMMENTARY
1900-2000

Stephen C. Angle and Marina Svensson
editors

An East Gate Book

M.E.Sharpe

Armonk, New York
London, England

An East Gate Book

Library of Congress Cataloging-in-Publication Data

The Chinese human rights reader : documents and commentary, 1900–2000 / edited by
Stephen C. Angle and Marina Svensson.
   p. cm.
Includes bibliographical references and index.
ISBN 0-7656-0692-5 (alk.paper)—ISBN 0-7656-0693-3 (pbk. : alk. paper)
   1. Human rights—China—History—20th century. 2. Human rights—China—
History—20th century—Sources. 3. Civil rights—China—History—20th century.
4. Civil rights—China—History—20th century—Sources. I. Angle, Stephen C., 1964–
II. Svensson, Marina, 1961–

JC599.C6 C485 2001   2001020699
323′.0951′0904—dc21   CIP

Printed in the United States of America

BM (c)   10   9   8   7   6   5   4   3   2   1
BM (p)   10   9   8   7   6   5   4   3   2   1

Contents

Part I. Last Years of the Qing Dynasty: 1900–1911

Part II. The New Culture Movement, May Fourth, and the Twenties: 1914–1926

Part IV. War with Japan and Civil War: 1937–1949

Part V. 1949–1975

viii

Part VIII. The 1990s

Stephen C. Angle is Assistant Professor of Philosophy at Wesleyan University. He is the author of *Human Rights and Chinese Thought: A Cross-Cultural Inquiry* (2002) and of articles on early Chinese rights thinkers and on Confucianism. His work focuses on understanding cross-cultural ethical differences and the possibilities for dialog, and on the relations between Confucianism and twentieth-century Chinese ethical and political values.

Marina Svensson is Assistant Professor at the Department of East Asian Languages, Lund University. She is the author of *Debating Human Rights in China, 1899–1999: A Conceptual and Political History* (2002), and of articles on human rights, democracy and Chinese politics. Her work focuses on the theory and practice of human rights in the PRC, legal reform, political and institutional changes, and social and political protests.

Acknowledgments

First and foremost we would like to thank those who have helped us with the translations in this volume. We are very grateful to Elizabeth A. Cole, Stephen S. Chou, and Zhou Yiyun, who produced excellent draft translations for a majority of the texts in the *Reader*. This project could not have been completed without their considerable efforts. Special thanks are also due Joan Judge, who suggested and translated the essay by Ma Weilong, and Timothy B. Weston, who suggested and translated the selection from Zhang Shizhao. Tim in turn would like to thank Shen Zhijia and Jia Jinhua for their help with his translation. The editors are responsible for the final state of all translations and for any mistakes that remain.

During this work we have also been helped and encouraged by many other people. Students in various incarnations of the class "Human Rights and Chinese Philosophy" at Wesleyan University were the initial impetus for a translation project, and we thank them for their comments on the drafts they used. For encouragement and comments on other aspects of the *Reader,* we would like to thank Chine Chan, Ron-guey Chu, Andrew Nathan, James Seymour, Sophia Woodman, and Peter Zarrow. We are also grateful to Mab Huang and Peter Huang for suggestions and help with texts from Taiwan, to James Whitman for helping us identify a number of German legal scholars, and to Keiko Kockum for help with transcribing the names of Japanese scholars. We would also like to thank Zhu Xiaomiao and Li Jian for assistance with obscure passages in some of the texts.

Some of the texts first appeared in a special issue of *Contemporary Chinese Thought* for which we acted as guest editors, and we are very grateful to Carine Defoort and Nicolas Standaert for giving us that opportunity, as well as for cheering on the book project. For useful ideas on how to pull off a work like this, we want to thank Michael Schoenhals.

Our thanks, finally, to Doug Merwin and the staff at M.E. Sharpe for working with us to bring this project to completion.

General Introduction

I. Rights and Chinese Thought

The past decade has seen a vigorous discussion of human rights both within China and between China and other nations. It is easy to think of China as a latecomer to human rights discourse, in part because during most of the post-1949 period, rights and human rights were taboo subjects in the People's Republic. In fact, however, over the last one hundred and more years China has had a rich and contested discourse about rights. By translating essays on rights and human rights from throughout the twentieth century, we aim to reintroduce themes from this forgotten discourse into contemporary debates. These essays show that the discussion of rights in China has long been motivated by indigenous concerns, rather than imposed from without, and it has been interpretive and critical, rather than passive and imitative. This introduction aims to situate the essays we have translated by discussing the terms of the discourse and then briefly sketching its history.

Until the mid-nineteenth century, there was no single term in Chinese that corresponded to the English term "rights" or its cognates in other European languages. This disparity was not accidental: classical and postclassical Chinese discourses on politics, ethics, and law were configured differently from their European counterparts, so the concerns that led to rights talk in Europe were handled in different ways in China. While there is ample discussion of privileges and powers in classical and postclassical Chinese philosophy, we find rights in none of the senses encountered in modern Western thought: no explicit claims correlative to duties; no protected claims essential to individual personhood; and no antimajoritarian trumps on the general interest. Admittedly, these are rather new and contested ideas in the West, but their roots run deep. Most conceptions of rights in the West take for granted that the human world is made up of independent individuals whose duties or personhood can be independently assessed. Classical Confucianism, along with most other Chinese schools of thought, denies that the sole unit of ethical or political assessment is the individual. Instead, theorizing begins from relationships and roles within relationships. Confucian thinkers stress reciprocal responsibilities rather than correlated rights and duties.[1]

Let us not leave you with the impression that Confucianism—or indeed, the Chinese tradition more generally—was unitary or static. During the same centuries that modern rights discourse was emerging in Europe, a number of Confucian thinkers were criticizing their tradition for inadequately recognizing and protecting legitimate self-interests. A variety of social changes underpinned these philosophical developments, ranging from increased calls for local self-rule to a flourishing commercial economy and a concomitant rise in the status of merchants. These trends helped to pave the way for the Chinese interest in and interpretation of rights when they began to read European and American texts dealing with rights in the nineteenth century.

II. The Emergence of a New Vocabulary

Discussion of rights in Chinese required new terminology, part of a tremendous surge of linguistic innovation in China and Japan during the nineteenth century. As we read texts employing this new vocabulary, it is important to keep in mind what the novel words do, and do not, represent. In Lydia Liu's study of what she calls "translingual practice" in nineteenth- and twentieth-century China, she talks of translation from a "guest language" into a "host language"—rather than the more conventional "source language" and "target language"—in order to stress the active role played by Chinese and Chinese speakers in the processes that she studies. She defines the study of translingual practice as examining the ways in which "new words, meanings, discourses, and modes of representation arise, circulate, and acquire legitimacy within the host language due to, or in spite of, the latter's contact/collision with the guest language," and argues for the appropriateness of her guest/host terminology, which we endorse, since:

> the translator or some other agent in the host language always initiates the linguistic transaction by inviting, selecting, combining, and reinventing words and texts from the guest language, and, moreover, . . . the needs of the translator and his/her audience together determine and negotiate the meaning (i.e., usefulness) of the text taken from the guest language.[2]

Throughout its history, Chinese rights discourse has continued to have complex interrelations with discussions of rights in other languages, and Chinese have increasingly participated in international discussions, for instance in the drafting of the Universal Declaration of Human Rights in 1948. We now turn to analyses of some of the terms central to the translations that follow.

One of the earliest words to stand for "rights" is *quan*, and it has retained its connection to rights down to the present day, though today it usually appears in compound terms which we will discuss below.[3] The earliest meanings of *quan* are concerned with weighing, both literally and figuratively. In a famous passage from the fourth-century B.C.E. Confucian classic *Mencius*, it is used to refer to the moral judgment of a virtuous person when deciding to bend a rule in order to achieve a greater good.[4] In many contexts, though, *quan* has no connection with morality, and often comes to mean simply power. It begins its relationship with "rights" in a translation by the American missionary W.A.P. Martin of Henry Wheaton's *Elements of International Law*. The translation, which was titled *General Laws of the Myriad Nations* (Wanguo gongfa) and published in Beijing in 1864, would prove to be quite influential on Chinese (and Japanese) rights discourse in the years ahead. The word most frequently used to translate "rights" in the *General Laws* is *quan*. *Quan* does not always correspond to "rights," however; in a number of places it is used to translate "authority." In addition, it appears as part of the compound *zizhu zhi quan*, literally "the *quan* of self-mastery," which is used to translate "independence."[5]

A Chinese reader of the *General Laws* would immediately understand that there was something special about *quan*. The *quan* of a nation or individual are not simply the powers it happens to have: it is clear that *quan* is a normative notion, dependent on reason, justice, and agreements. That is, one can talk about the *quan* a nation has to equality or independence whether or not it is equal or independent. These are things nations ought to have. Martin well understood the difficulties that readers would have with this term (and with the related term *quanli*, on which see below), writing in a headnote to a slightly later translation, which similarly dealt with international law:

> International law is a separate field of knowledge and requires a special terminology. There were times when we could not find a proper Chinese term to render the original expression, so our choice of words would seem less than satisfactory. Take the character *quan*, for example. In this book the word means not only the kind of power one has over others, but also the lot (*fen*) that moral principle (*li*) prescribes to each person. Occa-

sionally, we would add the word *li* [to form a compound], as, for example, in the expression "the original *quanli* of the common people," etc. At first encounter, these words may seem odd and unwieldy, but after seeing them repeatedly, you will come to realize that the translators have really made the best of necessity.[6]

The term that has come to be most widely used to stand for "rights" is not *quan*, but the compound *quanli*. This usage also dates back to the *General Laws* of 1864 where it is occasionally used as a direct translation for "rights." At one point in Wheaton's text, for instance, we read: "A state is a very different subject from a human individual, from whence it results that obligations and rights, in the two cases, are very different." Martin's translation puts the matter this way: "Now the various states and the multitudes of people (*shuren*) are widely different, and thus their obligations (*mingfen*) and rights (*quanli*) also have differences."[7] The term *quanli* has been discussed extensively by scholars, many of whom have pointed out that *quan* and *li* have a history of being used together in Confucian literature to mean the "power and profit" that can tempt one away from morality. Such a meaning obviously is far from what Wheaton meant by "rights," and this has led some to suggest that *quanli* was simply a bad translation for rights. The problem with calling *quanli* a bad translation, though, is its implication that the only process at work in the origins of Chinese rights discourse is a (failed) attempt to mirror and adopt Western concepts and standards. We believe that Chinese rights discourse shows a complex interaction between people discovering and interpreting foreign ideas that they take to be of universal significance, on the one hand, and people building from a foundation of native terms and concerns, on the other. Very often these people are one and the same, and the two modes of thought interpenetrate one another, as when native terms are used to explain what the foreign ideas mean. At the same time, participants in rights discourse reject many native ideas and practices, often in the name of new, at least partly foreign (universal) ideals. In addition, the discourse is extremely dynamic, developing in response to changes in both intellectual and political contexts.

One way to observe this dynamism is through the important term *minquan*. It was coined in Japan sometime in the late 1870s, and first used in Chinese soon thereafter by two diplomats familiar both with the Japanese usage and with political institutions in various Western countries. It was not widely adopted in China until fairly late in the 1890s, when reformers in Hunan, Hubei, and Shanghai began to invoke it as one of the goals of their proposed institutional changes. "People's authority" is probably the best way of rendering its initial meaning, but let us note one respect in which this may be misleading. *Minquan* was not about complete popular sovereignty. No one in China in the 1890s advocated full-scale democracy. The goal of *minquan* advocates was instead an institutionalized, consultative role in a constitutional monarchy. They saw participation in national and provincial assemblies as a means to strengthen the nation. One Hunanese reformer put it this way:

> If we do not establish a national assembly there will be no uniting the citizen's voices. . . . When asked, "What would it be like to establish a national assembly now?" we answer, "the national assembly represents the people's public duty (*gongyi*)." "But is the national assembly not then a representation of the people's authority (*minquan*)?" We say that the [imperial] order we have now received, the instructions we have taken, of the public duty to enlighten each other and revive learning is a public undertaking of the people. Considering the public duty to be a public undertaking, and the public undertaking to be a public assembly, what else can we call it but the people's authority? It precisely means the people's authority! Besides, people's authority is people's duty. "People" cannot be separated from "authority." The people devote themselves to their duty and the people engage in their own undertakings, while the ruler's authority draws together these myriad undertakings. "People's authority" is to manage our own undertakings. If the people lack authority, they cannot devote themselves to their duties. If they do manage their own undertakings, then the sovereign's authority will also reach its utmost.[8]

In subsequent rights discourse, the term *minquan* has taken on several different meanings. It features centrally in Sun Yatsen's political thought, in which context we translate it (following Sun's explicit analysis, translated below) as "people's power." Part of Sun's point is to restrict such "power" to those who embrace his party's revolutionary goals; many have followed him in restricting *minquan* to citizens (*guomin*) or to the ideologically correct. This understanding holds true of both Sun's Guomindang (Nationalist Party, GMD) and the Chinese Communist Party (CCP). Others have made it clear that they mean something quite different by *minquan*, though, in which case we translate it as "civil rights," which are regarded as applicable to all people in the country without distinction.

Renquan, the compound of "human" (*ren*) and *quan*, is the term now widely used for "human rights." For the earliest rendering of "human rights" into an Asian language, though, we again return to the *General Laws*, wherein Martin translates "human rights in general" as "the natual (*ziran*) rights (*quan*) of the people of the world."[9] Martin's equation of "human rights" with "natural rights" shows a grasp of Western rights discourse, which in the mid-nineteenth century was still much more comfortable with the idea of natural rights—which were often thought to be willed to us by God—than with the more ambiguous "human rights." The connection to a kind of divine will is echoed more explicitly in another Chinese term, *tianfu renquan*. Literally "heaven-endowed human rights," this term was used by Japanese scholars as early as the 1870s, and became widely used by Chinese around 1899. One of the earliest Chinese claims that rights derive from heaven (though not using the word *renquan*) ran as follows:

> As for "*quan*," it is not [a word for] military power, nor for bureaucratic influence. *Quan* is that with which one pursues the great norms and laws under heaven, and that with which one establishes the greatest justice and fairness under heaven. There must be something with which one accomplishes these things, and lacking any other name for it, we can simply call it "*quan*." Given that we are speaking of the great norms and laws, the greatest justice and fairness, thus *quan* must be given by heaven, rather than being established by people. Heaven gives people their lives, thus it must also give them the *quan* with which to attend to their lives.[10]

In the early 1900s, a whole range of terms was used to refer to natural and/or human rights, some of which put "heaven" in the foreground, others of which stressed "natural," and still others of which simply implied that these rights were seen as due rights (*yingxiang zhi quanli*), or as innate (*guyou*), sacred (*shensheng*), inviolable (*buke duo*), and/or inalienable (*buke paoqi*). In fact there is a strand in the Chinese tradition that has long insisted on naturalizing "heaven"—in effect making it into something much closer to "nature"—so it should come as no surprise that all these terms were used more or less interchangeably. In all these cases, even when particular authors did not view *renquan* as innate, *renquan* were nonetheless understood to be based on people's natures rather than being given by the state.

Many writers from throughout the century associate rights and human rights with the new term "personality" (*renge*), also emphasizing that rights are necessary in order to "be a person" (*zuoren*). In this context, personality does not refer to superficial qualities like whether one is an optimist or pessimist, but rather to fundamental characteristics deemed essential to full-fledged humanity. To deprive people of their rights or human rights, or for people themselves to forsake their rights, is to violate their personalities and to reduce them to the level of slaves or beasts. The term *renge* originated as a late nineteenth-century Japanese translation of European words that meant "personality," and it was quickly adopted by a number of Chinese rights theorists at the beginning of the twentieth century. Its centrality in Chinese discussions of rights can be explained by the confluence of a number of factors, the relative contributions of which are often difficult to separate. Personality in something like the Chinese sense played an important role in Western discussions of rights influenced by Hegel, and a number of these Western discussions turned out to be attractive to Chinese thinkers over the years. The resonance between *renge* and Confucian notions of personal development and humanity also cannot be overlooked, though this connection is rarely if ever made explicit.

A final term that we would like to highlight, although it entered Chinese rights discourse somewhat later than the others, is *shengcun quan*: the right to *shengcun*. *Shengcun* can be translated as "subsist," "exist," or "live," but in the context of this right, "live" and "exist" are too narrow. The right to *shengcun* is not about merely existing or merely being alive. It is about living in a fuller sense: having food, shelter, clothing, access to healthcare, and even, in some formulations, some considerable political and cultural opportunities. We will thus uniformly translate it as "right to subsistence." This right has become one of the central foci of debate both within Chinese rights discourse and in the interpretation of that discourse. Some scholars believe that this right has long been a part of the Chinese tradition. This notion is based primarily on texts like the Confucian classic *Mencius*. We believe that while this text (and others like it) clearly supports the idea that the people's well-being is something of paramount importance, to which any ruler must be committed in order to merit his position, no general notion of rights is intended or implied. The *Mencius* indicates that while people who act against a bad ruler cannot be blamed for what they do, they still do not act rightly. The stress throughout is on the ruler's responsibility to the people, rather than on any correlative right that the people might have.

Even if classical Confucianism does not ground a right to *shengcun*, this does not rule out the possibility that the very real concern we see in Confucianism for the well-being of the people might have led to an early focus in Chinese rights discourse on the right to such well-being, as opposed, perhaps, to civil and political liberties. The texts collected in this *Reader* do little to support such an idea, however. First of all, rights to civil and political liberties have been central to the significant majority of Chinese rights thinkers in the twentieth century, though some have been more willing than others to restrict these liberties when important national concerns are at stake. Second, explicit discussion of the right to *shengcun* did not begin until approximately 1920. There may well be antecedents to this explicit concern in earlier texts, and we may even be able to trace such antecedents to Confucian sources, but the fact remains that Chinese rights discourse has not focused exclusively, or even primarily, on economic issues.

One final note about the right to subsistence: in its early uses, it was understood as a right held by individuals. Some authors suggested, for instance, that in a capitalist society it entailed the right of all able-bodied people to be employed and various welfare rights for those who could not work. In more recent CCP discourse, in contrast, the right to subsistence is interpreted primarily as a collective right: rather than being a claim of individuals against their state, it is in the first instance a claim that states make on behalf of all their citizens against the world community.

III. Chronological Sketch

Last Years of the Qing Dynasty: 1900–1911

The earliest rights discourse in China was shaped and motivated by a rethinking of tradition and a search for new, more efficient ideas and methods to save China. The writings of people like Liang Qichao and Liu Shipei reveal conscious attempts to critically reflect on the Chinese ethical and political heritage in light of the new political situation in which China found itself at the turn of the last century. Their discussions of rights built upon Confucian ideas and concepts while at the same time trying to develop them by drawing on and incorporating foreign ideas. Other Chinese writers were engaged in more explicit borrowing and adaptation of foreign concepts, sometimes also turning their backs on tradition and attacking it, a tendency that would later become more pronounced. These writers felt that certain Confucian ideas and concepts were hindering China's modernization and threatening its survival. They sought inspiration in a whole range of Western philosophers, although their acquaintance with Western theories was sometimes very superficial. This early exposure to Western political theory, including human rights ideas, was influenced by and transmitted through Japan. The majority of the texts we translate in this section were thus written by Chinese who spent some time in Japan.

The Chinese student community in Japan at this time was enthusiastically engaged in translating Western political, legal, and philosophical works, in many cases relying on Japanese translations, or themselves writing pieces based upon the reading of Japanese works. Names of authors such as Jean Jacques Rousseau, John Stuart Mill, Rudolf von Jhering, and a whole range of other, today less well-known, writers fill the pages of the magazines published by Chinese students in Japan. These early twentieth-century writers regularly referred to freedoms of thought, speech, and publication in their essays, while paying little attention to economic rights. Numerous essays, two of which we have included in the *Reader*, asserted that the French, Germans, and English all had different understandings of rights, usually defending one or another of these conceptions.

The language of human rights did not attract Chinese students for purely academic reasons. These essays were penned by passionate young students for whom human rights spoke to their own situation and to the realities of Chinese society. Invoking one's rights made sense to them in the context of their struggle against their Manchu rulers. Both reformers, who wanted to restore the Guangxu emperor to the throne and resume the aborted reforms of the 1898 Hundred Days Reform period, and revolutionaries, who advocated the overthrow of the Qing dynasty altogether, accused the Manchus of violating people's innate and sacred rights to freedom of speech, assembly, and so on. The revolutionary Zou Rong, who wrote a short but influential pamphlet that electrified his readers, excerpts of which we translate here, accused the Manchus of having deprived the (Han) Chinese of their inalienable rights and called for a revolution modeled on America's. For him, as for others of his generation, it was not only a question of securing respect for individual rights; a more immediate and pressing concern was the need to safeguard national rights to sovereignty and save China and the Chinese race from extinction.

Rights and freedoms were not only demanded because they were beneficial to the nation, but also because they were regarded as necessary for individuals to live as autonomous persons and to fulfill their humanity. At the same time, the close relationship between rights discourse and nationalism can be seen in the emerging feminist discourse that took shape in China during these years. Chinese reformers and revolutionaries were eager to include women among their followers as they believed that the contribution of women was needed in order to complete the mission to save China. Many writers, both male and female, advocated equality between the sexes and equal rights for women. The language of rights was thus closely related to both personal liberation and national salvation, a trend that would continue to inform Chinese human rights debates over the coming decades.

The New Culture Movement, May Fourth, and the Twenties: 1914–1926

Throughout the New Culture and May Fourth movements, rights and human rights were central features of much progressive political and ethical theorizing. Both Communists-to-be, such as Chen Duxiu, and liberals, such as Gao Yihan, discussed and advocated rights and human rights. Rights discourse now lost most of its previous connections to the Confucian tradition, which itself came under sharp, albeit often simplistic, attack. Still, it is easy to understand and sympathize with the strong feelings that motivated these vehement attacks on tradition. Many Chinese were struggling to liberate themselves from the oppression of family and tradition and to assert themselves as autonomous individuals in charge of their own lives; they were impatient and scornful of tradition and eager to overthrow the "Confucian shop." The May Fourthers called for emancipating the individual (*geren jiefang*) and protecting personality, both of which depended on respecting human rights. They were not only seeking their own personal liberation, but like earlier generations also believed that this would be beneficial to social progress and modernization.

These were years in which Western ideas were interpreted and adopted with increasing sophistication, as numerous young people now had studied in and then returned from Western countries, and important American and European thinkers such as John Dewey and Bertrand Russell visited and lectured in China. Western influences helped to propel Chinese intellectuals in a whole range of directions. Hu Shi and Gao Yihan were prominent liberals, the former having studied extensively with Dewey at Columbia; Liang Shuming, in contrast, drew on his knowledge of Western schools of thought to criticize their excesses and advocate a revised form of Confucianism. It was also during these years that socialism and communism made inroads in Chinese society, leading to the founding of the CCP in 1921. Chen Duxiu and Li Dazhao were among the earliest converts to Marxism and they were also active in the founding of the CCP, with Chen becoming its first general secretary.

When the Western powers at the Paris Peace Conference in 1919 decided to give Japan the German concessions in China's Shandong province, it provoked Chinese students and workers to take to the streets and protest against both the decision and their own government for once again selling out to foreigners. Demonstrations and strikes swept over China as other patriotic Chinese joined them. This May Fourth movement, as it is known, served to radicalize the political environment and to disillusion many Chinese with the West, helping pave the way for communism. Although Communists have sometimes invoked human rights, they have generally taken a more ambivalent or critical position toward such rights, which Tan Mingqian's essay in Part II of this volume illustrates. Communists and liberals have nonetheless occasionally been able to unite in criticizing violations of human rights and the lack of individual freedoms, as the Manifesto of the Struggle for Freedom translated in Part II testifies. It was not only the Communists who expressed some criticisms of the language of human rights; the Nationalists were also—sometimes for the very same reasons—skeptical of both its content and its appropriateness for China. In Part II we include some excerpts from the writings of Sun Yatsen, the leader of the nationalist GMD who died in 1925. In his famous "Three Principles of the People" he seems to reject human rights, a view that is echoed by Zhou Fohai a few years later, though some subsequent writers do claim that Sun's views were more favorable to human rights than it might otherwise appear.

Starting around 1920, economic rights, including the right to subsistence (on which see above), were commonly referred to by most Chinese discussing human rights. Both negative and positive rights—in today's parlance—were seen as required for the achievement of larger goals such as personality development and communal well-being. The harmony of interests between individual and collective was regarded as both attainable and desirable, although some, like Sun Yatsen, in contrast believed that the Chinese people had too much freedom and that national salvation required the sacrifice of their individual freedoms.

The Nanjing Decade: 1927–1937

The founding of the Nanjing regime in 1927 signified the nominal unifying of China under the GMD; prior to this, China had been split up among different warlords since 1916. The United Front between the GMD and CCP, which was set up in 1923 under the advice of the Comintern, now faltered as Chiang Kaishek, the new GMD leader, turned against his erstwhile allies and began to hunt down all suspected Communists. It was the Communists who bore the brunt of the repression during the Nanjing period, but liberals were also affected since Sun Yatsen's Three Principles of the People were elevated to state ideology. The increasing repression of dissident views was thus a concern of liberals and radicals alike. The political writings of Hu Shi, Luo Longji, and Liang Shiqiu in the literary magazine *Xinyue*, two articles of which we translate here, are examples of the liberal advocacy of human rights and critique of human rights violations. Interestingly enough, their stance on human rights and demands for a constitution earned them the criticism not only of the GMD but of the CCP as well. As subsequent selections in the *Reader* demonstrate, GMD ideologists dismissed human rights as outmoded, unscientific, and unsuitable to Chinese conditions, while the Communists criticized human rights for serving only the interests of the bourgeoisie. In the early 1930s, liberals and radicals were able briefly to unite in support of the victims of the Nationalist regime to form the China League for the Protection of Civil Rights. The organization proved to be short-lived as it was fraught with tension and also suffered from attacks by the GMD.

War with Japan and Civil War: 1937–1949

With the outbreak of war with Japan, national salvation once more became the overriding concern of the Chinese people, but, as at the beginning of the century, national salvation and demands for human rights went hand in hand for many people. This is evident in the human rights movement initiated by Zhou Jingwen in 1941. Zhou argued that respect for human rights was essential for a successful struggle against the Japanese, but he also emphasized that individual rights were important in order to safeguard one's humanity and therefore could not be sacrificed with the national interest as a pretext. The Communists also demanded respect for human rights in the belief that this would help the struggle against Japan. During the 1940s, as the Second United Front between the GMD and CCP broke down—eventually leading to open civil war—the Communists were vocal in criticizing the Nationalists for curtailing civil and political rights. In many CCP-controlled areas there were also several proclamations regarding human rights. All people except traitors, regardless of their class, were granted civil and political rights, although these rights could not be used to oppose the war against Japan. Criticism of socialism was also out of bounds and political opponents were purged and harshly punished.

Despite wars and domestic problems the Chinese people were not isolated from international developments in the field of human rights. In the 1940s, Zhang Junmai kept the Chinese people up to date on discussions of human rights in the West, including work in the United Nations. Nationalist China was also an active participant in the efforts to establish a new international organization in the aftermath of the Second World War. It sent a strong delegation, including a representative of the CCP, to the San Francisco Conference which adopted the Charter of the United Nations in 1945. A GMD representative, P.C. Chang (Zhang Pengjun), then served as a vice-chair of the committee responsible for drafting the Universal Declaration of Human Rights (UDHR). When the UDHR was put to a vote on December 10, 1948, China also voted in favor of its adoption.

1949–1975

In 1949 the People's Republic of China (PRC) was founded on the mainland, and the Nationalists retreated to Taiwan. Human rights violations were frequent on both sides of the Taiwan strait during this period as the mainland was caught up in one political campaign after another and Taiwan was in the grip of a White Terror under martial law. Political opponents to the two regimes continued to invoke the language of human rights in their criticism of the regimes' brutality and repression, but often at very high costs to themselves.

In Taiwan, liberal intellectuals kept the spirit of May Fourth alive in the magazine *Free China*, demanding democracy and respect for human rights. Since Nationalist China continued to take part in human rights work in the UN, the writers in the magazine consciously referred to international human rights standards in their writings, as can be seen in the piece by Yin Haiguang that we translate here. Critics of the regime on the mainland did not have as ready access to human rights language since the PRC stood outside of the UN. During the abortive Hundred Flowers Movement of 1957, several students and others nonetheless criticized the government for violating human rights and ignoring the constitutional rights of the Chinese people. Although these writings were brief and disjointed, as our selections show, they still reveal the continuing attraction and power of human rights language. The regime's reaction to their critics in the Anti-Rightist Campaign that followed was harsh and uncompromising: more than 500,000 people were labeled rightists, lost their jobs, and were very often also sent to labor camps. The CCP's negative view of human rights is revealed in the piece criticizing the "rightists" that is translated here.

The PRC was also subjected to external criticism over its human rights record, in particular after its quelling of the 1959 uprising in Tibet. The Tibet issue was raised in the UN and by different nongovernmental organizations (NGOs) abroad, and this provoked a response from China that bears comparison to its similar response after the 1989 crackdown on the democracy movement. The motives behind the West's human rights concern were scrutinized and dismissed, and their critique regarded as an interference in China's internal affairs.

1976–1986, Including the Democracy Wall Movement

During the 1970s international human rights work underwent important developments. The two human rights covenants, the International Covenant on Civil and Political Rights (ICCPR) and the International Covenant on Economic, Social, and Cultural Rights (ICESC), went into effect in 1976, thereby strengthening international human rights law. Human rights now also became a central issue in the foreign policy of many countries at the same time as international and national human rights NGOs played increasingly influential roles in protecting human rights around the world. These global developments influenced the human rights discourse and political situation in both Taiwan and the PRC, even though their human rights discourses were of course also shaped by domestic political and intellectual developments in the two societies.

In Taiwan, the so-called *dangwai* (outside-GMD) opposition was getting stronger and more vocal, partly as a result of Taiwan's rapid economic development. Intellectuals in Taiwan continued to write on and demand human rights in the same way as members of the *Free China* group had done during the 1950s; we here translate a representative piece by Mab Huang from 1976. Human rights activism in Taiwan also took the form of more open protest, as manifested in the demonstration in Kaohsiung on Human Rights Day, December 10, 1979, which led to the arrest of many of its leaders and the eventual organization of human rights groups such as the Taiwan Association for Human Rights (TAHR), set up in 1984 by some of those involved in the 1979 protest. The GMD also realized the increasing importance of human rights in international and domestic politics and in 1979 set up its own government-sponsored organization, the Chinese Association for Human Rights (CAHR), to try to control and take the initiative on this issue; we here translate an essay by one of its founders, Hang Liwu.

The democracy wall movement in the PRC had its immediate background in domestic developments after 1976. The death of Mao Zedong and the fall of the Gang of Four paved the way for a new political leadership under Deng Xiaoping, which advocated economic reforms, rebuilding the legal system, and protecting all citizens' constitutional rights. The rehabilitation of victims of earlier political campaigns and the new assessment of the Cultural Revolution as "ten years of chaos" and "ten lost years" encouraged Chinese citizens who had suffered during those years to speak out. In the autumn of 1978 great expectations began to build up among the Chinese citizenry as these new polices were elaborated upon within the leadership, culminating in the important Third Plenum of the Eleventh Party Congress held in December of that year. Young people spontaneously began to gather at a wall in central Beijing to discuss political events and advocate further legal and political reforms. They held speeches, wrote big-character posters, and began to publish their own magazines. Human rights surfaced as one important issue in these discussions and we here publish four essays on this topic to underscore the range of opinions among the democracy activists.

This unofficial human rights discourse provoked an official reaction. As the next two selections included in the *Reader* reveal, human rights was a thorny issue for the CCP. Was human rights merely a bourgeois slogan, or could it be of relevance and use to a socialist state such as

China? Were those calling for human rights people with "ulterior motives" aiming at overthrowing the regime, or did they have a point when
they criticized the Gang of Four for human rights violations? Was it
possible to elaborate on a Marxist conception of human rights that could
be useful in the struggle against imperialism and colonialism? In the
late 1970s, these were still open questions, but as the 1980s proceeded,
the PRC's position on human rights became more affirmative. This was
in a sense inevitable, since as a member of the UN (having taking over
the membership from Taiwan in 1971), the PRC had to become more
involved in international human rights work. But affirming human rights
internationally and allowing human rights debates at home were two
different issues. Many of the democracy activists were arrested beginning in 1979 and the others grew silent as a result.

The Late 1980s: Before and After Tiananmen

Although the PRC became increasingly active in international human
rights work in the UN during the 1980s—it became a member of the
UN's Human Rights Commission in 1982 and signed several conventions during the decade—human rights remained off limits in the domestic discourse. In the late 1980s, however, as China experienced a
period of political liberalization that began in late 1988 and culminated
in the spring of 1989, human rights surfaced in both academic discourse
and more political debate. Xu Bing's essay from early 1989 is an example of an academic piece celebrating the idea of human rights, whereas
Fang Lizhi's open letter is a direct call to the government to respect
human rights and release political prisoners. In the spring of 1989 a
democracy movement of unprecedented scale developed as first students
and then ordinary citizens took to the streets to demand an end to corruption and for more open and democratic rule. Calls for freedoms of
speech, assembly, and association were frequent and drew broad support from among different groups of people. Explicit reference to and
discussions of human rights were relatively rare, however. We include
one such example of a direct reference to human rights, a manifesto that
was published and circulated in Beijing during May of that year.

It is likely that thousands of people were killed in the suppression of
the democracy movement on June Fourth, though no official or reliable
figures are available; tens of thousands of people were arrested. The
regime defended its actions by describing the movement as a "counter-

revolutionary rebellion" and those killed and arrested as "counterrevo-lutionaries" and "hooligans." It dismissed foreign criticism as interference in its internal affairs and rejected any charges of human rights violations. In view of its increasing incorporation into the international human rights regime, however, it did not dismiss the language of human rights but instead insisted that China itself was the true defender of human rights, that foreign human rights concern was bogus and insincere, and that the students had been imbued with a bourgeois understanding of human rights that needed to be corrected and replaced by a Marxist one. One of the earliest and clearest examples of such a line of reasoning is Shi Yun's article, published in early July in the *People's Daily*, which we have included in the *Reader*.

The 1990s

One result of the international criticism provoked by the suppression of the Chinese democracy movement was to make human rights an important issue both in Chinese domestic political discourse and in China's relations with the international community. The Chinese political leadership decided that more research on human rights issues was needed and that its official human rights policy needed to be refined and strengthened. To this end human rights research, both within government organs and within academic institutions, has been encouraged and supported. The first and most visible result of the government's own efforts was the publishing of a *White Paper on Human Rights* in 1991, which was followed over the years by a whole range of other White Papers. The 1991 White Paper outlined the Chinese official position on human rights, setting the parameters for both the official and other more academic discussions. Apart from the White Paper, some parts of which we reprint here, another important official document was the Chinese statement at the UN World Conference on Human Rights in 1993, which we also include. The official blessing on human rights has resulted in a formidable flow of academic articles and books on human rights. We translate a representative sample of important articles written by establishment intellectuals to indicate the breath and scope of their writings on human rights. Some scholars elaborate on official documents, while others push at the limits of the official discourse.

The official position on human rights has also met with more radical resistance and challenges from others among the Chinese citizenry. Chinese dissidents and other citizens are increasingly attracted to human rights talk and willing to take the government to task over its human rights record. We include several examples of such writings, ranging from careful and elaborate attempts to reveal the contradictions and fallacies of the official position to brief, more manifesto-like statements signed by various groups of citizens. The *Reader* ends with two texts that originate from Taiwan—a draft proposal to establish a National Human Rights Commission and a speech by Taiwan's new president on human rights. These texts illustrate the promises of human rights work, but also the need, despite developments toward full democracy, to institutionalize human rights in order to guarantee their protection.

Notes

1. The role-based nature of Confucianism should not be exaggerated, however; as a number of scholars have recently pointed out, Confucian ethics also contains important nonrelational elements. See, for example, Joseph Chan, "A Confucian Perspective on Human Rights for Contemporary China," in Joanne R. Bauer and Daniel A. Bell, eds., *The East Asian Challenge for Human Rights* (Cambridge: Cambridge University Press, 1999), pp. 217–19.

2. Lydia H. Liu, *Translingual Practice* (Stanford: Stanford University Press, 1995), pp. 26, 27.

3. For notes on how to pronounce this and other Chinese words, see "Romanization, Pronunciation, and Abbreviations," below.

4. See *Mencius* 4A:17. Lau translates it in that context as "discretion"; see D.C. Lau, trans., *Mencius* (New York: Penguin, 1970), p. 124.

5. See W.A.P. Martin, trans., *Wanguo gongfa* [General Laws of the Myriad Nations] (Beijing, 1864), vol. 1, pp. 1b, 19b, and 16a, respectively.

6. See W.A.P. Martin, trans., *Gongfa bianlan* [Introduction to International Law] (Beijing, 1878), translator's headnote. This paragraph is translated in Lydia H. Liu, "Legislating the Universal: The Circulation of International Law in the Nineteenth Century," in Lydia H. Liu, ed., *Tokens of Exchange: The Problem of Translation in Global Circulations* (Durham: Duke University Press, 1999), p. 149, though we have modified the translation somewhat.

7. See Henry Wheaton, *Elements of International Law* (London: Stevens & Sons, 1878 [1836]), p. 12; and Martin, *Wanguo gongfa*, vol. 1, p. 7b, respectively.

8. Translation based on Frederic Wakeman, Jr., "The Price of Autonomy: Intellectuals in Ming and Ch'ing Politics," *Daedalus* (1972), p. 65, somewhat modified.

9. See Martin, *Wanguo gongfa*, vol. 1, p. 9b.

10. He Qi and Hu Liyuan, "*Quanxuepian* shu hou" [Postscript to *Exhortation to Learning*], in *Xinzheng zhenquan* [A True Interpretation of New Policies] (Shenyang: Liaoning renmin chubanshe, 1994), p. 397.

Notes on Further Readings and Selected General Bibliography

Each of the texts that follow has an individual Further Reading section, in which we have aimed to supply selected secondary works on the author and the period, as well as other works by the same author or by authors expressing similar ideas. In order to satisfy both the needs of general readers and of specialists, we have included references to both English and Chinese materials whenever possible.

We have ourselves written extensively on human rights, but to avoid repetition, have chosen not to refer to our own works in these Further Reading sections. When the readings we suggest are scant, readers are particularly encouraged to look to our works, which deal with many of these texts and authors in detail. Angle has focused in particular on the philosophical aspects of the discourse, on its relation to seventeenth-through nineteenth-century developments, and on promoting a dialogue between contemporary Chinese and Western thinkers. Svensson has written on the historical and political development of the Chinese human rights discourse, tracing the concept from the late Qing dynasty until today, and paying particular attention to the interaction between domestic and international aspects of the human rights debate. The editors also maintain a companion website, which serves as a supplement to the materials contained in this *Reader*. It contains additional texts, some by authors already represented in the *Reader*, as well as other resources for learning and teaching about rights and human rights in China. It is located at: http://www.chinesehumanrightsreader.org.

In the General Bibliography below, we also list a number of other works addressing topics ranging from the relationship between Chinese culture and human rights, to China's interaction with the UN and the global community, to the relationship between human rights and international trade, and so on.

Selected General Bibliography

Angle, Stephen C. *Human Rights and Chinese Thought: A Cross-cultural Inquiry.* Cambridge: Cambridge University Press, forthcoming.

Baehr, Peter R., Fried van Hoof, Liu Nanlai, Tao Zhenghua, editors in chief; Jacqueline Smith, ed. *Human Rights: Chinese and Dutch Perspectives.* The Hague: Martinus Nijhoff, 1996.

Bauer, Joanne R., and Daniel A. Bell, eds. *The East Asian Challenge for Human Rights.* Cambridge: Cambridge University Press, 1999.

Bell, Daniel A. *East Meets West: Human Rights and Democracy in East Asia.* Princeton, NJ: Princeton University Press, 2000.

Davis, Michael C., ed. *Chinese Values and Human Rights.* Hong Kong: Oxford University Press, 1995.

De Bary, Wm. Theodore. *Asian Values and Human Rights: A Confucian Communitarian Perspective.* Cambridge, MA: Harvard University Press, 1998.

De Bary, Wm. Theodore, and Tu Weiming, eds. *Confucianism and Human Rights.* New York: Columbia University Press, 1998.

Edwards, R. Randle, Louis Henkin, and Andrew J. Nathan, eds. *Human Rights in Contemporary China.* New York: Columbia University Press, 1986.

Foot, Rosemary. *Rights Beyond Borders. The Global Community and the Struggle over Human Rights in China.* Oxford: Oxford University Press, 2000.

Hall, David L., and Roger T. Ames. *The Democracy of the Dead: Dewey, Confucius, and the Hope for Democracy in China.* Chicago: Open Court, 1999.

Kent, Ann. *Between Freedom and Subsistence: China and Human Rights.* Hong Kong: Oxford University Press, 1993.

———. *China, the United Nations, and Human Rights: The Limits of Compliance.* Philadelphia: University of Pennsylvania Press, 1999.

Santoro, Michael A. *Profits and Principles: Global Capitalism and Human Rights in China.* Ithaca, NY: Cornell University Press, 2000.

Svensson, Marina. "The Chinese Conception of Human Rights: The Debate on Human Rights in China, 1898–1949." Ph.D. diss., Department of East Asian Languages, Lund University, Sweden, 1996.

———. *Debating Human Rights in China: A Conceptual and Political History.* Boulder, CO: Rowman and Littlefield, forthcoming.

Traeholt, Anne-Marie, and Errol P. Mendes, eds. *Human Rights: Chinese and Canadian Perspectives.* Ottawa: Human Rights Research and Education Centre, 1997.

Van Ness, Peter, ed. *Debating Human Rights: Critical Essays from United States and Asia.* London: Routledge, 1999.

Weatherley, Robert. *The Discourse of Human Rights in China: Historical and Ideological Perspectives.* London: Macmillan, 1999.

Alternative Thematic Table of Contents

There are a large number of themes that can be traced through the texts in this reader. To facilitate a thematic reading, we offer here a selection of themes and indications of relevant texts. This list should not be seen as exclusive, either in terms of themes or texts related to a given theme.

**Part III. Economic Rights (Including the Right
    to Subsistence)**

Part V. Constitutional and Legal Rights

Part VI. Individual and Collective Rights

Part IX. Sun Yatsen's Ideas and Their Interpretation

Part X. Chinese Marxism and Human Rights

Romanization, Pronunciation, and Abbreviations

We have employed the Pinyin system of romanizing Chinese words throughout the *Reader*, with only a very small number of exceptions— cases in which people are so well known by an alternative romanization of their names that it would be perverse to insist on Pinyin. Examples of such exceptions include Sun Yatsen (instead of Sun Zhongshan) and Chiang Kaishek (instead of Jiang Jieshi). Most Pinyin syllables are readily pronounceable in approximately the way that an English speaker would guess, but there are some exceptions, including sounds that appear in some of the Chinese terms that we refer to the most. Here are some brief, informal suggestions on how to pronounce these syllables:

Quan, which occurs in compounds meaning "rights" (*quanli*) and "human rights" (*renquan*), is pronounced "chwuan." *Q* in general comes close to ch.

X is pronounced hs.

All syllables are pronounced, and there are no silent letters; *renge*, for instance, is pronounced "ren-ge."

We use abbreviations sparingly, and most of them should be well known. As a reference, here are a few that some readers may not have encountered previously:

CCP	Chinese Communist Party
GMD	Guomindang, the Chinese Nationalist Party, often romanized as Kuomintang.
ICCPR	International Covenant on Civil and Political Rights
ICESCR	International Covenant on Economic, Social, and Cultural Rights
PCC	Political Consultative Conference
PPC	People's Political Council
UDHR	Universal Declaration of Human Rights

Permissions

Some of the translations included in the *Reader* have been published previously, and we gratefully acknowledge the copyright holders for granting us permission to reprint them:

Qian Si, "A Criticism of the Views of Bourgeois International Law on the Question of Population." Reprinted from Jerome Alan Cohen and Hungdah Chiu, *People's China and International Law: A Documentary Study* (Princeton, NJ: Princeton University Press, 1974), vol. 1, pp. 607–610.

Wei Jingsheng, "Human Rights, Equality, and Democracy." Reprinted from James D. Seymour, ed., *The Fifth Modernization: China's Human Rights Movement, 1978–1979* (Stanfordsville, NY: Human Rights Publishing Group, 1980), pp. 141–146.

Human Rights League, "A Chinese Declaration of Human Rights: Nineteen Points." Reprinted from James D. Seymour, ed., *The Fifth Modernization: China's Human Rights Movement, 1978–1979* (Stanfordsville, NY: Human Rights Publishing Group, 1980), pp. 83–86.

Chinese Human Rights Movement Committee, Beijing, "Declaration of Human Rights." Reprinted from Suzanne Ogden, Kathleen Hartford, Lawrence Sullivan, and David Zweig, eds., *China's Search for Democracy: The Student and the Mass Movement of 1989* (Armonk, NY: M.E. Sharpe, 1992), pp. 280–281.

Fang Lizhi, "Open Letter to Deng Xiaoping." Reprinted from Fang Lizhi, *Bringing Down the Great Wall: Writings on Science, Culture, and Democracy in China* (New York: Norton, 1990), pp. 242–243.

Wei Jingsheng, "Prison Letter." Reprinted from "Dear Jiang Zemin & Li Peng: June 15, 1991" in *The Courage to Stand Alone: Letters from Prison and Other Writings*, Kristina Torgenson, ed. and trans., pp. 164–76. Copyright (c) 1997 by Wei Jingsheng. Used by permission of Viking Penguin, a division of Penguin Putnam.

Liberal Democratic Party of China, "Statement on the Issue of Human Rights in China." Reprinted from FBIS-CHI-91–222 (18 November 1991), pp. 22–23.

Xia Yong, "Human Rights and Chinese Tradition." Reprinted from Peter R. Baehr, Fried van Hoof, Liu Nanlai, Tao Zhenghua, editors in chief; Jacqueline Smith, ed., *Human Rights: Chinese and Dutch Perspectives* (The Hague: Martinus Nijhoff, 1996), pp. 77–90.

Liu Huaqiu, "Vienna Conference Statement." Reprinted from James T.H. Tang, ed., *Human Rights and International Relations in the Asia-Pacific Region* (London: Pinter, 1995), pp. 213–217.

Liu Nanlai, "Developing Countries and Human Rights." Reprinted from Peter R. Baehr, Fried van Hoof, Liu Nanlai, Tao Zhenghua, editors in chief; Jacqueline Smith, ed., *Human Rights: Chinese and Dutch Perspectives* (The Hague: Martinus Nijhoff, 1996), pp. 115–130.

Ding Zilin, Lin Mu, Jiang Qisheng (spokesperson), Jiang Peikun (drafter), Wei Xiaotao, "Declaration on Civil Rights and Freedoms." The full text of the declarations (in both English and Chinese) can be found on the website of Human Rights in China: <http://www.hrichina.org>.

Liu Qing, "Moving in the Right Direction: China's Irreversible Progress Toward Democracy and Human Rights." Reprinted from *China Rights Forum* (Fall 1999), pp. 16–19, p. 47.

Part I

Last Years of the Qing Dynasty: 1900–1911

1
On Citizens (1901)

Anonymous

"Shuo guomin" [On citizens]. *Guomin bao* 2 (1901). Reprinted in Zhang Nan and Wang Renzhi, eds., *Xinhai geming qian shi nian jian shi lun xuanji* [A Selection of Materials from the Ten-Year Period Before the Xinhai Revolution] (Beijing: Sanlian shudian, 1963), vol. 1:1, pp. 72–77.

The anonymous article "On Citizens" was published in the magazine Guomin bao *in 1901. This interesting but very short-lived magazine came out with only four issues in 1901 before publication ceased. The magazine was published under the auspices of the Chinese National Society in Tokyo. Its goal was to inaugurate a national movement in China; it advocated liberal methods to achieve this end. As the editors wrote in English in the first issue: "We are liberal, unprejudiced, and impartial reformers. We promise to tolerate all sorts of religions and we also promise to protect the life and property of all people living within our jurisdiction. What we are trying to do is to defend our inalienable rights, the rights of independence and of humanity. Self-defense is our justification; 'China for the Chinese' is our motto." The magazine discussed politics and China's dismal state of affairs. It also published articles on Western philosophy, including the first translation of the* American Declaration of Independence.

. . . What is meant by rights (*quanli*)? Nature (*tian*) gives birth to humans and endows them with the rights of personal freedom and political participation. We are, therefore, justified to concern ourselves with the executive power of the nation, to intervene in its legislative power, and to supervise its judicial power. When our nation receives benefits, we each personally benefit, and so we must use our collective strength to pursue [national benefit]. When our nation receives harm, we each are personally harmed, and so we have to pledge our lives to eliminate [national harm]. Hence, the genuine rights of citizens (*guomin*) cannot be suppressed by tyrants, cannot be infringed upon by oppressive officials, cannot be taken away by one's parents, and cannot be overstepped by one's friends. But if we hand over our individual rights on a silver platter to someone else; or if a monarch has monopolized all our rights and we do not dare to challenge him; or if a few aristocrats have privately (*si*) possessed all our rights and we still do not dare to challenge them; or if even foreigners have stolen and cheated us of our rights, and we still do not dare to challenge them; that is what is called forsaking one's rights. Those who have no rights are not citizens.

What is meant by responsibility (*zeren*)? Slaves are concerned only with their own affairs and those of their families, whereas citizens are concerned with the affairs of the nation and the race. When slaves are confronted with something they are timid and resigned. At home, they shift the responsibility onto their fathers and elder brothers; at court, onto their monarch and ministers. When all the people in a nation are like this, then no one takes responsibility (*ren shi*). When citizens are confronted by something, on the other hand, they are brave and bold. They understand that national affairs are also their own, and that their own affairs are also the nation's. When all the people in a nation are like this, then everyone takes responsibility. However, those who do not know order from chaos, are indifferent to demotion and promotion, and are unconcerned about the gain and loss, weal and woe of the nation, and only diligently and avidly seek to protect themselves and their families—such people live ignoble and degrading lives in this world and have forsaken their responsibilities. Those who do not take responsibility are not citizens.

What is meant by freedom (*ziyou*)? Freedom is, roughly speaking, not to be subject to suppression. There are only two forms of suppression: suppression by monarchical power and suppression by foreign powers. France, for example, broke away from monarchical suppression and achieved freedom, whereas America broke away from the suppression of a foreign power and achieved freedom. Those who are suppressed by monarchical power and not able to do what the French did are not citizens, and those who are suppressed by foreign powers and not able to do what the Americans did are not citizens either. In order to free ourselves from the suppression of monarchical and foreign powers, though, we first have to free ourselves from suppression by our thousands of years of indestructible customs, thoughts, education, and learning. Breaking out from the suppression of monarchical and foreign powers is the manifestation of freedom; leaping out from [beneath] thousands of years of indestructible customs, thoughts, education, and learning is the spirit of freedom. Those without the spirit of freedom are not citizens.

What is meant by equality (*pingdeng*)? Nature gave birth to humans, and originally there was no distinction between noble and base, superior and inferior. Because the strong tyrannized the weak and the many violated the few, however, distinctions between noble and base, master and slave were formed. Consequently, the rulers become masters and the ruled, slaves; the aristocrats become masters and the common people, slaves; free people become masters and unfree people, slaves; men become masters and women, slaves. This is called a nation of slavery. The situation for citizens is not the same. When one tears apart the web that binds the ruler and the ruled, then everyone becomes both ruler and ruled. When one tears apart the web that binds aristocrats and common people, then everyone becomes both a prince and a functionary. When one tears apart the web that binds free people and unfree people, then there is no such word as slave in the law, and Chinese workers overseas are no longer called "coolies." When one tears apart the web that binds men and women, both men and women have the right to political participation. Afterwards everyone is equal in the nation and each receives his or her due. When the people are equal, then one has a nation of equality. Those who are not equal are not citizens. . . .

Further Reading

Chinese concepts of citizenship are discussed from various perspectives in Joshua A. Fogel and Peter G. Zarrow, eds., *Imagining the People: Chinese Intellectuals and the Concept of Citizenship, 1890–1920* (Armonk, NY: M.E. Sharpe, 1997). For a general view of the goals and experiences of Chinese students in Japan at the turn of the twentieth century, see Paula Harrell, *Sowing the Seeds of Change: Chinese Students, Japanese Teachers, 1895–1905* (Stanford, CA: Stanford University Press, 1992).

2
On Rights Consciousness (1902)

Liang Qichao

"Lun quanli sixiang" [On Rights Consciousness]. Part 4 of *Xin min shuo* [On the New People], originally published in *Xinmin congbao*, 1902–3. Reprinted in *Yinbingshi quanji* [Complete Works from an Ice-Drinker's Studio] (Shanghai: Zhonghua shuju, 1989).

Liang Qichao (1873–1929) was a leading political thinker and publicist. His manifesto, On the New People, *was published serially in Japan, where Liang—like many other progressive intellectuals in the late Qing—lived and worked for a decade in order to avoid governmental suppression. The present essay was published in 1902 as part of* On the New People. *Liang began writing about rights as early as 1896; they came to occupy a prominent place in his theorizing after he arrived in Japan in 1898. He was influenced by the Social Darwinist ideas of Kato Hiroyuki, which can be seen most clearly in Liang's 1899 essay "The Right of the Strongest." Although some of these ideas are still present in the current essay, Liang had by this time developed a more complex position, partly through reading and interpreting the ideas of Rudolph von Jhering (1818–1892), a pioneering German legal theorist whose influence on Liang was significant, as Liang himself declares early in this essay.*

All people have responsibilities toward others that they ought to fulfill, and all people have responsibilities to themselves that they ought to fulfill. Not fulfilling one's responsibility to others is to indirectly harm the group, while not fulfilling one's responsibility to oneself is to directly harm the group. How is this? Not fulfilling one's responsibilities to others is like killing another; not fulfilling one's responsibilities to oneself is like killing oneself. If someone kills himself, then the group is decreased by one person. If there were a group all of whose members killed themselves, this would mean no less than the entire group's suicide.

What are one's responsibilities to oneself? In giving birth to things, nature (*tian*) endowed them with the innate abilities to defend and preserve themselves; all living things are examples of this. The reason humans are greater than the other myriad things is that they have not only a physical existence but also a metaphysical existence. There are numerous aspects to metaphysical existence, but the most important among them are rights (*quanli*). Animals have no responsibilities toward themselves other than preserving their lives, while in order for us who are called "human" to completely fulfill our self-responsibilities, we must preserve both our lives and our rights, which mutually rely on one another. If we do not do this, we will immediately lose our qualifications to be human and stand in the same position as the animals. Thus, the Roman Law's view of slaves as equivalent to animals was, according to logical theory, truly appropriate. (If we used a logical syllogism to make the reasoning explicit, it would look like this: [1] those without rights are animals; [2] slaves have no rights; [3] thus, slaves are animals.) Therefore, while in a physical suicide, only one person is killed, in the case of a metaphysical suicide, a whole society is turned into animals. Furthermore, the descendants of animals will continue on endlessly. This is why I say that not fulfilling one's responsibility to oneself is to directly harm the group.

Alas! I do not know how many times my fellow Chinese have willingly killed themselves!?

From where are rights born? They are born from strength. Lions and tigers always have first-class, absolute rights with respect to the myriad animals, as do chieftains and kings with respect to the common people, aristocrats with respect to commoners, men with respect to women, large groups with respect to small, and aggressive states with respect to weak ones. This is not due to the violent evil of the lions, tigers, chieftains, and so on! It is natural that all humans desire to extend their own rights and are never satisfied with what they have attained. Thus it is the nature of rights that A must first give them up before B can invade and gain them. For a human to be committed to strengthening himself or herself through preserving his or her own rights (*quan*)[1] is an unparalleled method for firmly establishing and doing well by his or her group. In ancient Greece there were those who made offerings to the god[dess] of justice. The statue of this god[dess] held a scale in her left hand and a sword in her right. The scale was for weighing the rights, and the sword was for protecting the manifestations of rights. To have a sword but no scale would be mean and wicked; but to have a scale without a sword is to make talk of rights empty and ultimately without effect. The German philosopher Jhering wrote *The Struggle for Law* (Der Kampf ums Recht). Jhering was a great philosopher of private jurisprudence who lived from 1818 to 1892. He wrote this book while he was a professor at Vienna University. In his own country, it was reprinted nine times, and it has been translated into twenty-one languages; [from these facts,] the value of this book can be ascertained. Last year the [magazine] *Yishu huibian* began to translate it into our nation's language.[2] Only the first chapter has been completed. I very much desire that they continue with it, so that this book can be used as a medicine to cure the Chinese people's extremely urgent disease. It is because the essential points of my current essay are mostly taken from Jhering's book that I have provided an outline in this fashion. Jhering writes: "The goal of rights is peace, but the means to this end is none other than war and struggle. When there are mutual invasions, there is mutual resistance, and so long as the invasions do not cease, the resistance will also not end. The essence is simply that rights are born from competition." He also says: "Rights [require] unending effort. If effort is stopped even for a moment, the rights will be annihilated." From this it can be seen that attaining and maintaining rights is in no way easy.

If one wants to attain [rights], if one wants to preserve [rights], then the place to begin is truly with rights consciousness (*quanli sixiang*).[3] The body provides the essential condition for a person's physical existence. Consider an internal organ like one's liver or one's lungs, or an external digit like one's finger or toe: If one of these were not to be right, who would not feel pain and rapidly think about how to heal it? Now bodily pain is evidence that one's inner organs have lost their harmony. It is a sign that the organ has been invaded. Healing involves warding off the invasion in order to preserve oneself. At the metaphysical level there are also invasions like this, and for one possessed of rights consciousness, as soon as one has been invaded and oppressed, the painful feeling directly and violently stimulates one, and the motive [to heal oneself], once aroused, cannot be controlled. One urgently thinks of ways to resist the invasion and restore one's former state. Those whose bodies are invaded and who nonetheless feel no pain must be apathetic and unfeeling. As for those whose rights are invaded and who nonetheless feel no pain—who would choose to be like this? Thus, for those without rights consciousness, it is acceptable even to call them "apathetic and unfeeling."

The strength of rights consciousness truly depends on a person's character. A slave can withstand any insult with equanimity, while a noble warrior would sacrifice even his head in order to clear his name. A thief can put up with any insults to his honor, while a pure business person would think nothing of exhausting his wealth in order to clear his credit. Why is this? He cannot stop himself due to the formless, psychic pain that he feels on being invaded, oppressed, or insulted. Others have misunderstood the true characteristic of rights, believing that it involved nothing more than the continuous calculation of physical, material benefit. Ah! Isn't that despicable? This is the opinion of superficial people. For instance, suppose I have an item that I took from another by force. The one whose item was taken will angrily resist [my appropriation] in court, wherein his goal is not [attaining] the thing itself, but [attaining] sovereignty over the thing. Thus, it often happens that, before a suit begins, people will announce that in previous suits all the benefit they attained was subsequently used to perform charitable deeds. If the person had been bent on profit, then why would this have been done? Therefore, this kind of suit can be called an ethical question, not a mathematical question. If it were the latter, then it would first be necessary to add things up, saying: "Can that which I attain through suing cover what I lose from court expenses? If they'll cover my expenses, then I'll go ahead; if they won't, then I'll abandon the suit." These are the thoughts and actions of a lowly person. This kind of calculation can, however, be used with regard to harm that does not have metaphysical aspects. For instance, if some object has fallen into a deep pool, and you are contemplating hiring someone to search for it, the course recommended by reason is to rely on the relative cost of the object versus hiring the searcher. One's only concern in such a case is with the benefit of recovering the item. A case in which one is disputing rights is different. One's concern in such a case is not with the benefit of recovering the item. Thus, the natures of rights and benefits are clearly opposed. If one covets the momentary ease of things before one's eyes and is concerned with [avoiding] trifling inconveniences, one cannot but view rights as useless. This is precisely where the line is drawn between personalities (*renge*) that are lofty and pure, and those that are lowly and disgraceful.

In ancient times, Lin Xiangru[4] scolded the king of Qin saying: "Smash both my head and the jade disk!" Now, given the size of the state of Zhao, how could such love be expressed for a tiny thing like a jade disk? He was saying that Qin could smash the disk, kill him, invade his territory, endanger his state, and still he would not surrender. Ah! This was nothing other than "rights!" Jhering has also said:

> If an Englishman traveling to the European continent is one day asked to pay an irrational charge by the hotel's carriage driver, in every case he will resolutely scold [the driver]. If the driver will not heed his scolding, the Englishman will struggle for justice without tiring, always preferring to extend his stay; even if his room charges were to increase as much as tenfold, he would not cease. Unknowing people all laugh at this great fool, but none of them understand that this person's struggle over a few shillings is in fact a vital part of what allows the nation of England to stand tall by itself in the world. This abundance of rights consciousness and sharpness of feelings of rights are the great reasons behind the ability of the English to establish their state. Now let's consider an Austrian whose stature and financial power are similar to the Englishman's.[5] Were he to run into the same situation, how would he deal with it? He would certainly say: "This trivial affair—how could it be worth paining myself and creating trouble?" He would toss over some money and be off. Who would know that hidden between this Englishman's resistance to parting with a few shillings and this Austrian's tossing the same shillings away there is a connection of enormous importance? All that informs several hundred years of political development and social change in the two countries lies there.

Ah! Mr. Jhering's words are profound and insightful. If my fellow countrymen were to look at themselves with regard to our generation's rights consciousness, would we look more like the English or the Austrians?

[. . .]

In general, Chinese excel at talk of humaneness (*ren*), while Westerners excel at talk of righteousness (*yi*). Humaneness is concerned with others. If I benefit others, they will benefit me—the emphasis is always the other. Righteousness, on the other hand, is concerned with oneself. I do not harm others, and they are not allowed to harm me—the emphasis is always on me. Of these two ethics, which, in the end, is correct? As for what is correct in the great utopian world (*datong*)[6] of one thousand or ten thousand years hence, I dare not say. As for today's world, though, I want to say that the world-saving great ethic is truly that of righteousness. If I manifest humaneness toward another, although this does not invade the other's freedom, since it then makes me dependent on the other's humaneness, I in effect give up my own freedom. The opportunities to act humanely are certainly many, and thus the instances in which I will be dependent on another's humaneness are similarly many, and thus its abuse could well make people's personalities increasingly base.[7] If we apply this to humane government, we can see that it is not the best form of government. Chinese people simply hope for humane government from their lord. Thus, when they run into humaneness, they are treated as infants; when they meet inhumanity, they are treated as meat on a chopping block. In all times, humane rulers are few and cruel rulers are common, and so our people, from the time thousands of years ago when our ancestors taught this doctrine, down to the present, have taken being treated like meat as heavenly scripture and earthly precept. It has been a long time since the consciousness expressed by the word "rights" was cut off from our brains.

[. . .]

Rights consciousness does not concern only the duties (*yiwu*) that one ought to exercise toward oneself; in fact, it is also concerned with the duties that an individual ought to exercise toward a general group. For instance, consider two armies engaging in battle. Soldiers in the same army are all gambling their lives in opposing a common enemy. If one person individually covets leisure and, in order to avoid strife, throws down his weapons and runs, then it goes without saying that he has sacrificed his good name and reputation. But consider: How could this man have the good fortune to still preserve his life? As long as his disastrous [example] has not been extended to the whole group, his fellow soldiers will stand in for him and fight the enemy; but if the whole army's officers and men are of the same stripe as the coward, and struggle to be the first to flee, then before it is over this coward and his whole group will be slaughtered by their enemy until none are left. What is to be chosen between an individual's giving up his rights and the flight of this weak soldier? Neither is satisfactory! Rights are continuously disturbed and harmed from without, and thus one must continuously exert one's inner strength in resistance, for only then will rights begin to be established. The strength of one's rights will be in direct proportion to the amount of effort one exerts. Consider again the previous example. Given an army of a thousand men, if one soldier among them flees, it is an extremely small matter. If, however, a hundred or several hundred men were to break ranks and run, then what would the result be? The remaining soldiers who had not fled could not help redoubling their efforts to fight hard, striving to shoulder their responsibilities and replace those who were gone, but even if they were extremely heroic and committed, their strength must have limits. What difference would it make if the fleeing soldiers were to personally stab the resolute ones with their swords? Competition for rights is just like this! If citizens cooperatively all exhaust their part of the responsibility to compete, then it will naturally be impossible for them to be invaded or oppressed. If there are people who try to avoid their responsibilities, this is as good as rebelling against the whole entity of the citizenry. How so? Doing this increases the power of the general enemy and provides it an opportunity to do mischief. Superficial observers may think that an individual's giving up his rights is no more than that person's own misery and does not influence others; how mixed up they are!

Being untiring in one's competition for rights, and the establishment and protection of rights, all rely on laws. Thus, those who have rights consciousness must take as their most important principle the struggle for legislative rights. Whenever a group has laws, no matter whether they are good or bad, they are always established by those who have legislative rights in order to protect the group's rights. The laws of citizens who are strong in rights consciousness will be ever-improving, each day getting closer to perfection. This begins with a minority, who, using the rights of the strongest (*qiangquan*), strive to benefit them-selves; after this the majority will use their rights of the strongest to resist [the others], also in pursuit of their own self interest.[8] As rights consciousness becomes increasingly developed, people's duties grow increasingly strong. Strength meets strength, rights are weighed against rights, and, thus, equal, excellent new laws are created. In the period when both new and old laws are transmitted there is often the most intense and cruel competition. When new laws appear, those who had previously relied on the old laws to enjoy special rights must necessar-ily be particularly harmed. Therefore, those who promulgate new laws are, in effect, issuing a declaration of war against those people who pre-viously had power. Out of the wrangling between progressive power and reactionary power, a great struggle arises! This is actually a general rule of the evolution of organisms. At a time like this, will the new rights and the new laws succeed or not? This will be entirely determined by the strength of the warring parties! Excellence of reasons does not come into consideration. During this transitional era, neither those who rely on the old laws nor those who promote the new can avoid receiving great harms. Try reading histories of the development of laws in the various nations of Europe and America: Which great law—whether it be the establishment of constitutions, the rejection of slavery, the set-ting free of serfs, the achievement of freedom of labor or religion—did not come through trial by fire? If the promoters [of the new laws] have among them careless, lazy, or pandering types, then gradually the move-ment will become theirs. This [mentality] "we retreat a step, you ad-vance a foot" will eventually result in the destruction of the so-called new rights. For thousands of years we Chinese have not known what rights were; we've always strictly followed the pedantic, Confucian talk of harmony. In essence, the birth of rights comes more or less together with the birth of humans. The pain of childbirth cannot be avoided. At-taining it is difficult, and we are therefore vigorous in protecting it: Be-tween citizens and rights, there is a love like that between a mother and her baby. A mother's giving birth to a child is truly like staking her life on it, and thus no one or nothing can change her love for it. Conse-quently, the rights that are attained only after a trial by fire will never be relinquished. If you do not believe me, please consider the ability of the Japanese people to protect their constitution: When compared to the ability of the English and American people, which strength is greater? Given all this, we can see that merely talking about "humane government" is not a sufficient means of establishing a nation.

Only considering humane government will not do; it goes without saying that a cruel government is still worse. In general, when people are born they are endowed with (*tianfu*) rights consciousness, which is due to innate good-knowing (*liangzhi*) and good ability (*liangneng*).⁹ And why is it that there are great inequalities—some are strong while others are weak, some lie low while others are destroyed? It always follows the history of a nation and the gradual influence of government [in making the nation inferior]. Mencius said it before I did: "It is not that there were never sprouts [on the mountainside], but cattle and sheep continuously graze there, so that it becomes barren."¹⁰ If one observes the histories of nations that have been destroyed—whether East or West, ancient or contemporary—one sees that, in the beginning, there have always been a few resisting tyrannical rule and seeking freedom. Again and again the government seeks to weed out [those resisting its tyrannical rule], and gradually those resisting get weaker, more despondent, have [their resolve] melt away, until eventually that violent, intoxicating rights consciousness comes increasingly under control, is ever more diluted and thin, to the point that any possibility of a return to its former strength is forgotten and it is permanently under control. After a few decades or centuries of this situation, rights consciousness will have completely disappeared. This definitely is owing to the people's weakness, [given which] how could the government's evils be avoided? As for this kind of government, suppose that there had been one [individual] who was able to continue his or her life pulse and exist down to the present day. [Even] if there are one or two, certainly their candles are burning low as they wait for their demise. When a government uses this method to kill people, it is really just using [the method] as a weapon to kill itself. In the suicide of a government, one does something to oneself; what is so terrible about that? If we look for the painful aspect, it is that the tragedy extends to the whole body of the nation, which cannot be saved. A citizenry is a collection of individuals. A nation's rights are formed from the rights of individuals. Thus, if one wants to seek the consciousness, feelings, and actions of "citizens," if one forgets about the consciousness, feelings, and actions of individuals, one will never find that for which one looks. Where its people are strong, one finds a strong nation; where its people are weak, one finds a weak nation. Where its people are rich, one finds a rich nation; where they are poor, one finds a poor nation. Where its people have rights, one finds a nation with rights; where its people have no shame, one finds a shameless nation. As for those who would make the three characters "shameless nation" into a technical term and hope, [on its basis], to establish their nation—is there such a possibility? Is there such a possibility?

[. . .]

Notes

1. As discussed in the general introduction, the term that we generally translate as "rights" is *quanli*. Like other authors, Liang often also uses the first character of that compound, *quan*, on its own, but with the same meaning. In such cases, as here, we also translate *quan* as "rights." Here, as often in such contexts, Liang is making use of the fact that one root meaning of *quan* is "strength." A few lines down, in contrast, *quan* is used in a different sense, to mean "weigh."

2. The first parts of Jhering's article appeared in issue no. 1 of *Yishu huibian*, in 1900.

3. As can be seen from the balance of this essay, *sixiang* does not mean thought or ideology here, but something closer to feeling or consciousness.

4. According to the *Shi Ji*, in 283 B.C.E., Lin was dispatched by the king of Zhao to take the priceless jade of the He clan to the state of Qin. The king of Qin had offered to exchange twelve cities for the jade. When Lin realized that the king of Qin planned to keep the jade without relinquishing the cities, he took back the jade disk, backed against a pillar, and made the declaration to which Liang refers.

5. Jhering wrote and taught in Austria, so uses this example to stimulate Austrians. [Liang's note.]

6. *Datong* is the phrase, rich with classical resonance, that Liang's teacher, Kang Youwei, used to identify his utopia.

7. In Western Europe one hundred years ago, caring for the poor was taken to be a governmental responsibility, and the numbers of the poor steadily increased. Subsequently people realized this pattern and corrected the policy by eliminating [the state's responsibility], and the people returned to prosperity. Gentlemen are supposed to "love the people with virtue," but I have never heard that they are supposed to indulge the people! Thus, [we see that] the best policy is to make each person able to stand on his or her own without having to rely on others. If I were to say I will support people with my humaneness, isn't that just putting them a class below myself? [Liang's note.]

8. Readers may refer to the passage on rights of the strongest in the author's *Book of Freedom*. [Liang's note.]

9. *Liangzhi* and *liangneng*, both originally from *Mencius* 7A:15. Good-knowing became a central theoretical term for Wang Yangming.

10. See *Mencius* 6A:8.

Further Reading

For biographical information and for the background to Liang's *On the New People*, see Hao Chang, *Liang Ch'i-ch'ao and Intellectual Transition in China* (Cambridge,

MA: Harvard University Press, 1971). For Liang's earlier discussion of the "right of the strongest," see "Lun qiangquan" [On the Right of the Strongest], in *Ziyou shu* [The Book of Freedom]. Reprinted in *Yinbingshi quanji* [Complete Works from an Ice-Drinker's Studio] (Shanghai: Zhonghua shuju, 1989). Another of Liang's essays from *On the New People* has been translated; see "The Concept of the Nation," in Wm. Theodore de Bary and Richard Lufrano, eds., *Sources of Chinese Tradition*, 2d ed. (New York: Columbia University Press, 2000), vol. 2.

3
On Rights (1903)

Anonymous

"Quanli pian" [On Rights], *Zhi shuo*, no. 2 (1903). Reprinted in Zhang Nan and Wang Renzhi, eds., *Xinhai geming qian shi nian jian shi lun xuanji* [A Selection of Materials from the Ten-year Period Before the Xinhai Revolution] (Beijing: Sanlian shudian, 1963), vol. 1:1, pp. 479–84.

The anonymous author of "On Rights" originally planned a sequel to this article to appear in the next issue of Zhi Shuo. *But* Zhi Shuo *shared the fate of so many other magazines put out by Chinese students in Japan in the beginning of the twentieth century, and faltered after only two issues. The article is a very interesting transitional piece. The author shows a rather thorough understanding of the discussion of rights in the West. He thus contends that the English saw rights as interest (*liyi*), the Germans saw rights as power (*weili*), and the French saw rights as "one's natural lot" (*benfen*). In his enumeration of rights, besides the usual Western rights to freedom and political participation, we also find the right to marry, which originates in the Confucian duty to continue the family line. The entire discussion of "natural lot," in fact, resonates with Confucian themes. But the author is also a strong critic of Confucianism, especially its idea of rites (*li*). In his opinion, the emphasis on rites has harmed the Chinese nation and should be replaced with the idea of rights.*

It is my agony that in my China, with her 300 rites (*li*)[1] and 3,000 formalities, all the people have sunk into submission. No one suspects that anything is wrong, however, and far too many still boast "our land is the land of propriety." This is truly deep ignorance! Humans did not originally practice the rites; sages in the savage times worked them out as a means to guide (*quan*)[2] the affairs of their age. Villains in later generations wanted to seize the power common to all (*gongquan*) and turn it into their private domain. Fearing people's disobedience, the villains made a stormy sea stormier by borrowing the name of the sages' rites to create nets to trap all the people. There is nothing more absurd than this! Is it not because people have lofty characters (*zhige*) that we are said to be the [most] spiritual (*ling*) of all things? The greatest aspects of our characters are freedom and equality; these are what differentiate us from the birds and beasts. The distinctions of superior and inferior, noble and base, by contrast, have made people lose their lofty characters. The people talk about the ritual code at every turn, worship it as a divinity and dare not go beyond it; and they prate about the great law given by the sacred kings without daring to offend against it. How ignorant they are! The rites have been established in China for more than 3,000 years, and China's feeble civility has also lasted for thousands of years. During the Han dynasty, one worried about the *xiongnu* [northern barbarians—Ed.]; in the Tang, the Khitans. There has never been a generation without worry about the foreign barbarians' invasion and disturbance, which reached its greatest height during the Jin, the Liao, the Yuan, the Northern Wei, and the Later Tang dynasties, when foreign barbarians were even able to use their military might to enslave China. Why have we never heard of any Chinese hero going out and becoming a leader over barbarians? The answer is that propriety (*li*) has made it so. Propriety exhausts our blood and spirit, ceasing only at death. Those who seized power in China were vigorous and strong when they founded their states; as soon as they were infected with China's propriety, however, defeat and destruction soon followed. I am acutely aware of its harm, and am even more grieved for my 400 million compatriots who are drowning in this one word: propriety. I contemplate it, I agonize over it, and I want to reform it.

What can rescue our people's characters and break them free from the teachings of propriety is nothing else but rights consciousness (*quanli sixiang*). The consciousness of rights leads us to care about the difference between our own rights (*quan*) and the rights of others. I do not violate others' rights, and others do not violate mine. If someone comes to violate my right, I defend myself and restore it, leaving no space for false pretense, retreat, or submission: This is the principle of rights. In our China, conversely, white flags of capitulation shadow the sun when the enemy's drum beats are heard; people forget about the foreign flags flying overhead and eat and drink in the streets; even when peace is made and the foreign armies are about to leave, the elders beg them to stay. Behold, everyone on earth nowadays is able to be our master! A nation's life or death is always measured with the depth of its citizens' (*guomin*) rights consciousness. With our citizens as they are, how can our nation ever survive? Ah, that our people are so cowardly and submissive is not without its reasons. The distinctions between superior and inferior, noble and base, have led to each person's inheriting particular responsibilities. The inferior and base would not dare interfere with matters long regarded as the concern of the superior and noble. However, we humans who live between heaven and earth have our natural rights (*tianran zhi quanli*), which cannot be taken away by [our] parents, nor can they be intruded upon by ghosts and gods in secrecy. We stand on earth side by side; who is noble and who is base? We were all given birth by heaven; who is to be respected and who is to be despised? I long for my 400 million compatriots to abolish propriety, restore their rights, and stride enthusiastically into the real world. Have they not seen the constitutions and laws in the civilized Western countries? Every article, every word is made for protecting their citizens' rights, like a loving mother protects her son, always concerned lest he take sick and die. This is also the reason why the white man is running wild on Earth.

People cannot stand and walk all alone: They must have family, society, and the state to support them. Family, society, and state all come about from the integration of people. On the one hand, people are the mothers of family, society, and state; these cannot be established without people. Family, society, and state are, on the other hand, the mothers of people, who cannot live without them. Since family, society, and state are common properties owned by all people, people have duties (*yiwu*) toward these groups that [the people] must exhaust if they are to live amid [the groups]. If they do not, family, society, and state will one day no longer exist, and the people will soon follow them in extinction. What are duties? They are the inside of rights. There must be rights before there can be duties. To embrace rights is to embrace the foundations of duties, and there is no such thing as embracing duties without embracing rights. When all the citizens fail to recognize the importance of duty and renounce their duties to each other, isn't wishing for the nation's prosperity then like climbing a tree to catch fish? When 400 million people are busy splitting themselves into 400 million nations, forgetting about that which unifies them, isn't achieving national prosperity then [very] difficult?

Things have their beginnings and ends, their outside and inside. Laws are the outside of rights. Leibniz, the great German scholar said: "The science of laws is the science of rights." How piercing a remark it is! The outside of rights are laws, and the inside of laws are rights; the two sides cannot be divided. Now, some may wonder, do laws and rites not have similarities? Rites are instituted by sages, and laws are established by legislators; neither emerges from nature, but is instead made by the power of man. The essences of laws and rites are, nevertheless, as far apart as heaven and earth. Rites divide people into superior and inferior, noble and base, and lead to differentiation and divergence. Under their restrictions, everyone has to submit to elaborate formalities—to the extent that even those in intimate relationships, such as those between father and son or husband and wife, are alienated from one another. This is the essence of rites. The essence of laws is, by contrast, taking equality as quintessence and ruling out the justification of repression or violations of freedom. Rites have cultivated the attitudes of submission and obedience, such that subordinates must obey everything, regardless of how unseemly and how unlawful it is, as long as it is from the superior. A ruler can behave irresponsibly, yet his subjects are not allowed to be disloyal; a father can be loathsome, yet his son is not allowed to be unfilial. These are examples of what happens when importance is attached to rites. Alas, what an extreme of submissively obedient servility! As for laws, their hundreds of articles all originate from the principles of freedom and equality. Ruler and subject, father and son, husband and wife, man and woman, all are equals, without the distinction of aristocrat and commoner or slave and free man. People have the right of equality; people have the right not to be subject to others. How great is this rights consciousness! In this age of struggle for survival, rights are sharp weapons in one's struggles. Today, the monarchical power is not yet gone and the threat of foreign powers is already beginning; without rights to resist them, on what can we rely in order to survive on this tiny planet? Despite our numbers, on what will we live? Now I am going to illustrate the principles of rights, in the hope that it will attract a little attention from my fellow citizens.

The Definition of Rights

What are rights? Western scholars have all sorts of theories, each with its strengths and weaknesses. I have chosen to develop the French scholars' position. When the goal of rights, the function of rights, and the substance of rights are illuminated, the definition of rights will be clear.

The Goal of Rights

What is the goal of rights? It lies in the completion of human nature. Man has physical senses of the ears, eyes, mouth, nose, four limbs, and five internal organs, as well as psychical senses of intelligence and thought. The actions of these senses are like those of a machine that cannot stop as long as its engine works. That is to say, the eyes cannot help but see, the mouth eat, the ears hear, the nose smell, and the brain think. The ears, eyes, mouth, nose, and brain all have their natures, and hearing, seeing, thinking, and so on, are the functions through which they are completed. When the functions work to their proper degrees, human nature is complete, and human life achieves its goal.

The goal of human life is to complete human nature, and this is a universal principle regardless of time and location. The method to achieve this goal must, then, be measured by the level of evolution of the human race. How is this to be achieved? Shi Nuyou[3] notes: "All human endeavors come from humans and return to humans; all enterprises are undertaken by humans, and their goals are inevitably to satisfy human needs." [Herbert] Spencer also pointed out: "By knowing an individual one can understand society and all its phenomena, because social phenomena are just external manifestations of the individuals' natures." How insightful are these two scholars' words! Religion, morality, politics, science, industry, and trade all originate from and return to human nature as their home. Is it not the goal of agriculture, industry, and trade to supply us with food, clothing, housing, and transportation? Is it not the goal of knowledge to enlighten our intelligence? Is it not the goal of medical science to remedy our illnesses? Is it not the goal of religion to pacify our hearts? Is it not the goal of politics to protect our well-being? Is it not the goal of war to fulfill our desires to outshine others, and that of marriage to satisfy our feelings of love? The goal of every human endeavor is to complete one part of human nature; human nature is so precious! It is like a woman of matchless beauty who is adored by many suitors. All want to marry her and bring her home to the wedding chamber. They come from everywhere to vie for her, while the beauty stands amid them, the object of everyone's thoughts. Human nature's relation to all human endeavors is like the beauty's to her admirers, and this is the reason why humans are noble.

The goal of rights is, like those of religion, politics, and so on, to complete a part of human nature, but rights, as humanity's safeguard, seem to be more valuable than politics, agriculture, trade, and the like. The ancients said: "Ritual propriety is more important than fulfilling the desires for food and sex."[4] I would say: "Without rights to support us, our lives themselves are in jeopardy; how can we be concerned with food and sex?" I am puzzled as to why we Chinese know only the importance of fulfilling the desires for food and sex, and fail to grasp that we ought to value rights. As a result, our property is plundered and our wives and children are abused and killed. How sorrowful!

The Function of Rights

How sorrowful! The descendants of the Yellow Emperor and the Holy Farmer, who take submissiveness as their teaching and forbearance as their scripture, all are quiet slaves. Lou Shide's "letting the spit on his face dry of itself"[5] and Zhang Gongyan's "The Hall of a Hundred Forbearances"[6] are our representatives. If you can crawl between someone's legs and become a laughingstock in the streets, you are regarded as a hero.[7] If someone slaps your left cheek and you turn the right one, you are then called a gentleman. Alas! How can Chinese heroes and gentlemen be so submissive? The reason is, I believe, that the pages of the ancient sages and kings' decrees, regulations, and codes are filled with words of prohibition, but words of encouragement are very scarce. They told you not to go beyond the restrictions, not to commit adultery, not to impose on others what you yourself do not desire.[8] "Do nothing" (*wuwei*) is the doctrine.[9] Never is it said that when your rights are violated by others, you have to restore them. Is it not owing to this lack of positive support that people remain forbearing and modest without being able to break through? People fail to recognize that the words of the sages were intended for use with respect only to one's own race and group, but never with respect to other nationalities and races. What sort of age is this, when we take forbearance and submissiveness to be the noblest character? Throughout the land, all of our texts, both at home and in school, laud forbearance and submissiveness as great virtues. We struggle to surpass one another in our cultivation of this character. What sorrow! Is it not appropriate that Westerners call such people "quiet slaves"? Do we Chinese want to be quiet slaves, or resolute free men? If you want to remain quiet slaves, there is no discussion. If you want to be free men, however, then you must know the function of rights.

What are the functions of rights? They are competition and compulsion. Competition is the sign of a nation's prosperity and power. When humans are born, there are none but who want to satisfy their desires. Desires and the desired things are infinite, but the resources on earth are finite. Because of this contradiction between infinite desires and finite resources, people deceive and bully one another, invade one another's property and seize things back and forth. The principle of competition is born from these struggles. As polishing a mirror makes it brighter, intensified competition promotes the ceaseless development of people's thought and intelligence. The most brilliant and talented Chinese were most numerous long ago in the periods of the Spring and Autumn, the Warring States, and the Three Kingdoms; the lack of competition since then has led to an enormous decline in talent. The European powers started with military competition, followed this with competition over knowledge, and today competition has come into all areas, including politics, law, agriculture, industry, and the arts—yet China still rests content with propriety and yielding! In this world of evolution, the ones who struggle to survive are superior, while the ones who do not are inferior. We love the virtue of submissiveness, but what can we do with those who do not? Submissiveness is, in reality, the foundation of the weak and the inferior. Our vast fertile land is soon going to be the white man's colony! What sorrow!

What does it mean to compel? To compel means to control others instead of to be controlled by others. Each person's rights have their dominion, and one [person] cannot intrude upon the rights of another. When someone commits a great wrong and violates the universal principle of natural rights (*tianfu renquan*) without scruples, we must defend [the principle] and endeavor to restore it. Despite our limited power and wisdom, we have to fight desperately without hesitation. Life comes from the victory over death; the life that has not endured this ordeal is not a life but an ignoble existence. Can we call those, whose rights are not protected, whose nature is incomplete, full-fledged persons? Those who are controlled by others lose their rights; those who have lost their rights do not have complete human natures. Those who cannot control others must be controlled by them—there are these two possibilities only, and compulsion thus cannot be neglected for even a day. Louis XIV is an example of a monarch who violated the people's right of compulsion; the Austrian chancellor Metternich is an example of an administrator who violated the right as well. The power of compulsion is so great; how can we allow the lowly tradition of forbearance to continue in this world?

The Substance of Rights

There have been various interpretations of the substance of rights: English scholars promote the theory that the substance of rights is interest (*liyi*), while German scholars argue that it is power (*weili*). I am not going to lay out all these opinions here, but shall confine myself to the ideas of the French scholars. According to this view, the substance of rights is a person's natural lot (*benfen*).[10] People in this world have not only their physical beings but also their natural lot, [which lays down] what they ought to do and ought not to do. What ought one to do? Those things discussed above that complete human nature. What ought one not do? Those things that harm others. Together, completing one's own nature and not harming others comprise our natural lot. Natural lot is therefore the substance of right, and rights originate from natural lot. It is people's natural lot to preserve their physical and spiritual beings, and so they have material rights. It is people's natural lot to produce subsequent generations, and so they have the right of marriage. It is people's natural lot to play roles in national politics, and so they have the right of political participation. It is people's natural lot not to be controlled by others, and so they have the right of freedom. All these rights originate from our natural lot. When one fulfills one's natural lot, despite one's limited capacity, one is never harmed or violated. Under these circumstances, even the inscrutable creator would retreat into powerlessness.

The above three points have thus made the definition of rights clear. I will now conclude: Rights are that through which we compete with and compel others, in order to complete our human natures. The storm on this continent is becoming wilder and wilder; the white men are everywhere. What rights do my poor compatriots have when their wives, children, and property are being taken from them, and national doom and racial extinction are nearing? Think of it, my dear reader!

Notes

1. Depending on context, we translate *li* as "rite(s)" or "propriety."
2. *Quan*, which we translate as "rights" when it is intended as an abbreviated form of *quanli*, has root meanings of "weigh" and "power." The latter meaning is

used a few lines farther down; here the idea is that the rites were used to weigh choices in savage times, and thus to "guide" people.

3. Identity unclear.

4. See *Mencius* 6B:1.

5. According to the *Old History of the Tang Dynasty*, Lou Shide and his younger brother had a discussion about the importance of being forbearing. The younger brother said: "I see. If someone spits on my face, I just wipe it (without showing any sign of being offended)." "That is not enough," Lou Shide said. "Wiping the spit is still opposing the other person's anger. Just let it dry of itself."

6. Zhang Gongyan (or Zhang Gongyi), a man in the Tang dynasty, whose family of nine generations lived under the same roof. When an emperor asked Mr. Zhang how he could ever manage such a complicated matter, the latter said nothing but wrote down the character *"ren"* (forbearance) more than a hundred times.

7. This is a story in Han Xin's (b.?196 B.C.) early life. A scoundrel challenged Han Xin to crawl between his legs and Han did it without hesitation. He later became a general who helped establish the Han dynasty.

8. See *Analects* 12:2, 15:24.

9. "Do nothing" is a fundamental idea in Daoism, wherein it is understood as performing no unnatural action rather than as being completely passive.

10. The author's use of the term *benfen* is a bit confusing in this text. It may have been influenced both by an early Japanese gloss for rights and by Confucian ideas. In 1862, Tsuda Mamichi had translated the Dutch term *naturregt* into Japanese as *tenzen no honbun* (*tianran zhi benfen* in Chinese), although this gloss does not seem to have become widely used in Japan. Fukuzawa Yukichi, in a work written in 1878, had also discussed rights in relation to the notion of *bun* (*fen*). For the Japanese context, see John Allen Tucker, "Confucianism and Human Rights in Meiji Japan" (paper presented at the East–West Center Conference on Confucianism and Human Rights, Honolulu, Hawaii, 1996). An article in *Zhejiang chao* in the same year as the current essay (1903) translated "duties" as *benfen* and "obligations" as *yiwu*, although it did not analyze the differences. In an article reprinted in *Dongfang zazhi* in 1906, a distinction was made between *yiwu*, referring to duties held by an individual in relation to the state, and *benwu*, which were understood as duties between individuals. Zhang Shizhao, in the article translated below, also makes use of the term *fen*, in talking about people having the right to enjoy *xiangdang zhi fen* (their appropriate lot) as citizens.

Further Reading

For information on the Chinese discusssion on human rights during this period, see He Yimin, "Lun Xinhai geming qian jindai zhishi fenzi renquan de juexing" [The Awakening of an Understanding of Human Rights Among Modern Intellectuals Before the Xinhai Revolution], in Hu Weixi, ed., *Xinhai geming yu Zhongguo xiandai sixiang wenhua* [The Xinhai Revolution and Modern Chinese Thought and Culture] (Beijing: Zhongguo renmin daxue chubanshe, 1991), pp. 64–83.

4

The People's Legal Right to Freedom (1903)

Zhinazi (Pseudonym)

"Falüshang renmin zhi ziyou quan" [The People's Legal Right to Freedom], *Zhejiang chao* 10 (1903).

This essay was published in the magazine Zhejiang chao, *which was put out by students from China's Zhejiang province who were studying in Japan; the magazine lasted only one year. The essay draws extensively—and to some extent, critically— on nineteenth-century German jurisprudence, and bears comparison with Text 2, above. Like Liang Qichao, the present author stresses the need to develop "rights consciousness." Also like Liang, we see here some ambiguity over the ultimate justification of rights: we are told in no uncertain terms that rights come from state law, but also that there are rights that "civilized" people know they "ought" to enjoy, and thus demand their states codify into law. It is important to note that the specific freedoms to which the author thinks people ought to have rights are all what we would now call civil and political rights.*

The right to freedom (*ziyou quan*) is one of the rights (*quanli*) that people hold against the state (*guojia*). If we examine the history of Europe, we will see that this right could not have been obtained if [European] states had not gone through numerous revolutions and their people had not gone through endless bloodshed. Uncivilized, despotic states feared only one thing: the freedom of their people, which would be able to limit the states' despotic powers. So long as the people's knowledge was deficient, their intellectual and physical strengths did not suffice to defy their states, and therefore they could not but lower their heads and obey [their rulers]. As people became more civilized, and also as they were pushed by the trends of the times and pressed by social changes, they were no longer willing to be fooled and manipulated. They mounted opposition movements aimed at recovering the rights that they ought to enjoy (*yingxiang zhi quanli*). The people of modern civilized countries are all [able to] bustle about under the aegis of their constitutions. Their states not only do not dare to interfere arbitrarily, but actually pay particular attention to protecting them. Isn't all this the result of fantastically ardent efforts by their predecessors?

Alas, our people always speak of freedom, freedom. Yet what after all is the right to freedom? And what eventually distinguishes the limit of freedom? I am afraid that our people are still utterly ignorant of these things. If we want to speak of the right to freedom, we cannot but start by explaining the definition of rights.

What are rights? Western scholars have more than one theory. Here I will raise four of the major theories. The first theory says that a right is that which is institutionalized by law and has coercive power. This was introduced by the German philosopher Kant, and jurists followed and echoed him.[1] The representative figure is A.J. Thibaut.

The second theory maintains that a right is the people's will (*yisi*) as acknowledged by law. This was also propounded by a German philosopher, Hegel, and other jurists followed and echoed him as well. The representative is Windscheid. Many scholars, however, object to this view, saying that if will is taken to be the [basis of] rights, then nonadults, legal persons, and the like will not be the subjects of rights. Thereupon the doctrine of utilitarianism (*liyi zhuyi*) emerges.

The third theory speaks of rights as the interests (*liyi*) that the law protects. The origin of this view dates to long ago. The German jurist Rudolph von Jhering advocates it. People who oppose it say that interests can satisfy our desires and are the most valuable things to us, but interests have both monetary and nonmonetary values. Which kind of value do "rights" have? To say that rights are interests seems to conflate the two. One of the maxims of Roman law says that rights go together with interests; if there is no interest, there is no right to litigate. Despite the fact that this principle was enshrined in Roman law, we should not on this basis conclude that interests simply are rights.

The fourth theory holds rights to be power (*shili*). It is advocated by Dernberg, who maintains that a right is a power given by law. Quite a few scholars refute this view and here we do not need to spend too many words on it.

These four views each have their biases; none can be called a true and lasting theory. Now I will elucidate that which I have come to deeply believe can be regarded as a [superior] model. A right is an interest that a personality (*renge*) possesses, as allowed by the law, with regard to a state or an individual. In general, this captures the essence of rights. Nevertheless, scholars still debate about what counts as "public rights" (*gongquan*) and "private rights" (*siquan*). One person puts forward a theory and then another refutes it; there is no consensus. I do not have time to enumerate every one of them. Based on what people in the realm of law today have agreed upon, rights in a relationship between individuals are called private rights, while rights in a relationship between state organizations and individuals are called public rights; the right to freedom is one of the public rights. There are, however, more than a few opposing arguments. I will briefly list them below for your reference.

Max Seydel maintains that the function of the right to freedom is to regulate state power (*guoquan*), not to regulate the rights of people. This is perhaps to say that freedom is no more than that which the law does not prohibit; it is not any special kind of freedom. C.F. Gerber says that the right to freedom does not delimit the rights of people. He believes that the right to freedom does not serve a specified purpose. Otto Mayer says that the right to freedom is not a true right; it is only supposed to restrict the state's rights of control (*zhipei quan*).

These few theories all follow the school of natural law. They do not understand the right to freedom as a right, nor are they aware that the right to freedom is by no means a heaven-endowed freedom prior to the existence of a state, as the school of natural law maintains. Neither is it the freedom of human interactions as physiology suggests. [In fact,] the concrete scope of the right to freedom is completely specified by law. The freedom of an individual with respect to the state can become a legal freedom only if it is acknowledged by the state, and thus put into the sacred, inviolable constitution. So long as the state's constitution does not cease to exist, people's rights to freedom will not vanish, for the state is under this inviolable duty. [After all,] rights are spoken of in contrast to duty. What else could it be that causes the state to have duties, if not rights? Such Eastern and Western scholars as Georg Jellinek, K. Walcker, Georg Meyer, Douzhinaier,[2] and Fukushima Giichi all agree with this opinion, [so] it is very believable and unquestionable. Here I list the kinds of rights to freedom below.

1. The freedom of residence and movement. The most essential among people's rights to freedom is the right of residence. The state is composed of people. Whoever resides in the territory of a state is its subject. Therefore the state allows its people to freely move without any restriction within its territory.

2. The freedom of physical security. In a civilized country people have noble personalities. Even a hair or a tress should not sustain any unreasonable restraint, so the state does not dare to improperly act to arrest, imprison, or punish anyone. Crimes in violation of the law, of course, are separate matters.

3. The freedom of safe residence. "Residence" is the place that people use for their daily living. Legally speaking, "[safe] residence" means not to damage a person's safety within his abode. So long as people are not suspected of a crime, the state ought not to intrude upon and search their residence without a reason, in order to protect their safety.

4. The freedom of secrecy in correspondence. "Correspondence" is when a particular person conveys his ideas to another particular person in written words. It is sealed carefully, unlike public mass advertisements that are intended to be known to all people. Thus the state's administrative organs, except as required by law, should not purposely open correspondence or show it to others, no matter what the enclosed content.

5. The freedom of assembly and association. "Assembly" is the gathering of a large number of people for a common end. "Association" is a contractual relationship; in order to fulfill their common end, a large number of people gather and contract to permanently and continuously seek their objective. During the old despotic era, the state prohibited and forcefully guarded against this right, fearing that people would initiate acts of resistance. In modern constitutional states, on the other hand, so long as the peace and order of the state and society are not harmed, the state should never interfere with this right.

6. The freedom of thought and expression. Certainly the law has no way to interfere with a person's inner thoughts. Only after the thought is published externally does it become the object of law and the state is able to limit or protect it. That which is put forth orally is called speech; that which is put forth in written words or illustrations is called writing; that which is put forth using stone-block, wood-block, or lead-block [printing] is called printed matter. So long as they do not transgress the limits of law, the state ought not arbitrarily interfere.

7. The freedom of ownership. The right to ownership (*suoyou quan*) is a relation between individuals in public law. As stipulated in the constitution, the right to ownership has two meanings. The first restricts the operation of the state's power, making it unable to violate people's freedom of ownership. The second protects people's freedom; if the state's administration violates [someone's property], [he or she] is permitted to be compensated by way of an administrative lawsuit.

8. The freedom of worship. Prior to the eighteenth century, the power of the Roman Pope was unlimited. Even all the rulers of European countries were subject to his power. Therefore politics and religion were

hardly separable, and his strength was able to force the people not to convert to other religions. In the modern age, after many revolutions and with the advancement of civilization, the state's politics and religion have become absolutely separate and independent. The state grants its people freedom of worship and does not interfere, though [religious activities] should not cross the boundary of peace and order.

In all, then, there are eight kinds of rights to freedom. They are set down in the law code, declared in the constitution, and all have sworn to comply and do not dare to disobey. But where are these rights [actually] respected?

Alas, when I think about this, I cannot help sighing deeply. Please consider: have the four hundred million people of our China completely enjoyed these rights? Should our citizens desire to put into practice their freedom of assembly and association, and so gather a large number of people to form an organization, the government would certainly label it as a rebellion, uprising, or riot, and would employ its despotic force to dispel them, arrest them, imprison them, and would not stop until all are stamped out. Should our citizens desire to put into practice their freedom of thought and expression to make manifest the common principles of mankind, the government would definitely hold [the principles] to be rumors, heterodoxies, insults to the court, or sacrilege, and would proscribe them, destroy them, and would not be content until the principles can no longer be heard.

I do not blame the arbitrariness of the government, though; I only blame the ignorance of our citizens. Which among the so-called civilized governments was not barbaric and despotic before their reforms? Why is rights consciousness (*quanli sixiang*) so weak in the minds of our citizens? Why do they treat rights so casually that they do not fight to reform the law, to stipulate clearly the limits of law, and hence to recover the rights due to them (*yingyou zhi quanli*)?

I cannot but blame those today who call themselves advocates of freedom (*ziyouzhe*). They do not have a sense of the civic consciousness (*gonggongxin*) nor a capability for self-rule (*zizhi*). They make the destruction of the community their purpose and regard the transgression of rules as freedom. They indulge themselves in individual selfishness and harm the rights of the commonality. Even up to the day they lose both fortune and honor, they still speak boastfully to others about "freedom, freedom," whereas they have degraded the value of freedom to nothing. Could they possibly know that what is called freedom and what are called rights in civilized states are [in each case] acknowledged by the law that has been approved publicly by the citizens? People together make up a state. If the elements of a state are all [passive and lacking in rights consciousness,] as I described above, then there will never be a day when the citizens recover their freedom. If the elements [have no civic consciousness nor sense of self-rule,] as I just described, then there will never be a day when the citizens peacefully enjoy their freedom. Civilized countries have no people who merely fulfill duties, nor do they have governments that exclusively enjoy rights. Those under heaven most capable of fulfilling duties while not enjoying rights are slaves and animals. If our citizens are willing to be slaves or animals, and allow a shepherd to reprimand them and thrash them, then there is nothing more to say. Otherwise, they should rise up at once.

Notes

1. We have attempted to identify all the scholars cited in the essay—thanks in large part to the help of James Whitman of Yale Law School—though some identifications remain tentative.
2. Identity unknown.

Further Reading

Richard Minear has written a careful study of the interpretation of German law by a prominent Japanese jurist in the late nineteenth century; see *Japanese Tradition and Western Law* (Cambridge, MA: Harvard University Press, 1970). For an authoritative account of the German tradition on which the present author draws, see M. Stolleis, *Geschichte des oeffentlichen Rechts in Deutschland* (Munich: Beck, 1988–92), vols. 1–2.

5
The Revolutionary Army (1903)

Zou Rong

Geming jun [The Revolutionary Army]. Originally published in Shanghai, 1903. Reprinted in Zhou Yonglin, ed., *Zou Rong wenji* [Collected Works of Zou Rong] (Chongqing: Chongqing chubanshe, 1983), pp. 59–62, 71–71. For textual variants, the editors have consulted the Chinese text reprinted and translated in John Lust, ed. and trans., *The Revolutionary Army* (Paris: Mouton & Co., 1968).

Zou Rong (1885–1905) received a classical education but, uninterested in an official career and frustrated by the irrelevance of his schooling to the day's issues, traveled to Japan in 1901 to further his studies. There he wrote The Revolutionary Army, *which was published in Shanghai after his return to China in 1903. The* Revolutionary Army, *which was scathingly critical of the Manchu rulers of China, enraged government authorities who sought his immediate arrest. Zou was protected by authorities of the International Settlement in Shanghai, and eventually sentenced to only two years in jail. Be this as it may, Zou contracted an illness in prison and died in April of 1905.* The Revolutionary Army *is far more than an anti-Manchu racist tract. It advocates political and social revolution, and Zou's account of the justification for and goals of these revolutions rests in no small part on natural rights and independence, as discussed in the two chapters from the work that we translate here.*

Revolutionary Education

There are barbarian revolutions and there are civilized revolutions.

Barbarian revolutions are the revolutions that destroy without construction; violent and unrestrained, they are enough to create reigns of terror. The Boxer Rebellion in 1900 and the activities of the Carbonari secret society in Italy are [examples of barbarian revolutions] that brought added chaos and misfortune to the citizens (*guomin*).

Civilized revolutions are the revolutions that destroy as well as construct. They destroy in order to construct, aiming to provide the citizens with all [their] rights (*quanli*) of freedom, equality, and autonomy (*zizhu*). They bring greater happiness to the citizens.

Revolution is the natural duty (*tianzhi*) of citizens. It is rooted in and originates from citizens and is not the private property of a few individuals. It may well be asked: Why are we making revolution today? The answer is that there surely are devils that hinder our citizens [from enjoying their] natural rights (*tianfu quanli*). We have to remove them and restore our natural rights. Revolutions remove misfortunes and seek happiness. To remove misfortunes and seek happiness is something to which my compatriots ought to pay homage. To remove misfortunes and seek happiness is a civilized revolution, to which my compatriots ought to pay even more homage.

If one wants thorough construction, one must first engage in destruction. If one wants thorough destruction, one must first engage in construction. This is a timeless principle. The revolution we are carrying out today is a revolution that destroys for the sake of construction. If one wants to engage in destruction one must first have the means of construction. The great man Giuseppe Mazzini, the founder of Italy, said: "Revolution and education go hand in hand."

I therefore appeal to my compatriots for "revolutionary education." This means that: "Education must precede revolution, and revolution must be succeeded by education."

Today's China is a nation without education. I have no heart to put down on paper all the ugly, mean, loathsome, and disgusting phenomena in society, but honor them with a posthumous title, with the remark: If the five sense organs are not perfect and the four limbs are not complete, then a man's personality (*renge*) is not complete. I have heard that education in France before its revolution was as developed as that of her neighbors, and that education in America before its revolution was as developed as that of England. The pasts of these prospering nations are things of which we Chinese cannot even dream. I have heard that education in India before its subjugation was as absent as it is in China, and that when Judea was consumed, its education was also as lacking as is China's today. China has arrogated to itself the pasts of these subjugated nations. But there is more to it than this. When we read the history of the revolutions [leading to] the independence of the thirteen colonies in America, the federation of Germany, and the unification of Italy, [we learn that] they all aroused people's enthusiasm so that war was declared against the monarchy, the mother country overthrown, and the aristocrats killed. They advocated freedom and forcefully upheld self-rule (*zizhi*). Internally they prepared for war, and externally they resisted strong neighbors. Although these were times when these nations were ravaged by successive wars and rotten to the core, [nonetheless] from parliaments and constitutions at the top to regional institutions at the bottom, they continued making great plans, administering the nation, and [thus] setting the highest standards for humanity. In a single instant, these valiant revolutionary fighters, heroic founders of nations, great men who shed their blood, were able with their morality, wisdom, and learning to shake out their clothes at the summit of the Kunlun mountains and to bathe their feet in the Pacific Ocean.[1] I worship them, I adore them! When I inquire into the reasons for these feats, I conclude that it can be nothing but education.

This was the case with Washington and Napoleon, who are worshipped as heroes all over the world. But if there had not been millions of Washingtons and Napoleons who responded to their call, what would Washington and Napoleon have done then? Even those with more ability, knowledge, or learning than Washington and Napoleon—what could they have done [alone]? There are known heroes and there are unknown heroes. Although Washington and Napoleon threw caution to the winds and shed their blood, they were just the representatives of innumerable unknown Washingtons and Napoleons. In today's China, a single Washington or a single Napoleon cannot deal with our problems. We have [first] to create innumerable unknown Washingtons and Napoleons, if the [suffering] masses are to be aided. I see many committed intellectuals (*zhishi*), who are patriotic and concerned about the times, always deeply reflecting [on its problems], who esteem themselves as Washingtons or Napoleons; whether their knowledge is superior to that of Washington or Napoleon I dare not say, but [in any event], I can only respect known heroes. As for these innumerable unknown heroes who reside in obscurity, each one respecting the other; alas, none among them can make a name [and lead the rest]. Today, all I can do is to publish my principles and expand on their inner meanings so that, together with my compatriots, we can urge their adoption.

—China should be the China of the Chinese. China is the land inherited from the Yellow Emperor. From child to grandchild in an unbroken line, we have been born, raised, and nurtured on this land, and we alone have the responsibility to preserve it. There are inferior foreign races, who contaminate our nation and violate the rights of our sacred Han race; we must not hesitate to sacrifice our lives to drive them out and to restore our rights.

—Everyone should know the principles of equality and freedom. At birth, there are none who are not free and equal. In the beginning there are neither rulers nor subjects. Yao, Shun, Yu, and Ji fulfilled their duties (*yiwu*) toward their compatriots; through their filial respect for their compatriots, Yao and the others were able to provide their compatriots with the greatest benefits, and were therefore viewed by them as representatives and treasured as leaders. But they were only the leaders of the group, and freedom and equality existed as before. Later generations were ignorant of this principle. Once coming to power countless autocrats, traitors, robbers, and bandits monopolized what belonged to the masses and made it the private property of their families and clans. They called themselves rulers and emperors, so that nobody under heaven was equal and free. The result was that men like Genghis Khan and Jueluo Fulin[2] led their inferior, nomadic races to invade and make themselves masters of our country, humiliating our ancestor the Yellow Emperor in the Nine Springs. Hence, [the goals] of our revolution are: to drive out the other races ruling us, to wipe out the autocratic monarchs, to restore our natural rights (*tianfu zhi renquan*), to stand under the sky of humanity and the sun of intelligence, and together with our compatriots to wander happily around in the cities of equality and freedom.

—[Everyone] should have concepts of politics and law. Politics is the management of national affairs by a central organization, and it cannot be the monopoly of one or two individuals. Every part of a machine, for example, is dependent on a general pivot. If other parts are damaged, however, the pivot cannot work either. The people's relationship to politics is like this. If the people have no political concepts, subjugation will follow. Please examine the cases of India, Poland, and other subjugated countries—is this not the case? The law is something that [establishes] an appropriate scope [for our actions], so that we will not err [in our treatment of] one another. XX[3] said: "Barbarians have no freedom." Why do the barbarians have no freedom? It is because they have no laws. I can kill people and others can kill me, so neither side has any freedom. Why are the Teutons more competent in self-rule than other races? It is because they have the concept of law.

[Revolutionary education entails:]

The cultivation, from the heavens above to the earth below, of a spirit of unfettered self-respect and independence.

The cultivation of a spirit of boldness and adventurousness, of going [forward] through fire or water, cheerful in the face of death.

The cultivation of love for one another, love for the people, self-respect, and a tireless duty of civic virtue (*gongde*).

The cultivation of individual and group self-rule (*zizhi*) in order to develop the personalities (*renge*) of the people.

The Principle of Revolutionary Independence

The excessive rights (*quanli*) given to the aristocrats, the harm done to the people's livelihood, the unauthorized increase of taxes, the extorted public debt, and the twice-levied ship tax—these were the reasons why the English Parliament revolted against King Charles and advocated revolution. The aristocrats' abuse of privileges, which led to the great disparity between noble and base and between rich and poor, the abandonment of the principle of the protection of the people, and [the state's] unrestrained taxation—these were the reasons that French people with lofty ideals did not flinch from violence and upheaval, and these were the causes of their revolution. A heavy tea tax, the forcible imposition of a printing tax without the consent of the legislative assembly, and the quartering of troops among civilians—these were the reasons that the Americans protested against the British, flew the American banner of righteousness at Bunker Hill, and loudly advocated revolution until independence was achieved. I do not mind repeating once more: Domestically we are the slaves of the Manchus and we are suffering from their suppression, externally we are suffering from the harassment of the Great Powers; we are therefore doubly enslaved. In addition, our race is on the verge of extermination. These are the reasons that our sacred Han race, descended from the Yellow Emperor, today calls for revolution and independence.

With the constant development of the natural sciences, the heresy that nature (*tian*) endowed Emperors [with rulership] can be obliterated. With the constant maturing of the civilizations of the world, the system of a one-person dictatorship ruling over the land can be overthrown. With the constant enlightenment of man's wisdom, everyone will be able to enjoy their natural rights. If today—today!—our sacred Han race is to break free from the Manchus' fetters, to restore all our lost rights, and to take our position among the strong countries of the world, all because we want to realize our natural equality and freedom, we have no choice but to carry out a revolution and to defend our right to independence. Alas, I am young, ignorant, and shallow, and not up to the task of expounding the great principles of revolutionary independence. I have conscientiously imitated the principles of American revolutionary independence, summarized into [the following] points. I again prostrate myself and respectfully offer these to my revered and dear 400 million compatriots of the sacred Han race to prepare them for the chosen way:

—China is the China of the Chinese. We compatriots should identify ourselves with the China of the Han Chinese.

—No alien race shall be allowed to trample on the slightest rights of our country.

—All the obligations to the Manchus should be abolished.

—First of all, the barbarian Manchu regime in Beijing shall be overthrown.

—All Manchus residing in China shall be driven out or killed as revenge.

—The emperor set up by the Manchus shall be executed as a warning to all despotic monarchs that this [system] cannot be revived.

—Foreigners as well as nationals who interfere with the Chinese revolution and independence shall be opposed.

—A central government shall be established as a general institution to conduct national affairs.

—The whole country shall be divided into areas and provinces, and all provinces, through public elections, shall select deputies to a legislative assembly. From the members of each provincial legislative assembly there shall be elected a provisional president as the national representative. A vice-president shall also be elected. Prefectures and counties shall also elect deputies.

—All [people] in the country, both men and women, are citizens.

—All men in the country have a duty to serve in the citizens' army.

—Everyone has a duty to be loyal to the newly founded state.

—Everyone is obliged to pay state tax.

—All citizens are equal; men and women are equal before the law, and there are no distinctions between superior and inferior, noble and base.

—All inviolable (*buke duo*) rights are bestowed by nature.

—Life, liberty, and all [other] interests (*yiqie liyi*) are natural rights.[4]

—Individual freedoms, such as speech, thought, and publication, cannot be infringed upon.

—Individuals' rights must be protected. The government that [shall be] established by virtue of the people's consent must use all its powers solely to protect people's rights.

—Whenever the government's conduct violates the rights of the people, the people are entitled to revolt and overthrow the old government in order to fulfill their wish for security and well-being. After regaining their security and well-being, the people also have the right to engage in public discussions, to consolidate their rights, and to establish a new government.

Once the government is established, there may be minor things that conflict with the people's wishes so that they may want to revolt and change things morning and night, similar to the rapid changes that can transpire in a chess game. This is definitely not the [proper] way [to conduct] a newly established government. In general, affairs cannot be completely without problems. If one values peace and harmony and does not let these problems cause serious harm to the people, then rather than rashly subverting the government and seeking to promote one's rights, it is better [to preserve] peace and harmony. But in the case of consistent governmental brutality and corruption, when the whole country comes under a despotic system, the people will rise and overthrow it and establish a new government in order to secure the aim of protecting their rights. This is not only the people's great right but also a duty to which they themselves attach great importance. The hardship and suffering we Chinese have endured have now reached their peaks. Today we [aim] to gain our revolutionary independence; although we still suffer under dictatorship, we should, under no circumstances, resign ourselves to this situation! It is, therefore, imperative to change the old form of government.

—The name of the nation should be settled as "The Republic of China." ("Qing" is the name of a dynasty, and "China" is what foreigners call us.)

—The Republic of China is a free and independent nation.

—Our independent and free nation has full rights and is equal to other major nations in the world in all affairs pertaining to an independent nation, such as proclamations of war and peace, the concluding of treaties, and the negotiating of trade.

—The constitution shall be based on the American Constitution, respecting Chinese characteristics (*xingzhi*).

—The law of self-government shall be based on the American self-government [i.e., federal] system.

—All matters concerning collective and individual issues, negotiations, establishment of departments and official duties in the nation, shall be based on American principles of management.

Let heaven and earth be my witnesses.

Notes

1. In other words, their morality and wisdom reached everywhere; as far as the mountain top and as deep as the ocean.

2. The name of the first emperor of the Qing dynasty, Shunzhi, who reigned from 1644 to 1661.

3. The person's name is left blank in the original.

4. This refers to the stipulation of the American Declaration of Independence: life, liberty, and the pursuit of happiness. In the first Chinese translation of the Declaration, published in *Guomin bao* in 1901, the pursuit of happiness was translated as "all interests" (*yiqie liyi*).

Further Reading

For the complete text and bibliographical information on Zou Rong, see John Lust, ed. and trans., *The Revolutionary Army* (Paris: Mouton & Co., 1968).

6
Textbook on Ethics (1905)

Liu Shipei

Lunli jiaokeshu [Textbook on Ethics]. Originally published in 1905. Reprinted in *Liu Shenshu yishu* [The Collected Works of Liu Shipei] (Shanghai, 1936).

Liu Shipei (1884–1919) received an outstanding classical education and obtained the juren *degree in 1902. After failing the metropolitan exam in the following year, however, he went to Shanghai where he became involved in revolutionary activities and wrote a number of political, ethical, and historical treatises, including the* Textbook on Ethics. *In his* Textbook, *Liu sets out a more systematic presentation of an ethical theory than any we find in earlier centuries. His goal is a complete reworking of Confucian ethics, and his methods and conclusions merit comparison to the similar objectives of Liang Qichao in the more popularized* On the New People *of three years earlier. Like Liang's "new ethics," Liu's ethical theory is shorn of much of the metaphysical apparatus that accompanied earlier neo-Confucian ethical teachings, and, like Liang, Liu is to some extent familiar with Western philosophical trends and concepts. Finally, like Liang, Liu finds "rights" (*quanli*) to be centrally important to his new ethics, as the following chapters from the* Textbook *make clear.*

On the Dividing Line Between Rights and Duties

The people of the earliest times were aware only of concepts related to the self. However, [while it is the case that] from the beginnings of human life, people all have thoughts of seeking their own interests, producing benefit and avoiding harm are not things that a single person can successfully do on his or her own. People must rely on others if they are to be able to preserve their selves. [At first, then,] there are no general concepts; people know that benefiting themselves does benefit themselves, but they do not realize that benefiting others also benefits themselves. Then the group of people progresses and comes to understand that benefiting others also benefits themselves. This is the origin of the relationship between oneself and others.

According to Han Feizi, in ancient times when Cang Jie created words, he called seeking oneself "private" (*si*), and he called turning one's back on the private "public" (*gong*). The doctrine of seeking oneself comes close to the Western doctrine of rights (*quanli*). The teaching of turning one's back on the private comes close to the Westerners' [notion of] duties (*yiwu*). In ancient Chinese thought, rights and duties were always divided as two separate roads. Confucius said, "The gentleman speaks of righteousness (*yi*), while the small man speaks of benefit (*li*)."[1] In so doing, Confucius took righteousness as public and benefit as private. From this beginning, all proponents of the Mutual Benefit School (*jiao li xuepai*)[2] looked down on the term "benefit" and refused to speak of it. They daily exhausted their duties toward others but did not then go to take rights as their reward. . . . Those who belonged to the Self-Cultivation School[3] [went even further], holding that striving for one's private benefit was a great wrong. (An example of this is the Song dynasty Confucians who taught that heavenly principle [*tianli*] and human desire could not coexist. . . .[4])

The Mutual Benefit School comes close to Mozi, of whom it was said that he would "shave his head and show his heels if it would benefit the empire"; this is to exhaust one's duties while not enjoying one's rights.[5] Those of the Self-Cultivation School come close to Yang Zhu. Yang spoke of the value of benefit, emphasizing the preservation of oneself; at the same time, he denigrated putting forth effort, saying that invading others was despicable. He similarly said that if he could benefit the empire by harming a hair on his head, he would not do it. [In short,] he advocated not invading others' rights and not exhausting one's duties toward others.

This is to misunderstand the principle of the relationship between oneself and others. In the mutual relations between oneself and others, rights and duties are necessarily equal. As the Western philosophers say, "For there to be great benefit, there must be two sides benefiting." In ancient times, Yanzi[6] [similarly] said, "Righteousness is the storing up of benefit." This is to say that one's exhausting of one's duties is the foundation for one's enjoying rights. The *Book of Changes* says: "If things are benefited, it will bring about harmony and righteousness." In other words, if people are provided with rights, it will make them exhaust their duties.

Who could be unclear about the border between rights and duties and yet be able to call [their theory] "ethics"? The border between rights and duties is created from the relations between people, so [it is clear that] it is from the relations between people that the principles of ethics are born. . . .

On Good-Knowing

The doctrine of good-knowing began with Mencius and was brought to completion by Wang Yangming. Mencius said: "What one can do without having to learn it is good ability; what one knows without having to reflect is good-knowing."[7] Zhu Xi interpreted good ability and good-knowing as things that did not depend on anything and thus came from heaven, rather than from humans. Lu Xiangshan's teaching also emphasized good-knowing. It was in Wang Yangming's teaching, however, that good-knowing came to represent his central idea.

The notion of good-knowing has three main advantages, [one of which will be spelled out in detail in the remainder of this chapter].

[It leads to] the manifestation of the people's will. Yangming said: "From sages to the dullest people, from the mind of a single person all the way out to the four seas, from ancient times to the distant future, there has been no difference in it—this is good-knowing." He also said: "One knows without reflecting; one is able without learning—these are [due to] the 'good-knowing.' Good-knowing's presence in the minds of people is not different in a wise man or a dull one; all under heaven, from ancient times to the present, are the same."

Lu Xiangshan used "establish the will" to encourage later students. (Lu said: "In the past thousand years there has not been a single person who established his will, but blaming [those who did not establish their wills] will not do; one must have the will to understand before one can have the will to hope.")

Many scholars who followed Lu's teachings arose and exerted themselves, and eventually Yangming created his doctrine of good-knowing and taught that it was the way of the sages. [According to Yangming,] one's mind is sufficient on its own; one need not search outside it. If one is able to extend one's good-knowing so that external things do not obscure it, then anyone can be a sage. . . .

Chinese people all believe that sagehood is something imparted by nature (*tian*), not something that one can stand up and grab. Since the doctrine of good-knowing was first proposed, [though, they] have believed that the good-knowing of everyone is the same, and that whatever a person receives from nature is always the same. That which people receive from nature is what is referred to in "Yao and Shun are the same as all people." Thus, lowly and poor people can look within and seek to enter the Way. . . .

[They] can, therefore, no longer use their [lowly] characters to restrain themselves. Recently the Westerner Rousseau invented the doctrine of "natural rights" (*tianfu renquan*), according to which goodness is the root nature of all people. [He] hopes that all people will willingly desire the public [good] and that all things will return to equality. . . .

Although Wang Yangming did not say [precisely] this, in practice, the doctrines of "good-knowing" and that of "natural rights" are the same. That which people receive from nature is the same, and, thus, that which [their] rights attain ought to be without any differentiation. [In such a situation,] can their freedom be limited and can they be made unequal again? Therefore, the doctrine of good-knowing not only encourages lowly people to manifest an active spirit, but it also encourages the common people's disposition to compete for rights. (Evidence for this can be found in Huang Zongxi's both advocating Wang's teachings and attacking unmerited rulers' rights.) This is the goodness of the doctrine of good-knowing.

On Righteousness

Freedom of thought and freedom of action—these are definitely an individual's rights. Freedom is what Zhuangzi meant by "let it be, leave it alone."[8] But freedom cannot be without limits. Thus, Chinese ancients always talked of humaneness and righteousness together. "Humaneness" means to strive to do good things. "Righteousness" means to avoid doing that which one should not do. To benefit others is "humaneness"; to avoid harming others is "righteousness."

In ancient writings, the character *li*, [meaning ritual, or decorous appearance] was written as follows, like our modern term righteousness. . . . Our term righteousness, in turn, was written as follows, which meant "appropriate."[9] Thus, when affairs reach their appropriate state, that is righteousness. . . . "Affairs reaching their appropriate state" means that both oneself and others have equal control over their own freedom, such that no one harms another in order to benefit oneself. . . .

The term "righteousness" is the same as that referred to in the *Analects* as "ordering oneself."[10] If one is able to order oneself, then one will not slip into evil, and if one can avoid slipping into evil, then one will not harm anyone else. Taking another's wealth, invading another's freedom, and slandering another's reputation are all examples of nonrighteous behavior. Thus, righteousness is a virtue, because it restricts an individual's freedom and ensures that he or she does not invade another's freedom. . . .

Yang Zhu said, "among the respects in which making an effort is despicable, invading another is the worst." "Invading another" is another way of saying applying one's strength to another. When one does not understand controlling oneself, one will simply follow one's nature in all one's actions. Instances of one's not restraining oneself and harming another all come from this [kind of defect].

The Song dynasty Confucians' talk of conquering the self and cutting off one's private interests was an extremely severe version of controlling the self. Not only did it mean that people would not interfere with others' rights, it also led to the loss of one's own freedom. This led the Ming Confucian Zhao Nanhuang to say that "Later Confucians [i.e., the Song Confucians] thought of the self as a shackle." The ancients' talk of the virtue of righteousness was of control added in the midst of freedom. They did not say that controlling oneself would also mean losing one's right (*quan*) of bodily freedom.

Notes

1. *Analects* 4:16. Here, Liu is relying on the connections between righteousness and duty, based on the fact that both contain the character *yi*, and between benefit and rights, which both contain the character *li*.

2. This was discussed in an earlier chapter. Liu lists Zhang Zai, Wang Yangming, Yan Yuan, and Dai Zhen as examples.

3. This was also discussed in an earlier chapter. Liu cites Dong Zhongshu, Han Yu, Xu Heng, and Wu Yubi as examples.

4. Here and below, Liu adds lengthy citations to the writings of various Confucian thinkers. Most of the ellipses in this text are omissions of such citations.

5. See *Mencius* 7A:26.

6. A prime minister during the Spring and Autumn Period.

7. See *Mencius* 7A:15.

8. "Let it be, leave it alone" is Watson's translation of *zai you* from *Zhuangzi* (*Chuang Tzu: Basic Writings*, trans. Burton Watson [New York: Columbia Univer-

sity Press, 1964], p. 114). This is how we believe Liu understood Zhuangzi, since this is a traditional interpretation of *zai you*, and fits the context well. On the correct interpretation of this phrase in Zhuangzi, however, see D.C. Lau, "On the Expression *Zai You*," in *Chinese Texts and Philosophical Contexts*, ed. Henry Rosemont (LaSalle, IL: Open Court, 1991).

9. The characters have been omitted.

10. See *Analects* 13:6 and 13:13.

Further Reading

For biographical details on Liu, as well as discussions of his subsequent anarchism and conservatism, see: Chang Hao, *Chinese Intellectuals in Crisis* (Berkeley: University of California Press, 1987); Peter Zarrow, *Anarchism and Chinese Political Culture* (New York: Columbia University Press, 1990); and Martin Bernal, "Liu Shih-p'ei and National Essence," in Charlotte Furth, ed., *The Limits of Change* (Cambridge, MA: Harvard University Press, 1976).

7
First Speech of Miss Xu Yucheng from Jinkui to the Women's World (1907)

Xu Yucheng

"Jinkui Xu Yucheng nüshi duiyu nüjie diyici yanshuogao" [First Speech of Miss Xu Yucheng from Jinkui to the Women's World], *Zhongguo xin nüjie zazhi* [China New Woman's Magazine], no. 5, June 5, 1907. Reprinted in *Jindai Zhongguo nüquan yundong shiliao* [Historical Materials on the Modern Chinese Women's Rights Movement] (Taipei: Biography Literary Publishing Company, 1975).

We know little about Xu Yucheng other than what she tells us in this essay, a speech published in the magazine Zhongguo xin nüjie zazhi *[China New Woman's Magazine]. The magazine, which was published by Chinese students in Tokyo, came out with six issues in 1907 before it was closed down. The magazine was less radical than many of the other magazines on women's issues and women's rights put out at the time, such as Qiu Jin's* Zhongguo nübao. *Its closure by the Japanese police, though, was prompted by an article on political assassinations as a method to promote revolution. Like many others at the time, the magazine demanded equality between the sexes and advocated equal rights for women. Xu was one of a number of authors who used the language of rights to advocate the liberation of women. She sees the right to freedom as central to women's ability to respect themselves, and believes that the right to freedom, in turn, rests on possessing what she calls "the qualifications for freedom." One possesses these qualifications only when one knows that in seeking freedom for oneself one must also respect the freedom of others; only this can be called true freedom. To depend upon others, a fate women were particularly prone to, would imply a degrading and slave-like existence without self-respect and honor. In light of the attacks that rights thinkers will subsequently level at Confucianism, it is notable that Xu quotes Confucius quite favorably. Other women were more radical and more political than Xu; the anarchist He Zhen, for example, advocated a more thorough going social revolution as the best path to realizing women's freedom.*

That which I admire most in my life is a pair of colloquial phrases. Not only have these two phrases been heard by and are known to everyone, but they are also often on everyone's lips. They are not, however, phrases that one speaks lightly without meaning to accomplish anything. You need to know that these two phrases denote a very important truth [universal to] the past and present, the five continents, and the myriad nations. Every single person should understand the meaning of these phrases, study their principles, and carry out the rights (*quanli*) they [represent]. If someone can understand these two phrases, study them, and carry them out, I can conclude that this kind of person is a complete person (*wanquan ren*) and is extremely fortunate. If someone does not understand these two phrases, does not study them, and does not carry them out, this kind of person is an incomplete person (*weicheng ren*) and is unfortunate. These two phrases have such significance, such seriousness, and such importance to the principles of our acting as people (*zuoren*) and to our personalities (*renge*), that whenever I think of them I cannot restrain myself—and so I must speak to you all today. . . .

What are the two phrases which I admire so very much? They are "Respect oneself and make oneself honorable" (*zizun zigui*) and "Debase oneself and make oneself low" (*ziqing zijian*). Are not these two phrases heard by everyone, known to everyone, and frequently spoken by everyone? Allow me to explain these two phrases a little more. What is it to "respect oneself"? It is to be able to retain one's right to freedom (*ziyou quan*). This right to freedom means that as long as one is a human and has knowledge, regardless of whether one is a man or a woman, one should be entitled to a share of the right to freedom; this right is sacred and inviolable. . . . That one can retain one's right to freedom, therefore, means that one respects oneself; being able to respect oneself, naturally one is an honorable person. What is it to "debase oneself"? It is to be unable to retain one's right to freedom. In no respect is one master of oneself; one is commanded and directed by others on every matter, just as the saying goes: "Order him to go east, [he] dares not go west; order him to beat the dog, [he] dares not beat the chicken." One only understands relying on others and obeying others, and does not know to seek one's own rights, hence one's right to freedom is stolen by others. Since one's right to freedom is stolen by others, one is not able to respect oneself. The inability to respect oneself means to debase oneself. One who debases oneself is naturally a low person. This is why I said that these two set phrases denote a very important truth [universal to] the past and present, the five continents, and the myriad nations. . . .

In antiquity, Confucius once heard a child sing: "If the water of the Canglang is clear, / It is fit to wash my chin-strap; / If the water of the Canglang is muddy, / It is only fit to wash my feet."[1] He then told his disciples: "You must remember these few lines. The meaning of this song is that if the water of the Canglang River is clear, I will wash my chin-strap. If the water of the Canglang River is muddy, I can only wash my feet." You may say that the water is the same; why should the chin-strap be washed if it is clear, but only the feet if it is muddy? You must understand that [the decision to] wash the chin-strap or wash the feet is not based on an artificial distinction (*weixin*), but in fact is because the water brings this treatment on itself.

The two phrases [I discussed above] also mean this same thing. If one can see oneself as worthy of respect, others will naturally regard one as something of value. If one sees oneself as debased, others will naturally take one to be a lesser being. In this light, we can see that the difference between "honorable" (*zungui*) and "despicable" (*qingjian*) is not the result of artificial distinctions, but is a fact brought on by oneself. Accordingly, since we are persons, we definitely cannot but respect ourselves and endeavor to obtain freedom, and we definitely should no longer debase ourselves or give up freedom. [We] now realize that the word "freedom" and those two phrases—"Respect oneself and make oneself honorable" and "Debase oneself and make oneself low"—are just like the chemists' elementary particles of atoms: no matter what one is talking about, they cannot be escaped. From this we can see that if we want to respect ourselves and be regarded as things of value, and do not want to debase ourselves and so behave like lesser beings, there is no alternative to endeavoring to obtain freedom.

Be this as it may, the word "freedom" is really very difficult: not only difficult to practice but also difficult to explain. Why is this? You must understand that one can only be free when one has the qualifications (*zige*) for freedom; without these qualifications, one can never be free.

If one tries to forcibly obtain freedom despite not having the qualifications, this is called "tyrannical freedom" (*qiangheng ziyou*) and "savage freedom" (*yeman ziyou*). A tyrannical and savagely free man still does not know freedom. Some may say: "His tyranny and his savagery are exactly the freedom that allows him to act as he desires. Why do you say instead that he does not know freedom?" I would answer that I have already said that one can only be free when one has the qualifications for freedom. What are these "qualifications for freedom"? Generally speaking, free people definitely will be delighted to let others have the same freedom as they do, and definitely will not infringe upon others' freedom or obliterate others' freedom. When people can act thus, it is called true freedom. As for those with tyrannical and savage freedom, they only know to invariably act as they please, but have no idea what is meant by freedom, what is meant by others' freedom, what is meant by violating others' freedom, nor what is meant by obliterating others' freedom. If this is taken to be freedom, then even killing people, setting things on fire, being a thief, or being a bandit would all be included in freedom. If everything can be counted as freedom, then it is no longer necessary to study what freedom is all about; one only needs to study what Satan is all about. How sad!

At this point, the question of whether we are free or not in China comes to mind. Who do you think are the freest people in our China? It is the men. Who are the least free people? Naturally it is the women. Of course our women in China are the least free people, but can the men in China really meet the definition of being free? No. Why not? Because they do not have the qualifications for freedom: they do not know what is meant by freedom, what is meant by others' freedom, what is meant by violating others' freedom, nor what is meant by obliterating others' freedom. They only know how to act as they please and practice their tyrannical and savage freedom—and they use covert maneuvers and explore all possible methods to deal with the freedom of we women. Therefore I say that [Chinese] men should be regarded as still not knowing freedom. They also do not realize that the right to freedom of we women has been violated and obliterated to the furthest extent by them. My sisters, you have to think about these things yourselves. Men have already violated and obliterated our right to freedom to this extent. Is it conceivable that we should just let things follow their own course and henceforth forget everything? Should we do this, then it is inevitable that others will comment that we "debase ourselves and lower ourselves...."

[What, then, is to be done?] I myself am neither particularly talented nor learned. I can think up no methods but the following: in my humble opinion, there is only one method to vigorously obtain self-respect (*zizun*) and self-esteem (*zigui*). If one wants to respect oneself, one must first gain the right to freedom. To gain this right to freedom, one must first acquire the qualifications for freedom. And how shall we acquire these qualifications for freedom? There is only one way, I think. What way is it? It is simply that we must seek learning. I think that if one has learning, one can acquire the qualifications for freedom. With these qualifications, one can enjoy the right to freedom. [If one] enjoys the right to freedom, one can be called "self-respected and self-esteemed." If we in the world of women are able to "respect ourselves and honor ourselves," even if they in the world of men want to practice their arbitrary and savage freedom, they will not dare. Even if [they] want to violate our freedom, they will have no way to violate it. Even if [they] want to obliterate our freedom, they will have no way to obliterate it. Since they will not be able to violate our freedom, obliterate our freedom, and will not dare practice their arbitrary and savage freedom, from then on, if anyone dares utter the sentence that we "despise ourselves and debase ourselves," I will not believe it. [Since] you all have heard these comments of mine and the explanation to this point, I trust that you do not take my words as unreasonable.

A sister, however, once came up to me and said: "Your words are no doubt correct, but how is it that we as women have to be free in order to be called 'self-respected and self-esteemed'? I do not quite understand [your] reason for this." I then asked her: "What is it that you do not understand?" She said: "Take me as an example. When I was young, living with my parents, though I did not get to study and seek knowledge, I still lived as a precious daughter for ten or twenty years. After I grew up, I was married to a scholar. This scholar was not only a young gentleman [from a good family] but also well learned and very talented. Within one year he passed his first exam, and I then became a Mrs. Licentiate. The first time he took the provincial examination, he got the degree of a provincial scholar, and I thus became a Mrs. Provincial Scholar. Later he went on to obtain the degree of advanced scholar and was selected into the Hanlin Academy, and I achieved the status of a Mrs. Hanlin. Of course I didn't get to study nor to seek knowledge, and I do not understand what is meant by freedom and thus cannot respect myself nor honor myself. But if [anyone] wants to put the words 'despicable' and 'low' on me, it seems to me that they do not fit. An ancient proverb says well: 'The wife becomes noble by relying on the husband; the ship is elevated by relying on the water.' Therefore I wonder why we must have the right to freedom in order to be called respected and honored. Me, for instance, although I do not have the right to freedom and cannot claim to have respected myself and honored myself, it is impossible not to speak of me as respectable and honorable (*kezun kegui*). From my point of view, then, it would be fine whether we women can claim the three words 'right to freedom' or not; it does not seem to be necessary. Now I have heard you say that it was so important, and I have become a little confused and wish to ask for your instruction."

After I had listened to her remarks, I almost burst into laughter. I suspect that each of you cannot help laughing after hearing this story. Yet we ought not laugh at her, but rather need to understand that these remarks of hers are the result of not having studied and not having sought learning. Accordingly, the words that she utters will induce others to laugh. Nevertheless, a person like her should really be seen as pitiable. There is in fact no shortage of pitiable people like her in our China, but people who speak out like she does are rarely seen. As for those who do not speak out but have this sort of idea in mind, I fear that they are too many to count. Because of this, though I felt like laughing very much when I first heard these remarks of hers, after a moment's thought, not only did I not feel like laughing, but I actually felt like grieving. I realized that our world of women has been poisoned to such a grave extent without our realizing it. The imprisonment techniques of the world of men have bound our world of women so tightly that people in our world of women—who have become slaves, become utensils, become toys, and even had their lives entrusted to the hands of others—do not even have any idea of this. Instead, she is quite elated; she calls herself respectable and honorable. Every sister, please think very carefully about this. Isn't this the most grievous thing for our compatriots in the world of women?

Therefore I did not laugh at her, but peacefully answered her: "Sister, your remarks do show a bit of thought, but because you have not thought it through carefully enough, you cannot understand my words about the self-respect, self-esteem, and freedom. . . . You said: 'The wife becomes noble by relying on the husband; the ship is elevated by relying on the water.' You have become the wife of the chief court historian and you seem to think of yourself as respectable and honorable. If a learned person were to view [your situation], however, he or she would probably say that your respect and honor are not reliable. Why is this? You need to know that since the heaven and earth have given birth to humans like us, we are entitled to a share of rights of freedom. This right to freedom is sacred and inviolable. Only [that which] is sacred and inviolable can be regarded as respectable and be regarded as honorable. As for those things we accomplish and those honors we receive by relying on others, no matter how respectable and honorable, they cannot be regarded as [genuinely] meriting respect and honor.

"Now I will make another analogy. Suppose one of us women were married to a man who is truly rich and noble. Although he is rich, however, he does not allow you to spend any part of his money. Although he is noble, he does not allow you to share any part of his good fortune. How can you cope with this? Even if he allows you to spend his money and to share his good fortune, if at some moment he wants to apply his tyrannical and savage freedom, again, how can you deal with him? This is why I said that your respect and honor are not reliable. If we want reliable respect and honor, we must retain the right to freedom. You have to know that we are simply women. Is there any relation of superiority and inferiority between men and women that we have to obey him, depend on him, and lead him to think of us as a utensil or a toy? Is this regrettable or not, do you think? The two phrases 'The wife becomes noble by relying on the husband; the ship is elevated by relying on the water' are not wise sayings but rather extremely unkind expressions. The first phrase means that we women are base by nature and we will become noble only by relying on men. The second phrase identifies we women with the ship, which will be elevated only when the water is rising; if there is no water, then [the ship] cannot move. Do you not agree that these words can enrage us? Because I cannot restrain my anger, I thus hold on to an idea of freedom (*ziyou de zhuyi*). The idea of freedom is sacred and inviolable."

After I told her these things, that sister did not say more. As for whether she could understand what I told her, I have no idea. My speech today is simply a casual talk based on my humble opinions; without realizing it I have spoken quite a lot. I wonder what you think after hearing all this? If the theory has some merits despite the vulgar diction, then all my elder and younger sisters, every one of you has to make up your mind and try your utmost to seek knowledge. Everyone must study until you have the qualifications for freedom and enjoy the right to freedom. From then on, the good words "self-respect" and "self-esteem" will naturally apply to you, while the bad words "self-contempt" and "self-degradation" will naturally fade away. The *Analects* says: "I seek humaneness and humaneness is at hand."[2] This means that as long as I want to do this, there is nothing that cannot be accomplished. My elder and younger sisters, [you] simply need to mindfully and vigorously do it at once.

Notes

1. *Mencius* 4A:8. See D.C. Lau, *Mencius* (New York: Penguin, 1970), p. 121. Lau is probably right that *canglang* should be translated as "blue," rather than naming a river, but Xu Yucheng clearly reads it as the name of a river.
2. *Analects* 7:29.

Further Reading

For a good collection of writings from this period on women's issues, see Li Youning and Zhang Yufa, eds., *Jindai Zhongguo nüquan yundong shiliao* [Historical Materials on the Modern Chinese Women's Rights Movement] (Taipei: Biography Literary Publishing Company, 1975).

For materials in English, see the two essays by He Zhen translated in Wm. Theodore de Bary and John Lufrano, eds., *Sources of Chinese Tradition, 2d ed.* (New York: Columbia University Press, 2000), vol. 2, pp. 389–94; and for articles from a slightly later period, see Hua R. Lan and Vanessa L. Fong, eds., *Women in Republican China: A Sourcebook* (Armonk, NY: M.E. Sharpe, 1999). For information on the women's press in the early twentieth century, see Charlotte L. Beahan, "Feminism and Nationalism in the Chinese Women's Press, 1902–1911," *Modern China* 1, no. 4: 379–416.

8

If the Citizens Want to Rid Themselves of the Evils of Autocracy, They Must Have Political Power (1908)

Ma Weilong

"Lun guomin yu tuo zhuanzhi emo yi ju zhengzhi zhi shili" [If the Citizens Want to Rid Themselves of the Evils of Autocracy, They Must Have Political Power], *Shibao* (March 7–8, 1908).

Ma Weilong's article appeared in the Shanghai daily newspaper Shibao *[The East-ern Times].* Shibao *was an organ of late Qing constitutional reformists founded in June of 1904. Little is known about Ma since he was not a regular* Shibao *journalist. Ma was not the first to mention issues of rights in the pages of* Shibao. *Between April and July 1907 the newspaper devoted a series of editorials to the subject of constitutional rights. This included a translation of the full text of the French Decla-ration of the Rights of Man, which was prefaced by a brief explanation of the con-cept of natural rights and its implications for the citizens of a constitutional nation. While Ma says that natural rights are innate, he simultaneously requires that citi-zens develop adequate "political abilities" before they can merit any rights.*

Today, civilized (*wenming*) nations in the world have abolished auto-cratic politics in favor of the politics of public opinion (*yulun zhengzhi*). There are two established reasons for this. One is theoretical, the other practical. Speaking from a theoretical perspective, in the politics of public opinion, the opinion of the people is used to implement national politics because all rights (*quanli*) originate with the people. This is the most practical of natural laws (*ziran zhi faze*). The nation is an aggregate of the people, and the people are individual members of the nation. The national interest is thus the same as the interests of each individual. Therefore, when a person intervenes in national politics, it is as if he is intervening [on his own behalf]. This is the necessary condition for indi-vidual self-preservation. [The ability to] fulfill this condition is what must be called humankind's innate (*guyou*) natural right (*ziran zhi quanli*). However, in all situations rights must be implemented in accor-dance with ability. Those with no ability have no rights. Therefore the level of ability determines the scope of rights. This is a theory on which all advanced nations of the world agree.

I will not go into the matter of the savagery of high antiquity, but will only discuss its contemporary remnant, autocratic politics. For example, in our nation the citizens (*guomin*) lack freedom of speech, association, and publication. As a result, the people cannot intervene in national poli-tics in the slightest way. Instead, national politics are implemented on the basis of one man's ideas. Citizens' conditions for survival can be stripped away as a result of one man's ideas. Therefore, it cannot be said that the people's survival is guaranteed. To sum up then, autocratic poli-tics violates natural laws. This is a grave error.

When natural law is established, those who lack ability are not granted rights. Therefore, citizens who lack political ability certainly cannot have political rights. As for the implementation of public-opinion politics, citizens who lack ability are not under [a regime of] public-opinion politics but [a regime] of autocratic politics. This is not a violation of natural principles, rather it is a proper application of them. However, if the citizenry's political knowledge were to suddenly develop, this would make individual citizens [members] of the nation. The interests of the nation would then be the interests of the citizens. In order to preserve their personal survival, the citizens would know that they had the right to intervene in national politics. And since they would know to exercise this right, public-opinion politics would be an appropriate system. If the people's abilities were to advance even further and they were capable of actually implementing this system, public-opinion politics would be the necessary result. Then, even if the government used all kinds of methods to hinder [this public opinion], they would ultimately have no effect. Up to this day, in all countries in which autocratic politics have perished and public-opinion politics have arisen, although mutual wrangling could not be avoided at the time [of the transition from one regime to the other], in the end, public-opinion politics has been the best instrument for victory. Does this not prove that [if] the political ability of the citizens [reaches the necessary level], then this ability will serve as the foundation of power, capable of overturning all oppressive force?

Public-opinion politics thus has a correct theoretical basis. However, from where does the correctness of this theory come? It comes from the progress of scholarship and from scholarly research. In studying the historical reasons for the development of public-opinion politics, [however,] its foundation does not come from theory but from practical necessity. This can be ascertained. Overlooking the Teutonic race, which resided in the forests of Germany in high antiquity, [we find] the reason for the development of the sprouts of public-opinion politics dates back to the beginning of the thirteenth century. [At this time] the Magna Carta was promulgated in England, resulting in the convening of parliament.

Then, in the beginning of the seventeenth century, rights law (*quanli fa*) was first announced, followed by the Declaration of Rights (*quanli xuanyan*).[1] This marked the gradual beginning of public-opinion politics. Its doctrine is none other than guarding against the evils of autocratic politics. This is perfectly natural. However, [the actual capacity to guard against the evils of autocratic politics] depends on the ability of the citizens. If [the government] recognizes freedom of speech, freedom of publication, and freedom of association, then when public opinion is expressed, it either agrees with the government or opposes the government. It must be one or the other. If public opinion opposes the government, does the government follow public opinion and change its policies? If so, then this is no longer an autocratic government but a constitutional government. If not, if the government does not take the public opinion of the people into account and uses its autocratic power to [suppress it], then the government and the people would be in a constant state of conflict. If [the people] want to overturn the government's power, [they would have no choice but to follow] the path of political revolution. I fear that if the government and the people do not reach an accommodation then we would be awaiting the complete breakdown of the government. Therefore, public-opinion politics is more than empty theory. In fact it could have dangerous results.

Furthermore, public-opinion politics does not develop by accident. [It must have] a foundation. This foundation lies in the people having vigorous opinions. If their opinions are vigorous, then their abilities are vigorous, and this is the source of strength. [Because] the source of strength lies in the citizens' vigorous opinions, if a collective body is not founded on vigorous opinions, then its so-called strength would be false rather than real strength. Although [this collective body] would be in a position to supervise the government, the government would in fact manipulate it. Although it would be in a position to admonish officials, the officials would in fact dominate it. This kind of public opinion does not have the slightest value. In the extreme, the damage it would cause would overflow into autocratic politics. This, too, is something to which our citizens should pay attention and should not forget.

Although we want today's citizens to have real strength, this is an extremely difficult problem. Why is this? Our citizens have been sheltered by the autocratic political system. For several thousand years, the slightest public opinion could not be expressed about anything concerning the interests of the individual or the interests of the collective. It is, therefore, natural that [the people's] powers of thought and powers of action have not developed. However, when things are at their worst they will surely mend, [as] spring follows winter. Today, at last our people have suddenly awakened from their ignorant and confused dreams and there is common public opinion (*yiban zhi yulun*) concerning the government's conduct. However, this is what is called the immature phase of public opinion. I can say emphatically, if we want the citizens' public opinion to further develop and become vigorous public opinion, [we must] organize vigorous political parties. [Once] we have vigorous political parties, then [the people] will project real strength that will reach to all matters of politics and law. The vigorous ideas [put forward by the political parties] would be developed every day in essays that would encourage the hearts of all under heaven and infuse the minds of all the nation's citizens with the reasons that public-opinion politics is beneficial and autocratic politics is harmful. Subsequently, large political associations would be formed among the people, manifesting the shared feelings of public opinion. At this time, even if the government asserted its powers of intimidation, the associations would remain intact. [Even if the government] beguiled the associations with profits, the associations would maintain their integrity. This kind of firm association with rights that cannot be usurped would resist [the government] to the end. I fear that within a few years a great national citizens' movement will surge up and demand the opening of a national assembly. Although the government will want to wipe out public-opinion politics and preserve autocratic politics, how could it?

Note

1. Ma is probably referring here to the English Petition of Rights (1628) and the Bill of Rights (1689).

Further Reading

For an excellent study of the journalists of *Shibao*, their cultural context, and their political goals, see Joan Judge, *Print and Politics: 'Shibao' and the Culture of Reform in Late Qing China* (Stanford, CA: Stanford University Press, 1996).

Part II

The New Culture Movement, May Fourth, and the Twenties: 1914–1926

9

Self-awareness (1914)

Zhang Shizhao

"*Zijue*" [Self-awareness], *Jiayin zazhi* [The Tiger Magazine], July 10, 1914. Reprinted in Li Miaogen, ed., *Wei zheng shang yi lun: Zhang Shizhao wenxuan* (Shanghai: Shanghai yuandong chubanshe, 1996), pp. 177–84.

Zhang Shizhao (1881–1973) was deeply involved in anti-Manchu revolutionary politics in the earliest years of the century. Between 1908 and 1911 he studied law, politics, and logic at the University of Edinburgh, during which time he became enamored of Western liberalism. After the 1911 Revolution, as before it, Zhang was closely associated with the revolutionary forces, but he never officially joined them. In founding The Tiger Magazine [Jiayin zazhi] *in 1914, Zhang reinforced his reputation as a political independent, for in that journal he criticized China's radicals and conservatives alike, calling for moderation and greater tolerance in public life. As is evident in the piece translated here, Zhang also took a strong stand in support of the rights of the individual, arguing that countries become strong not when they repress the rights of their citizens in the name of a strong state and unified society, but instead when they protect those rights (which he sometimes referred to as human rights, or* renquan*), thereby enabling the people to develop their full potential.*

Human beings are political animals. These days everyone says, "I don't talk about politics because politics has nothing to do with me." But everything they do takes place within the realm of politics and will be directly or indirectly influenced by good or bad politics. [Some of] those who avoid all talk of politics had previously showed concern but failed [to change anything], and thus became extremists, disliking society's foulness and remaining aloof and haughty. [Others] realized that their own power was insufficient and that they had no place to air their views, so they resorted to making up excuses to comfort themselves. As for how they feel in their hearts, no one fails to recognize that the current political situation is unstable; there is a definite disconnection between the way they genuinely feel things ought to be, [on the one hand,] and the situation into which they have been forced by actual events, [on the other]. . . . Everyone is concerned about careful study of the reasons for the present political instability, and the reasons for the disconnection [between the way things ought to be and the way things are]. But virtually no one is able to express these logically or to expound upon them systematically. It is not that they truly cannot do it, but that they are afraid of injuring feelings, are restricted by vulgar and conventional theories and by the appearance of the situation, and therefore lack the courage to make judgments based on reason. Opportunities to disprove and confirm are rare, and this results in a situation whereby all currents of thought lose their order, become vague and unclear, and are unable to penetrate to the bottom of things. When this happens for a long period of time society takes on an apathetic appearance.

My views originate in the desire to unlock the means to peace and harmony. If such principles remain unclear then all other talk is pointless. This is truly the key point with regard to politics. Readers who have read this far, if you ask anybody from where peace and harmony are derived, they will undoubtedly respond: "The country is the most important thing, so if politics is able to safeguard the country, then that means peace. Night and day we hope for peace and prosperity for the country. If the political arrangement is able to bring about prosperity, harmony will result." Perhaps their responses won't be this straightforward and clear, but if one studies them carefully, they will all follow this line of thinking. In other words, with regard to such matters, people's outlooks are all the same. But how in fact are nations to survive, and how can they achieve peace and harmony? The common answer is: "In order to secure the country, it is necessary to sacrifice the interests (*liyi*) of the individual. In order to give highest place to the country, it is the citizens' primary duty (*yiwu*) to prioritize the public (*gong*) over the private (*si*)." This is truly the manner of speaking, and we are all accustomed to hearing it. But, if this thinking is taken to its logical extreme, will it really lead to peace? Will it really deliver harmony? I don't believe it will. . . .

The country's fortunes have been rising and falling for thousands of years. Within that span there have been hundreds of heroes known to all, and sages with foresight have appeared over and over as well, yet the vast majority of them have overlooked the inclination toward growth and change that the people carry in their hearts, instead advocating convention and restraint, and everyone has followed this, no one even daring to think it wrong. Given that no one dares to think this is wrong, and that no one can express their individual wishes, public and private have gotten out of balance, freedom and social control are managed inappropriately, and, thus, the country's fundamental problems cannot be resolved. True peace and happiness are silently crushed by a sense of one's decreed lot (*mingfen*), the Confucian canon, customs, classics, and rites. But, if the people are not allowed to express their desires openly, they will express them in a twisted way; if they are not allowed to express them at a measured pace, they will, of course, express them by explosive means. Throughout the country's long history, changes of dynasties and foreign invasions can be traced to such reasons. . . .

I have sought to understand why this is so. Our conceptions of nation and sovereign (*junzhu*) are very unclear. We believe the sovereign stands for the nation and that devotion to the nation is the same thing as devotion to the sovereign, that giving one's life for the sovereign is no different from offering it for the nation. Xunzi interpreted the viewpoint of the Confucian scholars of his time: "Confucians follow the model of the ancient kings, esteem rites, carefully carry out their official duties, and esteem those of higher rank."[1] This "esteeming those of higher rank" unquestionably amounts to giving all of one's energy and all that one owns to the sovereign. Confucian scholars have propagated this lesson and merciless autocrats of each dynasty have also praised it in order to benefit themselves. As a result, all the wise and talented people in the country are restricted and no one dares put forth dissenting ideas. . . .

My purpose in this article is not simply to cite ancient lessons; rather, I say all this in order to clarify that our state was founded on the idea that the interests of the common people are to be sacrificed for the benefit of those at the top of society. This sacrifice and exclusive gain was originally brought about by force, but gradually it came to be accepted by Confucian scholars. In his *Yuan Dao*, Han Yu wrote that commoners who fail to serve and esteem their rulers by producing grain and cloth and making household utensils and money should be put to death; this statement is so preposterous that not even a child could be made to accept it. Yet for a thousand years esteemed scholars have come forth to praise Han Yu's work for carrying on the way of Yu and Tang—one can imagine how much harmful influence this outlook has had on society.

However, the notion that the sovereign and the nation function as an organic whole has changed over the past ten years—the idea that the inferior should sacrifice [in order to support] the superior has now been transformed into the admonition that the private be sacrificed [in order to support] the public [good]. But when the developmental path of this new idea is investigated it becomes evident that Confucian constraints are still in place to such an extent that those pursuing private interests must always falsely do so in the name of the public [good], even while denying the people's wishes in order to pursue their own repulsive goals and damaging the people's interests for their own gain. At every turn they avail themselves of sublime words while behaving like despotic emperors; the laws have no power and public opinion has no effect. If this is what is meant by "nation," it is hollow and meaningless. Though mine is not a great mind, how can I fail to bring forth what knowledge I do possess to express my grief and warning to my fellow countrymen?

... When people speak of "politics" they reveal considerable misunderstanding and a wide range of opinions. The first person uses it to refer to the nation, the next to speak of society; since the basic concepts remain unclear, how is it possible to arrive at the proper approach? And the consequence of this is that extremists rise up in violence, moderates blindly grope their way forward, the powerless are forced to let things drift, and those who are harmed must suffer in sorrow, that's simply the way it is. . . .

A nation is a type of political organization. All people in the country are part of this organization. The first requirement is that everyone in the country approves of their organizers. Even if not every single person accepts them, the vast majority must. At the point when everyone can live in peace with each other, the nation will have hope for peace and progress. It is possible that the tiny minority who do not accept the system will be able to move the majority, or cause the majority and the nation as a whole to yield to some extent in order to accommodate their desires and relieve their doubts. If that cannot be done, they should free themselves of their ties to the country and seek another place to live. This is precisely why freedom of nationality was established. These, then, are the fundamental principles upon which nations are established; they will scandalize pedantic and conservative Confucians, but Legalists will commend them. The reason for these principles stems from the fact that it is extremely difficult to unify the opinions, feelings, interests, and wishes of people dwelling [together] in a group (*qun*). Mozi's statement that "it is not possible to clearly understand the values and interests of people in far off lands"[2] comes close to the same sense. When one cannot fully understand the other, it is necessary to judge according to the other country's level of civilization. In Mozi's time it was truly that way. But if a constitutional system and media organs for the expression of public opinion have already been established, and transportation and the various professions are developed, it is not possible to hide [different views] within the country as to what is right and what is beneficial. In fact, the nation's value lies in its bringing together different viewpoints so they can compete, make concessions to one another, and together achieve the goal of a common path to peace. . . . If a nation does not function as a proper nation, it should be destroyed; if a government does not function as a proper government, it should be abolished. Today's Legalist thinkers all maintain that the nation exists for the sake of justice (*gongdao*). What, then, is justice? Each citizen in the nation has an appropriate lot (*xiangdang zhi fen*). What do I mean by "appropriate"? To the extent that fulfilling my lot is right, I should do it; to the extent it is wrong, I should abandon it. To the extent that fulfilling my lot is beneficial, I should enhance it; to the extent it is harmful, I should reject it. . . .

Somebody may say: "Making use of people's own considerations of what is right and what is beneficial to build a country in which the whole group is able to live together peacefully—that can only work if people do not transgress one another's [views of right and benefit]—but that will never be the case. And if that will never be the case, disaster and chaos will certainly result in the end. How do you respond to this?" Here is my answer: That is precisely why a nation depends on organization. The organization must arise from a group of people who recognize their innate interests (*guyou zhi li*) and seek a means of protecting them. At the same time, they realize that the only way to protect their interests is to form a single entity, establish an agreement (*guiyue*), and then to respect it in common. Thus the nation's responsibility (*zhiwu*) is to consolidate individuals' personal rights (*siquan*), on the one hand, and to uphold social order, on the other. The nation that effectively combines and unifies the principles of human rights and freedom (*renquan ziyou*) with those of public order (*gong'an*) and national benefit will produce the very highest level of cultural attainment. . . .

Today I wish to make it very clear to one and all: If the people's interests (*li*) are not promoted, how is the nation going to pursue its interests? If the people's strength is not substantial, from where will the nation's strength come? When the people pursue their self-interests, that, in fact, is beneficial to the country. When the people increase their strength, that, in turn, safeguards the nation. All those who propose damaging the people while worshipping the nation are false nationalists. Regardless of the motivations of those who promote that sort of bogus idea, we must dismiss it and keep away from it. . . . One sentence can sum it up: If we are determined to seek peace, then the nation should consider our peace as the standard of peace; if we know how to achieve harmony, then the nation ought to take that standard for harmony as its own. If it is otherwise, then the nation is not an organization appropriate to humanity, and whether it survives or collapses makes no difference. But if we are certain that we want the nation to survive, we must consider the extent to which it accords with humanity's needs. How exactly we are to accomplish this is not something this article can address, and neither can it predict whether we can accomplish it rapidly. However, there is one sure method that can aid our search for an organization that meets human needs, and that can be summarized in one sentence: If people invoke nationalism or similar kinds of slogans, and come to talk with us about [them], we should immediately criticize their hypocrisy, and absolutely not allow that kind of talk to disturb our hearts. All proposals reflecting a desire for rights (*quan*) should be stated directly; there is no room for hemming and hawing or for limiting or obstructing them. That is what this article has tried to emphasize repeatedly, and it is hoped that my fellow countrymen will deeply understand the article's aims. If there are people who truly understand the meaning of this article, they possess self-awareness (*zijue*).

Notes

1. *Xunzi* 8.
2. *Mozi* 11 (*Shangtong pian shang*).

Further Reading

For more on Zhang Shizhao and the intellectual debate in *The Tiger Magazine*, see Timothy B. Weston, "The Formation and Positioning of the New Culture Community, 1913–1917," *Modern China* 24: 3 (July 1998): 255–84.

10
The French and Modern Civilization (1915)

Chen Duxiu

"Falanxiren yu jinshi wenming" [The French and Modern Civilization], in *Xin qingnian* [New Youth] 1:1 (1915). Reprinted in *Chen Duxiu wenzhang xuanbian*

[Selected Essays by Chen Duxiu] (Beijing: Sanlian shudian, 1984), vol. 1, pp. 79–81.

After a thorough classical education, Chen Duxiu (1879–1942) went on to be a pioneering reform writer and activist, leader of the New Culture Movement, Dean of the arts and sciences at Beijing University, and co-founder of the Chinese Communist Party. His writings are usually brief and polemical, and he rarely pauses to expound on the meanings of central theoretical terms. He is nonetheless an astute and coherent author, not easily pigeonholed as "nationalist," "individualist," "cosmopolitan," or any of the numerous other categories under which scholars have filed him. Prior to 1921 his writings regularly touched on rights and human rights; the following well-known essay provides a flavor of his concern for equality and individual self-determination. Chen moved away from talk of human rights during his career as a leader in the Chinese Communist Party, although he did return to the ideas of freedoms and rights later in life, after expulsion from the Party.

"Civilization" is the opposite of uncultured savagery. The French word *la civilisation* is rendered into Chinese as civilization (*wenming*), enlightenment (*kaihua*), edification (*jiaohua*), and so on. No nation in the world, no matter whether Eastern or Western, ancient or modern, can be considered uncivilized, provided it has edification. Nonetheless, because of geographic differences and historical developments, civilizations are of different kinds. An ancient civilization contains, to name its primary elements, no more than religion to hinder killing and brutality, laws and prohibitions to control people, and literature to cultivate the people's spirit. This rule applies to all nations; none can flaunt their particular superiority. Unlike ancient civilizations, modern civilizations are sharply divided into two types: the Eastern and the Western. India and China are representative of Eastern civilizations. These two civilizations are largely the same, despite minor differences. They have not yet undertaken the essential transformation from ancient civilization into modern. They are "modern" by name, but ancient in reality. "Modern civilization" is exclusively European or Western civilization. It is European civilization that has been transplanted to America and is all the rage in Asia. All European peoples have made contributions to European civilization, but its leaders have been the French.

Modern civilization has three characteristics that played the greatest roles in changing the way (*dao*) of ancient [civilization], and, thus, in marking a new era in human thought and society. These are the ideas of human rights (*renquan*), evolutionism, and socialism.

Prior to the French Revolution, all European nations were founded on the privileges (*tequan*) of the monarchs and aristocrats. Only members of this minority were regarded as individuals with independent and free personalities (*renge*). The majority of people were the slaves of those with privileges, and had no freedom or rights to speak of. Since *The Declaration of the Rights of Man* (La déclaration des droits de l'homme) was published in 1789 by Lafayette, the author of the American Declaration of Independence, the Europeans awakened, as if from a dream or drunken stupor, and recognized the value of human rights. They rose up and fought against their monarchs, threw down the aristocracies, and established constitutions. Charles Seignobos once said: "Ancient law is the law of aristocracy. It divides men into unequal classes and requires each to keep his station. Modern society is democratic; everyone is equal before the law. Although inequality has not yet been eliminated completely, the only remaining problem is the inequality of private property. So we can say that public equality has already been established."[1] The ability of humans to be persons (*weiren*) and not to sink forever into slavery—is this not a gift of the French?

The meritorious services of religion, such as holding back brutality and encouraging goodness have surely benefited human society, but superstitious belief in divine right (*shenquan*) and the suppression of intelligence are its shortcomings. The faith of Europeans in Jehovah, the creator of the universe, was like the absolute obedience of the Chinese to the Confucian ethical code in leaving no room for doubt or criticism. This began to change with England's Darwin and the theory of evolution, which maintained that humankind was not God's creation. Darwin's successors continued to advocate this theory of competition for survival and it gradually reached the people, who abandoned sacred doctrines and trust-to-fate indolence and began to use their intelligence to surmount natural obstacles, invent scientific principles, create their own good fortune, and control their own destinies. As a result, the material strength and human achievements of Europe have increased enormously. Therefore, many say that biology is the special characteristic of nineteenth century civilization. If we look for the origin of Darwin's evolutionism, we find it in the work of a Frenchman, Lamarck. In 1809, Lamarck published his *Zoological Philosophy*, which was an unprecedented masterpiece that scientifically investigated the evolution of species and the origin of humankind. His theories tell us that the original ancestor of living things is the most primitive simple organism, which, in turn, originated from inorganic substance; he also teaches that adaptability and heredity are the principal functions in the evolution of living things. The Darwinism that shook the world fifty years later was, in reality, a successor of Lamarck. This is another great contribution of the French to humankind!

The rise of modern civilization completely destroyed the traditional systems in European societies, excepting only the system of private ownership. Although this system began in ancient times, its harms have become ever greater since the rise of human rights, competition, and the employment of industrial capital. Political inequality has become social inequality, and oppression by monarchy and aristocracy has become suppression by capitalists. This is a shortcoming of modern civilization, which there is no need to conceal. Socialism is, therefore, a theory of social revolution succeeding political revolution; its aim is to eliminate all inequality and oppression. We can call it "contemporary" European civilization, which opposes the [merely] "modern." The theory was born in the age of the French Revolution, when Babeuf advocated the abolition of the right to private property and the establishment of a system of public ownership (*la communauté des biens*).[2] Little attention was paid to this theory until the early nineteenth century, when it was revived in France. The most famous socialists were Saint-Simon and Fourier, who proposed founding a new society in which the state or society owns property, each individual contributes according to his ability, and each receives benefits according to his or her work. They disapproved of private ownership because [they felt] that it ran counter to humanism. In the following decades, the German thinkers Ferdinand Lassalle and Karl Marx expanded on their French predecessors' theories, the conflict between labor and capital became increasingly intense, and the voice of social revolution rose ever higher. European society teetered on the edge of collapse. Although private property was not abolished all at once, politicians and tycoons began to recognize that extreme economic polarization was definitely not in society's interest. They began to implement "social policies" such as mediation between capital and labor, protection of workers, and restriction of annexation. As a result, more recent economic theories give equal importance to production and distribution. If these policies and theories work, the situation of the poor might be improved. This is yet another benefit that humankind has received from the French.

Without these three elements of modern civilization, all of which were granted by the French, today's world would still dwell in such darkness! France, the creator of civilization, is now fighting against militaristic

Germany, and the winner cannot yet be foreseen. The German sciences that we respect are no more than products of modern civilization. Whether the Germans have any particular civilization that may benefit humankind, we do not know; what we do know is their opposition to the French ideas of liberty, equality, and fraternity (*bo 'ai*). Now the ideals of people in a civilization such as Germany's are greater than those to which we Eastern nations can aspire. Surely, for example, there are German literary giants, philosophers, or socialists who love liberty, equality, and fraternity and have concern for the world! In the majority of Germans' minds, though, the love of liberty and equality has been squeezed out by the love of national and racial strength. The French people, in contrast, have had the fondness for liberty, equality, and fraternity become part of their natures and customs. Admittedly, the British and Russian intention of attacking Germany is not clear, but eight or nine out of ten Frenchmen are fighting for liberty, equality, and fraternity. Even if France loses the war, we cannot forget its great contribution to humankind. In the past, when Germany won a war over France, Nietzsche, the German philosopher, noted: "We Germans should not be made dizzy with our victory. The French genius is to win with their inherited civilization." I would repeat this remark again and again.

Notes

1. Charles Seignobos (1854–1942), French historian. Chen cites the quote from the conclusion of *Histoire de la Civilisation Contemporaine*, p. 415. A translation by Chen of part of Seignobos's book appeared elsewhere in the same issue of *Xin qingnian*. (The errors present in Chen's French quotations have been corrected in this article.)
2. French in original. François Noel Babeuf (1760–1797), French political agitator.

Further Reading

For Chen's life, see Lee Feigon, *Chen Duxiu: Founder of the Chinese Communist Party* (Princeton, NJ: Princeton University Press, 1983). Chen's famous "A Call to Youth" is translated in Ssu-yu Teng and John K. Fairbank, eds., *China's Response to the West: A Documentary Survey 1839–1923* (New York: Atheneum, 1967). Translations of selections from three of Chen's other essays appear in Wm. Theodore de Bary and Richard Lufrano, eds., *Sources of Chinese Tradition*, 2d ed. (New York: Columbia University Press, 2000), vol. 2. The classic study of the New Culture and May Fourth movements, in which Chen was a leading figure, is Chow Tse-tsung, *The May Fourth Movement: Intellectual Revolution in Modern China* (Cambridge, MA: Harvard University Press, 1960).

11
The Constitution and Confucianism (1916)

Chen Duxiu

"Xianfa yu kongjiao" [The Constitution and Confucianism], *Xin qingnian* [New Youth] 2:3 (October 1, 1916).

The previous selection gives a sense of Chen's endorsement of human rights; this selection elaborates on his opposition to Confucianism. Like the very next selection by Li Dazhao, Chen is here reacting to the enshrining of respect for Confucianism in the Temple of Heaven Draft Constitution *(1913). In contrast to many scholars from Chen's day to the present, Chen argues that the elements of Confucianism that make it incompatible with democracy and human rights were in it from the beginning, rather than being added by later, more reactionary thinkers. Chen's criticism of Confucianism bears comparison with the more favorable view of Liang Shuming (Text 17) and with arguments by some contemporary scholars that certain versions of Confucianism, at least, are compatible with or congenial to human rights.*

"Confucianism" (*kongjiao*) is fundamentally an inefficacious idol and a fossil of the past. It should cause no problems for the constitution of a democratic country. Yet thanks to the ill consequences of Emperor Yuan [Shikai's] interference with the constitution, a section honoring Confucius was added to the nineteenth article of the Temple of Heaven Draft Constitution in order to recklessly satisfy the desire of the "traitor of the people" (*minzei*).[1] This has led to today's senseless dispute. But since this dispute has arisen, it cannot help but become an extremely significant issue in our country. Why is this? It is because the issue of Confucianism not only relates to the constitution, but is also an issue basic to our real life and ethical thought.

I have once said: "Starting from the time when Western civilization was imported into our country, the first thing to stimulate our awakening (*juewu*) was [Western] scholarship, in comparison to which [our scholarship] was found to be deficient, and this has been well known throughout the entire country. The second thing was politics. As recent political circumstances have demonstrated, it has become clear that [we are] no longer able to cherish broken and worn-out things. Beginning now, the thing that our citizens should question and on which we have not yet made up our minds is the ethical issue. If in this respect [we] are unable to awaken, then the prior so-called awakening cannot be complete awakening; perhaps we are still in the state of dreaming and seeing obscurely."[2] Basically so long as the issue of ethics is not resolved, politics and scholarship remain merely secondary issues. It is both natural and inevitable that even though for the moment we abandon the old and pursue the new, if our fundamental thinking is not changed, the old views can [always] be instantly restored.

The essence of Confucianism is called the "ritual teachings" (*lijiao*), which are the foundation of our country's ethics and politics. Our country must soon resolve whether they shall continue to exist or will be rejected; this issue should be prior to the resolution of questions concerning our state system and constitution. I already regard today's discussion of it as very tardy. Since my countrymen have now discussed this abundantly, it is probably superfluous for me to add more, but I cannot help but add my impressions.

Increasing knowledge of the natural sphere is the right path today to benefit the world and to awaken people. We might just boldly announce that all religions, if not of use to governance or to civilizing transformation (*zhihua*), are simply idolatry (*ouxiang*). For the sake of argument, though, let us consider the claim that religion will never be abandoned by the less civilized peoples. [Among] the various religions that circulate in our country, however, is something like the rigor of the Buddhist monastic rules and the profundity of its doctrines not valuable? Take a further example: Christianity only worships one God, its religious awareness is clear, and Christians' conduct is pure—very often far superior to that of those scholar-officials who venerate Confucianism. Today, does it not damage the freedom of religious worship to disdain other religions and venerate only Confucianism?[3]

Let us now consider, for the sake of argument, the claim that Buddhism and Christianity are not our traditional spiritual (*jingshen*) [beliefs], while Confucianism is the national essence (*guocui*) of China. In fact there were nine schools in the old teachings, however, and Confucianism occupied only one place. The Yin-Yang School understood calendars and astronomy. The Legalists objected to the "rule of man." The Sophists distinguished between name and actuality. The Mohists had theories about universal love, frugality in burial, and the rejection of destiny, as well as a concern with military technology and bravery in battle. The Farmers' School emphasized agriculture and feeding onself through one's own labor. These are all [elements of] the national essence which are superior to Confucianism and Confucius. To imitate the method of Emperor Wu of the Han—to proscribe the Hundred Schools and venerate only Confucius—today would be despotic in learning and thought. Its obstruction of the human intellect and the severity of the disaster it would cause would be even greater than [the harm done] to our politics by having an emperor.

Now consider the claim that Confucianism embraces the hundred schools and that venerating only its view would be sufficient to transform the people and improve their customs. Well, refuting others while asserting ourselves is a fashion common to all schools. If the church of Confucianism (*kongjiaohui*) establishes its teaching in the society as a private organization, the nation should of course grant it freedom equal to all other religions. We would even more readily welcome the convening of something simply called a "Confucian Society" (*kongxuehui*).[4] Instead, however, [advocates of Confucianism] are so arbitrary and unreasonable that they want to make the country, commonly shared by four hundred million people of various religions, worship Confucius alone, and they want to make the constitution, commonly shared by the four hundred million people of various religions, stipulate that the Way of Confucius should be the great foundation of self-cultivation. Alas! It was not so long ago that the use of state power to coerce religious faith led to the religious wars in Europe. Even though it may be said that our people love peace deeply, so that [coerced faith] is unlikely to provoke open warfare, [such coercion] would certainly cause a wide variety of disturbances and unrest in our daily lives.[5] [Mandating the worship of Confucius, in sum,] falls far short of transforming the people and improving their customs.

None of the constitutions of the myriad nations are so arbitrary and dictatorial as to regulate what is to be the great foundation of education. And whether the Way of Confucius is [even] appropriate for the spirit of republican education is a second question [to which I will turn in a moment]. Constitutions are the guarantors of the rights of the entire country's people, and should not be adulterated by privileging one race, one religion, one party, or one faction. [Even] with the advancement of modern scholarship and thought, no matter how many erudite scholars are gathered to meet and discuss whose theory should be the great foundation of education, I know that they would not dare make the decision hastily and write a book to declare it to the public. As for seizing upon the dignified constitution in order to coerce the assent and agreement of the whole nation and to thwart the freedom of thought and worship—is not such deliberate provocation a bizarre tale?

All these reasons are very clear and simple; anyone with a bit of knowledge will know them. Some of the contemporary eminences who venerate Confucius in fact do not think of Confucianism as a religion because of these [reasons]; there are also some who think of it as a religion but do not propose to coerce people's faith by means of the constitution. Although this group of Confucius-venerators does not have the bad habit of forcing people to be like themselves, I do not dare blindly follow their basic view, either. What I must discuss now, therefore, is not the question of whether Confucianism is a religion, nor simply the question of whether Confucianism should be written into the constitution, but rather the fundamental question of whether Confucianism is appropriate to the spirit of the republican education. This fundamental question penetrates the ethics, politics, social system, and everyday life of our nation both deeply and broadly; we must try to resolve it rapidly. In order to resolve this question, it is advisable to proceed directly and tackle its core.

What is its core? [Three things:] what exactly the spirit of the republican education is, what exactly the Way of Confucius is, and whether the two can be compatible.

The most important spirit of states in the West, where the rule of law [is practiced,] is that every person is equal before the law, absolutely without any distinction between superior and inferior or between noble and base. Even monarchist states take this as the right path for constitutionalization; it goes without saying that the democratic republics endorse it. Thus there should not be any doubt that the education of the people of a republic should actualize the spirit of human rights (*renquan*) and equality. Next we want to know what exactly the Way of Confucius is. Both those who venerate Confucius and those who reject him should have a precise idea of this; we should neither praise nor censure him using loose, generalized arguments.

Those who venerate Confucius can basically be divided into two groups. The first group regards the Three Bonds and Five Constant Virtues (*sangang wuchang*) as a great barrier that should never be transgressed, no matter whether in China or in foreign countries, in the past or in the present. The material civilization of the West is doubtlessly valuable, but when compared to the ritual teachings of the Confucian school, it can be seen as inferior. [These teachings] are the civilization distinctive to China; it is improper to recklessly discuss forsaking them. The second group believes that the theory of the Three Bonds and Five Constant Virtues came from apocryphal texts and was eagerly promoted by the Song dynasty [960–1279] Confucians, which in turn led to their problematic [belief in] the all-mighty power of the ruler. Original Confucianism (*yuanshi rujia*), [this second group believes,] was different. No one has advanced this view more carefully than Gu Shijun, who says that the Confucianism after the Song dynasty was a false Confucianism that had been assimilated by the ruler's power; the original Confucianism was the true, popularized Confucianism. While [Gu] thinks that the Three Bonds and Five Constant Virtues belong to the categories of false Confucianism, [he] accepts the view of Sima Qian that the Four Teachings,[6] Four Abstentions,[7] and Three Cautions[8] are categories of true Confucianism.[9] I personally agree with the first group and criticize the second.

Although the terms "Three Bonds" and "Five Constant Virtues" do not appear in the classics, that the substance of these theories did not originate in the Han, Tang, Song dynasties or afterward is an indisputable fact. The inculcation of loyalty (*zhong*),[10] filial piety (*xiao*), and obedience (*cong*)[11]—are these not all one-sided obligations (*yiwu*), representing an unequal morality, a system of hierarchy between the noble and the base, and the actual substance of the Three Bonds? "Not to serve is not righteous. Distinctions between age and youth may not be set aside; how can duties of ruler and subject be set aside?"[12] "Beaten till the blood flows, [the son should be] more reverential and more filial."[13] "The one who is called a wife is subject to the man."[14] "When the husband had gone out, she puts his pillow in its case, rolls up his top and lower mats, puts them in their covers, and lays them away in their proper receptacles."[15] How are we to suppose that these sentiments of revering the ruler, honoring the father, revering the male, and revering the husband date only since the Song? . . . Dong Zhongshu, Ma Rong, and Ban Gu were all great Confucians of the Western and Eastern Han dynasties [206 B.C.E.–220 C.E.]. Dong produced the *Luxuriant Gems of the Spring and Autumn Annals*, Ma wrote a commentary on the *Analects*, and Ban compiled the *Comprehensive Discussions in the White Tiger Hall*, all accepting the theory of the Three Bonds. Zhu Xi[16] merely kept using the traditional meaning. How can we blame the Song Confucians alone?

I believe that not only was the theory of the Three Bonds not counterfeited by Song Confucians, but it actually should be understood as the fundamental doctrine of Confucianism. On what basis do I say this? The essence of Confucianism is called ritual. What is ritual? The *Fangji* says: "It is by the rules of ritual that what is doubtful is made manifest and what is minute is distinguished, that they may serve as barriers for the people. Thus it is that there are the grades of noble and base, and the distinctions of dress."[17] It further says: "There are not two suns in the sky, nor two kings in a territory, nor two masters in a family, nor two superiors of equal honor; this is to show the people that the distinction between ruler and subject should be maintained."[18] The *Aigong wen* states: "Of all things by which the people live, ritual is the greatest. Without it they would have no means of regulating the services paid to the spirits of heaven and earth; without it they would have no means of distinguishing the positions proper to father and son, to high and low, and to old and young."[19] The *Quli* says: "Ritual is to determine whether relatives are close or remote, to settle points which may cause suspicion or doubt, to discern similarity or difference, and to make clear what is right and what is wrong."[20] It further states: "The [relations between] ruler and subject, high and low, father and son, elder brother and younger brother, cannot be determined without ritual."[21] The *Liyun* says: "Therefore, ritual forms a great instrument in the hands of a ruler."[22] The *Liqi* states: "Those rituals that come closest to our human feelings are not among the highest."[23] The *Guanyi* says: "Requiring from [him] all the observances of a full-grown man means to require from [him] the performance of all the duties of a son, a younger brother, a subject, and a junior."[24] These are all essential meanings of "ritual."[25] The theory of the Three Bonds originated in the [principle] by which the high and the low, as well as the noble and the base, are divided.[26]

We ought not blame Confucianism for this kind of class system, which distinguished the high and low and clearly stipulated the noble and the base, nor for the clan-based society or feudal age [in general], which served similar functions. [At the same time,] we ought not dissemble and insist that [these values] were absent in the original Confucianism. In fact I believe that only after its evolution in the Han and Song dynasties, when the categories of its bonds and constant virtues were clearly established, did Confucianism become an ethical view with a complete structure. This is Confucianism's outstanding characteristic and China's unique culture. Our many virtues, on the other hand—such as gentleness (*wen*), integrity (*liang*), respectfulness (*gong*), temperateness (*jian*), humility (*rang*), faithfulness (*xin*), righteousness (*yi*), purity (*lian*), and shame (*chi*)—have all been observed by experts in practical morality all over the world; we cannot boast of differences and accentuate some special course of our own.

If today we still lived in the era when our borders were closed, and thus had no access to the West's theory of equal and independent human rights for comparison, certainly no one would be in a position to discuss the faults of Confucianism. If today someone were to say that we Chinese are a lower race, with a culture very different from that of the white people, and that we cannot successfully force ourselves to imitate them, I would disagree in my heart but could not argue with him orally. But what greatly confuses me is when those who clearly identify themselves as the citizens of a republic, and who personally urge the importation of Western civilization, do not wish to abandon Confucianism, which differentiates high and low and distinguishes noble and mean in a way that is absolutely contrary to a republican state system and to Western civilization. To be a legislator while [still] venerating the Way of Confucius is to be extremely unreflective about the position one occupies. Basically the [traditional] law maintained that a commoner should not discuss [politics].[27] So how can Confucianism approve of a representative polity and a publicly elected parliament?[28] If the constitution has an article on venerating Confucius, all of the remaining articles can be abandoned. The constitution today, on the other hand, is entirely based on European systems, and the spirit of European systems is none other than equality and human rights. I can see that among the one hundred or more articles of the draft constitution, articles that are not contradictory to the Way of Confucius are very rare. How are [we] going to make them coexist?

If we thought that the [traditional] Chinese laws and the Way of Confucius were sufficient to organize our state, control our society, and make them fit to survive in the modern, competitive world, then not only would the republican constitution be revocable, but we would have to regard as superfluous and erroneous [a great deal of] the past ten or more years: the Constitutional Reform and Modernization Movement [of 1898], the bloody revolution, the establishment of a parliament, legal reforms,[29] as well as all the new political and educational [reforms]. They should all be annulled, and we should hold to the old law in order not to waste our [pre-existing] wealth. On the off chance that we are not content with our original lot (*benfen*), however, and rashly wish to construct a Western-style new state and organize a Western-style new society in order to seek an existence suitable for our modern times, then the fundamental issue is that we must import the foundation of a Western-style society and country, that is to say, the new faith in equality and human rights. [In addition,] we must completely awaken to the fact that Confucianism is incompatible with this new society, new country, and new faith, and still have the dauntless resolution to proceed. Unless [the Way of Confucius] is suppressed, [the new Way] will not prevail; unless [supporters of Confucianism] are stopped, [the new Way] will not be practiced.[30]

Notes

1. See *Mencius* 6B9.
2. See "My Final Awakening." [Chen's note; the article is "Wuren zuihou zhi juewu" [My Final Awakening], *Xin qingnian* [New Youth] 1:2 (February 15, 1916).]
3. The freedom of religion and worship is allowing people to worship whatever religion they freely choose, as well as making sure all religions enjoy equal treatment by the state without any discrimination. Recently the legislator Wang Xiejia suggested that if the worship of Confucius is abandoned, this would harm people's freedom of religious faith. His comment is really incomprehensible. Our state has not worshipped Buddha nor Jesus Christ, and nowadays it does not worship Confucius, either. [They are all] treated equally, and this is exactly what is called "respect for the freedom of religious faith." How can one say "harm"? Fundamentally, Mr. Wang overlooks Buddhism and Christianity and only knows Confucianism. He has never even dreamt of [genuine] freedom of religious faith [Chen's note].
4. Westerners very often have societies to worship great philosophers of previous generations [Chen's note].
5. For example, suppose that Confucianism is established as the national religion, then to the Presidential Election Law and the Civil Office Appointment Law should be added an article that a pagan is not qualified to be elected. Otherwise, for those pagans who become president or officials, it would be against the law not to worship Confucius and against their faith to worship Confucius; neither one would be correct. For another example, consider those students in school who believe in religions like Buddhism, Daoism, Christianity, or Islam; it would be against the school rules not to worship Confucius, yet it would damage their faith to worship Confucius; again, neither one is correct [Chen's note].
6. Culture, conduct, loyalty, and fidelity [Chen's note; see *Analects* 7:24].
7. No fixed opinions, no foregone conclusions, no stubbornness, no self-absorption [Chen's note; see *Analects* 9.4].
8. Abstinence, war, and illness [Chen's note; see *Analects* 7:12].
9. All of the above is the argument of Gu Shijun. For details, see his "Shehui jiaoyu ji gonghe guopo zhi kongjiaolun" [A Confucian Discussion of Social Education and the Soul of the Republic], *Minyi zazhi*, no. 2 [Chen's note].
10. Loyalty has two meanings: one is to all the people, and the other to the ruler.

[We] can be sure that the one juxtaposed with filial piety has to be the devotion to the ruler [Chen's note].

11. The *Jiaotesheng* says: "The woman follows the man: in her youth, she follows her father and elder brother; when married, she follows her husband; when her husband is dead, she follows her son" [Chen's note; see *Book of Rites* 11; see James Legge, *Li chi*, vol. 1, p. 441].

12. *Analects* 18.7.

13. *Book of Rites* 12. The whole sentence reads: "If the parent be angry and [more] displeased, and beat him till the blood flows, he should not presume to be angry and resentful, but be [still] more reverential and more filial." See James Legge, *Li chi*, vol. 1, pp. 456–57.

14. Source unknown.

15. *Book of Rites* 12. See James Legge, *Li chi*, vol. 1, p. 470.

16. A famous Song dynasty Confucian who lived from 1130 to 1200.

17. *Book of Rites* 30; see James Legge, *Li chi*, vol. 2, p. 285.

18. Ibid.

19. Ibid., p. 27; see James Legge, *Li chi*, vol. 2, p. 260.

20. Ibid., p. 1; see James Legge, *Li chi*, vol. 1, p. 63.

21. Ibid.

22. Ibid., p. 9; see James Legge, *Li chi*, vol. 1, p. 375.

23. Ibid., p. 10; see James Legge, *Li chi*, vol. 1, p. 406.

24. Ibid., p. 43; see James Legge, *Li chi*, vol. 2, p. 427.

25. That which was [famously] criticized by Yan Ying—that is, "laying such stress on appearance and costume, elaborate etiquette, and codes of behavior that it would take generations to learn his rules; one lifetime would not be enough!"— nevertheless belongs to the less significant parts of ceremonial elaboration [Chen's note; see *Shiji* 47].

26. The meaning of the Three Bonds was originated in ritual's distinction between the high and low. It begins with the husband and wife and ends with the ruler and subject. They are strung together and share the same structure, and it is impossible to abolish any one of them alone. People of our time want to abolish only the [bond between] ruler and subject. When the root has been destroyed, how could the other two bonds exist? Miss Li of Liuyang proposes the equality of husband and wife and believes that this would not harm the two bonds between ruler and subject and between father and son. (See the editorials of *Funü zazhi*, no. 5, this year.) All these people do not understand that the coexistent, basic spirit of the Three Bonds comes from the [basic Confucian] ritual teachings [Chen's note].

27. Chen here alludes to *Analects* 16:2, which reads: "When the Way prevails in the world, the ordinary people will not confer among themselves." In its original context, this passage means that when the Way prevails, the people will not plot rebellion.

28. The *Liyun* speaks of "A common spirit rules all under heaven; the worthies are selected and the able are recommended," but this refers to private exchanges of [power] among the elite in the era of Yao and Shun. It was something like Yuan Shikai's system of the "golden case and stone chamber," and was absolutely different from modern people's possession of suffrage [Chen's note].

29. In the *Great Qing Code* in force before the Republic, there was no article on the Way of Confucius [Chen's note].

30. The final sentence alludes to Han Yu, "Essentials of the Moral Way." See Wm. T. de Bary and Irene Bloom, *Sources of Chinese Tradition*, 2d ed. (New York: Columbia University Press, 1999), vol. 1, p. 573.

Further Reading

For an introduction to contemporary discussions of the relation between Confucianism and human rights, see Wm. Theodore de Bary and Tu Wei-ming, eds., *Confucianism and Human Rights* (New York: Columbia University Press, 1998). See also references from the previous text.

12
The Constitution and Freedom of Thought (1916)

Li Dazhao

"Xianfa yu sixiang ziyou" [The Constitution and Freedom of Thought], *Xianfa gongyan*, no. 7 (December 10, 1916).

Like many of his generation, Li Dazhao (1889–1927) spent some time studying in Japan. Upon his return to China he devoted himself to writing and teaching. Li was a central figure during the May Fourth period when he worked as a librarian at Beijing University and organized study circles on Marxism. One of the first Chinese converts to Marxism, Li wrote some of the earliest theoretical articles on Marxism published in Xin qingnian, *and he was a co-founder of the CCP in 1921. Li's early writings reflect a belief in constitutionalism and civil and political rights, and a familiarity with Western philosophers such as Rousseau, Montesquieu, Mill, and others. In comparison with Chen Duxiu, however, Li was much less preoccupied with the concept of human rights. The article translated here is one of Li's early writings and reveals a strong concern with the freedom of thought, which he regarded as the most fundamental freedom. Li strongly criticizes Yuan Shikai's attempt to elevate Confucianism to a state religion, arguing that this would threaten people's freedom of thought. Despite this critique, however, Li was not as critical of Confucius as many of his contemporaries. In this and a second article from the same year Li argued for the absolute freedom of speech, regardless of form and content, but he would in his later writings retreat from this conviction. He thus comes to argue that religion shackles people's minds and is itself a totalitarian belief system at odds with freedom of speech. Li therefore insists that attacking religion does not constitute an interference with other people's freedom of thought, but is actually a way of defending it. This conclusion is at odds with his insistence in the current article that people have the freedom to believe in whatever they want to, however dangerous or absurd this thought or belief might seem to others.*

A Western proverb says: "Give me liberty or give me death."[1] Now all people dislike death and want to live. Since they are willing to pay even with the sacrifice of their lives in order to seek freedom, the value of freedom must be as great as that of one's life, or perhaps even greater. As our lives go, it is possible to subsist (*shengcun*) without freedom, but it is intolerable. If we look, we will find that none of the great efforts in the history of human life fails to derive from the search for freedom. Setting aside others' experiences, take our country's continual revolutions as an example: previous generations' efforts, which did not stop even when threatened with grievous harms, can all be said to have been aimed solely at freedom. Today the worthies engaged in the public discussion on the constitution, who have worn themselves out and become querulous, exhausting their thoughts and reflections in their endeavor to devise the grave and sacred constitutional code, can also be said to aim solely at the reliable protection of freedom. Freedom is a necessary requirement of human life; without freedom, there would be no value in living. Constitutional freedom is a necessary requirement of a citizen's life in a constitutional state. Without constitutional freedom, life would have no value for the citizens of a constitutional state. If we wish to become the fortunate citizens of a constitutional state, we must first seek an excellent constitution; if we wish to acquire an excellent constitution, we must first make certain that the constitution is capable of protecting our complete freedom.

Ever since the human rights declaration in the British Magna Carta became the guarantor of modern human freedom, each country's constitution has taken it as a model. A [wide range of freedoms] are all clearly specified in these constitutions, including those of body, property, residence, privacy in correspondence, publication, teaching, assembly and association, and worship. Our Temple of Heaven Draft Constitution also imitates these existing standards, although it uniquely omits the freedom of teaching, and also attaches to the nineteenth article the sentence: "The Way of Confucius is the great basis of self-cultivation for citizens' education." This sentence not only amounts to implicitly canceling parts of the freedom of teaching, freedom of speech, freedom of the press, and freedom of worship; it must also mean that the gentlemen [who drafted the constitution] were taken in by the deceit of some villains who, harboring despotic ambitions, secretly manipulated the outcome. This is certainly the most lamentable thing. The [earlier] disaster of Yuan Shikai's tyranny was simply to kill our bodies, rob us of our property, and deprive us of our freedom of residence, correspondence, assembly, and association. This disaster did not go beyond the body and the individual, and was limited to a certain period of time. But this [new constitution] will kill both the life and thoughts of our race. The widespread poison will penetrate the society and be handed down for a hundred generations to come. Alas, this is brutal!

In our country, from the Qin dynasty onward,[2] the only enemies of our freedom have been our emperors and sages. In the last years of the Qing dynasty [1644–1911] there were discussions about establishing a constitution, but naïve and credulous scholars wished to force a relationship between the constitution and the emperor, and intended to imitate [the concept of] the "unbroken line of emperors for ten thousand generations" specific to the national condition of Japan. In the end, the constitution was not established and because of this the Qing House fell from power. After the beginning of the Republic, Yuan Shikai took all power in his hands, closed down the legislature, disbanded the political parties, destroyed the provisional constitution (*yuefa*), and killed [many] party members; his poisonous flame blazed up to heaven and could neither be faced nor approached. The gentlemen of the nation therefore catered to Yuan's whims and advised him to use his sizzling-hot authority to force a relationship between the constitution and the emperor. In the end, before the monarchy was established and because of [his attempt to become an emperor], Yuan died.

From this perspective, we can see that the emperor and the constitution cannot exist together. In an imperial era, a constitution will definitely not be allowed to develop, while in a constitutional era, emperors will certainly not be allowed to exist. Those who, holding the banner of the emperor, sought to penetrate the realm of the constitution have failed completely. They nonetheless did not awaken. They realized that the emperor was not effective, but still sought help from the sages, not stopping until they had found a place for their idol in the constitution. Please know that the constitution is established [to protect] the freedom of the citizens, not [to promote] the authority of emperors and sages; it is established [to ensure] the welfare of living people, not [to provide] a place for an idol. In our China, with its most ancient history, the power of various kinds of authorities and impositions that have accumulated over the centuries in the thoughts of citizens is extremely strong. Foreigners [often] say that [nothing more exists] in the territories of countries like China, India, Greece, and Rome than stone stele with their inscriptions and the tombs of the dead. Hence if we want to fully realize our citizens' freedom, [we] must not limit ourselves to using our currently existing [freedom] to protect the constitution; we should instead exhaust the maximum possible freedom in order to seek constitutional protection of the origin [of freedom]. What is [freedom's] origin? It is the freedom of thought. If there are any who hide themselves behind an idol and suppress our freedom of thought with the empty words of a sage, we should know that the disaster would be even greater than any harm that the authority of the emperor might do to our bodies; the resolution and force with which we face [such opponents] should also be still stronger than in the battle to defeat the emperor.

The sage who has the greatest authority in China is Confucius. When it comes to respecting Confucius as a great man in our nation's past, we give no ground even to those gentlemen who venerate Confucianism. Confucian teachings have genuine value even today; we definitely do not dare to disdain them. So long as one uses the Confucian teachings to aid in self-cultivation—making Confucius one's own Confucius—it is perfectly acceptable. It is unacceptable, however, to offer oneself before the idol of Confucius—in effect, making oneself belong to Confucius. It is acceptable to make Confucius become the Confucius of young people, but it is unacceptable to make all the young people become the young people of Confucius. When I was in Japan, I witnessed a commentator who publicized the theory of the uselessness of religion, and his words were very interesting. He said that Confucius, Buddha, Christ, and Mohammed are no more than kinds of food to us. Confucius as beef, Buddha as poultry, Christ as shrimp, and even Mohammed as crab are our various nutrients. We feed on beef and poultry in order to make them become muscle; we feed on crab and other food in order to make them part of ourselves. We similarly feed on Confucius, Buddha, Christ, or Mohammed in order to make their spiritual characters replace and become our own spiritual characters. But humans are omnivores; for the development of muscle we have to feed on beef, poultry, shrimp, and crab together; it is exactly similar that for the development of the spirit we have to adopt all the teachings of Confucianism, Buddhism, Christianity, and Islam together, as [this commentator] said. Though this argument is mostly a joke, it also contains quite a bit of truth. Given the strong digestive power (that is, thought power) of modern citizens' spirits, no single school from among Confucianism, Buddhism, Christianity, or Islam can possibly satisfy their desires. Those who desire today to use the very constitution that protects freedom in order to maintain the authority of Confucius are ignoring the strength of the citizens' thought power, which can never be stopped by the force of the constitution. Even if the result is exactly what they would wish, the consequences will be that the citizens' self-confidence (*ziwo zhi quanwei*) will gradually weaken and the liveliness of the citizens' thought power will gradually diminish. In the end, we will be forsaken by the world's evolutionary trends and made extinct by natural selection. We appreciate their loyalty to Confucius, but this is not, in fact, the way to show loyalty to Confucius's Way. . . .

I apologize if my argument here has seemed too radical. Having peered into the depths of our country's intellectual world, I have realized that if I do not shout loudly and hastily to spread the doctrine of self-liberation (*ziwo jiefang*), we will be unable to roll back the effects of circumstances that have long accumulated and are difficult to reverse. . . . The liberation of self in our country relies upon destroying the restraint Confucius [has put upon us]; hence I have spoken of it without regard to how painful it may be. There is room for negotiation with regard to all the other parts of the constitution that is now being composed; the only unequivocal demand [we must make] is for the protection of the freedom of thought.

Notes

1. This is a reference to Patrick Henry's famous words: "[I]s life so dear, or peace so sweet, as to be purchased at the price of chains and slavery? Forbid it, Almighty God!—I know not what course others may take; but as for me . . . give me liberty, or give me death."

2. The Qin dynasty lasted from 221 to 207 B.C.E. By choosing this starting point, Li seems to be exempting earlier figures, like Confucius and Mencius, from his criticism.

Further Reading

Li also addresses the freedom of thought three years later, in "Weixian sixiang yu yanlun ziyou" [Dangerous Thinking and Freedom of Thought], *Meizhou pinglun*, no. 24 (June 1, 1919). On the other hand, he argues for the adoption of Bolshevism in "The Victory of Bolshevism," in Wm. Theodore de Bary and John Lufrano, eds., *Sources of Chinese Tradition, 2d ed.* (New York: Columbia University Press, 2000), vol. 2, pp. 404–6. The classic study of Li Dazhao is Maurice Meisner, *Li Ta-chao and the Origins of Chinese Marxism* (New York: Atheneum, 1982).

13
The State Is Not the Final End of Life (1915)

Gao Yihan

"Guojia fei rensheng zhi guisu lun" [The State Is Not the Final End of Life], *Xin qingnian* [New Youth] 1:4 (1915).

Gao Yihan (1884–1968) was among the Chinese thinkers most familiar with Western political thought during the May Fourth period. He graduated from Meiji University in Japan in 1916, returned to China and was appointed professor of political science at Beijing University in 1918, where he remained until 1926. He subsequently taught at the Law School of the China National Institute of Shanghai, served as a member of the Control Yuan, and after 1949 was Dean of the Law School of Nanjing University. He wrote extensively on political theory, evaluating and synthesizing various trends in Western political thought. Rights figure prominently in Gao's writings; in addition to being one of the most subtle analysts of the general notion of rights writing in China, Gao was among the earliest advocates of economic rights, as we will see in Text 16. The present essay is among Gao's earliest writings and articulates the central features of the conception of rights he discusses throughout his career: rights are to be protected by the state, but they are neither innate nor ends in themselves. He strongly argues that the state exists for people, rather than vice versa; one of the central purposes of the state is to safeguard people's rights and freedoms.

Among my countrymen who advocate statism (*guojia zhuyi*), many today model themselves on the ancient principles of thousands of years ago and advocate harming the individual in order to benefit the state (*guo*). They believe that so long as it benefits the state, one need not hesitate from reducing [an individual's] rights (*quanli*) down to nothing. We can infer that the objective of such a policy is to make the state the final end (*qixiang*) of human life. Human life depends on the state, or in other words, humans are born for the state. If it is true that the final end (*guisuo*) of human life is the state, then outside of the state, human life has absolutely no value. The actions of the state are not limited by any clear standard. Individuals (*xiaoji*) have absolutely no qualifications for independent consideration alongside the state. Indeed, this kind of thinking gives birth to an ideology of state omnipotence. My purpose in writing this essay is to make clear wherein the final end of the state actually lies and to prove that the doctrine of state omnipotence is internally inconsistent. It is my good fortune to be able to instruct the gentle-men of the land.

Prior to the early nineteenth century, the final end of the state was an issue on which everyone had an opinion; it was virtually the point around which all political theories revolved. In addition, even until recent times, there have been those who say that laissez-faire-ism (*wuzhilun*) is nec-essary, and then there is the popularity of the doctrine of state bureau-cratism (*guojia guanpin*). In each of these cases, the state was seen as a natural thing. It was understood to grow and develop because it was a natural subject; aside from this subjectivity, we could never speak of its having a final end. Is there, though, anyone who does not understand that the state is something created by humans? Its actual substance is a system strictly deployed by humans as an aid in their seeking the final end of human life. No state can be established, therefore, without having humans to establish it. There are reasons for which people establish and maintain states, and the birth, existence, development, decline, and death of states are not without reasons. None of these are natural processes.

The state [is composed of] activities, rather than being a thing. When activities arise, there must be a reason for which they arise. Activities are [like] guests, while the reasons that give rise to the activities are [like] hosts. Things are different [from this]. Does a thing have a reason in accord with which it is born and grows? Its birth and growth simply follow its nature. It has no "ought" (*dangran*) that it needs to follow. It acts for nothing outside its own substance. In this it differs from activi-ties, which are done for some further reason. Thus physicists often rely on facts to change their theories, but never use theories to change their facts. They rigorously infer their theories from the things. As for those who study the governing of human activities, all the activities of manag-ing and organizing that they study must first have goals (*zhi*) that the management and organization seek. These activities are means of sup-porting the realization of the activities' goals. As far as humans are con-cerned, the goals of management and organization represent the final end of these activities. To put it simply, activities support people, and people are the final end of activities. The study of states is just the study of human activities. From the moment a state is founded, there must be a reason why it was founded. That which is founded is a state; that for which it is founded is a question about human life itself. The final end of the state is thus none other than the final end of human life. This is the fundamental reason why many scholars [now] reject the theory of state bureaucratism and maintain that states must have final ends. . . .

As political theories have developed, there has been a proliferation of different ideas of the final end of the state, none agreeing with any other. The Japanese [scholar] Ono Tsukayoshi says: "Doctrines of state ends have been a central topic of political theorizing since ancient times. The proliferation of different interpretations has increased over time."[1] Burgess writes: "Opinions concerning [state] ends are rich and plentiful, but all are mutually opposed to one another, and in addition are often incomplete."[2] What is the reason for this? It must be that studies of human activities change with the times, rather than following ancient models. [Such studies] are unlike physics, which remains the same for all time. The Japanese [scholar] Ukita Kazutami states: "The actual end of the state differs according to the difference in the times, environment, and power [relations]. Its changes follow people's self-enlightenment and the needs of the day."[3] The state is something established by humans in order to seek the final end of their lives. Its responsibility must always be to see what current shortfalls concern its founders, then bring people together so that their common strength can be used to repair and supplement the shortfalls. Measures the state undertakes should not, therefore, be aimed at crises of the moment, but rather at fundamentally and effectively repairing the people's shortcomings. [Anything that] opposes the final end of the people—[in particular,] a state whose end opposes the ends of the people—is thus not fit to be a collective institution. Institutions that are not fit to be collective institutions lack any qualifications for existence, and in the end will necessarily cease to exist. Furthermore, founding a state in opposition to the final ends of the people will mean that the concerns of the state and the people will be unable to attain harmony or unity. Can one harm the rights (*quanli*) of the people in order to benefit the state? If one sets aside rights-bearing people, and yet seeks to create a state that has rights, in what will the rights of the state inhere? Now any given thing has its particular nature. If it is broken up into parts, the collection will still have the same nature as that of the entire entity. Why is this? Because the nature of the entity is made up of the combined natures of its parts. Although combining together the [individual] people's rights (*renmin zhi quanli*) does not create a state's rights, when constructing state rights, one must rely on people who grasp their rights and are able to govern themselves. Only with people who can protect their individual rights (*yiji quanli*) can one found state rights. Those who today would like to use citizens (*guomin*) stripped clean of rights (the parts) to construct a state with extraordinary rights (the whole) are like someone who puts together a group of blind people in order to make a Li Lou[4] or who puts together a group of deaf people to make a Shi Kuang.[5] Thus state ends which peversely oppose the people's ends are not simply improper; they are also unachievable. [As I have said before,] the people's final ends should change with changing times and environments: they are definitely not eternally the same. Scholars therefore distinguish between the relative and absolute ends of states.

From ancient times to the present, those who advocate absolute ends for the state can perhaps be divided into two schools, namely "morality or happiness" and "protecting rights." Greece's Plato and Germany's Hegel both took morality to be the absolute end of the state. Aristotle took happiness to be the absolute end of the state. Numerous subsequent scholars criticized these theories, however, and sought to establish a clear scope for the state, thus limiting the degree to which the state could interfere in the people's lives. They asserted that assuring the rights of individuals, maintaining order through laws, and other such matters were the only ends of the state. Among the most prominent of these scholars were Locke, Kant, Humboldt, and Spencer. Locke wrote that the end of the state was preserving the people's lives, property, and liberty. Kant said that the central goal of the state was to develop the rights of humankind. Humboldt believed that the highest aspiration of humankind was to completely develop our abilities. Spencer's theories were similar to Humboldt's; he wanted people to use the strength of the state as a means to develop and encourage the rights of collective ethics.

Other theories seek to distinguish state ends according to the order in which they ought to be put into effect; we can call these theories of "relative ends." The following are among the well-known proponents of such theories. Holtzendorff believes that there are three state ends, which are all needed and which mutually support one another, but which must follow a certain order. First there is state strength (*guoli*), then individual freedom, then human culture (*renlei wenhua*).[6] Bluntschli agrees with the main outline of Holtzendorff's ideas, but puts a greater stress on the doctrine of public order (*gong'an*). He divides the state ends into direct and indirect. The former concern the entity of the state itself, and include increasing state strength and ensuring the well-being of the people as a whole (*wanquan minsheng*). The latter concern individuals, and include the maintenance of freedom and public order (*zhi'an*).[7] The American Burgess divides state ends into beginning, middle, and final. He says that the final end is the completion of human-ism (*rendao*) and of world culture. The middle stage is the full manifes-tation of a nationality's character and the people's nature and livelihood. The beginnings lie in government and freedom.[8] Garner believes that the maintenance of everyone's equitable, orderly, and peaceful general good is the original goal. Next comes seeking the public order of all humanity. The final end is the achievement of a world culture.[9] The Japanese scholar Mr. Ono Tsukayoshi similarly divides the ends into original and final. The former includes the establishment of state strength and law; the latter includes developing the people's bodies and minds and furthering social culture.[10] In addition to these authors, there are countless others who similarly hold that state ends must be gradually achieved in a certain order. They begin from the foundation of respect for the state's survival, continue by seeking the rights of individuals to be free in society, and conclude by advocating the flourishing of world-wide human civilization.

I want to look over all these theories, categorize their similarities, and analyze their agreements. To do this I must first see wherein they disagree in order to understand their commonalities and to thoroughly comprehend their strengths and weaknesses. From among their differ-ences, I want to discover their shared means and common goals, and I dare not do so in an arbitrary fashion. Before evaluating all these theo-ries, I shall first briefly elucidate my stand: The state is not in itself the final end of life, but a means for seeking that end. The people and the state can each make legitimate demands on the other: the state has rights against the people, and the people against the state; the people have duties to the state, and the state has duties to the people. What the state can require of people is to sacrifice their lives, but not their personalities (*renge*). The people's loyalty to the state ends in sacrificing their indi-vidual lives, but never their individual personalities. Personality is the master of rights. Without personality, rights have nothing on which to rely. Those without rights are like birds, beasts, and slaves—not citi-zens. In order to define the end of the state, therefore, we have to ask for what end the state exists, and also to understand the mutually dependent relationship between the state and the people, wherein either party's injury to the other is illegitimate. These are the premises of my analysis of the following theories concerning the end of the state.

The theories of morality and well-being have, of course, their foun-dations, but in practice these theories inevitably violate individual freedoms. Why is this so? The theory of morality defines the end of the state as the realization of moral ideals; the theory of well-being takes as its maxim the greatest happiness of the greatest number. In both these theories, though, morality and well-being lack appropriately delimited spheres of application. It follows that, when we empower the state to be in charge of morality or well-being, state power would apply everywhere without limit. Throughout history, whenever a state's powers (*guoquan*) have been too great and without clearly defined limits, the state has never failed to invade the people's powers (*minquan*). Based on these two theories, we can conclude that all actions of the people against the state, insofar as they are in the realm of morality or well-being, are within the scope of state interference. Such power will inevitably harm the people's freedom and reduce them to straw dogs.[11] Thus, the first principle with regard to the mutual confrontation of state power and personality is that each has its limits and its scope of appropriate application; therefore, they can mutually harmonize rather than mutually invade. In view of the above, we have to say that theories of morality and well-being run exactly counter to this principle.[12]

The theory of protection of rights is best able to remedy these defects by emphasizing the clear establishment of a limited scope for state action. Rights are not the final ends of life either, but rather a necessary means for achieving the final end of life. The state's efforts to realize ultimate ends must, at some point, come to a stop. The state's ends can be divided into ideal and practical.[13] The state can support the people's pursuit of their final end, but the state itself cannot pursue this end on the people's behalf. The state can endeavor to control everything that people manifest externally, but can do nothing about what is internal, such as thought, feeling, and faith. State power reaches form, but not spirit. The state can establish institutions to encourage people's actions, but the state cannot itself take actions on the people's behalf. The state can, with its power, promote the people's cultural and scientific motivations, but the state cannot itself develop these endeavors. For matters in the spiritual world, the state can only bring about causes, and, thus, motivations; it cannot directly perform actions, which alone lead to effects. This principle applies not only to spiritual matters; it is also valid in the practical world. With respect to the issue of population, for instance, the state can plan for national development and can issue orders to promote health in order to improve the people's well-being, but the state cannot, by itself, multiply the population and improve the people's health and wealth. Another example is livelihood. The state can implement good-will policies to support the prosperity of industries and to encourage the morale of laborers, but, once again, the state cannot, by itself, undertake production and investment.[14] The function of the state is, therefore, to stand amid the people, judging conflicts, mediating demand and supply, encouraging freedom and, thus, the development of autonomy, protecting personality, and looking forward to the results of independence. The only way that the people can make progress toward their final end is through their rights. Therefore, it is sufficient for the state to stand behind the people, using its powers to encourage and support the realization of the people's goals, and to remove harmful obstacles to such realization. Guanzi said, "Instead of walking on behalf of the horse, one should try to make the horse do its best. Instead of flying on behalf of the bird, one should make the bird fly until its wings tire." This is the genuine value of the theory of protection of rights.

As for the theories of relative end, though they differ in detail, in general their main points are similar. For instance, consider Holtzendorff's idea of state power and individual freedom, Bluntschli's keeping public security, Burgess's governmental freedom, Garner's ideas of primary and secondary ends, and Ono Tsukayoshi's primitive end. Some stress the survival of the state itself; some support the actions of the individual. But all hold that the state is only a means to the realization of people's final ends, like the relation between human life and clothing or food. Beyond this, these theories also hold that our ultimate final ends include complete realization of humanism and the establishment of a world culture. Above, [I discussed] practical final ends; these are ideal final ends. But both support the theory of protection of rights, and indeed, their core principles mutually illuminate one another. Protecting rights in itself exhausts the state's responsibility to pursue its practical end, and at the same time helps people to seek their ideal ends for themselves. Therefore, should not the end of the state simply be to protect the rights of the people? . . .

Notes

1. See the summary of the goal of the state in the *Outline of Politics* by the Japanese doctor of laws Ono Tsukayoshi [Gao's note].
2. Burgess, *Political Science and Constitutional Law*, vol. 1, p. 83 [Gao's note; full citation is: John Burgess, *Political Science and Comparative Constitutional Law* (Boston: Ginn, 1890–91)].

3. See the chapter on the goal of the state in *The Origin of Politics* by the Japanese doctor of laws Ukita Kazutami [Gao's note].

4. A man legendary for his sight.

5. A man legendary for his hearing.

6. *Der nationale Machtzweck, der Freihetits-oder Rechtszweck, der Gesellschaftliche Culturzweck* [Gao's note].

7. J. K. Bluntschli, *Allgemeine Staatslehre*, bk. V, ch. 4 [Gao's note].

8. Burgess, *Political Science and Constitutional Law*, vol. 1, p. 85 [Gao's note; see note 2].

9. Garner, *Introduction to Political Science*, ch. 10, p. 316 [Gao's note; full citation is: James Garner, *Introduction to Political Science* (New York: American Book Company, 1910)].

10. See the summary of the goal of the state in the *Outline of Politics* by the Japanese doctor of laws Ono Tsukayoshi [Gao's note].

11. Straw dogs are discarded after being used in sacrifices.

12. Ukita Kazutami, *A Theory of Politics*, chapter on the goals of the state, section 2 [Gao's note].

13. Holtzendorff, *Principien der Politik* [Gao's note].

14. J.K. Bluntschli, *The Theory of the State*, section on "Limitations of State Action" [Gao's note].

Further Reading

Gao wrote a number of essays on rights starting in 1915, several of which appeared, like the present essay, in *Xin qingnian*. Two of the most interesting are "Minyue yu bangben" [The Social Contract and the Basis of the Nation], *Xin qingnian* [New Youth] 1:3 (1915), and "Lelizhuyi yu rensheng" [Utilitarianism and Life], *Xin qingnian* [New Youth] 2:1 (1916). In 1919 Gao was very involved in John Dewey's visit to China, serving as Dewey's translator at an important series of lectures in Beijing, on which see Robert W. Clopton and Tsuin-chen Ou, trans. *Lectures in China, 1919–1920* (Honolulu: University Press of Hawaii, 1973). In 1930, finally, Gao published a book on Western political science that synthesizes many of his views on rights to that date; see *Zhengzhixue gangyao* [Outline of Political Science] (Shanghai: Shenzhou guoguang she, 1930).

14
Manifesto of the Struggle for Freedom (1920)

Hu Shi, Jiang Menglin, Tao Menghe, Wang Zheng, Zhang Weici, Li Dazhao, Gao Yihan

"Zheng ziyou de xuanyan" [Manifesto of the Struggle for Freedom], *Dongfang zazhi* [Eastern Miscellany] 17:16 (1920).

In 1920 a group of Chinese citizens deeply distressed at the oppressive policies of the warlords running Beijing issued the following "Manifesto." Hu, Li, and Gao all have articles elsewhere in this volume; see those entries for their biographical details. Jiang Menglin (1886–1964) completed a Ph.D. thesis on Chinese education under John Dewey at Columbia, wherein he advocated combining the best elements of Chinese culture with certain Western ideals, among which he included the safeguarding of individual rights. Jiang served several stints as chancellor of Beijing University, the first in 1919, and spent the rest of his career in educational administration, including serving as minister of education in 1928. Tao Menghe (1887–1960) was a British-trained sociologist who taught at Beijing University and subsequently became the director of the Institute of Social Sciences of the Academia Sinica in Taiwan. Wang Zheng was secretary of the New American Consortium, and Zhang Weici was a professor of political science at Beijing University. Two years later, a similar group tried again, signing onto "Our Political Proposals," a document written by Hu Shi and published in the periodical The Endeavor. *"Our Political Proposals" is less concrete than the "Manifesto"; rather than calling for specific regulations to be rescinded because they violate people's freedom, it calls in general for the protection of the freedom of the individual and suggests a framework within which a "good government," which would have the interests of the citizens in mind, could be implemented. Neither the "Manifesto" nor the "Proposals" were backed by political action or significant political power, and in the end neither had any appreciable result.*

Basically we have been unwilling to discuss practical politics, but there is not an instant when practical politics does not intrude and jeopardize us [in some way]. It is now nine years since the Xinhai [1911] Revolution. In this time, we have suffered bitterly from lack of freedom under the governance of a false republic. Even when the political situation changed and one party drove out another, the entire nation nonetheless continued to suffer from lack of freedom, just as before. Politics have forced us to this day in which there is no road we can travel. We have no choice but to promote a kind of complete awakening. We are convinced that if government does not proceed from the people, then a true republic cannot exist. However, if we wish government to proceed from the people, we must first have an environment in which the people's genuine spirit of free thought and judgment can be cultivated. We believe that in the history of human freedom, there is no country where the people have not paid for it with their blood. Without a people who are willing to struggle for it, it is impossible for true freedom to appear. That in recent years the warlords and political parties have dared to run amok in the way they have is proof that the people lack the genuine spirit of free thought and judgment. We now proclaim that there exist certain basic freedoms that are critical to the very existence of people and society, and thus we earnestly raise them here. May our Chinese compatriots rise and struggle!

A: Negative Aspects

1. The regulations for the public security police took a whole range of the people's freedoms—those of political association, assembly for political discussions, outdoor gathering, mass movement, demonstrations, speech, proclamation, labor rally, political participation by women, and so on—and handed them over to police officials to deal with as they wished. The result has been the total destruction of the movements for political reform, for the dissemination of ideas, for labor, and for women. The freedom of assembly and association guaranteed in the Provisional Constitution is now meaningless. Thus the regulations for the public security police proclaimed on March 2, 1914, should be abolished.

2. The law on publishing gave the public security police and local officials the [authority] to deal with the people's freedom to write, print, publish, disseminate, and circulate written materials and artwork. This not only completely ruined the tools for disseminating culture and instilling knowledge, but [in effect] abrogated the freedom to publish that was guaranteed in the Provisional Constitution. Thus the publication law, publicly proclaimed on December 4, 1914, should be swiftly abolished.

3. The regulations for newspapers have placed the freedom of speech of all publications—those appearing daily, weekly, fortnightly, monthly, yearly, and occasionally—in the hands of the police organs. The police have frequently demanded that the publications pay them a large fee to be held as security—a practice borrowed directly from the Japanese special laws [for the press]. The result is that the rights of both individuals and society to express their opinions have been subjected to the whims of the police officials. Thought cannot be free, nor can public opinion be independent. How can the freedom of expression guaranteed in the Provisional Constitution be effective? Thus, the regulations for the press, promulgated on April 2, 1914, should be swiftly abolished.

4. The regulations governing the publishing industry have utterly violated the freedom of publishing houses. This has completely undermined the freedom for publishers proclaimed in the Provisional Constitution. Thus the regulations for the publishing industry that were publicly proclaimed in 1919 should be abolished.

5. The precautionary regulations contain crimes such as "harming the social morality" and "obstructing a locality's general interests." The scope of and standards for these regulations are up to the decision of the police or provincial authorities, and they need not be applied only to those who have already committed crimes. The regulations can be applied to anyone the police or provincial authorities feel is "likely" to commit such an act. Those against whom "precautionary" measures are taken do not enjoy any freedom of residence, movement, employment, or behavior. This completely violates the regulations for freedom of residence and movement in the Provisional Constitution. Therefore, the precautionary measures promulgated on March 3, 1914, should be abolished.

6. The items set down in article fourteen of the order implementing martial law interfere with every one of the following freedoms, among others: person, residence, speech, publication, assembly and association, privacy of correspondence, residence, movement, property, and business activities. Such important questions as these should not be left to the administrative organs to handle. We must demand that in the future, so long as there is neither an imminent external threat nor a state of war, unless the national and provincial assemblies decide upon it or the citizens demand it, martial law should not be declared indiscriminately.

B: Active Measures

1. With respect to the following four kinds of freedoms, no laws may restrict them further [than they are limited] in the constitution:

(1) Freedom of speech;
(2) Freedom of publication;
(3) Freedom of assembly and association;
(4) Freedom to private correspondence.

2. In the last few years, the executive organs, the military, and the police have frequently detained and punished people without due process. They have thus utterly violated people's personal freedoms. We must put in place a law on "The Protection of the Human Person," in order to protect the freedom of the individual.

3. In the past few years, election fraud has reached an extreme. An "Election Oversight Committee" should be created from among citizens with no party affiliation, and they should undertake inspections

while elections take place. They should publicly request lawyers to look
into the criminal registry, as well as oversee [any related] lawsuits.

Further Reading

The background to the Manifesto is discussed briefly in Chow Tse-tsung, *The May Fourth Movement* (Cambridge, MA: Harvard University Press, 1960), pp. 239–40. See also entries for each of the text's authors in Chow's index. "Our Political Proposals" is discussed and partially translated in Jerome Grieder, *Hu Shih and the Chinese Renaissance* (Cambridge, MA: Harvard University Press, 1970), pp. 189–93. For an analysis of the political situation in Beijing in the early 1920s, see Andrew Nathan, *Peking Politics, 1918–1923: Factionalism and the Failure of Constitutionalism* (Berkeley: University of California Press, 1976).

15
The Spirit of Contemporary Democracy (1919)

Tan Mingqian

"Xiandai minzhizhuyide jingshen" [The Spirit of Contemporary Democracy], *Xin chao* [New Tide] 2:3 (March 1920).

Tan Mingqian (1886–1956), also known as Tan Pingshan, was a leading member of the CCP until 1927 when he lost out in factional struggles. He was later active in the Revolutionary Committee of the GMD, one of a number of democratic parties competing with the GMD and CCP. After the establishment of the PRC in 1949, Tan served in various governmental positions. The article translated here was written during May Fourth for the magazine Xin chao, *published by students at Beijing University. Tan's article is a Communist critique of the French Declaration of the Rights of Man and the Citizen. As Karl Marx's own criticism of the Declaration might lead one to expect of a Marxist, Tan is explicitly critical of the rights granted in the French Revolution—and implicitly critical of many of the rights proposals made by liberals in his own day. The French Revolution was about the bourgeois wresting privileges from the aristocrats, but it did not institute genuine democracy because it did not realize true equality and freedom. Despite their sacrifices for the revolution, proletarians gained no political rights; indeed, the rise of capitalism has meant that proletarians have lost any self-mastery (zizhu) that they ever had. Tan argues that the real spirit of contemporary democracy lies in two things, equality and freedom. True equality requires giving people equal opportunities, and thus true freedom means allowing for both the satisfaction of one's own self-regarding desires and the similar satisfactions of others: all people must have equal opportunities if freedom is to be meaningful.*

Protagoras was the first person in history to speak of democracy (*minzhizhuyi*). He said, "The gods in heaven give the spirit of justice [*gongzheng zhi xin*] and the spirit of shame (*xiuwu zhi xin*) to people simultaneously, and give them both to all people equally, without distinction of high or low, or large or small. Human society is thus best suited for the development of democracy." We can see that from its first steps, democracy did not depart from the idea of equality. In the Roman era, the majority of scholars felt alike: "Democracy comes from the opposition of common people to aristocratic privilege (*tequan*)." Because everyone belongs to humanity, everyone has the desire to seek equality. In the Roman era, aristocrats and commoners were completely unequal politically, so commoners seized democracy as a standard under which to struggle with the aristocrats for political equality. At the time of the French Revolution, [the people] similarly adopted a declaration to the effect that "all humans are equal." This makes it easy to see that during both the Roman and French revolutions, the idea of equality served as a foundation for democracy. Turning directly to contemporary democracy, if we look solely at the actual facts, we can see that it is not completely the same as the democracy of the French revolutionary era, but if we look at their two fundamental goals—their similar objectives of freedom and equality—we can say that there are no obvious differences. This is because contemporary democracy comes from the laboring class's struggle for freedom and equality against the nonlaboring class; this is the point of departure for contemporary democracy.

When we look at the actual facts, however, can we say that contemporary democracy and the democracy of the French revolutionary era are the same? Originally there were both political and social groups among the French revolutionaries. In the end, though, the social revolutionary group was defeated, so that from its first appearance, the Declaration of the Rights of Man did not, in fact, oppose the complete monopolization and plundering of, and entrenchment in, supreme political hegemony (*baquan*) by the capitalist classes. During this period, proletarians shed more blood and sacrificed more lives than we will ever know, but the result was that they were left politically without even a scintilla of rights. Can this be counted as free and equal? In the end, it was nothing more than overturning the so-called "trust" of the aristocracy in order to create a trust for the capitalists—one specially designed to preserve their hegemony. Although we cannot deny the contributions it made in overthrowing the aristocratic class, the original intentions behind the French Revolution certainly included neither allowing today's capitalist class to grasp all political prerogatives for themselves, nor establishing the strict line that now divides capitalists from workers.

What is capital's "trust"? To put it simply, capitalists have completely monopolized political, industrial, and social hegemonies. The result of this is that the systems of human life—from the national assembly, government, laws, and policies, to military organizations and industrial organizations—are all used to support this group of capitalists, who do not allow the proletarians to enjoy even a little of the surplus. There is a technical name for this kind of system: "capitalism." When capitalism flourishes in the world, those without capital entirely lose their self-mastery. Because of this, they are oppressed and forced to the lowest levels of all forms of human life, including the political, industrial, and social; people in this stratum are called the "proletariat" (*laodong jieji*). Seen from this perspective, the equality declared in the French Revolution was illusory rather than actual, partial rather than universal, and left the great majority of people sunk at the very lowest levels of society seemingly permanently. This has gradually led to the contemporary understanding of democracy.

By now it has been at least a hundred years that proletarians have been controlled by the power of the capitalists and forced to suffer. If we compare the cruelties the [French] citizens prior to the French Revolution were suffering due to aristocratic violence and papal hegemony, such as lack of freedom of speech, belief, work, residence, assembly, association, publication, and so on, they were about the same as is now the case for the proletarians. Even so, these cruelties were only political, and so cannot count as completely ubiquitous. Today, the harms proletarians suffer at the hands of capitalists are not merely political problems. They are problems that most deeply concern the benefits and harms of human life, namely the problems of everyday life: issues concerning clothing, food, and shelter, as well as issues concerning the lives of their fathers, mothers, and children. I do not know how many times greater these cruelties are than cruelties merely caused by political autocracy. For these reasons, the contemporary [understanding] of democracy has arisen. Contemporary democracy thus takes human life as its foundation and point of departure. This foundation and point of departure is both concrete and just.

In order to truly understand the sufferings of human lives, it is necessary that each individual experience a thorough awakening, without which such an understanding cannot be successful. This is because contemporary democracy is not something to be toyed with in the books of scholars; still less is it a new tool for the use of ordinary politicians and careerists as they seek to seize political power (*zhengquan*). Those visionaries who can talk of abstract principles but whose feet never touch the ground—they naturally cannot genuinely understand; even worse are the lawyers and politicians who idly cling to formalisms. It is essential that each person individually introspect so as to see clearly the sufferings of the human spirit; one must realize that the sufferings are both profound and urgent, and that no one can escape them. After this, one will become enraged and wholeheartedly strive for the liberation of one's own life. This is the spirit of contemporary democracy.

The spirit of contemporary democracy has, roughly speaking, two distinctive characteristics. The first is that opposition to the capitalist trust is the point of departure for contemporary democracy; labor centralism is thus its backbone, and it seeks true freedom, true equality, and true liberation. Second, [it recognizes that] today's capitalists not only monopolize industrial hegemony, but also control every single realm of human activity, from political to industrial to social. Thus when today's proletarians seek liberation, they cannot but completely separate from and shake off the capitalist trust's seizure and forcible occupation of all realms of human life, including the social, industrial, and political. In other words, contemporary democracy does not simply aim at competing with the capitalists for some positions and some power in the political realm. It requires that one seek to satisfy [everyone's] human spirit by plunging into society and industry with fearless resolution—this is the second distinctive characteristic of contemporary democracy.

That which has just been described, namely that contemporary democracy seeks social, industrial, and political freedom and equality, is naturally not in error, but [I must emphasize] that its goal is only to ensure that the class currently controlled by another—that is, the proletarians—completely satisfy their [needs] for concrete freedom and concrete equality. We do not think that after the exploited class throws off the capitalists, it should seize their power and occupy their hegemony. Those who seek hegemony of course seek to put it into effect, which means to suppress others and to subjugate others. If this happens, it has turned into autocracy, into aristocracy, and is no longer in accord with the spirit of democracy. To put it even more clearly: no matter which class seeks hegemony, it is wrong. Why is this? When the aristocratic class forcibly held hegemony, they created an aristocratic autocracy. When the capitalists forcibly held hegemony, they created an ideology of capital's omnipotence. If the proletarians today were to seize hegemony like the aristocrats and the capitalists before them, wouldn't they just create an autocracy of the majority? Contemporary democracy, therefore, ought only to speak of seeking freedom and equality, and it ought to seek them for all people. It is absolutely opposed to the forcible hegemony of any class whatsoever.

What is equality? Thinking about the answer to this question leads one automatically to think of Lincoln, the man who during America's Civil War of the mid-nineteenth century ended the system of slavery, though unfortunately leaving only his name to posterity. He deeply hated the cruelty of his day's slave system. He expressed the most profound empathy with the slaves subjugated by that system. He rejected the majority opinion and gave all his strength to advocating equality between whites and slaves. In a speech he gave in Independence Hall in 1861, he explains equality in a few sentences, as follows: "All people today, no matter what their class, ought to throw off their cruel shackles. All people ought to enjoy equal opportunities, and these equal opportunities definitely ought not be imaginary or merely verbal. This [is what it means] for people to have an equal chance[1] in life."[2] The idea of people's equal opportunities is thus the true meaning of Lincoln's [understanding of] democracy. According to contemporary democracy, therefore, we must ensure that each person has equal opportunities politically, industrially, and socially to develop his or her intelligence and abilities. We must ensure, finally, that no class has special demands (*tequan*) put on it that would lead to its oppressing itself, nor to its desiring prerogatives (*tequan*) that would allow it to oppress others: only this is genuine equality, [for it is] the genuine equality of all people.

What is freedom? To understand its true characteristics, we must understand that contemporary democracy places great importance on respecting the free opinions of each individual. Controlling any undertaking depends on the free opinions of each individual. In the social realm, relying on the control of individual free opinions is thus called social democracy; in the industrial realm, it is called economic democracy; and in the political realm, it is called political democracy. But what are "free opinions" (*ziyou yisi*)? And what is "control by free opinions"? To put it simply, no class subjugates others or is subjugated by others; everyone belongs to humanity, and there is no distinction between subjugator and subjugatee. In addition, in the realm of moral justice, there is no talk of subjugating oneself and obeying another. [Together,] this is the definition of free opinion. Similarly, in social, industrial, or political realms, no one is allowed to have prerogatives such that they interfere with or coerce themselves or others, and this is known as heeding the control of individual free opinions.

France has a famous legal scholar named Montesquieu who once defined freedom as follows: "Freedom has its origins in each person's desires, as well as in each person not needing to forcibly restrain his or her own desires." This definition is simple, inclusive, and perspicacious. There is one point, though, that we must note very carefully: although he says that freedom is born from each person's desires, this is not the complete manifestation of selfish desires, shorn of all limitations. Human lives do indeed have an aspect with its origins in our natural desires to benefit ourselves; we need not hide this fact. If, however, people rely solely on their desires to benefit themselves as guides to action, without a bit of restraint or any set limits, they will inevitably reach the point of inhibiting the free actions of others. At this point, humanity will contain people who subjugate others, which naturally also means that there will be those who are subjugated by others. This will be because an individual (or a small group of people) is willing to obliterate the desires of others—to make others sacrifice on his or her behalf—in order to satisfy his or her individual desires. Is this kind of behavior any different from there being a single "trust" in the world? To sum up, freedom, as it is understood by contemporary democracy, does not demand that we completely abandon our self-regarding desires, but it is also not completely without limitation. Thus if we want to attain the goal of genuine freedom in human life, we must ensure that each person has equal opportunities in all areas of human life, from social to industrial to political. Only this really counts as freedom—as freedom for all people.

Returning to the facts of the French Revolution, because in the end it was biased toward the political and made little effort in either industrial or social arenas, all the various means of life—from vast factories to miraculous technologies to abundant capital—ended up in the sole possession of a minority of society. On top of this, the laws that protected people's rights, the policies designed to develop businesses, the police whose job it is to ensure our security, and even the warships charged with guarding our citizens overseas—all are established solely for those in society with prerogatives. Not only this, but the vast majority in society without prerogatives are little more than draft animals. True freedom of opportunity is nothing like this.

The fundamental principle of the French Revolution is completely contained in the Declaration of the Rights of Man; the spirit of the Declaration is completely expressed in its advocacy of human equality. It says: "All humans, without distinction of age, strength, intelligence, or virtue, equally possess heaven-endowed human rights (*tianfude renquan*); among these human rights, the most important position is occupied by people's right to property."[3] "The right to property is sacred": these words were the banner with which each leader of the revolution incited the common people to struggle violently against the aristocrats and clergy; they were the weapon that toppled the aristocracy and ended the power of the church. However, it was as if the common people had warded off a tiger at the front door only to let in a wolf by the rear: soon enough, political, industrial, and social hegemony had been seized by the capitalist class. As soon as the old-style trust had been abolished, a new-style trust was created in its place. The essential factors in the formation of this [new-style] trust were the intention [of the capitalists] to benefit themselves—that is, to completely satisfy their individual desires while rejecting the interests of others—as well as the intention to control others with only [the capitalists'] own concerns, rather than any [wider] social functions, in mind. We can sum up their intention by saying that it emerged completely from their self-regarding impulses. Contemporary democracy absolutely cannot allow such intentions to exist. . . .

The liberation of life! The equality of opportunity! From abstract to concrete, from partial to universal: only these count as the spirit of contemporary democracy.

Notes

1. "Equal chance" in English in original.
2. Tan's version can be compared with the original, in which Lincoln, talking about the "great principle" that has motivated his country, said that it was "something in the Declaration giving liberty, not alone to the people of this country, but hope to the world for all future time. It was that which gave promise that in due time the weights should be lifted from the shoulders of all men, and that *all* should have an equal chance." Abraham Lincoln, *Speeches and Writings, 1859–1865* (New York: Literary Classics, 1989), p. 213.
3. The Declaration does not say this. Article 2 comes closest, but does not elevate the right to property above others: "The final end of every political institution is the

preservation of the natural and imprescriptable rights of man. These rights are those of liberty, property, security, and resistance to oppression." See Albert Blaustein et al., eds., *Human Rights Sourcebook* (New York: Paragon House, 1987), p. 744. Property is characterized as an "inviolable and sacred right" in the Declaration's last article, number 17. See Blaustein, *Human Rights Sourcebook,* p. 745.

Further Reading

For information on the students writing in *New Tide*, see Vera Schwarcz, *The Chinese Enlightenment: Intellectuals and the Legacy of the May Fourth Movement of 1919* (Berkeley: University of California Press, 1986). For Marx's criticism of the French Declaration, see Karl Marx, "On the Jewish Question," in Robert Tucker, ed., *The Marx-Engels Reader* (New York: W.W. Norton, 1978).

16
The Question of People's Rights in the Provincial Constitutions (1921)

Gao Yihan

"Sheng xianfa zhong de minquan wenti" [The Question of People's Rights in the Provincial Constitutions], *Xin qingnian* [New Youth] 9:5 (1921).

In the text translated here, Gao Yihan criticizes earlier human rights declarations for exclusively focusing on civil and political rights. Gao points out that since it was the bourgeoisie who in the seventeenth and eighteenth centuries were responsible for these declarations, they failed to stipulate the economic rights needed by the proletariat. This critique was shared by the Communist Tan Mingqian (see Text 15), but it was the liberal Gao Yihan who elaborated a "right to subsistence" [shengcun quan]. Gao argued that civil and political rights would be empty if people's livelihoods were not protected via rights to subsistence. Around the same time as Gao began to talk of the right to subsistence, others also did so, although sometimes out of different ideological convictions, as in the case of the GMD ideologist Dai Jitao. By the early 1920s, the right to subsistence had entered the Chinese rights discourse; it was thereafter embraced by people of different political persuasions, ranging from social liberals to socialists. The concept of and interest in a right to subsistence was thus not an invention of the CCP, as the invocation of this right since 1991 often makes it seem (see Text 52).

. . . Talking again about the right to freedom, the situation is the same. [That is, the right to freedom is as vulnerable in the face of social in-

equalities as the right to property, which Gao has just discussed—*Eds.*]
For example, the constitution stipulates only that "people have freedom
of speech and thought." We have to ask whether, in order to enjoy these
kinds of freedoms, people do not also need some corresponding life
capabilities? [If so,] then should society not have to provide each individual with the appropriate capabilities and facilities? The first precondition for all those who want to enjoy the freedom of speech and thought
is to be able to live. If not even one's life can be protected, then it is
impossible for one to receive an education. And even if one's life is
protected and an education received, and even if one does not have any
other problems, still, if there are no library facilities in society and no
scholars to advise one or to stimulate one's academic interests, or if
society, because of its industrial system or because of other customs,
does not give one convenient opportunities for study, then how can one
enjoy the high-sounding freedoms of speech and thought stipulated in
the constitution?

. . . [In other words,] the flaw in previous constitutions has been to
stress only fundamental political rights while neglecting fundamental
economic rights. . . . What is the content of basic economic rights? The
first is "the right to the whole value of one's labor," the second is "the
right to subsistence" (*shengcun quan*), and the third is "the right to work."
The right to the whole value of one's labor can be exercised only in a
communist system, whereas the right to work can be exercised in a
private-property system, and the right to subsistence can be exercised in
both a communist system and a private property system. . . .

What is the meaning of "a right to subsistence"? It is the distribution
of all wealth according to the needs of the people. If, for example, something is not of much use to person A but of great use to person B, then it
should be distributed to person B. According to the right to the whole
value of one's labor, the criterion for distribution of wealth is labor,
whereas, according to the right to subsistence, it is needs. To put it in a
nutshell, because people already exist (*shengcun*), they should have the
rights to protect their existence. It should not be the case that one group
of people cannot even protect their lives. Until a communist system is
adopted, we should use laws to protect those people who cannot obtain
the means for subsistence. Specifically, the law should acknowledge
the right of children to receive education and the right of the old, the
infirm, and those who have lost their ability to work to receive economic assistance. . . .

Further Reading

For additional writings by Gao Yihan, see Text 13. Gao's 1930 book on political science in particular gives an elaborate analysis of his view of economic and social rights. For a 1919 article by Dai Jitao mentioning the right to subsistence, see "Fa de jichu" [The Foundation of Law], reprinted in Tang Wenquan and Sang Bing, eds., *Dai Jitao ji, 1909–1913* [Dai Jitao's Collected Essays, 1909–1913] (Wuhan: Huazhong shifan daxue chubanshe, 1990). For a more detailed and thorough analysis that shows a clear influence from Gao, see Shi Weihuan, "Wo guo xianfa ying mingding guomin zhi shengcun quan" [Our Constitution Should Explicitly Lay Down the Right to Subsistence], *Dongfang zazhi* 19:21 (November 1922). See also the discussion of the "right to subsistence" in the General Introduction, above.

17
Eastern and Western Cultures and Their Philosophies (1921)

Liang Shuming

Dong xi wenhua ji qi zhexue [Eastern and Western Cultures and Their Philosophies]. Originally published 1921; reprinted as *Dong xi wenhua ji qi zhexue* [Eastern and Western Cultures and Their Philosophies] (Taipei: Jiuding Press, 1982), pp. 35–37 and pp. 177–78, 204–7, 208–9, 211–13.

Here are excerpts from two chapters of Eastern and Western Cultures and Their Philosophies, *a widely read book by Liang Shuming (1893–1988). An excellent biography of Liang identifies him as "the last Confucian," but no single label can encompass Liang's distinctive viewpoint. It is true that he famously sought to defend China's culture, and Confucianism in particular, from many foes. He keenly appreciated some of the central ethical and psychological insights of classical Confucianism, and strove to incorporate these ideals into a program of reform and education that would suit his new age. At the same time, though, Liang was an avid student of the sundry Western ideas that were being debated by his peers, and there can be no doubt that these ideas played roles in shaping his proposals and philosophy. Liang was as much a socialist as he was a Confucian . . . and then again, later in life he identified himself as a Buddhist. It is fascinating to note that he explicitly endorses many of the criticisms of Confucianism posed by Chen Duxiu, on which see Text 11. The central idea of Liang's book is that there have been three major cultural paths: the Western, Chinese, and Indian. He argues that each is appropriate at a certain stage of the evolution of human civilization. For Chinese of his day, his summary proposal is: "First, reject the Indian attitude without any reservation.*

Second, accept entirely the Western culture but modify its foundation; that is, change its attitude. Third, critically salvage the original Chinese attitude" (p. 202). This means, among other things, that rights must be recognized and fought for, but he thinks this can be done without falling prey to the problems that he (like many in his day) saw plaguing Western societies. After the publication of Eastern and Western Cultures, *Liang set out to put his ideas into practice. He was one of the instigators behind the liberal reform manifesto "Our Political Proposals," on which see by the introduction to Text 14, and subsequently made even more concrete efforts by promoting rural reconstruction and education. He discusses rights again in later writings, but much more critically: he seems to have lost confidence that rights can be insulated from the more problematic consequences of Western culture.*

Chapter 2: What Is Easternization? What Is Westernization? (Part 1)

. . . Chinese people are very startled when they see that in the Western way [of doing things], there is no single master. It is even more startling when they see that each person is equal, with no distinctions between high and low or superior and inferior. This is because they believe that the natural order between heaven and earth distinguishes between high and low, superior and inferior, and large and small, and that human affairs are supposed to conform to this order. The true basis for theories of the human realm, however, is how well they can be applied, not how credible they seem. In other words, any doctrine worth believing must be able to be applied successfully. The reason why [the Chinese] are convinced of [the distinctions] between high and low and superior and inferior, and regard the absence of these distinctions as odd, is because [they] wonder how people can live peacefully without such a distinction. This sort of suspicion is parallel with their [puzzlement about the absence of a master]. In the [case of the master], they expect failure without one person to govern the others—that is, without a ruler. In [the other case,] they expect failure if every individual does not contentedly comply with graded differentiation; that is, if [everyone is] not content with the low status of being governed. If none is low but [instead all are] equal, then no one would be able to govern others and no one would be governed by others, and there has never been a world [like that] that was not in chaos. It is beyond their imagination that such a world would turn out not to be in chaos. For several thousand years, that which has maintained the tranquility of Chinese society is the four words "high, low, large, small." They have never seen a society without "high, low, large, small." As I discussed above, the Chinese method is that those who make decisions and those who comply are two completely separate kinds, whereas in the West those who make decisions are those who comply, and those who comply are those who make decisions. Therefore the "governing" and the "governed" in China are two distinct classes, which creates the so-called "high and low." The [distinction between] "high and low" has to be rigorously observed, in fact, if this path is to be tenable. In the West every person is the "governing" and also the "governed"; there is naturally none of the so-called "high, low, superior, inferior," but instead everyone is equal. Thus rigorously observing high and low, on the one hand, and esteeming equality (*pingdeng*), on the other, are the two different spirits of China and the West.

When high and low are [people's] decreed lots (*mingfen*), they have the inequality of rights (*quanli*) as their contents. "Equality" itself is none other than the equality of rights. Accordingly, rights are the exact things for which people fight. Whether one has rights or not can be viewed in two different lights. From a comparative perspective, it is a question of equality and inequality. From an individual perspective, it is a question of whether or not one is free (*ziyou*). The result of the path that China has taken is that people are not equal, nor are individuals free. Although the original intention of the Chinese path was merely to allow one person to lead and make decisions regarding the continuing, common livelihood of all the people, it has in fact led to each individual's personal livelihood depending on the master, rather than on the individual's own self-mastery (*zizhu*). Not only have public affairs been entrusted to [the master], while individuals have no right to inquire into [his handling of them]; individuals also do not have the right to freely [decide on] their own speech and action. This is what is meant by "not free." Even though [an individual] can be very free in practice, this is only because [the master] does not interfere, not because [individuals] actually have rights. From the beginning this path would have been untenable had the master decision maker not been able to make unlimited decisions, and had the [common people] not absolutely complied with his orders. I have already touched on this previously. Therefore [the development] which everyone should [pay attention to] is from:

> The first level, when those with rights (*quan*) and those without rights are cleaved into two divisions, to:

> The second level, when there is no limit on the rights of those that have them, and no limit to the lack of rights for those who lack them.

The two words "no limit" are very important. Chinese completely fail to understand the [idea of] "limits." [Chinese] have never even conceived of concepts like "rights" and "freedom," and even now that they have encountered [such concepts], they still fail to comprehend them. The rights (*quan*) [that they speak of] are all powers (*quan*), as in "authoritative powers (*weiquan*)," the powers which do such-and-such to other people; all these powers are precisely opposite to "rights" (*quanli*). As they are spoken of in the West, rights and freedoms fundamentally require strict observance of limits, but Chinese regard them as "beyond limits" or "without limits." Thus they always have one of two kinds of attitude toward Western people's demands for freedom. The first is indifference, since [the Chinese] do not understand what [freedom] is for. The other is astonishment, since they assume this would send the world into chaos. From the beginning, their life experiences have not made them aware of this need [for freedom], which in addition would be sufficient to destroy [their particular path of life]. The Westerners' path is different from this. Their path originally grew out of seeking rights and the protection of freedom. Their path is thus necessarily able to respect individual freedom: rights are possessed by all the people themselves—that is, by each individual. [If] each individual is not willing to let others interfere with him, how could there be any problem? Hence that which we should note here also has two levels:

> The first level is that everyone has the right to participate in and be master over public affairs.
>
> The second level is that nobody has the right to interfere in others' individual affairs.

This is the reason why I mentioned above that decision-making must have a limited scope, as must the compliance with orders. [Just like when Chinese consider the Western path,] when Westerners see how the Chinese refuse rights and ignore freedom, they are also astonished and confused. This was similarly because their lives would fail without these things, and therefore they regard them as indispensable. Hence the relinquishment of human rights (*renquan*), on the one hand, and the love of freedom, on the other, manifest the extreme differences between China and the West. . . .

Chapter 5: The World's Future Culture and the Attitude That We Should Hold

[*Editors' note*: Liang has argued that the West is shifting toward more Eastern attitudes in many ways, among them: relativism instead of absolutism, emotions instead of knowledge, intuition instead of rationality, and so on.]

. . . And in addition to these changes in direction, the Western world of thought today clearly wishes to change its established attitude toward life (*rensheng taidu*), and the direction that they desire points to the Chinese path and Confucian path. We must first understand how up to this point, through adopting their Western attitude, they have been injured spiritually and suffered physically. Generally when an attitude or direction is first adopted, it may not appear in any way unsuitable. When a road is followed halfway, most travelers will still find it to be excellent, having led to achievements. When they continue on toward its end, however, going ever farther along its twists and turns, everything comes to seem wrong as many problems and countless pains emerge. Previously everything seemed wonderful, but now everything is terrible. The Westerners today are like this. I pointed out in the third chapter how Westerners embrace an attitude stressing selfishness and progress, which in the spiritual realm creates cracks between man and nature and between man and man. Proceeding farther, the cracks become larger and larger and deep cleavages develop. The result of this is that nature seems very cold to man, and man is heartless toward nature. There is no returning to the [attitude] of ancient times, in which heaven and earth were humanized and felt to nurture the myriad things in the world; heaven and earth seemed kind to man and man respected them, [man and nature] treating each other with mutual dependence and affection. With their rational and analytical minds, [Westerners] have categorized all the [things] of the universe and converted them into material objects. Nature is looked upon as a pile of fragmented, inanimate things, and as man himself is included in nature merely as a compound of fragments, there no longer exists a complete and coherent cosmos nor any profound spirituality. The clarity of their distinctions and boundaries between men, the importance they put on calculation, and the division, rivalry, and competition between each of them is such that there is not much mutual dependence or affection even among the family members like father and son: it seems as if they are only aware of themselves, while others are all strangers or enemies. It is indeed unbearably sad for men to live in this cold, unhappy, monotonous, and tedious universe, in which everything of interest has been completely obliterated.

[As they proceed] along their progressive path, [they] invariably seek for things outside [themselves], allowing their individual spiritual lives to go to waste. Their external lives are radiant, but their internal lives are so impoverished as to be completely empty. Accordingly they are uniformly anxious to escape from the narrow and cruel world that reason has imposed upon them. The wise among them consistently warn their fellow Westerners about the death of their spirits, in response to which they bustle about, [looking for salvation in things like] the rekindling of religion, the encouragement of arts, the universalism of "love," or the ideal that the soul and the body are one, but they cannot find a way out. The only savior now is the school of the philosophy of life (*shengmingpai de zhexue*). Although all the various measures [they have tried] aim at changing their preexisting attitude, only the philosophy of life really has the audacity and methodology to change their attitudes. For only the philosophy of life has the daring to fuse their fragmented universe into a whole; only its method can truly free them from narrowness and cruelty, restore their vigorous interest in life, and restore their universe, which had been made material, back to the spiritual. There is originally no such thing as matter. As things are placed under reason's categories and converted into calculable entities, they become material. When reason reigns supreme, everything is converted into the calculable and everything becomes material. Seen from the perspective of intuition (*zhijue*), on the other hand, all things have unique meanings and different characteristics, cannot be calculated or compared, and thus all become nonmaterial or spiritual. It perhaps goes without saying that all their narrowness, cruelty, monotony, or tedium can be transformed by intuition. And the method of this school [of philosophy of life] is intuition. In today's world intuition is going to take the place of reason and prosper, and the turning point consists in this school of philosophy. . . .

[*Editors' note*: Liang now turns to China, where he sees a need for some of the very insights from which Westerners are now beginning to turn away. China's situation is different: it needs more of a dynamic, progressive attitude, albeit not exactly the same as that found in the West.]

From my earlier description of the reasons we [Chinese] made mistakes and the pains we have suffered, it is almost possible to infer what kind of attitude we should hold now, but it still may be necessary to explain further our present needs and the current situation in China and abroad. Our needs are many. There is no point in enumerating them one by one; more urgent than any others is [learning] how to allow individual rights (*geren quanli*) to stabilize our social order. Not only is this more precious than anything else, but if any of our needs are to be obtainable at all, we must begin with this. Without doing so, we cannot consolidate the foundation of our country and become a nation in the international world. Without doing so, we cannot ensure that all our social undertakings proceed smoothly. In this case, isn't it possible to infer what kind of attitude will enable us to achieve these ends? Furthermore, look at the situation outside our country. Westerners have also suffered great pains from their culture. In the near or distant future, this will influence the tremendous transformation of the world [now beginning,] and open up the second cultural path.[1] In the past we worried about the destruction of our country and the extinction of our race. It seems now that the current situation is different, and the ideology of "enriching the state and strengthening the military" (*fuqiang*) [that we previously embraced] no longer needs to be practiced. The issues we should heed as we decide what attitude to adopt, therefore, are first, what lessons to draw in light of the drawbacks of Westernization, and second, the need to prepare for and advance toward realization of the world's second cultural path. I shall now critically discuss whether the intentions of various people today are compatible with these conclusions.

It is common today to speak of the so-called "new school" and "old school." The new school roughly refers to those who advocate Westernization, while the old school roughly refers to those who object to such advocacy—as this latter group hardly ever has something that they positively champion. In fact I think that there is also a third group that has gained some power without people noticing, namely the school of Buddhasization (*fohuapai*). Let us first look at what the new school says. It advocates none other than Mr. Chen Duxiu's "science" and "democracy," as well as Mr. Hu Shi's "critical spirit." I agree with all of these, but if this is all, they are inadequate to give people a fundamental attitude toward life (*rensheng taidu*). As water without a source cannot become a river, petty measures have no hope of providing a complete solution. This is the reason why Mr. Jiang Menglin's article "Change Our Attitude Toward Life" attracted my attention, though I would not agree with [him] uncritically or unconditionally. The first few volumes of the *Xin qingnian* magazine had several articles that advocated a certain kind of life, and there is also Mr. Chen Duxiu's essay "The True Meaning of Life."[2] [It is true that] the result of advocating science, democracy, and a critical spirit is that some will come to lead a certain kind of life. But I cannot unconditionally agree with any of [these views]. After all, the Westerners' preexisting attitude toward life has now been shown to have many shortcomings and has been severely criticized, but [the new school] still wants to adopt the whole of it without discretion. Despite the fact that this [Western] attitude will just worsen the plight of today's Westerners, it is indeed quite apt for dealing with the prejudices of the preexisting Chinese [attitude], but only after some [significant] modifications. Moreover, in order to prepare for and advance the development of the world's second cultural path, we also had better change the preexisting Western attitude a little. I will discuss later this corrected and modified Western attitude.

The old school is merely a reaction to the new school. They do not actually promote a return to the old (*jiuhua*). Mr. Chen Duxiu is the leader of the attacks on the old culture. Many people became angry and cursed after reading his articles and some wrote to argue with him. Yet the former did not go beyond anger and cursing, and the latter did not go beyond arguing. They simply have a kind of mental aversion and are not convinced, without any positive urge to joyfully promote a return to the old. As the contents of their ideas are unusually empty and they do not even comprehend where to find the fundamental spirit of a return to the old, how can they oppose Mr. Chen's clear mind and sharp writing? Naturally Mr. Chen has swept clean the field before him. I remember that in his article "Research on Confucianism" in *Meizhou pinglun*, Mr. Chen repeatedly asked: "Since it has been admitted that Confucianism is legally, politically, and economically incompatible with modern society and its mentality, I do not know what reason there could be for still wanting to venerate Confucianism. Other than the way of the ruler and minister, father and son, and husband and wife, as well as other explanations regarding the common morality, what exactly are the spirit, true appearance, and true meaning of Confucius?"[3]

The main idea of Chen's article is to say that Confucius's teachings are nothing other than either (1) conclusions derived from his contemporary society, or (2) general moral considerations. The former were only applicable to Confucius's contemporary society and are incompatible with modern society, and are thus out of the question. As for the latter, such as teaching people to be trustworthy and honest, teaching people to be benevolent and loving, or teaching people to be diligent and frugal: these are what moralists everywhere preach; what does Confucius in particular have to do with it? Outside of these, where does the true spirit and unique value of Confucius reside? I would like those of you who think Confucianism is treated unfairly to explain to me why. Such acute questioning has rendered the adherents of the old school tongue-tied; they really have nothing to say. The year before last year students at Beijing University began publishing magazines called *Xin chao* (New Tide) and *Guo gu* (National Tradition), as if representing the two schools of new and old. The *New Tide* could manifest a kind of Western spirit, while the *National Tradition* only accumulated a handful of outdated, useless things. Is it true that our real national tradition calls for China to become ancient again, and adopt an ancient attitude toward life? Is this kind of ossified, rotten material a worthy match for the [*New Tide*]? It has become embarrassing to talk about restoring anything of old China, and Confucius's doctrines dare not raise their heads—all this because there is no talent in the old school. What need could there be to discuss [traditional culture and the teachings of Confucius]? [In these circumstances,] the old school does not in fact advocate a return to the old, and so there is nothing there of which I can approve; as for their objections to cultural renovation (*xinhua*), I can only say that I disapprove. Their objections to cultural renovation are not well thought through. They recognize that society has to be reformed—which current institutions must accept—and that our scholarship is lacking while Western science seems to be good. But they nonetheless want to compromise and reduce the democratic spirit and the scientific spirit by half, not [allowing them] to be consistently practiced everywhere. As a matter of fact, these two spirits are completely correct; we should approve of them uncritically and unconditionally. This is what I mean by saying that we should "entirely accept" Westernization. How to introduce these two spirits is indeed today's top priority. Otherwise, we shall never be qualified to discuss personality (*renge*) or scholarship. As long as you examine carefully the pains we have suffered so far, you will understand that this comment of mine is not something provoked by the moment. This is why I have sighed that it is very fortunate for our world of scholarship and thought that these two years Dewey and Russell came to China first, while Bergson and Eucken did not come.[4] If Dewey and Russell had not come while Bergson and Eucken came first, please reflect on whether [the remedies] would have matched the existing chronic diseases. . . .

[*Editors' note*: Liang notes that his contemporaries have not only shown an interest in things Western, but also in Indian ideas and attitudes—and especially in Buddhism. For reasons similar to those we have just seen, he deplores this interest in Buddhism.]

Right now we urgently need to pacify our domestic turmoil and stabilize our individual rights of life, property, and so on. With what kind of attitude can these goals be achieved? Some people, such as Mr. Liu Renhang and others, believe that if everyone stops struggling for rights and profits the turmoil will cease; if given a dose of refreshing medicine by Buddhism, people will no longer struggle for rights and profits and the world will be in peace. In fact, however, this is a most incorrect opinion, perfectly contrary to the principles of affairs and to the true situation. Our current political system was adopted from the West, and in the West it was produced by their attitude of progressive pursuit. But the majority of our citizens still hold the old attitude that has existed for several thousand years, namely being indifferent to politics and not demanding individual rights, and this attitude is incompatible with [our political] system root and branch. Consequently a minority of people are allowed to compete with each other to seize and dominate power. The political situation is overturned incessantly and disturbances succeed one another without end. Therefore our concern today is not that [everyone] struggles [too much] for rights and profits, but that everyone struggles too little for rights and profits. Only if the majority of citizens come together to struggle with that minority can this political system be [effectively] established, can the yearly chaos be pacified, and can all our individual rights of life and property be protected. If [people] continue to obediently tolerate [the minority's excesses] and always scheme about ways to escape from the disturbances, then peace will never be achieved. The only possible course is to quickly adopt the Western attitude. Even our [current] attitude of bending oneself and yielding to others is not suitable. How much less [suitable] is Buddhism, which invariably exhorts people to give up the attitude of progressive pursuit? For this reason I warned, in my "Preface" to the *Elucidation of the Meanings of Consciousness-Only [Buddhism]*, that: "Should the Buddhist culture prosper, the turmoil of China will not end."[5] I hope that those who champion Buddhism have pity for the people being ravaged in Hunan and Hubei provinces, and do not again lead people to their third attitude and prolong the disastrous condition of the Chinese people. . . .

Let me now explain the attitude that I propose. The attitude that I propose is "firmness" (*gang*) as spoken of by Confucius. The sense of firmness [I have in mind] can encompass the whole of Confucius's philosophy and is quite difficult to explain clearly in a short time, but if we focus on the single point that most needs explaining, and use very simple language, we should be able to succeed. Roughly, firmness is activity that is replete with physical energy (*liqi*). Confucius said: "I have not seen a man of firmness."[6] Firmness is basically very difficult to achieve. Now it seems that we should not suggest extremely difficult attitudes to ordinary people, since if we want an attitude to be universally observed by everyone, it has to be very simple and easy: something which they can follow without even being aware of it, rather than requiring continuous efforts to be successful. But the firmness I am explaining here actually includes both the profound and difficult and the shallow and easy. Firmness is a direction of travel: in this direction, one can enter slightly or enter deeply. Thus it can also be a very simple and easy [attitude]. Naturally we would initially show people the simple and easy aspect, to lead them in this direction; if they have high potential, then they can advance themselves to the higher level.

What I ask of everyone today is no more than to move forward, so long as this movement is coming from one's direct sentiments rather than from any deliberation based on desires. Confucius said: "Cheng is subject to desire; how could he be firm?"[7] Generally both desire and firmness look like courageous, forward-looking activity, but one is full of strength while the other is completely false—neither full nor truly strong. In the former case, the movement emerges from the inside, while in the latter, the movement looks toward the outside for fulfillment. Confucius's statement "firm, resolute, simple, and reticent: near to humaneness" completely captures the person of lofty will and replete sentiments (*qing*).[8] The movements of such people probably all directly come from sentiments. Both for settling the present turmoil in order to protect life, property, and individual rights, and to promote the development of the future world culture in order to obtain a reasonable life, we must adopt the first attitude and everyone must vigorously press forward. But if this is not fundamentally fused with the second life attitude, the dangers and mistakes of the first path cannot be avoided and it will not be apt for the current transition period between the first and the second paths. Feeling unwilling to rest content with the situation and exerting ourselves [to fuse the two paths] is superior to heading straight at either of the paths alone.

I have pointed out this attitude to everyone in the memorial service for Miss Li Chao: "Seeking freedom is not done because [we] have calculated how much benefit or convenience is to be found in freedom, but because [we] feel unwilling to rest content without freedom."[9] One needs no more than this to meet my criterion of firmness. Firm movements are simply genuine perceptions and manifestations (*ganfa*). My intention was simply to promote the practice of vigorously pressing forward, while at the same time rejecting the decadent fashion of pursuing external material goods. I also said in that article: "Although the encouragement of desires can also move people forward, I do not support this." [What I say] now is not different from that idea. Mr. Shi Jinmo said to me: "Any movement is better [than no movement]." Many knowledgeable people today can see this much, but how do we make people move? It seems that in the last few years, people have primarily advocated movement stemming from desire. Recently there has been a slight shift in the direction of movement stemming from sentiments, but [I fear that] this is only a fashion following on certain social movements and a cliché that imitates Russell's creative and possessive impulses. The shift does not represent a clear-sighted choice [of sentiment over desire], and so [the situation now] remains disorderly, divergent, ambiguous, and vague, with no clear direction, much less the fundamental knowledge of how to proceed. There have been many [group] movements in the last two years, but the more people have moved, the more exhausted they have become and the more they have come to loathe moving. Now everyone is depleted and feels unable to continue. No one is delighted to move again; no one feels able to move again. All this is because external confusions seduce their desires and lure their sentiments into transient excitement; internally, they all share the Epicureans' (*yuwangpai*) ideas of life. They cannot stop until they are depleted and vexed.

It is not easy to move, and proper movement is harder still. In order to achieve [genuine] movements stemming from sentiment, one must first fundamentally open oneself up to a kind of life that completely transcends individual selfishness, envy of material things, ubiquitous calculation, and actions that expect [rewards], and emit a vital energy directly from the inside—Russell's creative impulse—that fuses with the forward-looking attitude and responds only in accordance with one's perceptions (*sui gan er ying*). Movement stemming from sentiment can only be achieved in this way. Only this kind of forward movement will truly be strong and maintain a vital energy. People will not become dispirited and weary; they will come to find joy through their own activities. Only forward movement of this kind can atone for what Chinese have lacked heretofore, relieve their current suffering, avoid the ills of the West, and satisfy the needs of the world, and it is fully consistent with what our foregoing studies of the three world cultures has indicated. This is what I call the attitude of firmness, what I call the proper second path of life. Originally the Chinese had taken this path, but they always leaned toward the negative (*yin*), flexible, receptive, and tranquil. This was close to Laozi, but not to the positive (*yang*), firm, creative, and dynamic attitude of Confucius. The firm attitude of Confucius is the proper second path of life.

Notes

1. That is, the Chinese path.
2. Several selections in this volume appeared in *Xin qingnian*; see Texts 10, 11, and 13. For Chen's article, see *Xin qingnian* 4:2 (February 15, 1919).
3. "Kongzi yanjiu," *Meizhou pinglun*, no. 20 (May 4, 1919). See also Chen's criticism of Confucianism in Text 11, above.
4. John Dewey and Bertrand Russell, both of whom Liang views as representatives of mainstream Western thought, visited China in 1919 and 1920. Henri Bergson (1859–1941) and Rudolph Eucken (1846–1926) both represent what Liang views as the trend toward Sinicization in Western thought.
5. Liang here refers to his book on "Wei shi" or "ideation only" Buddhism: *Wei shi shu yi* (Beijing: Beijing University, 1920).
6. *Analects* 5:11. Translation based on E. Bruce and A. Taeko Brooks, *The Original Analects* (New York: Columbia University Press, 1998), p. 24.
7. Ibid.
8. *Analects* 13:27.
9. See Liang's "Li Chao nüshi zhuidaohui yanshuo" [Speech at the Memorial Service for Miss Li Chao], in *Shuming saqian wenlu* [Writings of Liang Shuming Before the Age of Thirty] (Shanghai, 1924), pp. 76–78. The text of Liang's speech is also quoted in *Eastern and Western Cultures* itself, at pp. 188–90. Li Chao died in 1919 of tuberculosis, but this was attributed by Hu Shi and Cai Yuanpei to the social, economic, and emotional pressures placed on her by her family. See Hu's and Cai's famous essays, both of which are translated in Hua R. Lan and Vanessa L. Fong, eds., *Women in Republican China* (Armonk, NY: M.E. Sharpe, 1999).

Further Reading

For an outstanding biography of Liang, see Guy Allito, *The Last Confucian*, 2d ed. (Berkeley: University of California Press, 1986). Liang and several of his contemporaries are the subjects of Charlotte Furth, ed., *The Limits of Change: Essays on Conservative Alternatives in Republican China* (Cambridge, MA: Harvard University Press, 1976). Liang's views on rural reconstruction, one of the practical ways he attempted to implement his ideas, have been translated in "Reconstructing the Community," in Wm. Theodore de Bary and John Lufrano, eds., *Sources of Chinese Tradition, 2d ed.* (New York: Columbia University Press, 2000), vol. 2, pp. 382–86.

Liang's earliest discussions of rights appear in his 1917 pamphlet "Wucao bu chu ru cangsheng he?" [What Can the People Do If We Do Not Set Out?], in *Shuming saqian wenlu*, pp. 39–56 (Shanghai, 1924), and in "Lun xuesheng shijian" [On the Student Incident], *Meizhou pinglun* (May 18, 1919). After his extended discussion in *Eastern and Western Cultures*, he returns to rights, much more critically, in *Zhongguo wenhua yaoyi* [The Essentials of Chinese Culture] of 1949, rev. ed. (Taipei: Wunan Press, 1988), esp. pp. 91–92.

18
The Principle of People's Power (1924)

Sun Yatsen

"Minquan zhuyi," in *Sanmin zhuyi* [The Three Principles of the People]. Originally published 1924. Reprinted in *Sanmin zhuyi* [The Three Principles of the People], 18th ed. (Taipei: Sanmin Press, 1996).

Sun Yatsen (1866–1925) was a revolutionary activist, theoretician, and leader of the GMD. His Three Principles of the People, from which these lectures are excerpted, was his theoretical manifesto. Sun's formulations were extremely influential, as the many discussions, pro and con, in subsequent essays in this collection will confirm. The three principles are: nationalism [minzu zhuyi], people's power [minquan zhuyi], and people's livelihood [minsheng zhuyi]. Our concern here is with the second of these. Sun's understanding of quan, which in most other essays we have translated as "rights," as "power," is a central element of his thought that helps to explain his lack of interest in promoting further freedom for individual Chinese, as discussed below. "Minquan" is one of the most changeable and contested terms in all of Chinese rights discourse, though, and some of his subsequent supporters understand it to mean something much closer to "people's rights" than "people's power," even if they still differentiate it from human rights. For more discussion of this term, see the General Introduction.

Lecture One

Ladies and Gentlemen:

Today I am going to give an account of the principle of people's power (*minquan zhuyi*). What is the principle of people's power? In order to explain the meaning of the principle of people's power, we first have to know the meaning of "people" (*min*). In general, a mass of individuals that constitutes an organized group is called a people. What is the meaning of *quan*? *Quan* is force (*liliang*) or power (*weishi*); a power that is as strong as the state is called *quan*. The most powerful nations are called "the strong ones" (*lieqiang*) in Chinese and "the powers" (*liequan*) in foreign languages. Another example is that the force of a machine is called "horse force" (*mali*) in Chinese and "horse power" (*maquan*) in foreign languages. Hence, power (*quan*) and force (*li*) are the same, and the force that can carry out orders and direct others is called power. When we combine "people" (*min*) and "power" (*quan*), we get "people's power" (*minquan*), which means people's political force. What is political force? In order to understand this idea, we have to know something about politics. Many believe that politics is too subtle and abstruse for ordinary people to understand. China's military men often say, for instance: "We are soldiers and do not understand politics." Why don't they understand politics? They do not understand politics because they see politics as something subtle and abstruse. But politics is actually plain and easy to understand. It is alright to say that military men should not intervene in politics, but not to say that they should not understand it. Military men must understand and realize the meaning of politics because they are the driving force behind politics. [If we look at] the meaning of the two characters constituting "politics" (*zhengzhi*), to put it plainly, *zheng* means the affairs of everyone, and *zhi* means to administer. Politics is thus the administration of the affairs of all. A force that is capable of administering the affairs of all is called political power (*zhengquan*). Because today it is the people who administer political affairs, [this political force] is called "people's power." . . .

Lecture Two

. . . It is for profound [reasons] that we in the revolutionary party have always advocated revolution of the Three Principles of the People and not revolution to achieve freedom (*ziyou*). The slogan of the French Revolution was freedom, that of the American Revolution was independence, and ours is the Three Principles of the People. This [slogan] was expounded only after much time and effort, and does not copy the views of others. Why are the Chinese youth wrong to advocate freedom, and why were the Europeans right when they were doing so? . . . When we put forward a goal and exhort everybody to fight for it, this goal must [respond to] the pain that the people have keenly felt, for only then will they respond enthusiastically. The Europeans had suffered deeply from dictatorship, and therefore they assented with one heart and one mind as soon as the call for freedom was raised. If we now advocate freedom in China, however, people would not pay any attention, because they have never suffered from this kind of pain. If we advocate getting rich (*facai*), though, it will be met with much support. Our Three Principles of the People are similar to the principle of getting rich. To understand this logic, further explanation is needed. The reason why we do not directly advocate getting rich is that it does not encompass [all of] the Three Principles of the People, but the Three Principles of the People do encompass getting rich. The system of public property implemented in the early days of the Russian Revolution was close to a direct advocacy of getting rich. We in the revolutionary party, however, do not advocate only this one thing, and therefore [our objectives] cannot simply be encompassed by "getting rich," much less by the word "freedom."

Currently many European observers of China are of the opinion that the level of Chinese civilization is very poor. They claim that the [Chinese people's] political consciousness is so weak that they do not even understand freedom, saying: "We Europeans were already fighting and sacrificing ourselves for freedom one or two hundred years ago, performing countless magnificent and earth-shaking feats. But the Chinese today still do not know the meaning of freedom. From this can be seen that the Europeans' political consciousness is much more developed than that of the Chinese." Because the Chinese do not talk about freedom, their political consciousness must be weak. But this reasoning, in my view, does not hold. Since the Europeans respect freedom so much, why do they also say that we Chinese are like "a sheet of loose sand"? When the Europeans fought for freedom, their concept of freedom was naturally very strong. But after they achieved freedom and their goal was reached, perhaps their concept of freedom also gradually became weaker? I believe that if someone today again were to advocate freedom in Europe, it would not meet with as much support as before. Moreover, the European revolution for freedom is a method of two or three hundred years ago, which is no longer feasible.

What is so wonderful about "a sheet of loose sand"? It suggests abundant freedom: Without freedom, there can be no "sheet of loose sand." In the embryonic stage of European people's power the Europeans advocated struggling for freedom. When this goal was achieved, every individual had increased his or her own freedom, but this also meant that many problems appeared because of excessive freedom. So a British scholar named Mill argued that "only when [each] individual's freedom [stays within] the scope of not violating other people's freedom can there be real freedom." If one violates the scope of other people's [freedom], that would not be freedom. The Europeans and Americans used to advocate freedom without [specifying] any limits, but because Mill defined the limits of freedom, their freedom has also been significantly reduced. Based on these facts, we know that even foreign scholars have gradually recognized that freedom is not some sacred (*shensheng*) and inviolable (*buke qinfan*) thing, and that one has to draw limits to restrict it. The foreigners criticize the Chinese, on the one hand, for not knowing freedom, and on the other hand, for being like "a sheet of loose sand," but these two arguments are really mutually contradictory. Since the Chinese are like "a sheet of loose sand," this suggests abundant freedom. If being like "a sheet of loose sand" is something bad, then as soon as possible we should add water and cement so that they will mix together and become [as hard as] stone; [in other words,] we must unite ourselves into a solid group. This [would mean that] the loose sand could no longer move, having lost its freedom. The current Chinese sickness is not, therefore, the lack of freedom. If the essence of Chineseness is "a sheet of loose sand," this means that Chinese have always enjoyed abundant freedom. Chinese people, however, originally did not have a word for freedom, and thus they did not have this consciousness either. But what has consciousness to do with politics? Do the Chinese, after all, have freedom?

From our research into the facts of "a sheet of loose sand," we know that Chinese have enjoyed a great deal of freedom, and because this freedom has been excessive, they did not think of understanding it, even to the extent of not having a word [for the concept]. . . .

Why are we Chinese like "a sheet of loose sand," and what has made us so? It is because of excessive individual freedom. Because the Chinese have too much freedom, China needs a revolution. The goal of the Chinese revolution is different from those of the foreign [revolutions], and therefore the method is also different. Why does China need a revolution? To put it bluntly, [the reason] is the opposite of the reason for the Europeans' revolutions. The Europeans made revolution because of the lack of freedom, and accordingly fought for freedom. We Chinese, [on the other hand,] had too much freedom, lacked a [sense of] collectivity, and had no ability to resist [aggression], and so we became "a sheet of loose sand." Because we are like "a sheet of loose sand," we suffer from the imperialists' invasions and from the Great Powers' trade war, yet cannot offer any resistance. If we want, in the future, to be able to resist foreign oppression, we need to destroy individual freedom and unite ourselves into a solid group, just as when one adds cement to loose sand, it becomes [as hard as] stone. As the Chinese now have too much freedom, we suffer the ills of freedom. This problem exists not only among the students, but also inside our revolutionary party. The reason why we have not hitherto been able to establish our republic after overthrowing the Manchu Qing dynasty is all due to the abuse of freedom. . . .

Revolutions in foreign countries originated in the struggle for freedom. Only after fighting for two hundred or three hundred years and generating immense agitation, was freedom achieved and people's power (*minquan*) finally realized. The slogan of the French Revolution was "Liberty, Equality, and Fraternity." The slogan of our revolution is "Nationalism, People's Power, and People's Livelihood." What is the relationship between these two slogans? Our nationalism could, in my opinion, be said to be equivalent to their freedom, because to realize nationalism is precisely to fight for our nation's freedom. The Europeans fought for individual freedom, but now the application of freedom is different. How should we apply the word freedom today? If it were applied to the individual, we would turn into "a sheet of loose sand." It is therefore imperative to apply the word freedom not to the individual, but to the nation. The individual should not have too much freedom, but the nation must have complete freedom. When our nation is able to take free actions, then our nation is a strong and prosperous one. To achieve this goal, however, we must all sacrifice our [individual] freedom. When the students have sacrificed their freedom, they can work hard every day and put their efforts into their studies, and when their studies are completed, their knowledge developed, and their capabilities enriched, they can serve our nation. . . .

Further Reading

Sun's 1905 manifesto for the revolutionary party he founded is translated in Ssu-yu Teng and John K. Fairbank, eds., *China's Response to the West: A Documentary Survey 1839–1923* (New York: Atheneum, 1967). All six of Sun's lectures on the principle of people's power are translated in the somewhat dated *San min chu i: The*

Three Principles of the People (Shanghai: Commercial Press, 1928). For additional writings by Sun translated into English, see Julie Lee Wei, Ramon H. Myers, Donald G. Gillin, eds., *Prescriptions for Saving China: Selected Writings of Sun Yat-sen* (Stanford, CA: Hoover Institution Press, 1994). For Sun's biography and analysis of his thought, see Marie-Claire Bergère, *Sun Yat-sen*, trans. Janet Lloyd (Stanford, CA: Stanford University Press, 1998).

19
Foreword to *Renquan* Magazine (1925)

Anonymous

"Fakan ci" [Foreword], *Renquan* [Human Rights], no. 1 (August 1925).

The magazine Renquan *appeared in five issues between August and December 1925. The purpose of the magazine was to make people aware of the idea of human rights and to advocate a society based on respect for human rights. The magazine's editors regarded human rights as applicable to all countries and as characteristic of civilized and just societies. They argued that human rights were needed in order for individuals to be persons (*zuoren*), and held that without them humans would be reduced to the level of beasts. Human rights were based on our needs to preserve our lives and develop our personalities and intellects; they included economic, political, and educational rights. Human rights applied to all human beings. While the subjects of women's rights (*nüquan*) were women, setting them in contrast to men, and the subjects of people's rights (*minquan*) were the common people, setting them in opposition to rulers, aristocrats, bureaucrats, and warlords, the subjects of human rights (*renquan*) were all human beings. Human rights were opposed only to the minority who tried to suppress the rights of the majority.*

If we view the evolution of human society from the perspective of the conception of power governing society, we can detect a progress from divine rights (*shenquan*), to rights of the ruler (*junquan*), to rights of the people (*minquan*), to human rights (*renquan*). We can see that under the influence of these conceptions of power, with each stage of social evolution, humankind's tree of life has yielded different buds and flowers. . . .

> [Here follow paragraphs on governance by divine rights, rights of the ruler, and rights of the people. Metaphorically, in the first stage, humans were nothing compared to God and their tree was cut down. In the age of ruler's rights, only the ruler was allowed to flourish and the people were

used to nourish him. In the age of people's rights, although more people could flourish and bloom, the majority still could not.—Eds.]

How was it that [humankind] entered the stage of governance by human rights? It was then that people first dug the earth and sowed the seeds so that in the future sprouts and twigs would grow, leaves and buds would bloom, and trees would blossom and bear fruit. Even if this moment [of blossoming] has not yet arrived, we reckon, assess, and are convinced that in this stage of evolution, the tree of humankind will inevitably put out flowers everywhere and be full of sweet-scented osmanthus. This is because a society governed by human rights is imbued with three essential factors:

1. life sustaining (*shengcun*) functions;
2. the fresh air of freedom; and
3. a fertilizer of appropriate equality.

When one has these three essential factors there is no need to rely on the light of God, nor to protect the flower of the ruler, nor to one-sidedly attend to the budding representatives [of the people]. Just as long as one has the tree of life, then one can collectively and powerfully move forward. Only in this stage is life real, autonomous (*zizhu*), self-developing, universally flourishing, meaningful, and valuable.

How can one say that a society governed by human rights has the three above-mentioned essential factors? Because a society devoted to human rights protects three great natural rights (*tianfu renquan*):

1. the right to subsistence (*shengcun quan*);
2. the right to freedom; and
3. the right to equality.

Nature (*tian*) endows humans with these three great rights and at the same time gives us the abilities to unite and to protect [ourselves]. People then use their ability to unite to organize society with the goal of protecting these three great rights. Therefore, no matter which method is used to organize society, all hold that justice lies in actually protecting these three great rights. Any [method] that violates the three great rights is unjust and evil, and should be sentenced to death and then executed.

All just states that work to genuinely protect natural rights should, in their basic organic law (*genben zuzhi fa*), at the very least stipulate that all people enjoy the following three great fundamental rights:

1. fundamental economic rights;
2. fundamental political rights; and
3. fundamental educational rights.

Fundamental economic rights mean that all people should enjoy the necessary materials for subsistence—namely, that they should have rights to the minimum essential level of clothing, food, and housing. All of today's states acknowledge the right to existence (*shengcun*).[1] The laws of all states have stern stipulations that anyone who physically hurts another is punished, and anyone who kills another is executed. But in the realm of the economic system, laissez-faire free competition runs wild. The strong seize things [from the weak], so that the great majority [fail to sustain] the minimum essential level of clothing, food, and housing and [often] starve to death. This is no different from permitting people to starve others to death while regarding it as societal justice. Mencius said: "What is the difference between killing a person with a knife and killing him with politics? There is no difference."[2] This [saying] exposes the same kind of contradiction.

Fundamental political rights mean that all people have specific rights to freely express political opinions—namely, the right to make decisions in basic political [matters], the right to general elections, the right to freely express criticism, and so forth. Although the rights to political participation acknowledged by the laws of today's constitutional states can be interpreted in this way, in reality their scope is very narrow. For example, when it comes to basic reforms of domestic politics, or to proclamations of war and peace, the great majority of citizens can only follow blindly and obey. With respect to the right to elect and to be elected, there are restrictions based on sex, property, and education. As for the freedom of speech, extensive and vague legal explanations are often used to restrict it, and it is trampled upon by parties with the political aim of wiping out dissent. Therefore, even though peoples' rights to political participation are acknowledged in name, in reality this is nothing more than a minority usurping the state while claiming to base themselves on the general will, which is no better than helping bandits to obtain grain.[3]

Fundamental educational rights mean that all people have the right to receive a free and equal education, which starts with enlightenment and culminates in the ability to conduct independent research. The differences between humans and animals are our innate faculty of reason and our acquired education. A real human society is thus one that sees it as the height of justice to let all its members enjoy a complete and flawless [education], so as to protect and develop their innate faculties of reason. A just state must, within a fixed limit, allow all people fundamental educational rights. Only then should the people shoulder any legal and moral responsibilities. Those who oppose this are labeled [those who] "do not teach but kill." Socrates said: "Lack of knowledge is in itself evil." Similarly, we say: "Lack of education is in itself evil." Although modern states have so-called universal education, the level is extremely low and the scope is very limited. In reality those receiving education are only the children of the rich minority, whereas the majority are busy eking out an existence and have no opportunities to receive education. In this foolish and shabby state of affairs, humans are really only biological creatures [rather than social], and thus contemporary human societies cannot be understood as genuine human societies.

The three above-mentioned fundamental rights are the inalienable and minimal rights set down in the contract that established human society. If we forsake [even] one of them, then our three natural rights— that is, the right to subsistence, the right to freedom, and the right to equality—cannot avoid being encroached upon, which runs counter to the purpose of humanity's creation of society. Therefore, for all kinds of society and social organization, if these three fundamental rights have been violated, revolution is the appropriate means for ultimate salvation. Thus, a just state ought to have a basic system that genuinely protects all people's fundamental rights, namely, economic rights, political rights, and educational rights. This criterion applies to all systems.

In order to protect all people's fundamental economic rights, states should, at the minimum, adopt the three principles outlined below for their economic systems:

1. All people should have work that, at a minimum, enables them to support their lives. The state has the duty to assist those who have become unemployed or whose [work] is insufficient.
2. The level of private property should have an upper limit.
3. The distribution of production should be according to criteria laid down by the state.

In order to protect all people's fundamental political rights, states should, at the minimum, adopt the three principles outlined below for their political systems:

1. All basic domestic reforms and international proclamations of war and peace should be decided through general referendums.
2. The right to elect and to be elected should not be restricted with respect to sex or property.
3. Apart from any concrete and clear legal restrictions, people should have absolute freedom of assembly, association, and speech.

In order to protect all people's fundamental educational rights, states should, at the minimum, adopt the three principles outlined below for their educational systems:

1. The state shall establish institutions for universal vocational education and supplementary education up to the level of independent research. It shall not collect tuition fees.
2. All people have the right and duty to freely receive vocational education and supplementary education up to the level of independent research.
3. The state shall supply all people with the facilities to equally enjoy the opportunities of higher education.

The above tenets are the most natural, reasonable, and minimal tenets of societies governed by human rights. Real human societies and just states are founded upon and proceed forward from these tenets. A society or state that breaks these tenets and retreats [from them] is not a real human society or a just state. Modern societies and states evolve toward the stage of governance by human rights. In order to promote and hasten our development to this stage, the sooner to see the blooming tree of humankind, we publish the magazine *Human Rights*. We hope that people who have been enlightened and embrace these tenets will arise and sing together the march of the human rights society!

Notes

1. *Shengcun* can be translated as both "existence" and "subsistence," depending on context.
2. *Mencius* 1A:4.
3. "To help bandits obtain grain" is a saying from the *Shi ji* [Records of the Grand Historian], meaning "to help an enemy in their evil deeds."

Part III

The Nanjing Decade: 1927–1937

20

The Basis and Particulars of the Principle of People's Rights (1928)

Zhou Fohai

"Minquan zhuyi de genju he tezhi" [The Basis and Particulars of the Principle of People's Rights], *Xin shengming* 1:2 (1928).

Zhou Fohai (1897–1948) helped found the CCP but left the party in 1924 and aligned himself with the GMD. He then became one of the GMD's leading theoretical writers and was the editor of the monthly Xin shengming. *Zhou had earlier contributed to* Xin qingnian, *and, in an article published in 1922, voiced the opinion that freedom of speech and association should not be given to the bourgeoisie since they then could use these freedoms to thwart the revolution. Although Zhou in 1922 was a supporter of the CCP, and by 1928, when the article excerpted here was published, a theoretician of the GMD, his opinion on the need to restrict certain people's rights and freedoms did not change. Zhou argued against the idea of natural rights because it implied that all people, by virtue of their being human, would enjoy rights. The idea of "revolutionary people's rights" as advocated by the GMD, on the other hand, ensured that only those loyal to the revolution could exercise political rights.*

. . . Why are the people's rights (*minquan*) advocated by the GMD's principle of people's rights (*minquan zhuyi*) not the French type of natural rights (*tianfu renquan*)?[1] As we have explained above, a social system is neither absolutely good nor absolutely bad. If the system suits the needs of the time, it is a good system; otherwise, it is a bad one. This rule also applies to theories and doctrines. When a doctrine suits the needs of the time, it is the most powerful and effective one at the time. As times change, though, the needs of the times will change as well, and a doctrine that was once powerful and effective will lose its power and effectiveness. The theory of natural rights was powerful and effective in the period before the French Revolution because it suited the needs of the time. At that time Europe was rigidly stratified; from peasants to imperial kinsmen, everyone's [position] was hereditary. A peasant's son was born a peasant, a noble's son was born a noble, and it was absolutely impossible for a peasant to become a noble. Moreover, the ruling class at the time advocated the doctrine of the sovereign's divine right to defend this stratification. . . .

The theory of natural rights demolishes the doctrine of the sovereign's divine right. According to this [new] theory, humans are born free and equal. God's original intention is that all people are free and equal in status; the unequal phenomena that occur subsequently in human society are all artificial. A peasant's son is born a human being, not the son of a peasant; a noble's son is also born a human being, not the son of a noble. That one later becomes a peasant and one a noble is nothing but an artificial result, an artificial inequality. This artificial inequality runs counter to God's will. In order to obey God's will one must demolish inequality and return to natural equality. When this theory was put forward the doctrine of divine rights lost its influence and foundation. Exactly at that time, new developments emerged in the natural sciences one after another, and as they were put into effect, industry gradually developed, as did the third estate—that is, the class of industry and commerce. The third estate then advocated the theory of natural rights, which helped to bring about the French Revolution. The theory of natural rights was therefore an effective and powerful theory around the time of the French Revolution.

In today's China, however, the theory of natural rights is no longer suitable. The purpose of the current Chinese Revolution is not to realize natural rights. In the Declaration of the GMD's First National Conference, it says:

> The GMD's principle of people's rights is essentially different from so-called natural rights, and it alone suits the needs of the current revolution in China. People's rights in this Republic shall be enjoyed only by citizens [guomin] of the Republic. These rights shall not be granted to those who oppose the Republic, so that they cannot make use of the rights to sabotage the Republic. This principle could be further explained as follows: all individuals and groups that truly fight against imperialism can enjoy all freedoms and rights, whereas all those who betray the nation, deceive the people, and are loyal to the imperialists and warlords, regardless of whether this is as a group or an individual, may not enjoy these freedoms and rights.

Maybe some will be concerned that the principle of people's rights advocates political equality and the realization of politics by the entire people, but according to the explanation above, there is a group of Chinese who are not entitled to people's rights. Regardless of the size of this group, the nation will be divided into two groups of people: those with and those without people's rights. This means that inequality still exists. As long as some people are excluded from political participation, politics by the entire people cannot be realized.

This concern is easy to dispel. The abolition of political inequality and the realization of politics by the entire people are naturally the ends of the principle of people's rights, but ends are inseparable from means, and ends without means and theories without methods are empty. The principle of people's rights has its ideal as well as its method. Its ideal is surely the realization of political equality, but in order to attain true equality, it is necessary to pass through a period of temporary inequality. Temporary inequality is the means to realize true political equality. We know that to accomplish true equality, we first have to clear away its obstacles and to do away with those who damage equality. In China those who damage equality are still the warlords and the individuals and groups who "betray the nation, deceive the people, and are loyal to the imperialists and warlords." These people cannot be overthrown with one stroke. Although they are collapsing, they still hope for revival. If we allow them to continue to participate in politics and act freely, they will make use of their political rights to sabotage the revolution. Consequently, political rights shall not be granted to all "those people who oppose the Republic." When we have cleared these people away and there no longer are those "who oppose the Republic" in the nation, all people can enjoy political rights. This, then, is the abolition of political inequality and the realization of politics by the entire people. If we advocate the theory of natural rights, however, these people could also, following this theory, demand their people's rights, because even though they are counter-revolutionaries and opponents of the Republic, they are, after all, still human beings. And, being human beings, they are entitled to the natural rights of freedom and equality. We advocate, therefore, "revolutionary people's rights" (*geming minquan*). Only those who approve of the revolution are entitled to enjoy revolutionary people's rights, which are not granted to counterrevolutionaries. Under the slogan of "revolutionary people's rights," counterrevolutionaries have lost the theoretical foundation to demand people's rights. The theory of natural rights was enough to promote revolution during the time of the French Revolution. In today's China, however, the theory hinders the revolution and the realization of politics by the entire people. Hence, the principle of revolutionary people's rights is a necessary phase leading to politics by the entire people—there is no contradiction. . . .

Note

1. *Minquan* is translated here as "people's rights," not "people's power" as in the article by Sun Yatsen translated above. We choose this translation because it better reflects Zhou's discussion of why only certain kinds of people enjoy political rights during the transition period. See also the discussion of this term in the General Introduction.

Further Reading

For general background on the politics of this period, see Lloyd Eastman, *The Abortive Revolution: China Under Nationalist Rule, 1927–1937* (Cambridge, MA: Harvard University Press, 1974). For an earlier article by Zhou Fohai that also touches upon the subject and limit of freedom, see Zhou Fohai, "Ziyou he qiangzhi: pingdeng he ducai" [Freedom and Force: Equality and Dictatorship], *Xin qingnian* 9:6 (July 1, 1922).

21
Human Rights and the Provisional Constitution (1929)

Hu Shi

"Renquan yu yuefa" [Human Rights and the Provisional Constitution], *Xinyue* [Crescent] 2:2 (May 6, 1929). Reprinted in Hu Shi, ed., *Renquan lunji* [Collected Writings on Human Rights] (Shanghai: Xinyue Shudian, 1930).

Hu Shi (1891–1962) was one of the leading intellectuals of the twentieth century. After a classical Chinese education and then studying with John Dewey at Columbia University, he returned to China in 1917 to become a major figure in the New Culture Movement and an advocate of liberalism and gradualism. A signatory to the Manifesto of the Struggle for Freedom of 1920 (see Text 14, above), Hu nonetheless had a diffident relationship to politics throughout his life, often preferring to leave the compromises and disappointments of concrete political action to others. With this essay in the Xinyue *magazine, though, Hu launched a brief human rights movement that included both detailed criticisms of the practices of the GMD government and theoretical discussions of human rights (for an example of the latter, see especially the next text, by Luo Longji). Hu's main argument in this essay is that genuine protection of human rights requires a legal foundation that applies impartially to all, including members of the military and the government. He demonstrates that a balanced reading of Sun Yatsen's writings also points to the need for a "provisional constitution," though he neglects to say that Sun was no defender of unqualified "human rights" (see Text 18). Hu's position in this essay is criticized by the Communist Peng Kang, translated below as Text 23.*

On April 20, the Nationalist government issued an order concerning the protection of human rights. This is the text of the order:

> Human rights are protected by law in every country in the world. Now that our tutelage government is in existence, a foundation for the rule of law (*fazhi*) definitely needs to be established. All those entities within the Republic of China's legal jurisdiction, whether individuals or organizations, shall not engage in illegal behavior that harms the physical being, freedom, or property of others. Those who violate this order shall be harshly punished according to the law. Each department of the administrative and judicial organs are instructed to follow this order.

In this period when human rights have been so badly violated that they scarcely exist, the fact that an order was suddenly given to protect human rights caused our people unhoped-for joy. But when some time had elapsed after our initial happiness, a careful reading of this order brought us great disappointment. The causes for our disappointment are the following:

First, this order defines "human rights" as "physical being," "freedom," and "property." But these three concepts are not clearly defined. For example, what exactly is meant by "freedom"? And what kind of protection does "property" really receive? These are very important defects.

Second, the order forbids harmful behavior by "individuals or organizations," but does not mention government organs. Certainly neither individuals nor organizations should harm the physical being, freedom, or property of others, but every day what causes us the most suffering is abuse of the people's physical beings, freedoms, and property by governmental, quasi-governmental, or party organs. For example, our freedom of speech and publication has just been curtailed; all over the country, people's property gets confiscated; recently, electrical industries were confiscated. These were all carried out according to the orders of government bodies. The order of April 20th gave people no protection whatsoever against situations like these. Is this not like "only allowing prefectural officials to light fires, but not allowing the people to light their lanterns"?

Third, the order says "Those who violate this order shall be harshly punished in accordance with the law," but to what law does "in accordance with the law" refer? We do not know which law today is able to protect the people's human rights. The Republic of China's penal laws always had a "crime of interfering with freedom," but all kinds of interference with freedom have been carried out in the name of the government or the party, and in such cases people have absolutely no protection whatsoever.

Not long after this order was given, newspapers in Shanghai found out that there has been a discussion about whether "the activities of anti-Japanese organizations are included within the scope of the order." Japanese-language newspapers believe that the order applies to the activities of anti-Japanese organizations (otherwise known as organizations for national salvation), but Chinese-language papers, like Mr. Wei Lei's editorial in the newspaper *New Current Affairs*, assert that such activities should not be punished as a result of the order.

Is this just a problem for anti-Japanese organizations? In fact whenever any people are called "reactionary elements," "local tyrants and evil gentry," "counterrevolutionaries," "suspected Communists," or other similar labels, they lose all protection of their human rights. Their physical being can be violated, their freedom can be completely curtailed, and their property can be taken without any reason—and none of this is "illegal activity." Whenever any printed material is labeled a "reactionary publication," it will be banned, and this will not be considered to harm anyone's freedom. Whenever a school run by foreigners is labeled as a "cultural invasion," or one run by Chinese is labeled as an "academic clique," "reactionary," etc., then they can be closed and confiscated, and this will not be considered illegal or damaging. In any of these various situations, what kind of protection do we have?

I would like to discuss a recent event, which, although minor, is of great significance. On March 26 in Shanghai all the newspapers received a cable saying that Mr. Chen Dezheng, a representative of the Shanghai Special GMD Headquarters, had raised the suggestion during a meeting on how to "severely deal with counterrevolutionary cases." His general concern was that the courts were too bound by [the need for] evidence, so that counterrevolutionary elements often managed to escape punishment. Mr. Chen's suggestion was the following:

> Courts or other legal institutions permitted by law to hear cases should
> punish for counterrevolutionary offenses anyone who is certified as a

counterrevolutionary by documents from provincial or special municipal party branches. If [the courts] disagree, they can appeal [the matter to higher-level courts]. If higher-level courts or other legal institutions permitted by law to hear cases receive certificates [on the counterrevolutionary's status] from the Central Party Branch, they must squash the appeal.

That is to say, if a court is considering a case involving counterrevolutionary charges, they may not hold a hearing, but can only depend on the proof presented by the Party section and must convict and sentence the defendant. Isn't this a negation of the basic concept of rule of law?[1]

When I saw this suggestion, I felt I could not endure it and wrote a letter to the director of the Judicial Yuan, Dr. Wang Longhui. My basic idea was to ask him, "What are your thoughts about this incident?" and also, "In the history of the law all over the world, in what century and among which civilized people can we find this method either written in books or established as a system?"

I thought these questions were worthwhile presenting to the public and so sent a copy of the letter to the National Press Correspondents' Society to publish. After a few days, I received a letter back from the National Press Correspondents' Society, which said:

"Your letter has already been sent on to the newspapers, but it will not be published, as it has been withheld [from publication] by the news censors. We respectfully return your original with gracious thanks." I did not know that my letter could have such great military importance that it deserved to be investigated by the news censors and banned. That letter was one for which I took personal responsibility. I do not know why a citizen cannot take the responsibility for publishing something that discusses questions of national importance. But what recourse do we have against such irrational interference?

Or take the case of a dean at Anhui University, who, because he denounced Chairman Jiang [i.e., Chiang Kaishek], was detained for days. His family and friends had no recourse except to go to the relevant office and beg for leniency—they could not go to any court of law to sue Chairman Jiang. When people cannot sue but can only beg for mercy, then this is rule by people, not rule of law!

Recently, there was also the case of the shop closures in Tangshan, which began when Yang Runpu, the manager of the firm Liang Yi Cheng, was imprisoned and tortured by local troops on suspicion of buying and selling arms. According to an April 28th report in the *Dagong bao* [news-paper], twelve people representing the Tangshan General Merchants' Association went to the 152nd Brigade to beg for leniency for Yang Runpu, and for his release, but the military court would not agree to release him. Just as the representatives were leaving, by chance they caught sight of Yang being brought into the room by soldiers. "Yang's legs were hugely swollen, and they saw traces of blood. He could barely move, and when he saw the representatives, all he could do was cry without shedding any tears. He tried to speak but no words would come out. His pitiable state was almost impossible to describe." But when the Tangshan General Merchants' Association and eighty-eight stores to-gether sent a telegram to Tang Shengzhi, they too could do no more than beg for leniency for Yang. When their pleas proved to be fruitless, all they could do in the end was declare a shop closure in the city of Tangshan. Where are human rights here? And where is rule of law?

As I write this, I have just seen an article in the *Dagong bao* [news-paper] of May 2nd, which says that the result of the shop closure in Tangshan was the release of Yang Runpu. "But because he had suffered such severe physical abuse, he cannot walk and can only stand by leaning on the door frame for support. He has not returned to Liang Yi Cheng but went directly to a hospital for treatment." The *Dagong bao* journalist went himself to interview Yang, and his report contains the following:

> I saw Yang Runpu from the front and back wearing a short Chinese-style gown. Traces of blood were still visible. His clothes were stuck to his body and he was just trying to get them off so the doctor could work on him. I asked what was the situation after his detention. Yang answered that he could not stand to say much, but that they used an old-fashioned wooden bar originally used to punish thieves. I could not bear his suffer-ing! Yang continued that just when he reached the point when he could barely stand the pain, the wooden pole which was being pressed against his leg suddenly broke. They then switched to a bamboo board and beat him all over his entire body. This went on for a while. While Company Commander Liu was in the room, they primarily used an iron stick in-stead of the wooden one. Judge Zheng was afraid they would acciden-tally kill him, but they did not. After this, each interrogation brought on a beating. Today he has injuries to every part of his body. According to the doctor, Mr. Yang's injuries are serious, and if he is not carefully nursed for at least three months, he will not be able to recover.

This incident took place eleven days after the issuance of the order regarding the protection of human rights. I wonder what thoughts the gentlemen in the GMD have on the subject of this incident?

These few facts that I have randomly chosen all demonstrate that no single, murky order can achieve the protection of human rights nor the guarantee of rule of law. Rule of law means that the behavior of government officials may not in any way transgress the limits of the regulations set forth in the law. Rule of law recognizes only the law, not people. Under the conditions of rule of law, neither the chairman of the GMD nor the officers of the Tangshan 152nd Brigade may transgress the limits of the regulations set forth in the laws. If the chairman of the GMD can detain citizens at will, then naturally the officers of the Tangshan 152nd Brigade may also willfully detain and interrogate merchants. In China today, the government's conduct basically knows no boundaries based on laws and regulations, and so the people's rights and freedoms also have absolutely no protection based on laws and regulations. In this situation, how can we speak about protecting human rights?! How can we talk about establishing a foundation for the rule of law?!

Today, if we really want to protect human rights and establish the rule of law, our first task is to draft a constitution for the Republic of China, or at least, at the very least, to draft a so-called Provisional Constitution for the Tutelage Period. When Mr. Sun Yatsen defined his *Strategy for Revolution* he divided the measures needed for revolutionary reconstruction into three time periods:

> The first period is government based on military law (three years).
>
> The second period is government based on a Provisional Constitution (six years): "All the rights and duties (*quanli yiwu*) of the military government toward the people, and those of the people toward the military government, will be spelled out in the Provisional Constitution. The military government, local assemblies, and all the people will have to obey it; those who violate it will bear the consequences."
>
> The third period is constitutional government.

The *Strategy for Revolution* was completed in 1906, and was subsequently repeatedly revised. Mr. Sun Yatsen wrote his *Sun's Theory* in

1919, and in the sixth chapter he repeatedly emphasized the importance of "a transitional period" and, speaking very clearly, stated that "by this time, we should have a Provisional Constitution in order to instruct the people and implement regional autonomy." In January 1923, when Mr. Sun completed the *History of Chinese Revolution*, he still called the second period the "transitional period" and he paid special attention to it. He said:

> The second period is called the transitional period. During it, a Provisional Constitution should be drafted (which has not yet been done) and regional autonomy should be established, in order to promote the development of people's rights (*minquan*). When counties, acting as autonomous units, have released their soldiers upon the conclusion of hostilities, they should promulgate provisional constitutions in order to regulate the rights and duties of the people and the ruling powers of the revolutionary government. Within a time limit of three years, the people should be able to elect their county officials. . . . With respect to the these autonomous organizations, the revolutionary government may only exercise its tutelage powers (*xunzheng zhi quan*) in accordance with the Provisional Constitution.

One year later, in April 1924, when Mr. Sun wrote his *Outline of National Reconstruction*, he divided reconstruction into three periods, with the second defined as the "tutelage period." However, in the *Outline* he did not mention the "Provisional Constitution" of the tutelage government, nor did he set a time limit for the tutelage government. Unfortunately he died a year later. After his death, people read only his *Outline* but do not study the history of the "three periods" he mentions, so they believe that the tutelage period of government can be prolonged indefinitely and that China can be governed without a Provisional Constitution, which is a great mistake indeed.

Mr. Sun's *Outline* does not mention a Provisional Constitution, but from studying his works written before 1924, it is clear that he never believed such a large country as China could be governed without [such] a constitution (*genben dafa*). The *Outline of National Reconstruction* has numerous omissions and oversights. For example, the twenty-first clause says, "Before the Constitution has been promulgated, the head of each Yuan[2] is appointed and dismissed by the president." This shows that during the tutelage period there is a "president," but nothing in the *Outline* says where the president comes from. Another example is the announcement made by the first General Meeting of GMD Representatives in January 1924, which already speaks of "The Party controlling the central positions of political power," but nowhere in any of the twenty-five clauses of his *Outline of National Reconstruction*, from three months later, does Mr. Sun say anything about a one-party dictatorship. These examples prove that the *Outline of National Reconstruction* is only one plan that Mr. Sun considered at one time, and should be considered neither the final word nor an all-encompassing document. The *Outline* is a document that should have been changed long ago to suit the current situation. (For example, the nineteenth clause says that the Five Yuan should be established at the time the Constitution comes into effect, but they were in fact set up last year.) How can the inadequacies of the *Outline* best be addressed, taking into account the needs of the current situation?

Today, we need a Provisional Constitution, in order, in the words of Mr. Sun, to "regulate the rights and duties of the people and the ruling powers of the revolutionary government." We need a Provisional Constitution to put limits on the government's power; anything that exceeds these limits is "illegal conduct." We need a Provisional Constitution to protect the people's "physical beings, freedoms, and property." If the human rights set down in this constitution are violated, no matter whether they are violated by the commanders of the 152nd Brigade or by the Nationalist government's chairman, the people must be able to bring a complaint to the courts and all must submit to the rule of the law.

Our slogans are: "Swiftly draft a Provisional Constitution in order to assure a foundation for the rule of law!" and "Swiftly draft a Provisional Constitution in order to protect human rights!"

Notes

1. See also the discussion of this same incident in Text 36.
2. Sun talked about five branches (*yuan*): the executive, judiciary, parliamentary, examination, and censorial.

Further Reading

For background on Hu Shi, the classic work is Jerome B. Grieder, *Hu Shih and the Chinese Renaissance* (Cambridge, MA: Harvard University Press, 1970), which can be supplemented with Min-Chih Chou, *Hu Shih and Intellectual Choice in Modern China* (Ann Arbor: University of Michigan Press, 1984). An idea of the range of Hu's interests can be gained from the several brief translations of his writings contained in Wm. Theodore de Bary and John Lufrano, eds., *Sources of Chinese Tradition, 2d ed.* (New York: Columbia University Press, 2000), vol. 2

22
On Human Rights (1929)

Luo Longji

"Lun renquan" [On Human Rights], *Xinyue* 2:5 (1929). Reprinted in Hu Shi, ed., *Renquan lunji* [Collected Essays on Human Rights] (Shanghai: Xinyue shudian, 1930), pp. 33–59.

Luo Longji (1898–1965) was a political scientist who spent seven years studying in England and America, culminating in a Ph.D. from Columbia University in 1928. Together with Hu Shi and Liang Shiqiu, he published a number of articles on human rights in the magazine Xinyue *in 1929 and 1930. The present essay stands out as the most theoretically sophisticated of the numerous* Xinyue *articles. Luo draws on a number of themes and concepts he learned from mentors in the West, most especially from Harold Laski, whose social liberalism Luo found very appealing. Luo defends the idea of human rights against those from both the Communist and Nationalist camps who saw it as an abstract or outmoded idea. He understands human rights to be necessary in order to develop both one's own and others' humanity and well-being. Luo stresses that human rights have to safeguard both the physical and spiritual aspects of human existence; they therefore include both civil and political rights and economic and social rights. Also of interest is his insistence that human rights demands vary due to historical and social differences. While to some degree this makes for a relativistic understanding of human rights, Luo nonetheless believes that human rights are universally applicable.*

1. Introduction

The destruction of human rights (*renquan*) is a fact that cannot be concealed in today's China. The order protecting human rights by the People's Government on April 20 is ironclad proof of [the government's] acknowledgment that the human rights of the Chinese people have already been destroyed.[1]

Those Chinese who have set their wills on being persons (*zuoren*) have already committed themselves to strive and struggle for the return of human rights. In fact, therefore, the human rights movement has already begun. Its success will depend upon time. On this point, there is no need to make a special appeal.

Originally, the means to use in the struggle for the return of human rights were not set. Paper, pen, and ink were enough to establish England's Magna Carta of 1215; guns, cannon, and blood were needed to arrive at France's Declaration of the Rights of Man[2] of 1789. It is an historical fact that in different environments, the means of struggling for human rights change as well; the current essay will take this for granted. What are human rights? What are the human rights that we currently desire? These are, indeed, extremely important questions in the current human rights movement. I believe that the extreme importance of these questions is owing to three reasons, which can be summarized as follows:

1. The human rights movement naturally has its goals. These goals ought to be clearly and methodically written out. The order of the People's Government says: "Human rights are protected by law in every country in the world." What are these "human rights . . . in every country in the world"? Do those who made the order understand it clearly? The order also says: "[one] shall not engage in illegal behavior which harms the physical being, freedom, or property of others." What is the scope of these three items? Are human rights limited to these three items? Those who made the order have not answered these questions clearly. Compare this with other instances: most of the human rights of the English people are set down in the Magna Carta of 1215, or in the Petition of Right of 1628, or in the Bill of Rights of 1689. Most of the human rights of the French people are set down in the Declaration of the Rights of Man of 1789. What are the details of our current human rights? We have reached the time for an answer to this question.

2. There are some people whose human rights have already been destroyed who have deceived themselves into saying that human rights is an "abstract term." They use slogans like "starving and unable to eat, freezing, and unclothed" to claim that the human rights movement cannot be compared to the reality of the materialist, class revolution. These people have completely failed to realize what human rights are. Of course human rights encompass clothing and food; they also include many things still more important than clothing and food. Consider, after all, that if in his day Germany had enjoyed complete freedom of thought, speech, and publication, Marx would not have had to flee to London's British Museum in order to write *Das Kapital*! Those who criticize human rights as an abstract term have completely failed to realize what human rights

are. What are the details of our current human rights? We have already reached the time for an answer to this question.

3. Then there is the group of momentarily lucky tramplers on human rights. They ridicule human rights as a worn-out slogan, and laugh at the human rights movement as a relic of the seventeenth and eighteenth centuries in England and France. The undeserving people who have gotten their way for the moment try with all their might to model themselves on the seventeenth century of Charles I of England, or on the eighteenth century of Louis XVI of France: they are performing the old play "The state is I." In such an environment, we can only sing the old tunes of the Magna Carta and the Declaration of the Rights of Man. Actually, are human rights an old tune? If you look at the constitutions of the various countries newly created after the Great War, you will see that human rights have many new tunes. Those who have gotten their way for the moment and who use any means to stamp out human rights have completely failed to realize what human rights are. What are the human rights that we seek? We have already reached the time for an answer to this question.

2. The Meaning of "Human Rights"

Human rights, simply put, are the rights that [are needed] to be a person (*zuoren*). Human rights are those conditions necessary for one to be a person.

The meaning of "to be a person" on the surface seems very shallow, but in fact is extremely profound. Any animal that has five senses, four limbs, a head, internal organs, skin, bones, fingers, hair, the appearance of a person, and the shape of a person—any such animal ought to be called a person. Whether, however, this person is or is not "being a person"—can or cannot possess the conditions for "being a person"—this is a separate question.

A dead person is, of course, not "being a person." For "being a person," the first [requirement] is life. In other words, preserving life is the point of departure for being a person. As soon as we mention preserving life, we must immediately think of the conditions that are necessary for life. For instance, in order to preserve life, one must have clothing, food, and shelter. Put another way, the opportunities to acquire clothing, food, and shelter are necessary conditions for being a person. Having opportunities to acquire these things, therefore, counts as one part of human rights. The Westerner's "right to work,"[3] if it were these days to become part of human rights, would count in just this way.

If I have clothing, food, and shelter, then, as far as I myself am concerned, I can definitely be a person, but there is the further question of whether others can or cannot allow me to be a person. In a barbarian society, the strong control the weak and the many do violence to the few. One knife or one gun can end my life at any time. Thus, although I am a person, and although I want to be a person, I do not definitely have the opportunity to be a person. In other words, if one wants to preserve one's life, bodily safety is another necessary condition. Another part of human rights, therefore, is the protection of bodily safety.

According to what has been said, then, human rights are the necessary conditions for human life: the right of acquiring clothing, food, and shelter, as well as the protection of bodily safety. The scope of human rights, however, definitely does not end here. Preserving life is necessarily the point of departure for being a person, but it is certainly not the only goal of being a person.

Consider the millions of people living in today's China: They have their lives, but which few among them are truly persons? To be a person, speaking frankly, requires that one have the happiness[4] of being a person, and life requires that one have the well-being of life. In order to enjoy the well-being of life, the various conditions [mentioned above]—clothing, food, shelter, and bodily safety—are not enough.

Persons have their individual natures (*gexing*) and their personalities (*renge*). As long as one's individual nature and one's personality do not have opportunities to be developed and nurtured, one is not being a person. In the area of individual nature and personality, it will just not do to say that "all people can become Yao and Shun."[5] It cannot be denied that all people have, in their individual natures and personalities, strong points that can be developed. "Be myself at my best"[6] is a commonly heard Western phrase. To put it more colloquially, in being oneself, be a good person. Only in this way does being a person come to have meaning; only in this way can we have hope of achieving well-being in life.

Thus, the so-called necessary conditions for life definitely do not end with clothing, food, shelter, and bodily safety; we must add all the conditions that make for developing one's individual nature, nurturing one's personality, and becoming the best possible person one can be.

At the same time, we must realize that we are no more than single elements of humanity. My being a person cannot but be simultaneously related to humanity in many ways. My well-being is related to the well-being of the whole of humanity: When I am the best I can be and [fulfill] my responsibilities to humanity, the service of cementing together humanity allows humanity as a whole to attain the best possible [level]. Finally, this will enable humanity to attain the greatest well-being of the greatest number.

Consequently, the so-called necessary conditions for life cannot be limited to an individual's clothing, food, shelter, and safety, nor even to the conditions [needed for] him or her to become the best person he or she can be. On top of this must be added the conditions for attaining the goal of providing the great majority with the greatest well-being.

In accordance with what has been said above, the definition of human rights should be as follows: human rights are the necessary conditions for being a person. Human rights are the rights of clothing, food, and shelter; the protection of bodily safety; and the conditions for attaining the goals of an individual's "becoming the best person he or she can be," thus enjoying the well-being of individual life, and also of humanity's becoming the best that it can become, thus allowing the great majority to enjoy the greatest possible well-being.

This is my definition of human rights. It is very prosaic and straightforward. I did not trace back to the seventeenth-century doctrines of Hobbes, who believed human rights to be something for satisfying all desires. [After all,] people have many desires that fundamentally ought not to be satisfied. Many people who consider themselves to be great men have the desire to be despots or to have many mistresses; we cannot say that according to the theory of human rights, these kinds of desires should be satisfied. I have also not invoked the eighteenth-century doctrines of Rousseau. He believed that human rights were bestowed by nature (*tianfu*), and added that we must return to truth and simplicity, going to our natural environment and freely developing our original nature. I'll always believe, though, that Shanghai will not turn back into the wild state of 500 years earlier. I shrink even more from praising the nineteenth-century doctrines of Bentham, who believed that human rights ought to be based on the law. In China's past history, the wise have made the law and the simple have followed it. China's current situation, [though,] is that the strong establish the law and the weak obey it.

That the law and the correct ethical norms are two [different] things is a universal problem in the world's countries. From the perspective of law, the most that I can know is what my rights are; I have no way of finding out what rights I ought to have. China's old law permitted barbaric practices, [yet] people ought not to necessarily admit that these practices are human rights. Adult citizens of republics ought to have election rights, yet contemporary Chinese law does not permit the people to participate in government. Above the law there are human rights, and law does not necessarily completely exhaust human rights—these are obvious facts.

To speak a little more completely, in giving the meaning of human rights, I have relied entirely on the word "function."[7] All of the following three points are necessary functions, and all are necessary conditions for being a person: (a) preserving life; (b) developing individual nature and nurturing personality; and (c) attaining the goal of the greatest well-being for the greatest number of humanity.

Now, let me give an example to illustrate my point. Freedom of speech is [a] human right. The reason that freedom of speech has become a human right is not because it is able to satisfy people's desires, nor because it is endowed in people by nature, nor yet because it is permitted by law; the fundamental reason is its function. It is a necessary condition[8] for being a person.

All individuals have thoughts, and where there are thoughts, there is the desire to express those thoughts. In order to express the thoughts, one must speak. One wants to say what is in one's own mind, not what someone else wants one to say. Saying what one wants to say is a route to developing one's individual nature and nurturing one's personality. This is the path to being oneself at one's best.[9]

When I have freedom of speech, only then can I contribute my thoughts to humanity. This kind of contribution—even bracketing the question of whether the thought is good or not—is the responsibility of people to society. From the societal perspective, whether or not a thought is used, this kind of contribution provides [needed] reference material. This is the road to humanity's achieving its greatest possible good, [or in other words,] the road to the greatest well-being for the greatest number of humanity.

On the other hand, if one suppresses freedom of speech, then that which one has suppressed does not stop with speech, but in fact deals with thought. And it does not stop with thought, but touches on individual nature and personality. If one suppresses individual nature and personality, this is just slaughtering the life of an individual—wiping out the life of humanity.

It is in accordance with this kind of theory that I say freedom of speech is [a] human right. Human rights consist of all the necessary conditions for humans to be persons. Without these conditions, I cannot be myself at my best and humanity cannot reach its highest level.

3. Human Rights and the State

The state's existence has a particular function.[10] If it loses this function, it simultaneously loses its reason for existing. The state's function is to protect human rights, to protect those necessary conditions for citizens' being persons. Whenever the necessary conditions for my being a person have lost their protection, then as far as I am concerned, the state has lost its function and I have lost my duty to follow the state.

Article 2 of France's Declaration of the Rights of Man says: "The final end of every political institution is the preservation of the natural and imprescriptible (*yong bu momie*) rights of man. These rights are those of liberty, property, security, and resistance to oppression."

Down to the current day, while the scope of human rights has broadened, the object of governmental institutions has not changed. In his *Modern State*, L.M. Maciver[11] says:

> As for the state, we should not just think of it as one type of group, but also view it from a factual perspective and from the perspective of the logic of its function: it is an institution with the character of a company. It is because the state serves its citizens that it can command them; it is because it takes on responsibilities that it has rights (*quanli*). . . . It has the function of protecting human rights. In order to put this function into effect, it must have appropriate power. Its power ought to have limits, just as its function ought to have limits.

The English politician and scholar H.J. Laski, in his book *A Grammar of Politics*, has also said:

> The state is a landed institution that is divided between the government and the people. Its existence, its exercising authority, and its receiving obedience from the people, are all because only then can the people achieve their greatest possible good. In order to reach this goal, the people have their human rights. Human rights are those conditions without which citizens would be unable to achieve their greatest good. Thus human rights are quite obviously not a product of the law, but rather exist prior to the

law, and are in fact that law's ultimate goal. The standard for the level of excellence of a state is the degree to which human rights are successfully protected.

To put it simply, the theory of state omnipotence is bankrupt. In the twentieth century, the institution of the state is only one among many institutions in a society. The value of its existence shifts with the effectiveness of its serving its function. Its authority over people has limits, rather than being absolute. The scope of these limits is determined by its function. The people's obedience to the state has conditions, rather than being absolute. The most important of these conditions is that the state protect human rights, and thus protect the necessary conditions for people's lives. If ever the state does not serve this function, the people's duty to obey the state has ended.

The most common reason for a state ceasing to serve its function is that the state is taken over by some individual person, by some family, or by a number of people united into a group. [When this happens,] the state's function will have changed its fundamental nature: it will have become the state of an individual, or of a family, or of a private organization. It will have become a tool with which the individual, family, or private organization tramples on the human rights of the majority of the citizens. History has more than enough examples of this happening. For instance, from the perspective of function, the France of 1789 was Louis XVI's state, not the French people's state; thus the statement "The state is I." From 1640 to 1911, from the perspective of function, China was the Manchu royal family's state, not the Chinese people's state. . . . In these kinds of circumstances, in a mutated situation in which the state has become private property, the result—if the people are able to awaken—will always be revolution. This is also an historical fact.

Marx's statement that the state is a tool that the capitalist class uses to invade the proletariat is not without some one-sided reasoning. States have indeed at times been dominated by some individual, family, or organization. What needs to be noted, though, is that if one looks at the facts of history down to the present day, one will see that those who dominate [the power of] the state are not necessarily all capitalists.

Now what I want to speak about here is not the fact that states have been occupied in these ways, but about what citizens' attitudes toward a state that has already been seized should be. My answer is as follows: "The state's authority is limited. The people's duty of obedience to the state is relative. Whenever the state cannot carry out the responsibilities that I have entrusted to it, the state has thereby lost the right to order me, and I no longer have the duty to obey." My doctrine of human rights and the state is just that. It is very simple, prosaic, and straight-forward. I am not an adherent of Bakunin nor a disciple of Marx. Do not give me the criminal titles of destroyer of authority or overthrower of the state.

Laski has said:

> A state legitimates its name by protecting human rights. The most important method we can use to determine the quality of a state is to take as our basis the contributions it makes to the concrete well-being of its citizens. At a minimum, we must recognize that from the perspective of political philosophy, states are not monolithic entities that can use authority in order to force people to heed their will. Unless [we follow] the strictest legal theories, states can only request obedience from people on the basis of the benefit that this obedience to the state will bring the people. Citizens, simply because they are citizens, have the responsibility of inspecting the ultimate aims and character of all of the government's actions. The government's actions cannot be considered as holy simply because they come from the government. These kinds of actions have an appropriate standard for being inspected: the people must have the right to understand the intention behind the government's actions. Simply put, the state cannot create human rights, but only acknowledge human rights. Its quality, at all times, can be measured according to the level at which human rights are acknowledged.

Let this serve as a bit more of an explanation of my view of the relation between human rights and the state.

4. Human Rights and the Law

Law is created in order to protect human rights; law is created by human rights. The former refers to law's function; the latter, to law's origin. Those who, in struggling for human rights, promote the rule of law, are logically correct. The fundamental purpose of law is to protect human rights. Beccaria, a political theorist who based himself on jurisprudence, believed that the goal of law was to seek the greatest good for the greatest number. The Englishman Blackstone has also said that "an important goal of law is to protect and stipulate human rights" (*Commentaries*, book 1, ch. 1).

For those who struggle for the rule of law to first struggle for a constitution is also logically correct. If we put things simply, we can divide law into two types. One is constitutional law; one is the common law. Constitutional law is that law whereby the people control the government. Common law is that law whereby the government controls the people (see Maciver's *Modern State*, p. 25). In a state under the rule of law, the government controls the people, and the people simultaneously control the government. Thus the true meaning of rule of law is that in the whole state, there is not any individual, nor any group, that stands in a position above the law. If one wants to reach the position in which the government and the people simultaneously control each other, it is essential to have a constitution. In this respect I also believe that the following few lines of Mr. Hu Shi are very correct: "We must understand, the great function of a constitution is not only to stipulate the people's rights, but also more importantly to stipulate the limits on the powers (*quanxian*) of the various governmental institutions. The only training we can have for democratic politics is to establish a constitution (*genben dafa*), make sure the various governmental institutions do not go beyond the limits on their powers set for them by the law, and ensure that they cannot invade the people's rights."

If we take this a step further, we can say that when it comes to trampling on human rights, the harm done by individuals and private groups is actually small. When the People's Government ordered, on April 20, that "Neither individuals or organizations shall engage in illegal behavior which harms the physical being, freedom, or property of others. Those who violate this order shall be harshly punished according to the law," this was heeding the small at the expense of the big. In fact, although violent gangsters and murderous kidnappers may indeed "engage in illegal behavior which harms the physical being, freedom, or property of others," the fear they spread is far less than that of individuals, families, or groups who occupy the position of government, wear the trappings of government, and yet are not restrained by any law whatsoever. Of this, we can find many concrete examples.

It cannot be doubted that the function of law is to protect human rights. Those who struggle for human rights first struggle for the rule of law; those who struggle for the rule of law first struggle for a constitution. I believe that this order is very logical. Constitutions, [however,] can sometimes not only fail to protect people's human rights, but also be used by particular individuals, families, or groups as tools to trample on human rights. This, too, we can find examples of in history, and is a point on which those struggling for the rule of law should reflect. If we realize that before the French constitution of 1875, France had seven other constitutions, and if we recall that Napoleon I and Napoleon III both promulgated constitutions, we should pay attention to the next item that I will discuss.

Those discussing human rights cannot ignore the origin of law. Law is the expression of the people's general will.[12] I believe that this sentiment of Rousseau's is the fundamental principle of the law of a democratic (*minzhi*) state. It is at least the case that in the creation of the constitution—the law whereby the people control the government—this principle cannot be violated. Article 23 of Mr. Sun Yatsen's *Outline of National Reconstruction*, "Convene a people's assembly, determine a constitution, and promulgate it," is naturally evidence that he acknowledged that "law is the expression of the people's general will." Those who talk about human rights of course should talk about constitutions, but in addition to constitutions, it is necessary to add this condition about the origin of the constitution.

Human rights exist before law. A [central] principle of human rights is that only when people have themselves established law, do they acquire the responsibility to obey. The goal of law is to seek the greatest well-being of the greatest number, and only the people themselves know what is the greatest well-being for themselves, and are thus able to seek that well-being for themselves. Another of the [principles of] human rights is that one seeks one's own well-being. Thus we can say that law laid down by the people is human rights, and that law is the product of human rights. As far as the relation between human rights and law, therefore, my conclusion is that law protects human rights, while human rights produce law.

It is unfortunately an irremovable fact that law is, in the end, only words on paper, and while human rights can produce law, law's words on paper are not necessarily able to protect human rights. To give only the simplest of examples, France in 1851 of course had a constitution, but did that obstruct Napoleon III's restoration? China in 1911 of course had a provisional constitution, but did that stop Yuan Shikai's implementation of the imperial system? This is another thing that those who talk about human rights and law should heed.

What we need to understand is that while a constitution protects human rights, the constitution also relies on the protection of human rights.

France's Declaration said: "These rights are liberty, property, safety, and resistance to oppression." "Resistance to oppression" is one of [our] human rights, and it is also something protected by law. This is Locke's so-called human right of revolution. When things reach the dangerous moment in which the laws desired by the people cannot be produced, or in which the existing laws are no longer effective, the people must exercise their human right of revolution. When we look at how the Magna Carta was signed in England in 1215 or at how England's Petition of Right of 1628 or its Bill of Rights of 1689 were achieved, and then look at how America was begun in 1776 or at how unrest was incited in France in 1789, we will know that there are numerous examples in history of people seizing their human right of revolution in order to protect their human rights.

As far as China is concerned, while human rights like freedom and equality were developed surprisingly late, the right of revolution was early on acknowledged by most people. Mencius's "I have heard of the execution of a criminal; I have not heard of a regicide" was the first instance of acknowledging this right of revolution.[13] Mr. Sun Yatsen's forty years of effort to preserve human rights like freedom and equality by exercising the human right of revolution is a recent example. All human rights can be invaded, trampled, and expropriated by others. Only the human right of revolution is always in the hands of the people. This is naturally the people's very last hope for life, and this is also the most important aspect of the relation between human rights and law.

5. The Temporal and Spatial Characters of Human Rights

Human rights, as said above, are a number of necessary conditions for a person's life. In other words, they are necessary conditions for a person's living. Peoples' needs for living are different, depending on both time and place. In a particular era or location, the people's living standard will already include certain items and certain others will be missing. The content of the peoples' needs and the direction in which they struggle, therefore, cannot help being guided by the influence of their environment. Thus I say that human rights have both temporal and spatial characters.

What has just been said is a very obvious fact of history. For example, in England, the Magna Carta of 1215 and the [Bill of Rights of 1689] were both documents from the human rights movement, but the content of these human rights were completely different. The eighth article of the Magna Carta reads: "Any wife, if she is unwilling to be remarried, cannot be forced to remarry." This is such a trivial item, and yet in the England of 1215, it was a right that had to be struggled for, and it is a human right. . . .

The Bill of Rights of 1689 said: "For the King to suspend or institute a law as he wishes without receiving the agreement of the Parliament is unlawful. . . . For the King to collect monies without receiving the approval of the Parliament, or for him to exceed the approved time limit or methods in his collections, is also unlawful. . . . The freedom of speech of the members of Parliament shall not be subject to any outside interference. . . ." The environment in the England of 1689 was different from that of England in 1215 . . . , and so the human rights for which people struggled differed as well.

If we look at the whole of Europe, we will see this fact confirmed everywhere. The meaning of the term "human rights" differed between the seventeenth and eighteenth centuries, as it did between the eighteenth and nineteenth centuries. Human rights are the necessary conditions for people's lives. Necessities for living vary with different eras, and thus the scope of human rights changes, too. People having the right to work, workers having the right to strike: these are things of which Europe of the seventeenth or eighteenth centuries had not heard. They are evidence of progress in the meaning of human rights.

If people ridicule those of us of China's contemporary human rights movement, saying that we have our heads stuck in the seventeenth and eighteenth centuries, the reason is just that those ridiculing us know nothing of the temporal character of human rights. Human rights also have a spatial character. For instance, there are naturally differences in content between the English Petition of Right and Bill of Rights, on one hand, and France's Declaration of the Rights of Man of 1789. No one can deny that England's human rights demands in that day leaned toward economic issues; France's toward political issues. France's 1789 Declaration said: "In respect of their rights men are born and remain free and equal. The only permissible basis for social distinctions is public utility. The final end of every political institution is preservation of the natural and imprescriptible rights of man. These rights are those of liberty, property, security and resistance to oppression. The basis of all sovereignty lies, essentially, in the Nation. No corporation nor individual may exercise any authority that is not expressly derived therefrom."

Aren't these clearly emphasizing the political? Anyone who has studied history will know that the social environments of seventeenth-century England and eighteenth-century France were different. The main reason for the difference between England's and France's human rights movements lies with the spatial character of human rights. To carry this a step further, consider that the slogan of the American Revolution was liberty, equality, and the free pursuit of happiness. The French Revolution's slogan was "liberty, equality, fraternity." If we use historical hindsight to analyze these two slogans, we can see the origin of their difference. It goes without saying that the American "free pursuit of happiness" has a different meaning from the French "fraternity"; but even the terms like freedom and equality that [appear] the same in [their respective] laws had different meanings. The fundamental reason for all these differences is that human rights have a spatial character.

If people ridicule those of us of China's contemporary human rights movement, saying that we are simply copying the stale goods of Europe and America, the reason is just that those ridiculing us know nothing of the spatial character of human rights. . . .

Notes

1. For the full text of the order and critical discussion, see Text 21.

2. The full title is the *Declaration of the Rights of Man and the Citizen*. We leave off ". . . *and the Citizen*" because Luo's Chinese version of the title, *Renquan xuanyan*, makes no mention of citizens.

4. English in original.

5. Ancient sage kings: Confucians taught that all people could, in principle, reach the same level of cultivation as these sages attained. See *Mencius* 6B:2.

6. English in original.

7. English in original.

8. The text has "contract" (*tiaoyue*) instead of "condition" (*tiaojian*), but this appears to be an obvious misprint.

9. ". . . . be myself at my best" in English.

10. Both "state" and "function" in English.

11. *Sic*; should be Robert M. Maciver.

12. "Law is the expression of the general will" appears in English in the original.

13. See *Mencius* 1B:8. Mencius is explaining that because of his immoral rule, the king in question no longer counted as a genuine king, and thus his death was not regicide but execution.

Further Reading

For Luo's biography, see Terry Narramore, *Chinese Intellectuals and Politics: Luo Longji and Chinese Liberalism* (University of Melbourne, 1983), and Frederic J.

Spar, "Human Rights and Political Engagement: Luo Longji in the 1930s," in Roger B. Jeans, ed., *Roads Not Taken: The Struggle of Opposition Parties in Twentieth-Century China* (Boulder, CO: Westview Press; 1992). Luo's "What Kind of Political System Do We Want?" is translated in Wm. Theodore de Bary and John Lufrano, eds., *Sources of Chinese Tradition, 2d ed.* (New York: Columbia University Press, 2000), vol. 2, pp. 331–34.

23

The New Culture Movement and the Human Rights Movement (1931)

Peng Kang

"Xin wenhua yundong yu renquan yundong" [The New Culture Movement and the Human Rights Movement]. Originally published in *Xin sichao*, vol. 4 (February 28, 1931). Reprinted in Cai Shangsi, ed., *Zhongguo xiandai sixiang shi ziliao jianbian* [A Concise Edition of Materials in the History of Modern Chinese Thought] (Hangzhou: Zhejiang renmin chubanshe, 1983), vol. 3.

While in the early 1930s the CCP was extremely critical of the ruling GMD for its suppression of people's rights and freedoms, it nonetheless agreed with the GMD in criticizing the Xinyue *group's concept of human rights, on which see the previous two selections. Although GMD and CCP perspectives differed, they were in agreement in rejecting human rights as an excessively abstract idea which did not fit China's revolutionary needs. Zhou Fohai's essay (Text 20) gives a good picture of the nature of the GMD's critique of human rights. The CCP focused on the political and class standpoint of the* Xinyue *group as it revealed itself in the struggle for human rights. Communists argued that laws and rights are products of existing social relationships and therefore reflect the interests of those in power. The* Xinyue *group was only fighting for the freedoms of the individual and the bourgeoisie, whereas the Communists were fighting for the freedoms of the proletariat. CCP member Peng Kang furthermore claimed that the* Xinyue *group's critique of the GMD's violations of human rights was not convincing, and questioned the notion that respect for human rights could be brought about through the establishment of laws and a constitution. Rights and freedoms, the Communists argued, could only be secured through political struggle. What was needed was a political revolution and the overthrow of the GMD, rather than reform of the present political system. Although they criticized the concept of human rights, they nonetheless affirmed the value and importance of freedom of thought and speech.*

Since Hu Shi last May published an essay in *Xinyue* [magazine] called "Human Rights and the Provisional Constitution," the question [of human rights] has attracted the attention of many people, which just confirms that the current ruling class is intensifying its oppression and exploitation. The common people have lost every bit of their freedom. In these conditions of oppression and exploitation, using the viewpoint of the New Culture Movement, Hu Shi and others have raised some questions and lodged some protests against the current ruling class. The spread of this movement has enriched the contents of the New Culture Movement and given it a close relationship to politics so that the participants in the New Culture Movement have become participants in a human rights movement (*renquan yundong*).

It is a necessary principle that cultural movements come to be related to political movements. Since cultural struggles originally are part of political struggles, they have a political meaning and must take the same measures as a political movement. Only then can they penetrate deeply into the masses and be of practical use. Only when it becomes a movement can it take on something of this [political] essence. Thus, although the gentlemen associated with *Xinyue* tried at first to avoid politics, now they find they cannot help but discuss political questions—in fact, their movement has now become a political movement, the human rights movement. On this point, we do not resemble some people who believe that *Xinyue* has deserted its original goals and taken the path of politics, but see this as a necessary development that follows the intensification of objective conditions.

However, while we find no problem with *Xinyue*'s becoming political, we do have a problem with the kind of political meaning that Hu Shi and his compatriots' New Culture Movement has, and with the kind of thing that the human rights movement really is. To press the issue a bit, what is their class meaning and function? In all questions, the class standpoint must always be the major issue. . . .

According to Hu Shi, "A major undertaking of the New Culture Movement is the liberation of thought." This is naturally not a bad [goal]. Cultural movements are basically a kind of struggle, and the opponents in this struggle are the traditions of the old culture. The old political system is the shield of the old traditions, so in the struggle the old political system inevitably will increase its restriction and oppression of the new movement in order to protect the old traditions. Thus, in order to pursue its own development, the new movement has to resolutely oppose this restriction and oppression. Only through enjoying freedom can new developments come about. The demand for freedom of thought and speech is thus very meaningful for every New Culture Movement.

To demand freedom of thought and speech is a kind of struggle, but the opponent in this struggle is not actually the traditions of the old culture, but rather the political organizations that protect them. Thus, the significance of freedom of thought and speech is political, and the struggle is a political one. Cultural movements are from the beginning closely linked with political movements, and as the [cultural] struggle develops, it will certainly lead to an intensification of the political struggle and to the unification [of the two movements].

This is our understanding of cultural movements, and also of freedom of thought and speech. Based on this kind of understanding, let us see how to struggle for freedom in a time when there is no freedom of thought or speech.

Why should we struggle for freedom? Because we have no freedom. Why can't we have freedom? Because we are not allowed to have freedom. Who will not allow us to have freedom, and why won't they allow us to have freedom? A class culture is built on its economic base. Fundamentally, it is the manifestation of this class spirit, something that eulogizes, praises, and strengthens it. A change of the material base brings about the birth of a new culture, which causes the superstructure to vacillate. In order to protect its collapsing power, the ruling class must forestall or oppress anything that might hasten its collapse. That is why all new movements at this moment of time will meet with destruction at the hands of the controlling powers. The old powers become more oppressive and destructive as they become more unstable and closer to collapse. China today is in exactly this situation.

This is why, if we do not have freedom today, it is because the current ruling class does not allow us to have freedom. They do not allow us to have freedom because they want to prevent their impending fall from power. We are not allowed to reveal their ridiculous behavior or to expose their sinister projects. As long as you stand in opposition to their class thinking and their concrete interests you cannot avoid oppression.

Thus we do not have freedom of thought or speech.

But are we willing not to be free? No; "Give me liberty or give me death!"[1] From the viewpoint of the cultural movement, without freedom of thought, speech, and publishing, the New Culture Movement cannot develop. Right now we do not have freedom; this is a reality that everyone acknowledges. Our wanting freedom is not the issue; the issue is, how do we obtain it?

We have said that cultural movements are a form of political movement, and that the struggle for freedom of thought and speech is a kind of political struggle. The current political struggle is a struggle of a certain class to seize political power, and so the cultural struggle is a burgeoning class's struggle to replace the culture of the ruling class with its own culture. Thus, the important significance of the struggle for freedom of thought and speech in a cultural movement lies not in adopting an individualistic standpoint and advocating that individuals should have these freedoms to contribute to the improvement of society; it is rather in a class's—and today it is the proletariat's—advocating the freedom to criticize the ruling class in order to expose the rulers' reactionary thinking, educate the masses of its own class, form its own class's theory, and consolidate its own class battle line.

Freedom of thought and speech are the freedom to criticize. Criticism is a kind of weapon, a weapon to push the ruling class toward its own fall. When the ruling class finds itself facing such a weapon, it counters with its own weapon. There is no ruling class that will permit the class it oppresses to freely reveal [the ruling class's] reactionary nature. What is the weapon of the ruling class? This is clear: it holds the reins of political power in its hands, and can use political power to mobilize all its institutions and tools to oppress and control freedom of thought and speech. The greater the power of criticism, the more shaky the ruling class's hold on political power, and the more cruelly it will use its weapons. But already shaky political power cannot be saved, and ever-increasing criticism cannot be checked. At such a time, if you want freedom of thought and speech, you must enter into a total struggle with the political power that controls and suppresses freedom. Only by means of struggle can freedom of thought and speech be achieved.

Hu Shi and others like Liang Shiqiu are aware of the necessity of having freedom of thought and speech, but they do not know how to achieve it. Hu Shi hopes that the ruling class will "cancel all orders, systems, and structures that restrict freedom of thought and speech." Liang Shiqiu wants the law to "protect our freedoms." We cannot understand how this wagging of tails and fawning before the ruling class could have any effect. You want laws? Doesn't the GMD's political platform have an article which clearly affirms that "the people have complete freedoms of assembly, association, speech, publishing, residence, and belief"? But today the government doesn't implement these freedoms! The more you want them to [observe] the law, the more they will increase their oppression and restriction until they take your life; this is the GMD's only answer to all your tail-wagging and fawning!

We want freedom of thought and speech, but in the first place, we do not want the individualistic freedoms that Hu Shi and his colleagues demand from the standpoint of bourgeois liberalism. What we demand is the proletarian freedom to criticize the ruling class from the proletarian standpoint. In the second place, we do not seek this freedom through tail-wagging and fawning discussion, but rather we will seize it by means of struggle.

If we want the freedom to criticize, we must struggle, and our struggle must advance forward so we can overturn the regime that suppresses freedom. Only thus can we obtain complete freedom, since if the opponent we criticize doesn't disappear, the task of criticism cannot be completed. If the regime is not overthrown, all reactionary forces cannot be rooted out. Only with this kind of understanding and by these means can we achieve our goals and open the road of freedom by replacing [the old traditions] with the new culture.

"Freedom of thought and speech" are "crucial elements of human rights." The deprivation of freedom of thought and speech is the deprivation of important human rights, so the gentlemen of *Xinyue* have risen up to fight for them, turning [their struggle] into a movement. Their aim is to restore human rights, and the step to achieve this is to "draft a constitution for the Republic of China, or at least, at the very least, to draft a so-called Provisional Constitution for the Tutelage Period." Their slogan is, "Swiftly draft a Provisional Constitution in order to assure a foundation for the rule of law! Swiftly draft a Provisional Constitution in order to protect human rights!"[2] "Those who struggle for human rights advocate rule of law . . . and those who struggle for rule of law must first struggle for a constitution."[3] Thus, their human rights movement could also be said to be a constitutional movement.

We would like to discuss several questions in order to better understand the class meaning and function of this movement.

The first important question is, what are human rights? In order to say what human rights are, we must first explain what humans are.

Humans live in society; they are never wholly isolated things, but are a totality of their social relations. Relations of economic production, in turn, make society into class society, so that [rather than just] say that humans are part of society, it is more concrete to say that they are members of a certain class. Thus, we cannot know what humans are in the abstract, nor what human rights are in the abstract. "If the skin does not exist, how can the hair attach to it?" This is very simple logic. But the gentlemen of the human rights movement do not understand it, and so they have let loose some mistaken ideas.

These gentlemen are completely consistent; in their literature they express [the idea of] "human nature" (*renxing*) and in their politics they struggle for "human rights." "Human nature," "human rights," what abstract expressions! What bourgeois ideas! Here we insist even further on the connections between cultural movements and political movements. We have already criticized their views with respect to cultural questions, and will now proceed to be more concrete [in our critique] with respect to political questions.

Since human rights are the kind of thing [I have just described], it is natural that the questions they raise, such as the [relationship between] human rights and the state, or between human rights and the law, are similarly [problematic].

What is the state? Those who struggle for human rights say its function is to protect human rights. They refer to the Second Article of the French Declaration of the Rights of Man: "The purpose of all political associations is the preservation of the natural and imprescriptible (*yong bu momie de*) rights of man." We have already said that human rights is an abstract thing; it is even more true that there are no "imprescriptible rights of man." If a state is to protect such abstract things, it will itself become an abstraction. But if there really is such a thing as a state, then what kind of thing is it?

We will not discuss here the theory of the state, but will only look at the writings of the human rights movement member Luo Longji.[4] He acknowledges that "Marx's statement that the state is a tool that the capitalist class uses to invade the proletariat" is reasonable; "states have indeed at times been dominated by some individual, family, or organization." The state is an uncompromising product of a class society. It is a tool by which one class oppresses another, a structure that implements the orders of the oppressing class. However, class division in capitalist societies has reached the final form of [class] antagonism; class division has clearly reached an extreme point. Thus, the state in a capitalist society clearly shows its class nature and its form is extremely consolidated. So if we want to speak of the state, we must first speak of capitalist states. Luo Longji has not grasped this point, because he says, "What needs to be noted, though, is that if one looks at the facts of history down to the present day, one will see that those who dominate [the power of] the state are not necessarily all capitalists." But, in fact, those who dominate the state can only be a certain class, and certain individuals, families, or organizations are only representing that class.

The relationship of human rights to law is much the same as their relationship to the state. It is impossible to find a law that protects human rights; they only protect the private property of the dominant class—which today is the capitalist class—and defend the laws that are related to it and that oppress the class being dominated—which today is the proletariat. Laws do not arise from human rights, but rather from relationships in a specific society. Laws do not protect human rights, but rather ensure the class privileges (*jieji quan*) of the capitalists.

Simply put, this is the view of the state and laws that we Marxists hold. So-called human rights and other ideas of this kind were demands put forth by the bourgeoisie when they opposed feudalism; they were the major slogans during the bourgeois revolutionary period. Today, in the Chinese revolutionary phase, human rights advocates struggle for human rights and the drafting of a constitution, and it is naturally to the GMD, an organization representing the capitalist class, that they express their opposition and demands.

Therefore, we say that in their cultural movement, the gentlemen of *Xinyue* take the position of bourgeois liberalism, and in their politics, their position is the same. We only need to understand this point for the meaning and function of their movement to become evident.

They want human rights and have raised thirty-five articles.[5] Naturally we do not want to discuss each of them, nor do we need to. However, we must realize that in our current context of heterogeneous political powers, this is the national bourgeoisie's attempt to obtain full political power by opposing the ruling class and deceiving the broad laboring masses. They thus use such vague class terms as "all citizens," "all the people," or "the public will of all the people," but their expression "the state should protect private property." is much clearer. Who of the "citizens" have private property? Do proletarians have private property? If this is not speaking on behalf of the bourgeoisie, then on whose behalf is it?

We can go one step further and ask, if this human rights movement is such a pressing demand, how do they intend to obtain human rights? They stick to old ways and continue to talk about drafting a constitution! Drafting a constitution!? Who will draft this constitution? Do they want the GMD itself to draft it? The GMD has already answered that the

Outline of National Reconstruction works as the constitution, and as for human rights, they have already been drafted in all kinds of laws, so there is no need for a human rights bill. How do the human rights advocates feel about this?

China's history has already told us that constitutional movements are futile. The history of Europe and the United States tells us that if you want human rights, you must use revolutionary methods; was not the French Declaration of the Rights of Man written in blood? The human rights advocates know these realities very well, so they should wake up and face them directly.

From the above, the real face of the human rights advocates is already obvious. We also know that today we have no freedom whatsoever, and that [in such circumstances] we do not demand laws and human rights from the current ruling class. This is especially true of the masses of workers and peasants who have suffered the greatest oppression: they do not even know what "human rights" are. What they want is their own class's interests and rights, and in order to achieve and protect them, they want to move the struggle for political power forward.

The gentlemen of *Xinyue* want to struggle for human rights, but the masses of workers and peasants want to get political power.

Therefore, we cannot help but say that in this respect those struggling for human rights are reactionaries.

We have already analyzed above the relationship between the New Culture and human rights movements and their respective contents. We also know their true meaning. Now we will look once again at the position of those who take part in these two movements.

Everyone already knows that the current ruling class is reactionary and has betrayed the revolution. But the gentlemen of *Xinyue* and the human rights movement are somehow not of this opinion; they have struck a dirty deal to defend the ruling class. Although they have also said that the GMD is reactionary, this is only from the standpoint of the New Culture Movement. If the GMD suddenly gave in to all of Hu Shi's demands, then he would no longer regard it as reactionary and would immediately be perfectly satisfied.

But isn't this a trap, when they say on the one hand that the GMD is reactionary and on the other that it can be venerated as a revolutionary government? What kind of words are these? Isn't this all deliberately to confuse the masses? Originally [they felt that] the revolutionary government was very good, but now in the eyes of Hu Shi and his friends it is slightly improper. So they jump up and shout a bit, hoping the other party will answer. If they do receive their answer, they will have no more concern for the countless people who still suffer oppression and abuse. No wonder Liang Shiqiu says, "if a proletarian is at all promising, he only needs to work honestly and diligently all his life, and he will be able to amass a fair amount of capital. Only this is a proper way to struggle for livelihood."[6] What kind of words are these? Other than a lifetime of slave labor, the proletariat are not to participate in anything? Are they not to have a share in freedom of thought and speech, and are human rights not to be their rights?

We already know that those who call themselves human rights advocates and those they call the reactionary ruling class actually are one and the same. So when they see the mistakes of the ruling class, they "very thoroughly and honestly make a critique." This is so that [they] "can perhaps give a wake-up call to the younger elements in the GMD so that they will have the opportunity to consciously rectify these reactionary tendencies."

They do not know that when the broad laboring masses look at these reactionary tendencies, they desire to voice thoroughgoing and antagonistic criticism; they do not hope for a "conscious rectification," but rather for a complete overthrow of the system.

These are the characteristics of Chinese society today. The cultural movement inevitably reflects and heightens these features; the human rights movement should [therefore] be a political movement.

In a word, no matter from which side we look at these questions, we cannot avoid saying that the *Xinyue* gentlemen are reactionaries.

Notes

1. These words by Patrick Henry were repeated by many Chinese, ranging from Liang Qichao to Li Dazhao. Henry's original words run: "[I]s life so dear, or peace so sweet, as to be purchased at the price of chains and slavery? Forbid it, Almighty God!—I know not what course others may take; but as for me . . . give me liberty, or give me death."

2. From Hu Shi's article "Human Rights and the Provincial Constitution"; see above, Text 21.

3. From Luo Longji's article "On Human Rights"; see above, Text 22.

4. Peng cites two sentences from Luo's "On Human Rights"; see Text 22.

5. Luo Longji provided a list of thirty-five different human rights in his article, including both civil and political as well as social and economic rights.

6. *Xinyue* 2:6–7 (1930).

Further Reading

For another example of a Communist critique of the *Xinyue* approach, see Qu Qiubai, "Zhongguo renquan pai zhen mianmu" [The Real Features of the China Human Rights Group], *Buerweike* 4:6 (1931). Reprinted in Cai Shangsi, ed., *Zhongguo xiandai sixiang shi ziliao jianbian* [A Concise Edition of Materials in the History of Modern Chinese Thought] (Hangzhou: Zhejiang renmin chubanshe, 1983), vol. 3, pp. 35–41.

24
Two Excerpts (1933 and 1936)

Wu Jingxiong

"Sanminzhuyi he falü" [The Three Principles of the People and Law], in *Falü zhexue yanjiu* (Shanghai: Shanghai faxue bianyishe, 1933), p. 45.

"Zhonghua minguo xianfa caoan de tese" [Special Characteristics of the Republic of China's Draft Constitution], *Dongfang zazhi* 33:13 (1936): 9–10.

Wu Jingxiong (or John C.H. Wu, 1899–1986) was among the most influential Chinese jurists and legal thinkers of the twentieth century, and played an important role in the drafting of the 1946 Constitution of the Republic of China. Wu studied with leading authorities in the United States and in Germany, was a judge and dean of the Comparative Law School of China in Shanghai, and in the 1930s was the chairman of the Constitutional Drafting Committee of the Legislative Yuan. Wu's remarks in these two excerpts should be seen in the context of ongoing debates in the late 1920s and early 1930s about the way in which a constitution ought to protect rights. The Nationalist government had promulgated a Provisional Constitution in 1931— at least on paper, meeting the demand of Hu Shi from 1929 (see Text 21)—and work had begun in 1932 on drafting a permanent constitution. The first complete draft was finished in 1933 by Wu. In this draft, and in the eventual final version, the people's rights were allowed to be limited by simple legislation, so long as the restrictive laws were aimed at one of four vague social goals. Wu sees himself as implementing the ideas of Sun Yatsen, and he is clearly also influenced by the legal positivist conception of rights that he encountered in America in the 1920s. Wu sees rights as historical and relative: they are not universal, but have to suit the times and the needs of each individual society.

24a. From "The Three Principles of the People and the Law"

. . . During the eighteenth and nineteenth centuries, individualism (*geren zhuyi*) flourished in various Western countries, advocating that the rights (*quanli*) of individuals were innate (*tianfu de*) and therefore absolute. As a result of this, it reached the point that each individual was only aware of the ways in which his or her actions brought about his or her own rights, with no regard for the difficulties of others, still less for the interests of the whole society. This in turn brought about a society based on mutual competition. [As a result,] inside China we are wracked with a confusion of lawsuits, while internationally, there have been periodic wars, culminating in the great tragedy of the recent European war!

Mr. Sun Yatsen's idea of people's rights (*minquan*) is completely different from this individualistic concept of rights. Society, rather than the individual, is the point of departure for people's rights. According to Mr. Sun's ideas, rights are given to individuals by society, and society is the source that produces rights; if an individual leaves society, he has no rights to speak of. Society can grant rights; when necessary, it can take them away, or at the very least, it can limit the scope of rights. Thus, the idea of people's rights stresses that all rights are relative, not absolute. . . .

24b. From "Special Characteristics of the Republic of China's Draft Constitution"

Section 3: The Protection of People's Rights (renmin de quanli)

The people have very many different kinds of rights. Those stipulated in the Constitution are only the principal ones that are recorded as examples (as in Sections 8 through 23 in the Draft Constitution); it does not provide a complete list of every right that [the people] ought to enjoy. In addition to those stipulated in the Constitution, therefore, the people have still other appropriate kinds of rights, which the Constitution ought also to protect (for instance, the freedom of marriage). Thus, Section 24 of the Draft Constitution stipulates that "All the people's other rights and freedoms which harm neither the social order nor the public interest receive the protection of the Constitution: they cannot be limited except in accordance with law."

The Draft Constitution uses two methods to protect the people's rights. One is to restrict executive and judicial powers so that they shall not harm people; for example, Sections 9 through 24 all contain language like: "[these rights] cannot be limited except in accordance with law."

This means that only the legislative branch can implement measures to limit the people's rights and freedoms; the executive branch cannot recklessly attempt to limit them.

The second method is to restrict legislative powers so that they shall not harm the people. For example, Section 5 declares that "All laws which limit the people's rights and freedoms must be passed in order to defend national security, avoid a severe crisis, protect social order, or promote the necessary interests of society." From this section we can see that if the legislative branch uses the law to limit people's rights, it must be in conformity with [at least one of] the four goals stated above of "defending national security, avoiding a severe crisis, protecting social order, or promoting the necessary interests of society." It cannot pass laws to limit rights and freedoms simply because it wishes to. Looking at different examples of various countries' constitutions to see how they protect the people's rights and freedoms, we find that many place limitations only on executive and judicial powers' abilities to harm people, but do not limit legislative power. Our Draft Constitution places limits on all three branches—the executive, judicial, and legislative—and so it can be said to be very thorough.

When drafting a constitution there are two distinct ways in which people's rights and freedoms can be restricted; restriction by law and by the Constitution. In the former case, although the Constitution acknowledges that people have all kinds of freedoms, it nonetheless gives the law the complete power to interfere in these freedoms. Even though executive interference is not allowed by the Constitution, legislative interference is countenanced. Allowing this kind of restriction, therefore, affords only weak protection of the people's rights and freedoms. In addition, if one chooses the method of allowing legal restrictions, then only after laws of this kind have been promulgated can the people enjoy their stipulated freedoms: the Constitution alone is not enough. If, on the other hand, one chooses constitutional restrictions, then as soon as the Constitution is implemented, people will be able to enjoy their freedoms. The constitutional method of restricting rights and freedoms is stronger and more stable than the legal method. The best way to protect the people's rights, in short, is to have these restrictions arise from the Constitution.

Seen in this light, why does our Draft Constitution have legal restrictions instead of constitutional ones? It is necessary to clarify that earlier constitutional movements in Europe and the United States were movements in which individuals struggled for freedoms. Our current constitutional movement is one in which we Chinese as a group struggle to save our country. When those earlier Europeans and Americans struggled for freedom, they took the individual as their point of departure. Our struggle for freedom takes the collective as its starting point. The freedom we struggle for is the freedom of our nation and of our nationality (*minzu*). China's current situation is completely different from that of Europe and the United States when their people were struggling for freedom. At that time, Europeans and Americans were oppressed by feudalism or tyranny, which is not our situation today. At that time, the great question for Europeans and Americans was how to save themselves; our great question today is how to save our nation and our nationality. Our nation and nationality have long been oppressed and trampled upon, and the situation today is clearly worse than ever. To save our nation and our nationality, we have no choice but to ask individuals to spare no effort at sacrificing all their freedoms in order to seek the freedoms of the collective. Because of this, our Draft Constitution must choose the path of legal restrictions, and in each provision where it stipulates [the protection of] rights, it must add that "they cannot be limited except in accordance with law."

Further Reading

For a discussion of American and other influences on Wu, see Thomas E. Greiff, "The Principle of Human Rights in Nationalist China: John C.H. Wu and the Ideological Origins of the 1946 Constitution," *China Quarterly*, no. 103 (September 1985): 441–61. The Constitutional drafting process is discussed in Lloyd Eastman, *The Abortive Revolution: China Under Nationalist Rule, 1927–1937* (Cambridge, MA: Harvard University Press, 1974), pp. 159–80. The final version of the 1946 Constitution can be found in Ch'ien Tuan-sheng, *The Government and Politics of China* (Cambridge, MA: Harvard University Press, 1950).

For further discussion of Wu's philosophical perspectives, see his "The Status of the Individual in the Political and Legal Traditions of Old and New China," in Charles A. Moore, ed., *The Status of the Individual in East and West* (Honolulu: University of Hawaii Press, 1968). Wu's autobiography is *Beyond East and West* (New York: Sheed & Ward, 1951).

25

A Discussion of Constitutional Stipulations Concerning the People's Rights (1933)

Qiu Hanping

"Xianfashang guanyu renmin zhi quanli guiding zhi shangque" [A Discussion of Constitutional Stipulations Concerning the People's Rights], *Dongfang zazhi* [Eastern Miscellany] 30:7 (March 9, 1933): 96–97, 98–99, 102–3.

Qiu Hanping (1904–?), jurist, banker, and government official, was one of those active in the debate on constitutionalism in the early 1930s. Like some others such as Zhang Zhiben, and in contrast to Wu Jingxiong (see Text 24), Qiu emphasized that the constitution should fully protect people's rights and freedoms. He criticized earlier Chinese constitutions for falling short of fully guaranteeing the protection of people's rights, and also pointed out that these stipulations in any case had not been upheld and respected. The piece by Qiu translated here, although showing a strong concern with people's rights and freedoms, nevertheless also reveals something of an uneasiness with the language of human rights. Qiu is furthermore critical of the earlier narrow focus on civil and political rights. He advocates a more active state, applauding what he characterizes as the "process of development from passive to active, from individual to social, from abstract to substantial—to put it in simple terms, progressing from passive laissez-faire to welfare policies."

Of all the questions we might raise about the constitution, that which most concerns the subsistence (*shengcun*) of our four hundred million people are the articles on the people's rights (*renmin zhi quanli*). Seen from an historical point of view, this question is the core of the Constitution. In China today all law and discipline have been lost, and our "rights" have been violated until no trace of them can be found. We need not even ask whether subsistence is protected; nothing at all is protected! That is reality and it cannot be denied. If we wish to study how the people's rights can be protected, we cannot ignore this reality. In order to make this question easier to discuss, we can divide it into five parts. The first is the meaning and history of "human rights" (*renquan*). The second concerns the means of protecting human rights set forth in the constitutions of various countries. The third is the contents of so-called "human rights." The fourth discusses the provisions for "human rights" in past constitutions. The fifth part looks at future standards for drawing up a constitution. I will discuss these points in the above order. Before proceeding, I would like to clarify one point concerning the term "human rights." The expression "human rights" did not originally make sense, and today's fashionable scholars are in fact all discussing some sort of "duty standard" (*yiwu benwei*). Since I have found nothing better in Chinese dictionaries than "human rights," though, for the time being I will use it.

Section One. The Meaning and History of "Human Rights"

What are human rights (Right [sic] of Man, *Droits de l'homme*)? In Western history they have been considered extremely important. Human rights are the natural rights (*ziran quanli*) that come with birth. In other words, without these rights, humans cannot subsist. For this reason, people have shed blood without regret in the struggle for rights. In 1215, the English could no longer endure the heavy-handed abuses of tyranny, and so they rose up to oppose the king. As a result, King John approved the Magna Carta. On the one hand, the Magna Carta assured some basic rights, and on the other hand, it was an agreement reached between the people and the monarch. The most important thing was that the king would have to seek the agreement of the great landowners to levy taxes. Although this right was limited to the large landowners, it meant that the principle had been established, and afterward its scope could gradually be expanded. The contents of human rights were enlarged by such documents as the Petition of Right of 1628 and the Bill of Rights of 1619, among others, and their significance for human rights was equal to that of the Magna Carta. With the French and American revolutions, human rights became formally enshrined in constitutions, which is considered the most important [stage in the history of human rights]. This tide reached every Western country, and human rights became a key part of each constitution. If we study in detail the constitutions of each country prior to the late nineteenth century, there are three noteworthy phenomena.

First of all, in the age of despots, the existence of human rights was completely ignored, and the ruling class held the power of life and death over everyone. The human rights movement began by endeavoring to limit this kind of power and to compel the rulers to recognize the subsistence rights of the ruled. Most of the great atrocities of the last 200 years have been as a result of this struggle. In other words, human rights are the subsistence rights that the ruled class compelled the ruling class to acknowledge, and so these rights are passive. Why is this? It is because the subsistence rights of the ruled were obtained by demands placed on the rulers.

Secondly, the rights in constitutions are enumerated. That is, constitutions clearly acknowledge the rights people have. This makes it look like the rights people have are granted by the constitution: if there were no constitution, there would be no human rights; if one wants to have human rights, one must have a constitution. This, however, is illogical and contradictory. It is illogical because a person's subsistence rights exist prior to the constitution; it is contradictory, because if one acknowledges that human rights exist from birth, then the stipulations of a constitution should be unnecessary.

Thirdly, the goal in drafting a constitution is to limit the power of the rulers in order to protect human rights. The reason for this is entirely owing to the viciousness of past tyrants, which greatly provoked the people and led them to believe that a good government is one that grants the people a relatively large amount of freedom. The great vitality of individualism since the seventeenth century owes to this same reason.

[Omitted: Section Two. The Means by Which the Constitutions of Various Countries Protect Human Rights]

Section Three. The Contents of So-Called "Human Rights"

From the English Magna Carta down to today, the meaning and contents of human rights have undergone radical changes. We may say that, before the late nineteenth century, the contents of so-called "human rights" were confined to individual freedoms and the right to political participation. With respect to individual freedoms, the guiding principle was that they limited the government's right to intervene. More precisely, except for limitations imposed by society's interests, people should enjoy absolute freedom. This conception was completely influenced by natural law. From the point of view of today, it does not seem logical, but in the age of resistance to brute force, this doctrine was a most stimulating drug. In those days individual freedoms included no more than physical freedom, freedom of residence, freedom to work, freedom to own property, freedom to worship, freedom of thought, freedom of assembly, freedom to form associations, and so on. In the age of tyrants, these freedoms were suppressed or completely forbidden. Freedom of religion in particular was only achieved in Europe through the spilled blood of millions. The main goal in opposing brute force in general was the restoration of individual freedom.

Over the ages, each country's constitution has stipulated individual freedoms. More recently, though, as democratic governments have become prevalent, [people] have strongly felt that unlimited individual freedom impedes society's progress and impairs the interests of many; in newer constitutions, therefore, the words "human rights" are seen as somewhat dangerous. In Germany's new constitution, the words "human rights" were changed to "the fundamental rights and duties of the Germans," which greatly expands the scope of the concept. More detailed research reveals that Germany's constitution in reality has opened up a different path with regards to rights. Not only does it passively recognize people's freedoms, but also it actively helps individuals to secure their freedoms. Yet there is one shortcoming: do the various individual freedoms exist prior to the constitution, or should we say that they exist only because they are stipulated in the constitution? Because Germany's constitution still harkens back to older models, it cannot resolve this point, and so it loses a good part of the true spirit of constitutionalism.

From the time of the English Magna Carta, people have believed that participation in government was necessary for securing individual freedoms. In the age of tyrants, popular participation meant only that people had the right to express their opinions about the burden of taxation. Afterward, the application of this general principle was gradually extended, first to small landholders and then to the people as a whole. This was true in France as well. Originally, political participation only meant the right of the people to speak out. The next step was the right to vote, and the next step after that was the limited right to stand for elections. In modern times, a few constitutions give the people the rights of referendum and recall. From this we can see that the content of the right to participate in government has expanded with the evolution of political ideas.

Politics in the past few years has gradually begun to follow a certain path. Previously people felt that governments were things to which there was no alternative, but also that governments were impediments to individual freedoms. For this reason, their major demands were the limitation of the state's jurisdiction and the guarantee of their basic rights. The popularity of individualism in the nineteenth century owes to this reasoning. Only when this began to bear fruit did people discover that the evils of individualism are roughly equivalent to, if not even worse than, the results of tyrannical systems of government. This could not help but raise some doubts about so-called individual rights to freedom. In fact, since the birth of individualism as an institution, society suddenly began producing many empty-handed workers. The fruit of their bitter labor goes into the private coffers of the capitalists. In order to alleviate their suffering, one can only end the existing system, if not by overthrowing it, then by reforming it. Overthrowing a system, as in Russia, is revolutionary. Reforming it, as in the United States or Europe, is a moderate course of action. The poor of society (the proletariat) account for the majority of people, so their power to intimidate is naturally very great. In order to preserve social stability, one must put in place ways to improve their lot. So-called social policies arose as the times required, and faith in the state's omnipotence also increased every day; from the past down to today, this seems like an unalterable principle. This kind of thinking, however, is diametrically opposed to the previous, extremely laissez-faire attitude. The force of these new ideas is sweeping over the world like flood waters. Comparatively new constitutions have included these issues as important items. The people's basic rights have been expanded from the passive sphere of protection to a more active sphere of support. Examples include: people's right to an education that is practically free, special protection for workers, aid and comfort to women and the disabled, relief for the unemployed, and so on.

In summary, the content of "human rights" is in a process of development from passive to active, from individual to social, from abstract to substantial—to put it in simple terms, progressing from passive laissez-faire to welfare policies.

[Omitted: Section Four. Past Constitutional Stipulations Concerning Human Rights]

Section Five. Future Standards for Constitutional Regulations Concerning Human Rights

China's current problems are due to its having taken the wrong constitutional road. Every day, China sings the tune of freedom but it never finds the true road to freedom. The British constitutional expert Dicey said incisively: "To acknowledge the existence of people's rights to individual freedoms is not at all difficult; nor is it particularly advantageous. The real difficulty is rather in realizing the protection of these rights." This is a famous dictum which unfortunately is a great [and true] statement! The failure of China's past efforts at constitutionalization lay in singing the song [of freedom] without any way to realize its goal. From the Provisional Constitution of 1911 to the Tutelage Constitution of 1931, there was a period of twenty years, but rights to individual freedoms not only failed to find a realistic means of protection, but the lip service paid to them in the constitutions' texts actually grew ever weaker—even to the point of increasing exploitation. The Provisional Constitution's provisions for the people's rights to freedom had very limited standards. In the Tutelage Constitution, not only are there limits [on freedoms] that are without any standards whatsoever, there is also an article that [allows for] the suspension [of people's freedom]. This kind of "progress in reverse" is really alarming. Who knows what was in the thoughts of the drafters of these constitutions! I believe that future constitutions cannot but demand realization [of their principles], and if we wish to see them realized, we should clearly heed the mistakes of the past, while at the same time paying heed to our national character (*guoqing*). The following are the standards [I propose] for the drafting of the Constitution:

1. In the Constitution it can be stipulated that the state has the right to limit the people's basic rights, but it is necessary to set standards and degrees for these limits. In accordance with this principle, we should remove all [explicit] stipulations concerning the freedom of religion and [similar rights]. The section about the people's rights should begin with this kind of rule: "All the people's freedoms which do not violate the spirit of the constitution are affirmed." If this is the case, it will not be necessary to enumerate stipulations regarding [each freedom]. When the people's freedoms are in violation of the spirit of the Constitution, the state can rely on laws to limit them.
2. The "laws" mentioned in the Constitution should be clearly defined.
3. We should stipulate that "a person's right to life should not be violated even if guilt is determined after a trial and according to the law." Past constitutions forgot to include this provision.

4. The right to freedom of movement and privacy of mail and telegram can only be limited according to the law; there should be no provision for their suspension.
5. [The freedoms of] assembly and association should be adjusted in accord with the spirit of the first, second, and third sections of the French Constitution, as follows: "The people of the Republic of China have the right to gather peacefully and unarmed without first filing a report or getting special permission. Permission for outdoor gatherings must be granted by local authorities, and if there are security crises, such gatherings may be forbidden."
6. All the people of the Republic of China who do not violate the penal code have the right to form organizations and associations, and this right may not be limited by any preventative measures.[1]
7. If people's speech or publishing activities are found by public security organs to cause critical dangers, they may be limited by punishments or prevented in accordance with the law.
8. If the state uses or takes a person's property, that person shall be compensated at a price which reflects the value of the property, in accordance with the law.
9. Section 8, Clause 2 in the government's provisional constitution can be retained, but the following should be added: "When the responsible organs do not press charges, one must apply to the court for a written summons and investigate within twenty-four hours, or else free the suspect."
10. No matter whose right to freedom is limited, suspended, or violated, the person or persons involved may request that the court within twenty-four hours either issue a summons and investigate, or, if the court feels the complaint is not reasonable, release any detained person.
11. Courts have the privilege of issuing all summons, and this may not be limited or abolished by any law.
12. Only those currently on active military duty may face court-martial.
13. Special organs other than ordinary and administrative courts may not be established to try criminals.
14. Special penal codes, different from ordinary penal codes, may not be established.

15. Legislative methods shall not be used to penalize people; the law shall not penalize a person twice for the same crime.
16. If government officials deliberately violate the constitution, they shall be punished by life imprisonment.
17. Officials act as public servants. There shall be no one-party servitude. (German constitution, Clause 130.)

I feel that in the new constitution particular attention should be paid to the seventeen articles outlined above. We hope that this constitution can become a reality and be able to assure the protection of the rights of the people. Otherwise, the drawing up of this constitution will be a pointless exercise. If my rambling essay can serve to attract the attention of my countrymen, and hasten the completion of the new constitution, my greatest wish will be fulfilled!

Note

1. As to point number six, because I was pressed for time I could not go into the reasons for it. I hope to cover it more fully in a future essay. The above essay is an expression of one man's opinion, but written to express the position of the masses [—author's note].

Further Reading

Please see the suggestions following the previous reading.

26
Manifestos of the China League for the Protection of Civil Rights (1932 and 1933)

China League for the Protection of Civil Rights

"Zhongguo minquan baozhang tongmeng xuanyan" [Manifesto of the China League for the Protection of Civil Rights], *Shen bao* (December 18, 1932). Reprinted in Chen Shuyu, *Zhongguo minquan baozhang tongmeng* [The China League for the Protection of Civil Rights] (Beijing: Beijing chubanshe, 1985), pp. 150–51.

"Zhongguo minquan baozhang tongmeng Shanghai fenhui xuanyan" [Manifesto of the Shanghai Section of the China League for the Protection of Civil Rights], *Shen bao* (January 18, 1933). Reprinted in Chen Shuyu, *Zhongguo minquan baozhang tongmeng* [The China League for the Protection of Civil Rights] (Beijing: Beijing chubanshe, 1985), pp. 151–52.

The League was founded in Shanghai toward the end of 1932 on the initiative of Song Qingling, Cai Yuanpei, Yang Xingfo (also known as Yang Quan), Lin Yutang, and others; a section was later established in Beiping (the name of Beijing from 1928 to 1949), headed by Hu Shi. The League was established in response to the GMD's increasing repression of leftist intellectuals and suspected Communist supporters, and drew support from a broad range of the Chinese political spectrum. It sought the release of all political prisoners and also publicized violations of civil rights. Note that we here translate minquan as "civil rights"; for the complex background of this term, see the General Introduction. Throughout its brief existence, the League was fraught with internal strife due to the different goals and political beliefs of its members (see Text 27). The League came to an abrupt end after less than six months when one of its members was assassinated, presumably by the Blue Shirts, a clandestine organization in charge of intelligence operations against the GMD's political opponents.

26a. Manifesto of the China League for the Protection of Civil Rights (1932)

It is most painful that civil rights (*minquan*), which the Chinese people sought through the great sacrifice of revolution, have still not been realized. Newspaper accounts of [attempts to] control public opinion and of illegal arrests and massacres have practically become common sights. It has even gone so far that young boys and girls are sometimes suspected of being political criminals, after which they cannot avoid being secretly tried in military courts. Even if the trials were public, the minimal human rights (*renquan*) that the general will seeks from society in order to protect civil rights have already been lost. We profoundly understand that for this kind of situation to be effectively and completely reformed, we must work hard to change the environment that produced it. At the same time, we must also realize that all progressive countries have international organizations [devoted to the] protection of civil rights, such as [the organizations] led by [Albert] Einstein, Jueleisai,[1] [John] Dewey, [Bertrand] Russell, and [Roman] Roland.[2] The most important purpose of this kind of organization is to protect the freedoms of thought and society that are needed for human life and for social progress. Following this same reasoning, we propose the establishment of the China League for the Protection of Civil Rights. The aims of the League are:

1. To fight for the release of all political prisoners in the country, and for the abolition of illegal arrests, torture, and massacres. The League

will first of all devote itself to the majority of prisoners who are unknown and who do not receive any attention from society.

2. To give political prisoners in the country legal and other assistance, investigate prison conditions, publish the facts about violations of civil rights in the country, and arouse the general will.

3. To provide help in the struggle for the freedom of association and assembly, the freedom of speech, the freedom of the press, and various other civil rights.

[Here follows a final paragraph proposing an administrative structure and other details.—Eds.]

26b. A Manifesto of the Shanghai Section of the China League for the Protection of Civil Rights (1933)

From the beginning, all struggles for political, social, economic, and moral freedoms necessarily have had as their fundamental goals the demands for freedom of speech, freedom of the press, freedom from forceful interference, and freedom to express opinions regarding the social powers that violate the happiness of the majority, as well as the right to expose and criticize such powers. The concept of real democracy (*demokelaxi*) has been held up as the norm in all social struggles for 300 years; millions of people have spilled their blood and lost their lives for it. It is still at the heart of social and economic struggles. But when the result [of these struggles] involves only a minority, it cannot be hailed as a success. Only when the majority [also] enjoys their interests can democracy be said to have been established. That democracy is the goal of all struggles forward is beyond doubt. However, many of the forces obstructing the progress of humanity often seek to make the interests of the democratic system into [the interests of] their own petty selves, and, at the same time, deprive other people of their just civil rights. The meaning of such a struggle is especially important in China today. All humankind is suffering from a severe economic crisis. In addition to this worldwide crisis, the Chinese people must also endure the aggression of Japan and other imperialist [powers]. These threats strike deeply into the hearts of the Chinese people. Only the Chinese people themselves can take their fate in their hands and fight for the survival of the nation. The Chinese future completely depends on the Chinese people; the route [to this future] lies in the realization of freedom of thought, freedom of speech, and freedom of movement. If this does not come to pass, China will be reduced to the status of Africa. Even worse, it will become still more impossible to reach the future road of economic, social, and political development. This is an indisputable fact, which can be confirmed through both speech and writing and also through the history of iron and blood.

However, to this point, the Chinese people still do not have even the traces of minimal civil rights. To the contrary, periodically magazines and newspapers are shut down and assembly and association are forbidden. During the past five years, the publications that have been forbidden or have lost their [right] to publish number several hundred. The content of these magazines and newspapers includes a variety of political persuasions, both left wing and right wing, and are not limited to opinions and critiques by Chinese authors. Many pure literature and art magazines have also been forbidden; moreover, publications carrying foreign social and cultural struggles are not allowed to circulate in the country. [The repression is so extreme] that collecting these kinds of works can sometimes lead to imprisonment or assassination. The publications that have received such unfortunate treatment are not confined to those that criticize domestic or world affairs; we recollect that official party newspapers, such as *Beiping daobao* and *Minguo ribao*, also have actually been closed due to the unreasonable demands of the Japanese imperialists. At present, not even the opinions of the rulers can safely be expressed. The severity of the bans and the fineness of the net of censorship are such that editors of the banned magazines, even if they are fortunate enough to escape prison, still do not dare to protest. If China wants to resist its enemy and if the Chinese people want to advance to the realm of real democracy, then this oppression of new ideas and critiques, and these restraints on the freedom of speech, have to be abolished. The China League for the Protection of Civil Rights calls on the Chinese people to rise and to strive to realize the freedom of the press, the freedoms of assembly and association, and all interests [associated with] genuine civil rights, and to fight against all censorship and prohibitions. We call on the masses to demand both the universal enjoyment of minimal civil rights and an end to the suppression of writers, artists, and newspaper editors who work hard for the progress and liberation of China.

Notes

1. Identity unclear.
2. The organizations referred to here include the American Civil Liberties Union

(ACLU), of which Dewey was a member. Lin Yutang, for example, wrote about the ACLU and wanted to model the League on that organization.

Further Reading

For Song Qingling's biography, see Sterling Seagrave, *The Soong Dynasty* (New York: Harper and Row, 1985). On Cai Yuanpei, see William J. Duiker, *Ts'ai Yüan-pei* (University Park, PA: Pennsylvania State University Press, 1977). For additional documents on the League, see generally Chen Shuyu, *Zhongguo minquan baozhang tongmeng* [The China League for the Protection of Civil Rights] (Beijing: Beijing chubanshe, 1985).

27
The Protection of Civil Rights (1933)

Hu Shi

"Minquan de baozhang" [The Protection of Civil Rights], *Duli pinglun* 3:18 (February 1933).

Liberals within the Chinese League for the Protection of Civil Rights (on which see the previous text), such as Hu Shi, believed that the League should work within the existing political system, while radicals, such as Song Qingling, believed that this was a futile task and that the GMD was corrupt beyond reform. In keeping with his earlier position (see Text 21 above), Hu Shi adopted a narrowly legalistic approach to human rights and the League's work. Since he regarded the GMD as the legitimate ruler of China—especially since the adoption in 1931 of the Provisional Constitution, which he earlier had demanded—he advocated that the League confine itself to seeking the legal protection of human rights. In early 1933, Hu Shi and Yang Xingfo made an investigation of the prison conditions in Beiping. When the prisoners of one prison later wrote an open letter to the League demanding their help and deploring the conditions in the prison, Song Qingling and Agnes Smedley issued a public appeal and demanded "the immediate and unconditional release of all political prisoners" on behalf of the League. Hu Shi reacted strongly to this appeal, as the article translated here reveals, both because he felt that the conditions described did not match his findings, and also because he felt that asking for the "unconditional" release of all political prisoners was asking too much of the government. The furthest Hu Shi was willing to go on this issue was to seek guarantees that political prisoners were not treated cruely and that legal safeguards were upheld. The majority of the League's members criticized his position, and when Hu Shi did not bend on this issue, he was eventually expelled.

A couple of days ago, at the meeting of the Beiping Branch of the Chinese League for the Protection of Civil Rights, Mr. Yang Xingfo made a very profound statement: "The struggle for the protection of civil rights (*minquan*) is an eighteenth-century affair. Unfortunately, we Chinese living in the twentieth century must still undertake this eighteenth-century task."

The civil rights that progressive peoples should have are not bestowed by sovereigns or granted by the law. They are won by the struggles of people with foresight and written in blood into the law. They are protected by the constant vigilance of countless numbers of people. Without a conscious long-term struggle, there can be no rights set forth in law. If there are laws that grant rights, but no habit is cultivated to make people protect their own rights, then those rights are but empty words in legal [form]. Laws can only stipulate our rights but cannot protect them. The protection of rights depends on individuals' cultivating the good habit of never being willing to abandon their rights.

"Rights" (*quanli*) is a new word that has gradually come into use over the last thirty years. When this word began to be used in China, Mr. Liang Qichao and others pointed out that Chinese have historically lacked rights consciousness, and that we Chinese needed to promote this kind of rights consciousness.[1] The essential meaning of "rights" is that which a person ought to have; its correct translation should have been "just powers" (*yiquan*). Only later did it come to be [understood as] those "rights" given by law which individuals ought to enjoy. Ancient China did not entirely lack this concept of "just powers." Mencius expressed the thought most clearly: "If it was contrary to justice (*yi*) or the Way, he would neither give nor accept the smallest trifle."[2] This is exactly the meaning of "rights." "He would neither give . . . the smallest trifle" refers to respecting what is due to oneself; ". . . nor accept the smallest trifle" refers to respecting what is due to others. Expanding our analysis, Mencius's statement that "[the superior person] cannot be led into excesses when wealthy and honored, deflected from his purpose when poor and obscure, nor [convinced to] bow before force or might"[3] also means that an individual should respect that which is his due, and do that which he considers right. The Confucian and Mohist schools of philosophy also had this concept. However, [ancient Chinese also heeded] the lesson of the way of yielding, namely that in one's life one should yield rather than struggle and "be wronged, yet not retaliate";[4] one should take suffering misfortunes as the basis for cultivating virtue. Once this spirit was internalized, no one dared to protect what they ought to have, nor were they willing to struggle against powerful people for what they believed to be right. When Mr. Liang and others said that Chinese lack rights consciousness, they meant the habit inculcated by a tradition of preferring to "be wronged, yet not retaliate." Under the control of these habits, people can neither enjoy nor protect their human or civil rights, even if they exist in the law.

However, in the end, the knowledge and capability of ordinary people is limited. We cannot hope that everyone will understand what are his or her rights, nor defend them. The reason why the Chinese do not cherish rights is not just that they have been under the influence of religion and philosophy (*sixiang*), which [reject] struggle and [encourage] the enduring of misfortunes; an even more important reason is the lack throughout the history of law in China of the profession of legal defenders. Our ancient ancestors only knew how to worship upright officials such as Lord Bao; they did not advocate the profession of lawyers who could be the defenders of people's rights.[5] Except for the far-sighted politician Wang Anshi, most Confucian scholars were not willing to recognize the law as a subject of study.[6] The literati did not study law, and hence the specialists in law all came to be a class that was despised. The most lofty ones became yamen secretaries handling criminal cases, while the less exalted ones became legal pettifoggers writing legal complaints. The yamen secretaries helped officials to settle lawsuits; ordinary people had to rely on themselves for defense. The legal pettifoggers who bought legal complaints could not act as defenders; at the most they could write complaints for people and "handle cases" in the the shadows. In the play *The Four Imperial Scholars*, the famous character Song Shijie, a legal pettifogger, engages in a lawsuit for his adopted daughter. The complaint was written on behalf of an important person in the court, and Song Shijie appealed while appearing in court, yet he almost lost the entire case. When we see this drama, we can see that our ancestors even down to today have at least occasionally felt the need for legal defenders. The creator of *The Four Imperial Scholars* was an unknown talent, however; his views do not represent those of Chinese society in general. Ordinary Chinese know that legal pettifoggers like Song Shijie are hard to find, and so are those upright officials like Lord Bao. And so they only hoped that they would never in their lives have to enter an official gate or law court. If they entered a law court they only expected to meet with misfortune which they could not withstand and against which they could not defend themselves. To seek victory is a natural instinct, but to be willing to suffer misfortunes is against human nature. The Chinese people's willingness to undergo misfortune and reluctance to bring suit may not be due so much to religion or philosophy, as to the long-standing lack of a class of lawyers to defend people's rights.

The development of Westerners' thinking about rights is completely opposite to the teachings of their religion. Christianity also teaches people not to resist power: "If a man strikes your right cheek, offer him also your left cheek." However, Christianity could not stifle the legal spirit initiated by the Romans. Rome not only bequeathed Roman Law to Western civilization, but even more importantly, her legal teachings and institutions of legal protection. Western intellectuals were willing to study law and take on law cases on behalf of the people; they acknowledged that legal defense was a high professional calling and that the redress of wrongs was a glorious achievement. People only have rights worth the name when this kind of attitude and system are prevalent. We should not forget that in medieval Europe the oldest university, in Salerno, was originally dedicated to the study of medicine, and the second oldest, in Bologna, was founded for the study of law. Only the third oldest university, in Paris, was for theological studies. Our literati "studied ten thousand scrolls but never the law"; since they did not study law, we did not have any legal defenders, only legal pettifoggers who could not defend the people's rights.

The Chinese have only called for rights consciousness for a short period of time; legal education has existed for an even shorter period. The existence of Chinese public legal defenders has been still more recent, so the civil rights set forth in constitutions and provisional constitutions are still empty phrases. Military officers and officials do not know how to respect civil rights, and the people themselves know even less about how to enjoy and defend their own rights. When rights are actually violated, people can only busy themselves by calling on personal relationships and seeking the good offices of others, or else resort to bribery. They cannot take the just, higher road of following the law. In the last few years, political conflicts have reached a crisis point: on the one hand, the ruling party has used its power to punish the expression of public opinion throughout the country and to suppress dissenting parties and political factions, while on the other hand, there is dissatisfaction among all kinds of political forces with the present rule, ranging from well-intentioned criticism to armed resistance by revolutionary parties and groups. In this complex political conflict, the ruling power, in order to protect its own power, naturally uses all kinds of pressure tactics to suppress opposition forces, including many excessive measures such as the indiscriminate use of secret military trials, executions, mass arrests, and oppressive, inhuman imprisonment. These methods are all enough to cause an atmosphere of terror. In these conditions of ongoing political power struggles, especially in a situation where the regime is using all its power to oppose armed resistance, all sensibilities, friendships, and old ways of behavior have become meaningless. It is in times like these that people gradually have become aware of the need for protection of their civil rights. The movement for the protection of civil rights has begun to develop in our time because the battle lines have been most clearly drawn and the political conflict grown most intense. The historical background to this conflict becomes clear if we pay attention to the proclamation released in Shanghai by this movement, [which demands] "the release of all political prisoners in the country and an end to all illegal detentions, torture, and massacres."

I support this movement for the protection of civil rights. I acknowledge that it is the starting point for the Chinese people's awareness of the need for the protection of civil rights in their everyday lives. From this embryonic beginning, perhaps we can gradually inculcate the habit of cherishing our own human rights and respecting those of others, and thus gradually train ourselves to become a people who value the rights we should enjoy [as humans] and dare to struggle for what we believe is right. In order to achieve this goal, the Chinese movement to protect civil rights must be built on a foundation of law. On the one hand, we must be vigilant in order to assure the government's respect for the law and, on the other, we must discipline ourselves to use legal means to protect our own rights and those of others.

However, when we observe the words of those who take part in the movement to protect civil rights today, we notice a great flaw in their discourse. They regard the problem of the protection of civil rights as a political rather than a legal question. This is a mistake. Only by taking the law as one's basis in the struggle to protect civil rights can one achieve the goal of making politics take the road of the rule of law. Only the rule of law can achieve the constant and universal protection of civil rights.

If law is left out of the discussion of the protection of civil rights, then we will have a situation in which "the husband has his truth, the wife has hers"—that is, a dead end. According to yesterday's newspaper reports, the Central Committee of the League for the Protection of Civil Rights published a demand for the "immediate and unconditional release of all political prisoners." This is a good example of the problem. This is not defending civil rights, but demanding that the government grant the freedom to revolt. If a government is to exist, naturally it must punish all attempts to overthrow and oppose it. To demand that the government grant the freedom to revolt: is that not the same thing as asking a tiger to give away its own skin? He who asks a tiger to give up its own skin must be prepared to be bitten; those who take part in political movements have taken this responsibility upon themselves of their own accord.

We feel this is the wrong road to take. We approve of the defense of civil rights, but we believe that the rule of law is the only true defender of civil rights. We can only advocate that, in implementing the law, political prisoners also should receive the normal protection of the law. We would like to present four working principles in relation to this point:

First, we can demand that no matter what kind of political prisoner is being considered, there should be firm proof of his guilt, and only judicial organs can issue arrest warrants and make arrests. A person who wrongly accuses somebody should, after the facts have been proved, himself be sentenced for the same crime of which he has accused the other.

Second, we can demand that no matter what kind of political prisoner is being considered, according to Article 8 of the Provisional Constitution, he should be handed over to a formal court within 24 hours of arrest.

Third, we can demand that when the court accepts a case, all those against whom there is sufficient evidence to warrant prosecution should be prosecuted and receive a public trial, while all those whose evidence shows them to be innocent should be released.

Fourth, we can demand that after political prisoners are sentenced, they, like all other criminals, should receive the most humane treatment possible.

This is our basic legal position on the question of political prisoners. If we desert this position we cannot but become revolutionaries, in which case we can no longer be considered [participants] in the movement to protect civil rights.

As the above points reveal, I have only used the example of political prisoners to present my personal views of this movement. Besides the issue of political prisoners, the League for the Protection of Civil Rights could be engaged in countless other tasks, such as: the promotion of legal research; investigation into the judicial and executive branches; the abolition or reform of laws and decrees that impede civil rights; investigation into and reform of prison conditions; the facilitation of voluntary legal defense work; the promotion of the freedoms of speech, publication, education, thought, assembly, and association. These are all directions that we could energetically pursue.

Notes

1. Liang Qichao's essay "On Rights Consciousness" is Text 2, above.
2. *Mencius* 5A:7.
3. *Mencius* 3B:2.
4. *Analects* 8:5.
5. Lord Bao, Bao Longtu, was an upright official who conscientiously solved criminal cases and therefore has become a symbol and hero in criminal novels.
6. Wang Anshi (1021–86) is famous for a whole range of new fiscal, administrative, and military laws which he put into effect during a short reform period between 1069 and 1073 during the Song dynasty.

Further Reading

For a more radical member's view of the task of the League, see Song Qingling, "Zhongguo minquan baozhang tongmeng de renwu" [The Task of the China League for the Protection of Civil Rights], December 1932, reprinted in Song Qingling, *Wei xin Zhongguo fendou* [The Struggle for the New China] (Beijing: Renmin chubanshe, 1952), pp. 31–53. See also the references after Text 21.

Part IV

War with Japan
and Civil War:
1937–1949

28
The Human Rights Protection Regulations of Shandong Province (1940)

Provincial Council of Shandong Province

"Shandong sheng renquan baozhang tiaolie," Adopted, announced, and put into force on November 11, 1940. Reprinted in Dong Yunhu and Liu Wuping, eds., *Shijie renquan yuefa zonglan* [World Documents of Human Rights] (Chengdu: Sichuan renmin chubanshe,1990), pp. 764–65.

In the 1940s several of the Communist-controlled areas adopted declarations protecting people's rights within their jurisdictions. Some of them also explicitly used the term human rights (renquan). *The rights stipulated were predominantly civil and political rights, such as freedom of speech, freedom of publication, and freedom of assembly and association. The exercise of these rights was, however, contingent upon their being used in the struggle against Japan. Certain groups of people, such as traitors, counterrevolutionaries, and others were excluded from enjoying these rights. Rights were thus not regarded as belonging to people qua human beings, but were instead contingent upon correct political beliefs. Rights were valued for their usefulness in the revolutionary struggle and were more of a means to an end than an end in themselves.*

Article 1. For promotion of democracy, general mobilization of the nation, and implementation of the true spirit of judicial protection of human rights (*renquan*), this regulation is formulated based on the Program of Resistance Against Japan and National Reconstruction and on decrees of the National Government.

Article 2. All citizens of the Republic of China, without distinctions of sex, race, religion, profession, or class, are equal politically and equal before the law.

Article 3. The people of the Republic of China enjoy the rights set down in the Outline of National Reconstruction, to vote, recall, institute, and review, but traitors and those whose civil rights (*gongquan*) have been deprived are excluded from this category. Political prisoners sentenced before the War of Resistance are not restricted by this proviso.

Article 4. As long as people do not hinder the War of Resistance, they shall have the following freedoms:

1. The people have the freedom of their person and the freedom to arm against the Japanese.

2. The people have the freedoms of residence and movement.

3. The people have the freedoms of speech, authorship, publication, assembly, association, and correspondence.

4. The people have the freedoms of belief, religion, and political activity.

Article 5. The freedoms in the above article shall not be restricted except on the basis of the Program of Resistance Against Japan and National Reconstruction or the decrees of the National Government.

Article 6. When people are arrested and held in custody due to suspicion of criminal activities, the organ that executes the arrest and detention must hand them over to a judicial organ within twenty-four hours.

Article 7. No one suspected of having committed a crime is subject to arrest without a warrant.

Only organs of state power (*zhengquan*) from the county level and higher and military units from the regiment level and higher have the right to issue arrest warrants.

Article 8. Governmental offices and mass organizations at district, county, and village levels may not execute arrests or detentions, except in cases of serious charges or when there is a possibility that the suspect will escape.

Article 9. Regarding all prisoners condemned to capital punishment, they shall not be executed before the sentence is approved by the supervisory commissioner's office. In the regions without a supervisory commissioner's office, the county government may not execute capital punishment unless the sentence is approved by the prefectural commissioner's office.

Article 10. Governmental functionaries at all levels who violate the people's freedoms or rights, unless it is in accordance with legal procedures, shall bear both criminal and civil responsibilities. The victims of their misconduct are entitled to receive compensation for their losses in accordance with the law.

Article 11. The Provisional Council of Shandong Province has full rights of interpretation and revision of these regulations.

Article 12. These regulations are adopted, announced, and put into force by the Provisional Council of Shandong Province.

Further Reading

For similar documents from other CCP-controlled areas, see the work by Dong Yunhu and Liu Wuping mentioned above. For Mao Zedong's writings, see the next text and its suggestions for further reading.

29
On Policy (1940)

Mao Zedong

"Lun zhengce" [On Policy]. Originally written in December 1940. Reprinted in *Mao Zedong xuanji* [Selected Works of Mao Zedong] (Beijing: Renmin chubanshe, 1991), vol. 2, pp. 762–70.

Rights do not feature prominently in the writings of Mao Zedong (1893–1976). Mao did not view rights as innate or natural; they were instead merited on the basis of one's class position and political views. Whether rights should be given to any group of people was also determined by an analysis of the demands of the political situation. At the time Mao wrote the essay translated here, the CCP and the GMD had nominally joined in a United Front against the Japanese, who controlled large parts of China. The Communists were prepared to acknowledge the civil and political rights of all people, including landlords and capitalists, provided that they used these rights and freedoms to fight the Japanese. Although the language of human rights did not play an important role in the revolutionary rhetoric of the CCP, the Communists would nonetheless frequently refer to it throughout the 1940s when they criticized the GMD's repression of dissenting views.

In the current situation of anti-Communist high tide, our policy is of decisive significance. But many of our cadres still fail to realize that the Party's present policy must be very different from its policy during the Agrarian Revolution. It must be understood that under no circumstances will our Party change its United Front policy during the entire period of the War of Resistance Against Japan; many policies adopted during the ten-year period of the Agrarian Revolution should not simply be recommended again. This is especially so of the ultra-Left policies in the latter period of the Agrarian Revolution, which failed to understand two basic features of the revolution: The Chinese Revolution is a bourgeois-democratic revolution in a semi-colonial country, and it is a long-term revolution. Here are examples of these ultra-Left policies. There was the opinion that the GMD's fifth "encirclement and extermination" campaign and our counter-campaign were the so-called decisive battles between counter-revolution and revolution. There was the economic elimination of the capitalist class (the ultra-Left policies on labor and taxation) and the rich peasants (by allotting them poor land). There was the physical elimination of the landlords (by not allotting them any land). Furthermore, there were the attacks on intellectuals, the "Left" deviation in mopping up counter-revolutionaries, the Communists' monopoly of political power (*zhengquan*), the Communist doctrine in national education, the ultra-Left military policy of attacking the big cities and disapproving of guerrilla warfare, the putschist policy in the work in the White Areas, and the policy of attacks on organizations within the Party. These policies are not only wrong today, in the period of the War of Resistance Against Japan, but they were also wrong in the past. These ultra-Left policies were expressed as the error of "Left" opportunism, or exactly the reverse of the Right opportunism led by Chen Duxiu in the latter period of the First Great Revolution. It was all alliance and no combat in the latter period of the First Great Revolution, and all combat and no alliance (except with the fundamental elements of the peasantry) in the latter period of the Agrarian Revolution. These are striking manifestations of two extremist policies, and both resulted in enormous losses to the Party and the revolution.

Our current policy of an Anti-Japanese National United Front is neither all-alliance, no-combat nor all-combat, no-alliance, but a policy that combines alliance and combat. Specifically, it means:

1. All people who approve of the Resistance against Japan, or all anti-Japanese workers, peasants, soldiers, students and scholars, and businessmen, are united in the Anti-Japanese National United Front.

2. Within the United Front our policy must be a combination of alliance and independence.

3. As far as military strategy is concerned, our policy is independent guerrilla warfare within the framework of a unified strategy. Our basic strategy is guerrilla warfare, but no chance of performing mobile warfare should be lost when the conditions are favorable.

4. In the combat with the anti-Communist diehards, our policy is to make use of their contradictions, win over their majority, oppose their minority, and crush them one by one. Our combat must be conducted on just grounds, to our advantage, and with restraint.

5. In the Japanese-occupied and GMD ruling areas our policy is, on the one hand, to expand the United Front and, on the other, to select and conceal elite cadres. We should use the methods of both organization and struggle to conceal the elite cadres, lay in long-term ambush, accumulate strength, and wait for opportunity.

6. With regard to the relationship of classes within the country, our basic policy is to develop the progressive forces, win over the middle

forces, and isolate the anti-Communist die-hard forces.

7. With respect to the anti-Communist diehards, our policy is a revolutionary dual policy of uniting with them, insofar as they still approve of resisting against Japan, and of isolating them, when they are determined to disapprove of the Communist Party. With regard to the anti-Japanese aspect, the diehards also have a dual character. Our policy is, therefore, to unite with them, insofar as they are still anti-Japanese, and to combat them and isolate them when they vacillate (for instance, when they collude with the Japanese aggressors and are reluctant in disapproving of Wang Jingwei and other traitors). As their opposition to the Communist Party also has a dual character, our policy, too, should have a dual character. Insofar as they are still unwilling to break up GMD-Communist cooperation, our policy is to ally with them, but insofar as they execute high-handed policies and launch armed attacks on our Party and people, our policy is to struggle against them and to isolate them. Elements with this kind of dual character must be distinguished from traitors and the pro-Japanese faction.

8. Even among the traitors and pro-Japanese elements there are people with dual characters, toward whom we should likewise adopt a revolutionary dual policy. Insofar as they are pro-Japanese, our policy is to struggle against them and to isolate them, but insofar as they vacillate, our policy is to draw them nearer to us and win them over. Such elements with a dual character must be distinguished from out-and-out traitors like Wang Jingwei, Wang Yitang, and Shi Yousan.[1]

9. We have to make a distinction between the pro-Japanese big landlords and big bourgeoisie, who are against the resistance, and the pro-British and pro-American big landlords and big bourgeoisie, who are for the resistance. We also have to make a distinction between big landlords and big bourgeoisie with dual characters, who are for the resistance but vacillate, and those who are for unity but anti-Communist. Finally, we must distinguish among the less ambivalent national bourgeoisie, the middle and small landlords, and the enlightened gentry. Our policy is to build on these distinctions. The above-mentioned diverse policies are all derived from these distinctions in class relations. . . .

To correct the one-sided views of Party cadres on the question of tactics and their consequent vacillations between Left and Right, we must help them to acquire a comprehensive and integrated understanding of changes and developments in the Party's policy. Today, the principal dangerous tendency in the Party is still the trouble caused by the ultra-Left viewpoint. In the GMD-ruled areas, there are many who cannot enthusiastically carry out the policy of selecting and concealing elite cadres, lying in long-term ambush, accumulating strength, and waiting for opportunity, due to their underestimation of the GMD's anti-Communist policy. At the same time, there are many who fail to carry out the policy of expanding the United Front; they have in fact given up, due to their oversimplified view of the GMD as being entirely hopeless. In the Japanese-occupied areas there are also similar states of affairs.

In the GMD-ruled areas and the anti-Japanese base areas, there were those who used to stress alliance to the exclusion of combat, overestimated the GMD's anti-Japanese wishes, and hence blurred the difference in principle between the GMD and the CCP. They renounced the policy of independence and autonomy within the United Front, and accommodated themselves to the big landlords, big bourgeoisie, and the GMD. In effect, they willingly tied their own hands, and did not dare to expand the anti-Japanese revolutionary forces nor firmly struggle against the GMD's policy of opposing and restricting the Communist Party. These Rightist views were once a serious problem, but have now basically been overcome. However, since the winter of 1939, an ultra-Left tendency has occurred as a result of the conflict between the GMD's anti-Communist policy and our self-defense. This tendency has been corrected to some extent but has not been completely erased, and it still finds expression in many concrete policies. It is therefore necessary to examine and define our concrete policies.

As the Central Committee has already issued a series of directives on concrete policies, only a few general points will be given here.

Concerning organs of political power (zheng quan). It is essential to resolutely uphold the "three-thirds system," under which Communists have only one-third of the places in organs of political power, so as to attract non-Communists to participate in political power. In areas like the northern part of Jiangsu province, where anti-Japanese democratic political power is just beginning to take form, the proportion of Communists may be even less than one-third. Both governmental offices and the people's representative bodies must draw the petty bourgeoisie, the national bourgeoisie, and the enlightened gentry who are not actively opposed to the Communist Party into participation, and those members of the GMD who are not anti-Communists must also be allowed to participate. Even a small number of Rightists may be allowed to join the people's representative bodies. On no account should our Party monopolize everything. We aim only to destroy the dictatorship of the big compradore bourgeoisie and the big landlord classes, not to replace it with a one-party dictatorship of the CCP. . . .

Concerning anti-espionage policy. We must firmly suppress the confirmed traitors and anti-Communists; otherwise, we shall not be able to protect the anti-Japanese revolutionary forces. But there must not be too much killing, and no innocent people should be incriminated. Vacillating elements and followers among the reactionaries should be dealt with leniently. In interrogating any criminals, torture must be resolutely abolished; the stress must be on the weight of evidence, not on confession. Our policy toward prisoners captured from the Japanese, puppet, and anti-Communist troops is to set them all free, except for those who, having incurred the hatred of the masses, must be sentenced to capital punishment, once their death sentences have been ratified by higher authorities. Among the prisoners, those who involuntarily joined the reactionary forces, despite more or less revolutionary inclinations, should be won over in large numbers to serve our army. The rest should be released. If they go on fighting against us and are captured again, they should again be set free. We should not insult them, confiscate their belongings, or exact recantations from them, but treat them sincerely and kindly without exception. Carrying out this policy, despite how reactionary they are, is an efficient way to isolate the hard core of reactionaries. As for renegades, except for those who have committed severe crimes, they should be given a chance to make a fresh start, provided they discontinue their anti-Communist activities; if they wish to rejoin the revolution they may be accepted, but not readmitted into the Party. The ordinary GMD intelligence agents and the Japanese spies and Chinese traitors should be differentiated and handled accordingly. To establish a revolutionary order, the chaotic state in which any institution and organization can make arrests must end. It must be stipulated that, with the exception of army units in combat action, only government, judicial, and public security agencies shall be empowered to make arrests. . . .

Concerning the rights of the people. It should be laid down that all landlords and capitalists not opposed to the War of Resistance shall enjoy the same human rights (*renquan*), property rights, and right to vote, and the same freedoms of speech, assembly, association, thought, and belief, as the workers and peasants. The government shall take action only against saboteurs and those who organize riots in our base areas, and shall protect all others and not interfere with them.

Note

1. These three men all collaborated with the Japanese during World War II.

Further Reading

On Mao Zedong's political ideas, see Stuart Schram, "Mao Tse-tung's Thought to 1949," in *The Cambridge History of China.* Vol. 13, Republican China, 1912–1949 (Cambridge: Cambridge University Press, 1986), Part 2, pp. 789–870. For various CCP documents and texts by Mao and other CCP leaders, see Tony Saich, ed., *The Rise to Power of the Chinese Communist Party* (Armonk, NY: M.E. Sharpe, 1996).

30
The Program of the Human Rights Movement (1941)

Zhou Jingwen

"Renquan yundong gangling," *Shidai piping,* nos. 73-74 (1941), pp. 1–3

In 1941, Zhou Jingwen (1908–1985) launched a human rights movement in the magazine Shidai piping. *Zhou was motivated both by concerns about the human rights violations committed by the Guomindang and by a belief that the protection of human rights would enable people to make greater contributions to the war effort. As Zhang Junmai would be, Zhou was inspired by H.G. Wells's work to draft a new human rights declaration that could serve as an inspiration during World War II and as a manifesto for a future peaceful world. Zhou also attempted to relate the 1941 human rights movement to the May Fourth movement of 1919, in that he intended his human rights movement to awaken and liberate the Chinese. Positive reactions from readers prompted Zhou to publish a special issue on human rights, and some of the articles were also reprinted in book form. Zhou chose to remain on the mainland after 1949, and was severely criticized during the "three-anti" and "five-anti" campaigns in the early 1950s. He fled to Hong Kong in 1957 and there revived* Shidai piping.

Facing the crisis and darkness of our motherland, we, the good and honest Chinese people, cannot but roar with indignation and fight in order to rescue our nation and restore our rights to be persons (*zuoren de quanli*).

For almost a hundred years, the Chinese nation has been reduced to the status of a semi-colony. For thousands of years, a small minority has ruled the majority of our people, and in our age, the remnants of feudalism are still destroying our freedom and trampling upon our rights. From abroad, we are suffering the humiliations of might-makes-right (*qiangquan zhuyi*); at home, we are oppressed by feudalism. The humiliations are the losses of territory and sovereignty and the deprivation of human rights (*renquan*); the oppressions are unreasonable and illegal rule and the loss of human rights. We cannot allow this darkness to continue to exist in our motherland.

We should be as brave as our ancestors and protect the continuity of our great nation, fight with all our strength against might-makes-right, and achieve our great mission of national revolution. In the name of our humanity (*yi ren de zige*), we shall fight against dictatorship to complete the democratic revolution of the mutual rule of government and people. In the name of our humanity, and from the standpoints of mutual love among compatriots and equality among all people, we shall abolish the system of exploitation of man by man and establish an economic system of mass welfare. Human rights provide a just foundation for all three of these great ideals.

Only when our rights to be persons are fully developed can we dedicate all our physical, material, and mental resources to the great cause of national liberation. Only when our human rights are sufficiently protected can our nation be in a harmonious state of general progress in which all are responsible for national affairs. Only when our human rights are protected will the master-slave relationship be erased from China's history forever.

In order to rescue our country and nationality (*minzu*) and to restore our rights to be persons, externally we vow to oppose might-makes-right, especially the imperialism that opposes and invades our country. Domestically we oppose feudal forces, dictatorship, and absolutism, as well as the control of culture, thought, study, and teaching. At the same time, we oppose, even more vehemently, the old Confucian orthodoxy that fettered people. We oppose "clandestine tribunals," the extrajudicial deeds of special agents and police, and the evils of corrupt officials. Most important of all, we oppose the economic system of exploitation of man by man.

With these various oppositions, we manifest our fighting [spirit] and our sacred (*shensheng*) and inviolable (*buke qinfan*) rights to be persons.

The most sublime meaning of human society is to let each individual achieve a satisfactory and happy life, so that all can live as human beings. A slave society is not only brutal and miserable but also will end with its own downfall. Only a society whose members all live as human beings is glorious. Although the rights of people are rights enjoyed by them simply by virtue of their being human beings, the protection of these rights is sought not only by individuals alone but also through mutual respect between individuals, and especially through society, which is created by individuals to protect [their rights]. Without society, individuals cannot manage a public life, let alone the protection of their rights. The nation is an organization that manages public life and maintains social order for humankind. Its power originates from the individuals that form this group; it can also be said that it is the manifestation of the common will. The nation exists for people, rather than people existing for the nation. The fundamental motivation for the frequent sacrifices that people make for the national interest is that the interest of the group embraces that of the individual: the public (*gong*) interest embraces private (*si*) interests. The nation is the people's own group, and it is the people's responsibility to protect their own group.

History teaches us that in many circumstances the minority controls the nation's power, and that this minority harms the interest of the majority. This violates the purpose of the nation's existence. The government is only an institution that executes national affairs but national affairs are the affairs of the whole people. Those national affairs that run counter to the majority's interest are a transgression and an encroachment against which the people have the responsibility to rebel. Anyone who sees the nation as his private country or sees the government as an institution for private partisanship, and thereby violates the majority's interest and will, is a public enemy against whom the people have the absolute right to rebel.

Life is most meaningful when we can all live for ourselves but, at the same time, live for others as well. How shall we conduct our lives in order to be "persons," while, at the same time, helping our society to be a sublime society? The nation is an organization that seeks the people's welfare, and the government is an institution that executes national affairs. They should be evaluated based on the extent to which they promote our rights to be persons. As human beings and as citizens, we are entitled to enjoy the following basic rights in public life:

1. *The right to life.* Everyone has the right to life and each individual has a duty to mutually respect this right. The state and its agencies cannot arbitrarily deprive anyone of this right against the laws laid down by the people's will (*minyi*). Other groups and organizations have even less claim to violate this right.

2. *The right to personal freedom.* Everyone has the right to the freedom of personal movement. Insofar as his or her conduct has not broken the law determined by the people's will, an individual can move and travel freely without being subject to arbitrary arrest or detention by the government. The people may treat the so-called special agents who injure the people as bandits and take any necessary action in self-defense.

3. *The right to freedom of residence.* Everyone has the right to freedom of peaceful residence, free from intrusion and disturbance. Soldiers, police, and military police are absolutely forbidden to break into private residences without the legal formalities determined by the people's will. The people may treat the "special agents" who have broken into private residences as bandits and take any necessary actions in self-defense.

4. *The right to freedom of thought.* Everyone has the right to freedom of thought, that is, the right to research, reflect, and study. No teachings and studies are to be subject to restrictions. Governmental organs and parties cannot by force or through other means interfere [with this right].

5. *The right to freedom of speech and publication.* Everyone has the right to freedom of speech and publication. Public speech shall not be supervised and publication shall not be censored. Governmental organs and parties cannot use their position to wrongly interfere [with this right]. As for illegal speech and publication, the person concerned shall shoulder the responsibility.

6. *The right to freedom of religion.* People of different religious beliefs shall coexist in tolerance. Neither government nor political parties may compel people to believe in a particular religion or doctrine, much less compel them to join a political party.

7. *The right to freedom of assembly and association.* Everyone has the right to assembly and association with people who share the same ideals and interests. No assembly or association, insofar as it does not threaten the social welfare or cause direct social disorder, is to be subject to restriction. The government and political parties may not wrongly interfere [with this right].

8. *The right to freedom of employment.* Everyone has the right to choose a profession and the right to work. Government and political parties may not compel people into a [particular] occupation nor force them through various means to lose their jobs.

9. *The right to public trial.* Everyone is entitled to a just and public trial when his or her conduct has violated the law. The people are not to

be subjected to trials conducted by "clandestine courts," "special agent courts," or military and police offices. The arrested person shall not be subjected to detention in military or police offices, and must be handed over to a regular court within twenty-four hours. The arrested person and his or her family members have the right to request a hearing by the court [responsible for] the arrest. The accused has the right to a defense lawyer at the public trial.

10. *The right to oppose violence.* Everyone has the right to oppose violence. Regardless of whether it is the government, political parties, or individuals that use violence against him, the victim may rebel to defend himself and raise a legal charge.

11. *The right to enjoy a minimum livelihood.* Every working individual has the right to a guarantee to receive a minimum livelihood. The standard of individual minimum livelihood is defined according to the equal distribution of the national wealth.

12. *The right to management of national affairs.* Every citizen, as a constitutive element of the nation, has the right to manage national affairs. This management takes the direct form of election of the government, and the indirect form of supervision and the voicing of opinions regarding national affairs at any time.

We have proclaimed people's basic rights; without these rights to be persons, we cannot imagine that we could live as human beings, much less that we could live happily and satisfactorily. These rights are not only the guarantees for our lives as human beings but also the preconditions for social progress and cultural development. Only if these preconditions are fully developed can we realize national liberation, and [only then] will the greatness of the nation have a real basis. We believe that only a society formed by free people has a glorious future. Only free people are able to critically seek the correct orientation for culture and thought, letting their own experiences and interests be used to guide the way forward. A nation of free people alone is happy and harmonious; a slave society will never achieve such a great miracle!

We use our life experiences to understand the situation of our society and to more thoroughly understand the depth of the crisis and darkness of our motherland. Facing this situation, we solemnly put forward our basic rights to be persons. What remains for us now is only to take action. In order to fulfill this just and promising mission, without begrudging any kind of sacrifices, we, the good and honest Chinese people, without distinction of age, sex, race, or class, vow to fight for this glorious future. Let us raise our torches to light every dark corner; let our magnificent voices reach every remote silence; let our 450 million compatriots roar like lions. Our human rights and our motherland's glorious [future] are all depending on our great actions!

Further Reading

The magazine *Shidai piping* published many articles on human rights over the years, beginning with Zhou Jingwen's "Zhaokai renquan yundong" [Launch a Human Rights Movement], *Shidai piping*, no. 69 (1941). Another interesting piece from the special issue on human rights is Shi Zishan, "Renquan yundong de lilun he gongzuo" [The Theory and Work of the Human Rights Movement], *Shidai piping*, nos. 73–74 (1941). After his escape to Hong Kong Zhou wrote a book about his experiences under the CCP; see Chow Ching-wen, *Ten Years of the Storm* (New York: Holt, Reinhart and Winston, 1960).

31
Human Rights Are the Basis of Constitutionalism (1946)

Zhang Junmai (Carsun Chang)

Zhang Junmai, "Renquan wei xianzheng jiben" [Human Rights Are the Basis of Constitutionalism], *Zaisheng*, no. 125 (1946).

During the 1940s, Zhang Junmai (1887–1969) was a leader of the China Democratic Socialist Party and an important figure of the so-called third force in the struggle between the CCP and the GMD. Zhang kept himself informed about discussions on human rights in the West and the work in progress in the United Nations on the Universal Declaration of Human Rights. He also took part in the San Francisco conference which adopted the UN Charter. During the 1940s, Zhang discussed human rights in the magazines Zaisheng and Minxian; we translate parts of one of these articles here. In other writings, Zhang introduced and translated discussions of human rights in the West, such as the declaration of human rights adopted by the French organization Ligue des droits de l'homme in 1936, and a human rights manifesto written by H.G. Wells in 1939. Both these declarations were fairly radical in nature and called for economic rights, including the right to subsistence.

The origin of the human rights (*renquan*) movement in Europe and America is distant, but its first expression in official documents took place with the September 1774 Declaration of Rights of the state of Virginia in America, the July 1776 American Declaration of Independence, and the July 1789 French Declaration of Human Rights. These are the most important documents of the human rights movement. The revolution of our Chinese republic, although also influenced by the French Revolution and the American [War of] Independence, had as its most important goals the overthrow of the Manchu Qing [regime] and the establishment of a republic, which involved the formation of political parties to conduct politics. Before the last Great War [i.e., World War II], the human rights movement was not an important element of our political thought. Even though Sun Yatsen discussed the issue of human rights in his lectures on the Three Principles of the People, he was influenced by the denunciations of natural rights (*tianfu renquan*) by the historical school and by the Benthamite school [of utilitarianism] in Europe, and, therefore, advocated revolutionary human rights (*geming renquan*). It is important to be aware of the fact that [the idea of] human rights refers to the protection of the rights of all people in the country; that is to say, all [people] by virtue of their being human beings should have the same kind of rights (*quanli*). One cannot say that those who participate in the revolution should therefore enjoy human rights, whereas those who do not participate in the revolution should not enjoy any human rights, because the work of the revolution is to establish human rights and not to restrict human rights.

After the previous Great War [i.e., World War I], the Russian Communist Revolution established a government through proletarian dictatorship, and all people who were neither Communist Party members nor [members of the] proletariat were deprived of their freedoms of person, speech, and association, as well as their right to property. In the same way, in countries where fascism was popular, only [members of] the Italian Fascist Party and the German National Socialist Party enjoyed freedoms of person, association, and speech. [Members of] other parties—such as the Communist Party, the Social Democratic Party, and the Democratic Party—were deprived of all the freedoms to which they were entitled. We could say that since the Russian Communist Revolution and up to the last war, there has been a period of popularity for the European anti–human rights movement.

In 1939, at the beginning of World War II, Roosevelt and Churchill declared four freedoms in the Atlantic Charter: first, freedom from want; second, freedom from fear; third, freedom of speech; and fourth, freedom of belief and religion.[1] We could say that this was the beginning of the new human rights movement. Because of this, everyone suddenly saw the light and realized that if one wanted to talk about democracy one could not separate it from human rights. If one separates it from human rights, the results are the dictatorships of communism and fascism. After the meeting of the United Nations [UN] conference, it was clearly stipulated in the preface [of the UN Charter]: "We reaffirm our faith in fundamental human rights, in the dignity and worth of the human person, in equal rights which do not distinguish between large and small countries or between men and women."[2] Article 68 of the [UN] Charter mandates the establishment of an Economic and Social Council and promotes [the idea of establishing] a Human Rights Commission. At present this Economic and Social Council is working to propose a kind of international human rights law, using international treaties to protect human rights in all countries. From this it can be seen that human rights [work] in the twentieth century does not resemble [that of] the nineteenth century, when only stipulations were added to the constitutions [of individual countries]; today, we [are trying] to add a kind of international legal protection.

What, in fact, is the meaning of "human rights"? In a "country" (*guojia*), great power (*quan*) is gathered in the hands of that country. The people have no choice but to obey the orders of the government. But do the people have to obey all orders, regardless of what kind of orders the government proclaims? For example, if the country wants my life, do I have to give it up to the country? If the country wants my property, do I have to hand over my property to the country? If the country wants to seal my mouth, must I resemble the people of Jin and guard my speech?[3] If it is plainly east, the country will not permit you to say west. If it is obviously black, the country will not permit you to say white. In other words, only the country is permitted to say what is black or white and right or wrong, and the people are not permitted to distinguish what is right from what is wrong, what is black from what is white. Suppose this is the kind of obedience that the country wants from the people. If it wants [their] money then money has to be given; if it wants [their] lives then [their] lives have to be given; if it wants them to say "black" they cannot say "white"; if it wants them to say "east" they cannot say "west." If people are obedient to this extent, can there still be any justice (*gongdao*) to speak of in this kind of country? Mencius said: "If the ruler treats the vassal as mud and weeds, then the vassal will treat the ruler as an enemy."[4] This saying is based on the general truths of cause and effect and retribution (*baoying*). It can be seen that regardless of how strong a country's power is over its people, a sphere should be designated [within which] it can be said that this is your life, this is your property, these are your thoughts and actions; within this sphere, each one of the people has inherent (*tiansheng*) and inalienable (*buneng yirang*) rights. Within this sphere, the country cannot arbitrarily interfere with or coerce [the people]. All the rights enjoyed by each person within this sphere are called human rights. . . .

[. . .]

This human rights concept, however, has developed over time. For example, during the French Revolution and the American [War of] Independence, people paid attention to freedom of speech, freedom of belief, freedom of association, freedom of property, and so forth. But there were no discussions, at that time, of the right to work, the right to leisure, or the right to an equal livelihood. Today, in the twentieth century, everybody realizes that these kinds of rights are one part of people's rights (*renmin quanli*). . . .

[. . .]

I now want to bring this [discussion of] human rights to a close. I still have some conclusions to tell each of you. Only if human rights are protected will the position of the government be solidified. Because people have personality (*renge*), understand rites (*li*) and justice (*yi*), and have a sense of honor, they naturally comprise the backbone of the country. Respecting people is thus [a means] to protect the dignity (*zunyan*) of the government. If a country wants human rights to be protected, it must first treat people as human beings and not as slaves. Second, the power of the government must naturally be restricted, and because this is in order to raise up the position of the people, it is worthwhile for the country's future generations. Third, one can definitely not use one group of people as the tool of a political party to trample upon other people's rights. Such a procedure simply means that the government itself uses despicable methods, and this will only cause the country to fall into chaos; in no way can it attain the principle: "administer the country and rule the world" (*zhi guo ping tianxia*).[5]

Notes

1. The *Atlantic Charter* was actually proclaimed in 1941.
2. Zhang Junmai has changed the word order somewhat. His translation also differs from the later official translation of the Charter.
3. This saying originates from the work "Shuo fan" by the Western Han scholar Liu Xiang.
4. *Mencius* 4B:3. "If the ruler treats the vassals as his hands and feet, they will treat him as their belly and heart. If he treats them as his horses and hounds, they will treat him as a stranger. If he treats them as mud and weeds, they will treat him as an enemy."
5. From the *Great Learning*, one of the Confucian *Four Books*. Note that in the *Great Learning*, personal morality was the *sine qua non* for political success.

Further Reading

For the life and ideas of Zhang Junmai, see Roger B. Jeans, Jr., *Democracy and Socialism in Republican China: The Politics of Zhang Junmai (Carsun Chang), 1906–1941* (Lanham, MD: Rowman & Littlefield, 1997). For his own writings from a somewhat later date than the present text, see Carsun Chang, *The Third Force in China* (New York: Bookman Associates, 1952).

32
Proclamation on the Current State of Political Affairs (1947)

China Democratic League

"Zhongguo minzhu tongmeng dui shiju xuanyan" [Proclamation on the Current State of Political Affairs]. Originally published in 1947. Reprinted in *Zhongguo minzhu tongmeng lishi wenxian* [Historical Documents of the China Democratic League] (Beijing: Wenshi ziliao chubanshe, 1983).

The China Democratic League started out as the League of Chinese Democratic Political Groups, which was established by representatives of different minority parties in 1941. In 1944 it was reorganized as a political party based on individual membership. The League saw its task to be playing a moderating and mediating role as a "third force" between the CCP and the GMD. But when the GMD broke the agreements laid down at the Political Consultative Conference (PCC) in 1946, many of the League's members became disillusioned with the government. The proclamation translated here was written in April 1947 and reveals the League's dismay at the turn of events and its attempts to make the government live up to its promises. Since the day of its founding, the League had spoken out in support of human rights. It demanded freedom of the press and the release of all political prisoners, among other things. The League was itself affected by the GMD's repression; several of its members were arrested and a few prominent members, such as the poet Wen Yiduo, were murdered. The League was banned in October 1947, which resulted in its becoming aligned with the CCP. From 1949 onward, the League has continued to exist as one of the eight minor parties on the mainland.

The China Democratic League firmly and persistently advocates that belief in democracy, peace, and unity is the only road to salvation for China in her current crisis. This is the road that was unanimously laid down by the Nationalist and Communist parties, and other parties which together participated in the Political Consultative Conference (PCC).[1] This is also the common demand of all Chinese people. It is from this standpoint that we solemnly declare the following points to the recently reorganized government.

Firstly, the reorganized government is not in accordance with the program and spirit with which a government was supposed to be created according to the PCC.[2] Although the recently reorganized government is advertised as following the PCC resolution, both the measures it has taken and the elements constituting it are fundamentally not in compliance with the PCC resolution. The most important spirit of the PCC resolution is that all the parties participating in the PCC should enjoy equal and legal statuses in the formation of a joint government, whose goal is then to unite us so that we can realize constitutional democracy in China. Speaking very frankly, the goals of a joint government would be to end the armed conflict between the Nationalists and the Communists, and to persuade these two parties to cooperate peacefully. Today, the Nationalists and the Communists are in the midst of pursuing an all-out, violent civil war, and the new government is deeply divided. This fundamentally violates the spirit of the PCC.

Secondly, the reorganized government does not advance peace. The Guomindang, the Chinese Democratic Socialist Party, and the Chinese Youth Party jointly proclaimed a program for the peaceful construction of the country as their criterion for [successful] governance. This program makes the purpose clear from the very beginning; it raises the two words "peaceful construction" in a heartfelt and strikingly clear way. Thus, the civil war should be stopped before the new government is established; the new government should be organized only after peace is achieved. Today the three parties sign the program, [but then they insist that] a political solution of the CCP problem must wait until after the railway transport system has been restored, and since their means to restore the railway system remains armed force and war, how can one begin to speak of peaceful construction? Political solutions are the opposite of armed solutions. Political solutions promptly forsake armed force and war. Armed force and war thoroughly negate political solutions. The government led by the Guomindang, with the participation of the Chinese Democratic Socialist Party and the Chinese Youth Party, is jointly responsible for conducting war with the Communist Party. How can one even begin to speak of "peaceful construction"?

Thirdly, the reorganized government is not realizing democracy. In order to realize democracy, one must first bring rule by [a single] party to an end. Today the first article of the organizational law of the national government has been revised, but it still explicitly stipulates that it is based on the Provisional Constitution for the Tutelage Period. As long as the Provisional Constitution continues to be in effect, China will remain in the phase of political tutelage. So whether it is a tutelage government of one or of three parties, it will still be a tutelage government and not a democracy. On the other hand, if the new government completely denies the Provisional Constitution of the tutelage government period, then since the creation of the new government also essentially violates the resolution of the PCC, the legal basis for the new government will be even more problematic. The organizational law of the national government has no regulation regarding to whom the government is responsible, which means that the new government is not accountable to anyone. Therefore, where do we start in order to realize democracy? As the three above points demonstrate, the recently reorganized government runs counter to the road of democracy, peace, and unity. The China Democratic League believes that among all our current national issues, this is the most regrettable.

Speaking from another point of view, it is a reality that in China today the Guomindang, the Chinese Democratic Socialist Party, and the Chinese Youth Party have seized power together. Political power (*zhengquan*) is a right (*quanli*); even more, it is a responsibility. The political parties that already hold power should resolve the problems of the nation and relieve the suffering of the people. The China Democratic League believes that if the civil war is not stopped, politics cannot take its proper course, and the people's suffering will not be alleviated. To end the civil war and restore peace are the preconditions for the current government to recapture the faith and support of the people. Second, the minimal standard for a government of the twentieth century is to protect human rights (*renquan*). From now on, whether or not the Chinese people truly enjoy freedom of the person, thought, religion, speech, publishing, assembly, association, residence, movement, communication, and so on, will be real proof of whether the political party in power will remain in power. To give an example, at this late hour, all political prisoners should immediately be released and all publications that have been gratuitously shut down should be restored. This is only a small example, but from now on it will serve as a test of the government's protection of human rights.

Third, the government's greatest responsibility is to protect the people's opportunities for subsistence (*shengcun jihui*). It is common knowledge that the Chinese people today have reached dire economic straits of such proportions that they helplessly await death. Agriculture is in a state of ruin, industry has almost collapsed, but still the new government cannot halt the tyranny of conscripting soldiers, imposing grain levies, and raising taxes. And it cannot lay down plans for effective measures to stabilize prices in order to solve the question of people's survival. This political situation is accelerating the downfall of the nation. The three parties' signing their program [for the peaceful construction of the country] was said to be necessary in order to borrow money to achieve stability and improve the people's lives, but this was nothing but a pretext. If the civil war is not stopped, then all loans will either directly or indirectly be used to fund our massacring one another; this logic is most obvious. The China Democratic League persistently advocates that, before the civil war is stopped, the United States should not make any loans to China, since they will only increase the suffering of the Chinese people; and that the government should not use any foreign capital to engage in mutual slaughter. Today, the Chinese people have no means of subsistence; this is the real test of the government. This has been our third point. These three points constitute the present government's minimum responsibilities and the goals of the China Democratic League today in its forthright critiques and supervision of the government.

Today, with the establishment of the new government, the China Democratic League wishes to take this opportunity and present our position anew. Since the day the PCC was established, the China Democratic League has been an equal and legitimate Chinese political organization. In the past year, we have consistently preserved an independent, peaceful, and open position outside of political power. Our independence consists of our having our own viewpoints, political programs, and policies. Only in this way can we earnestly hope in our speech and actions to make a clear distinction between right and wrong: we cannot be called [merely] neutral, and still less can we be accused of bias. Our peaceful position refers to the League's rejection of the use of military force, and particularly to its rejection of military force in political struggles. As to our openness, this refers to the League's democratic style of work, its use of democratic methods, and its responsible critique and supervision of the government. This was the League's position in the past, and it is still our position today. Recently Chairman Chiang [Kai-shek] indirectly referred to the League when he said: "The government's implementation of democracy must be one hundred percent." The China Democratic League earnestly wishes to point out that one hundred percent democracy must start with respect for people's dignity (*zunyan*) and protection of their sacred (*shensheng*) and inviolable (*buke qinfan*) human rights. In a one hundred percent democracy, the political party that holds power must respect the equal and legal status of parties not in power. The League definitely accepts the obligations that an equal and legal political organization ought to have, and also definitely strives for the rights that such a political organization ought to enjoy. According to this principle, we strongly oppose the arbitrary arrest of League leaders and members, such as Du Bincheng, Luo Bingji, Wang Juren, and others, and demand their immediate release. We would further like to earnestly point out that whether peaceful, open political organizations can exist outside of those in power is a test of whether or not the country has a democratic political [system]. Today, the China Democratic League, no matter how the political situation changes, will use legal methods to struggle and maintain its equal and legal status. This resolution will never change. This is the "one hundred percent attitude" of the China Democratic League's struggle for democracy.

Notes

1. The Political Consultative Conference (PCC) was established in 1946. Its forerunner was the People's Political Council (PPC), set up in 1938 to work as an advisory body to the government. The PPC and the PCC were composed of representatives from the different major and minor parties and groups.

2. In January 1946, Chiang Kaishek convened the PCC to discuss a constitution.

But in November of the same year Chiang unilaterally and in clear contravention of agreements reached under the PCC convened a National Assembly to adopt a constitution that reflected the wishes of the GMD and its allies, the Youth Party and the Democratic Socialist Party, for a one-party government by the GMD. This badly disappointed the League, which refused to participate in the National Assembly. In February 1947, the government then forbade the presence of CCP representatives in Nationalist-controlled areas and soon thereafter full-scale war broke out between the GMD and the CCP.

Further Reading

For primary sources from the League, see *Zhongguo minzhu tongmeng lishi wenxian* [Historical Documents of the China Democratic League] (Beijing: Wenshi ziliao chubanshe, 1983).

For secondary reading on the civil war period, see Suzanne Pepper, *Civil War in China: The Political Struggle 1945–1949* (Berkeley: University of California Press, 1980). For studies of the different democratic parties, see James D. Seymour, *China's Satellite Parties* (Armonk, NY: M.E. Sharpe, 1987), and Roger B. Jeans, ed., *Roads Not Taken: The Struggle of Opposition Parties in Twentieth-Century China* (Boulder, CO: Westview Press, 1992).

33
Chinese Statements During Deliberations on the UDHR (1948)

P.C. Chang (Zhang Pengjun)

For the final deliberations on the UDHR, *see Official Records of the Third Session of the General Assembly, Part 1, Social, Humanitarian and Cultural Questions, Third Committee, Summary Records of Meetings, 21 September–8 December 1948* (Lake Success, NY: United Nations, 1948).

Nationalist China took an active part in the setting up of the UN, and was also quite supportive of the incorporation of human rights statements in the new international body's statutes and other instruments. When the Human Rights Commission in charge of drafting the UDHR was set up in 1946, headed by Eleanor Roosevelt, one of its two vice-chairs was the Chinese representative P.C. Chang (Zhang Pengjun, 1892– 1957). The first drafts were collaborative efforts done by the drafting committee based upon suggestions and drafts submitted by a wide range of individuals, states, and NGOs, which then were passed on to the Commission and back a number of times, before finally landing on the table of the General Assembly for a general discussion. When the UDHR was put to a vote on December 10, 1948, China without hesitating voted in favor. This positive view of international human rights work on the part of the GMD is somewhat surprising in view of its earlier skepticism of human rights, as manifested in the writings of Sun Yatsen and Zhou Fohai (see Texts 18 and 20), and its own violations of human rights on the mainland before 1949 (see Texts 21 and 26) and on Taiwan after 1947 (see Text 36). Its changing view might simply have been due to pragmatic considerations, including the fact that it needed the help and recognition of the Western powers in its struggle against the Communists. Be that as it may, while the GMD earlier had argued that human rights were inappropriate to China, it was now prepared to stress their universality and work toward establishing an international legal framework. In addition, P.C. Chang and other Chinese representatives were also eager to quote Chinese sources in order to show that Chinese traditional philosophy and the concept of human rights had much in common. In view of the fact that many contemporary scholars, as well as the PRC government, seem to believe that economic and social rights would be more acceptable and important to the Chinese, it is interesting to note that Chang and the other Chinese representatives to the UN did not focus on these rights, and at times even seemed reluctant to include them in the UDHR. At a later stage in the drafting process, however, China defended the inclusion of rights to food and clothing, but these rights were not originally proposed by China. We reprint below several of Chang's comments in the drafting process, together with brief, contextual introductions.

34a. In the discussion on the UDHR at the General Assembly on October 2, 1948, P.C. Chang made the following comments on the need for a universal declaration.

Mr. CHANG (China) stated that the draft international declaration of human rights which the General Assembly was about to adopt was a timely and noble document, for which there was urgent need. The Charter committed all Member States to the observance of human rights; the declaration stated those rights explicitly. It was only proper that their final formulation should take place in France, the birthplace of modern ideas of freedom.

In the eighteenth century, when progressive ideas with respect to human rights had been first put forward in Europe, translations of Chinese philosophers had been known to and had inspired such thinkers as Voltaire, Quesnay, and Diderot in their humanistic revolt against feudalistic conceptions. Chinese ideas had been intermingled with European thought and sentiment on human rights at the time when that subject had been first speculated upon in modern Europe.

Stress should be laid upon the human aspect of human rights. A human being had to be constantly conscious of other men, in whose society he lived. A lengthy process of education was required before men and women realized the full value and obligations of the rights granted to them in the declaration; it was only when that stage had been achieved that those rights could be realized in practice. It was therefore necessary that the declaration should be approved as soon as possible, to serve as a basis and a programme for the humanization of man.

A declaration of human rights should be brief and readily understandable by all. It should be a document for all men everywhere, not merely for lawyers and scholars. It was with that object in mind that the Chinese delegation had introduced, at the third session of the Commission on Human Rights, a brief declaration containing ten articles and it was gratified by the fact that the document had aided in making the present draft declaration clear and relatively brief.[1]

34b. On October 6, the relationship between rights and duties was up for discussion; it had been discussed on a number of previous occasions and was to come up again. Some states, such as those from Latin America, had wanted the declaration to include a list of the duties of individuals, while other states were opposed to such an inclusion. In view of the fact that many regard the Confucian tradition as duty-oriented, it is instructive to note that Chang did not push the issue of duties. Although Chang below speaks favorably of duties and argues for the necessity to strike a balance between rights and duties, it was actually he who later proposed that the article on man's duties toward his community should be placed toward the end of the UDHR. As he then put it: "An article which dealt with the limitations on the exercise of the rights and freedoms proclaimed in the Declaration should not appear at the beginning of the Declaration before those rights and freedoms themselves had been set forth." But on October 6, he had the following to say on the topic:

Mr. CHANG (China) . . . [stated that the] aim of the United Nations was not to ensure the selfish gains of the individual but to try and increase man's moral stature. It was necessary to proclaim the duties of the individual for it was a consciousness of his duties which enabled man to reach a high moral standard.

34c. On October 7, the discussions continued in the General Assembly, and apart from again taking up the issue of the proper role of duties in the declaration, Chang then followed up on the previous speakers' discussion on whether article 1 should state that human beings were endowed "by nature" with reason and conscience, as was being proposed. René Cassin, the French representative who, like Chang, also served as a vice-chair, had originally suggested that article 1 of the UDHR read: "All men are brothers. Being endowed with reason, they are members of one family. They are free and possess equal dignity and rights." Chang had then suggested that one should add the Confucian concept of "two-man-mindedness" (ren) to complement the reference to reason and underscore that man should act in consideration of his fellow human beings. Others approved of Chang's idea, and the UK and Lebanese representatives then suggested that the English word "conscience" be used to express the idea of ren *and added to Cassin's invocation of reason. The discussion on October 7, touched upon what had proven to be two of the most difficult issues in the drafting process. One was on whether there should be any references to God or natural law in the discussion of the origin of human rights, although in the end neither was mentioned. While the former rapidly was rejected as foreign to many cultures, many also raised objections to any references to "nature" whatsoever, as it was seen as building upon a Western philosophical tradition. The second issue was whether people really were born free and equal. Related to this issue was the question of whether people were born good, or, as Chang argued, whether they were born with both the ability to do good and to do evil. Cassin, in contrast, "urged that the word 'born' should be maintained. Men were born free and equal, although they might later lose those attributes. The sentence in its existing wording proclaimed the right of human beings to freedom and equality, a right which was theirs from birth."*

Mr. CHANG (China) felt that article 1 of the declaration should remain where it was, and that the two sentences which made up that article should not be separated. A happy balance was struck by the broad statement of rights in the first sentence and the implication of duties in the second. Should article 1 be taken out of the body of the declaration, it would not claim as much of the reader's attention as it deserved to do; moreover, the various rights would appear more selfish if they were not preceded by the reference to "a spirit of brotherhood." Similar reasoning applied to article 27 [the present article 29], which contained a statement of duties. Statements of rights and duties should form an integral part of the declaration.

Mr. Chang supported the deletion in article 1 of the words "by nature," as suggested by the Belgian representative. That measure would obviate any theological question, which could not and should not be raised in a declaration designed to be universally applicable.

While the declaration would no doubt be accepted by a majority vote of the Member States, in the field of human rights the popular majority should not be forgotten. The Chinese representative recalled that the population of his country comprised a large segment of humanity. That population had ideals and traditions different from those of the Christian West. Those ideals included good manners, decorum, propriety, and consideration for others. Yet, although Chinese culture attached the greatest importance to manners as a part of ethics, the Chinese representative would refrain from proposing that mention of them should be made in the declaration. He hoped that his colleagues would show equal consideration and withdraw some of the amendments to article 1 which raised metaphysical problems. For Western civilization, too, the time for religious intolerance was over.

Mr. Chang agreed with the Lebanese representative that the word "born" in the first sentence of the English text of article 1 should be deleted; without that amendment, the sentence was reminiscent of Rousseau and the theory that man was naturally good. For the purposes of the declaration it was better to start with a clean slate. . . .

The second sentence of article 1 called upon men to act toward one another in a spirit of brotherhood. That attitude was perfectly consistent with the Chinese attitude toward manners and the importance of kindly and considerate treatment of others. It was only when man's social behavior rose to that level that he was truly human. Decorum was an ideal which should not be lost sight of—as unfortunately it often was in the struggle to uphold noble principles.

34d. On October 9, the question of whether all men were born equal and free was again discussed. The Soviet representative, Mr. Pavlov, expressed doubts that the declaration was the proper place to deal with the origin of human rights. He also voiced the view that man's rights were not determined by birth but by the social structure of the state. In a society characterized by exploitation men would not be equal or be able to live in a "spirit of brotherhood," as the proposed article 1 had it; it was only in a socialist society where exploitation had been abolished that this became a fact. To this the Bolivian representative, Mr. Matienzo, replied that Western democracies didn't accept the USSR view that human rights were not inherent but simply derived from the social structure of the country in which one lived. He also pointed out that neither in the USSR did people live as brothers, and that the language of the declaration did not speak of present realities but only set a goal for mankind to try to realize this principle. After Mr. Matienzo, Chang took to the floor having the following to say on this point:

Mr. CHANG (China) thought that the basic text of article 1 . . . would be acceptable to the Committee if it were understood on the basis of eighteenth-century philosophy.

That philosophy was based on the innate goodness of man. Other schools of thought had said that man's nature was neutral and could be made good or bad, or again that his nature was all bad. The eighteenth-century thinkers, whose work had led to the proclamation of the principles of liberty, equality, and fraternity in France and, in the United States, to the Declaration of Independence, had realized that although man was largely animal, there was a part of him which distinguished him from animals. That part should therefore be given greater importance. There was no contradiction between the eighteenth-century idea of the goodness of man's essential nature and the idea of a soul given to man by God, for the concept of God laid particular stress on the human, as opposed to the animal, part of man's nature.

Mr. Chang urged that the Committee should not debate the question of the nature of man again but should build on the work of the eighteenth-century philosophers. He thought the Committee should agree to a text beginning "All human beings *are* free . . ."—using "human beings" to refer to the non-animal part of man—as proposed by the Lebanese delegation, and should further agree to delete the words "by nature," as proposed by the Belgian delegation. If the words "by nature" were deleted, those who believed in God could still find in the strong opening assertion of the article the idea of God, and at the same time others with different concepts would be able to accept the text. . . .

Mr. Chang paid a particular tribute to the contribution to the work of preparing the draft declaration made by Professor Cassin, the representative of France, who so ably exposed French doctrines of the eighteenth century.

Concerning practical reality, a point raised by the USSR representative, Mr. Chang said that all recognized the existence of wrongs, but the most efficacious way of correcting those wrongs was to set a common standard such as the draft declaration sough to establish. Recognition of the stark facts with which the world was faced should not, however, be termed realism but naturalism, for realism meant that which was truly real and which could be affirmed with the full force of the soul.

34e. At the meeting on October 15, Chang made a summary of the discussion and the idea behind the draft declaration itself.

Mr. CHANG (China) observed that all the amendments that had been submitted, even including those which had not been favorably received by the majority, had made a constructive contribution toward the preparation of a common declaration.

Members should not, however, lose sight of the draft declaration itself, which was the basic document before the Committee. That draft was the result of assiduous efforts and it had been reviewed with meticulous care. The original text prepared at Geneva had been submitted to the various governments for their comments. It had then been examined by the Commission on Human Rights and had been altered in the light of the various comments and suggestions to which it had given rise. The draft declaration before the Committee was the final product of all that work, and it constituted only two-thirds of the original Geneva draft. It had, in fact, been realized that the clearer and the more concise the declaration was, the more effective and lasting it would be. The declaration was not intended for legal experts or scholars but for the general public; it should therefore be as striking as possible, and, accordingly as concise as possible. It would be best if the declaration were limited to ten articles, but, if that were not possible, it should at least be limited to the twenty-eight articles which composed the draft under consideration.

Mr. Chang then stated that the Third Committee had not studied the structure of the declaration as a whole. In his opinion, such a study was essential and therefore, in examining the declaration, he would refer specially to its logical structure.

Articles 1, 2, and 3 expressed the three main ideas of eighteenth-century philosophy; article 1 expressed the idea of fraternity, article 2 that of equality, and article 3 that of liberty.

The idea of liberty was then analyzed and applied to the human being in article 3. Article 3 set forth a basic principle, which was then defined and clarified in the nine following articles. Article 4 dealt with slavery, article 5 with the right to recognition as a person before the law, article 6 with equality before the law, article 7 with the need to establish the legality of arrest, article 8 with the right to a fair trial, article 9 with the right to be presumed innocent until proved guilty, article 10 forbade interference with a person's privacy, and article 11 affirmed the right to freedom of movement.

In that series of articles the idea of liberty was gradually and progressively enlarged; it was applied first to the individual, then to the family, and finally to the country. That series of articles therefore served to develop and clarify the idea of liberty.

Articles 13 to 20 dealt individually with the various social institutions.

Article 20, like article 3, expressed a general idea which was explained and developed in the following articles. Article 20 set forth the idea of social security and that idea was defined and developed in articles 21 to 25.

Note

1. Chang is here referring to E/CN.4/102, China's amendments to the draft declaration of human rights, which was indeed presented at the third session on 27 May 1948. But its own draft proposal had been submitted to the second session and is cataloged as E/CN.5/AC.1/18.

Further Reading

For a meticulous study of the drafting process and all the suggestions and amendments proposed by different representatives, Johannes Morsink, *The Universal Declaration of Human Rights: Origins, Drafting and Intent* (Philadelphia: University of Pennsylvania Press, 1999), is the ultimate work. For a more readable history of the background to the UDHR, see Paul Gordon Lauren, *The Evolution of International Human Rights: Visions Seen* (Philadelphia: University of Pennsylvania Press, 1999). And for a study of China's early involvement with the UN, see *China and the United Nations,* Report of a study group set up by the China Institute of International Affairs (New York: Manhattan Publishing Company, 1959).

Part V

1949–1975

34
Rightist Statements (1957)

Pu Zhongwen, He Shifen, and Feng Guojiang

Originals reprinted in *Gaodeng xuexiao youpai yanlun xuanbian* [A Collection of Rightist Discussions from Schools of Higher Education] (Beijing: Zhonggong Zhongguo renmin daxue weiyuanhui shehui zhuyi sixiang jiaoyu bangongshi, 1958), pp. 90, 91, 585–87.

During early 1957, a political thaw began to develop in China. By late April, Mao Zedong had managed to get sufficient support within the leadership for a full rectification campaign of the Party in which non-Party people and members of the democratic parties were also encouraged to speak out against the three evils of bureaucratism, subjectivism, and sectarianism within the Party. During a few weeks in May of 1957, this political thaw culminated with speeches, wall posters, and heated discussions on issues ranging from administrative problems and bureaucratism to the paramountcy of the CCP in political affairs. The criticisms by those who would soon be labeled "rightists" (see the text) touched both upon systemic failures, such as the lack of democracy and rule of law, and on the actual execution of specific policies and the heavy-handedness of certain cadres. The language of human rights was occasionally invoked in connection with discussions of the constitution and the legal system. Many, for example, referred to the stipulation of citizens' rights in the 1954 constitution and argued that these rights were in effect being violated. Others talked about human rights violations when criticizing excesses committed during different political campaigns. In the rather disjointed pieces we have chosen to translate here, we hear the voices of some young students. It is interesting to note that the students, who after all had come of age in the new society and received a socialist education, should take up the language of human rights when criticizing the Party. Although the identities and fates of these students are unknown today, they nevertheless are quite representative of the general mood and views of the period.

38a. Statement from People's University Planning Department Student Pu Zhongwen

China has no legal system. The police and other security organs have the power to search people at any time; they constantly commit excesses while suppressing counterrevolutionaries. China's leaders have been influenced by the Stalinist model. The violation of human rights (*renquan*) is an everyday occurrence. Some lower-level cadres, in particular, feel that any opposition to them means opposition to the Party and the people. This is naturally a tragedy of their shallow intellect. We should respect the conduct and liberty of each member of the people. This situation is even more backward than the democracy of the bourgeoisie; it is a relic of feudalism, since the protection of human rights was put forward in the bourgeois revolution. Since the constitution was promulgated, it has been ignored by some Party members. We should strive for the equality of human rights in the law. Our [political] movements have often led to excesses. Today's struggle against Li Xin was also excessive. The leaders can taste for themselves the flavor of excess; why then do we so excessively pursue the destruction of people's spirits?

38b. Statement from People's University History Student He Shifen

During the Rectification [Campaign], I heard about some incidents when people were exposed which sent shivers down my spine and made me profoundly aware that human rights (*renquan*) are unprotected. The constitution of 1954 stipulated protection for the freedom of the person, as well as rights such as those of residence and correspondence, but since [its promulgation] the constitution has been ignored and incidents of human rights abuse have increased. Among [these abuses] are limiting the freedom of the person (as exemplified in the incident at the Number Five Construction Company during the Campaign of Elimination of Counterrevolutionaries),[1] the opening of letters, illegal searches of homes (as was done by some ministerial offices and government organs during the elimination campaign), illegal detentions, incidents of hanging, beating, and controlling people (as was done by some local leaders in the course of establishing state monopolies for purchasing and marketing grain, etc.); these are just a small number [of the incidents]. There have also been those who were driven mad by insulting criticisms and imprisonment (see the report by Lin Xiling),[2] and some who even after being hounded to death were still insulted as counterrevolutionaries and slackers. Where is national law in all of this? For these reasons, I call on the National People's Congress to formulate and pass a Bill of Human Rights which among other things would protect human rights, stipulate the legal handling of human rights violations, and [require] timely investigations of human rights cases. This would clarify the national law and settle the people's hearts.

38c. Statement of Qinghua University Student Feng Guojiang

What are the results of the Campaign of Elimination of Counterrevolutionaries? It deepened the contradictions among the people.[3] This is the first [result,] that it deepened these contradictions. And the second? Naturally, I haven't thought much about this—I only have had a few days, [so my thoughts are] very superficial. I have to think about it in more depth because there are many more questions! I would like to ask everyone to help me out and carefully think it over when they return home. Everyone has many opinions about the Party Committee. [In any event,] the second result was to confuse the distinction between ourselves and the enemy. The people: us; friends; you say he is a counterrevolutionary?! Struggle him! Yet it's clear he is a friend.

He committed no errors, none at all. He has made no mistake, but you say he is guilty. Young people love the truth. Frankly, during the struggle sessions our sense of truth and justice was raped. In fact, classmates, I know and he knows that his friend has done nothing wrong, but the activist elements taking the lead wanted to force him to shout slogans and betray his conscience. He betrayed his conscience by speaking. This is a very cruel thing to do to a young classmate. He obviously knows what is true, but you force him to say that it is not. Things that are clearly not true, you force him to say are true. A young person's pure soul has been stained!

What is the third result? The constitution and human rights have been violated from beginning to end. I want my classmates to know this! It is people who cultivate the belief in the constitution and human rights! The common people! This cultivation of belief is more complex than the building of a house or the construction of a city! To make people respect others and the constitution is not an easy task. But what should we say about the struggle sessions to eliminate the counterrevolutionaries? We can say that everything is finished—finished! What human rights, what constitution are left? Naturally we should use an historical point of view when analyzing questions; could one discuss the constitution or human rights with local despots in the countryside in Old China? It was a battle for survival—either you die or I die! It was not a question of having or not having a constitution! Of course one can struggle; of course one can kill! I'm saying in all honesty that in order to deal properly with those kind of counterrevolutionary elements and local despots, it would be best if I took care of them: I could strap on a gun. But that's history.

Now we are already talking about contradictions among the people. The Constitution of the People's Republic has already been promulgated. Do you still want to use the old methods of struggling with the enemy to struggle against your own people? Can this be changed? These methods should be dropped, they should be changed immediately! Otherwise it's just too dangerous. It's too dangerous to treat your own people as enemies! ... I criticize him (pointing at Qinghua University's Party Committee member He Dongchang);[4] it was he who said with great self-satisfaction: "We've clarified the history of a good number of people." I want to ask: is a [person's past] history important? Of course it is! But we must remember that history is the past; it's something which has died, and what you get is dead history. You've gotten dead history, you've clarified dead history, and what have you lost? The heart of the living people! The living and beating heart of the people is what you've lost! If you put these things together and compare them, which is more important? You think about it, all of you. I won't answer for you. . . . No, I had better answer. I tell you my opinion: my answer is that, in comparing what we've achieved with what we've lost, the loss is incomparably larger! I believe that if I were to investigate the [charges raised in the] speech of the Party Committee member today, there would be too many things to investigate. Yes—it's true! [People's] work results are revealed in their [personal] dossiers (dang'an). [He Dongchang sees all this,] but he doesn't see the [resulting] loss, the lost youth of these classmates! Should I advise the members of the Party Committee to investigate for the sake of the people and our nation, or should it be for the sake of one's own position? This is a penetrating question. . . .

I believe that after [they are completed,] the struggles against living people are more dangerous than if you had shot the people. Perhaps He Dongchang won't understand this. That's natural—how could one who separates himself from the masses understand their situation?

In this respect, classmates, I believe that the struggle sessions which have resulted in the wronging of four hundred innocent classmates is a leftist [deed]. A leftist deviation! I'm not a political scientist, but I can still express my opinion. In this context, to use such methods [of struggle sessions][5] against living people! This attitude, frankly, is that of rightists. The people are not like me: I am not capable of seeking revenge, ever—why should I seek revenge? But the people aren't like me, people who have been vilified—do you think they aren't capable of hatred? They are hate-filled, and it doesn't matter how much time passes. I would like to ask He Dongchang for advice on how to treat these people in a time of peace. We would often have to pacify them, or else we must be on guard against them. In reality we would have to be on guard against them. Someone told me—it was someone who had been struggled against—that Su Jianuo came and wanted another classmate to come and see him. [He said to Su Jianuo,] "Why bother! What do you want? You have lost the hearts of the people! I am still alive!" These are troubling matters, very difficult ones; in times of peace you must be on guard, as well as in times of chaos. Someone told me that it would be understandable if that classmate wanted to kill a Party member. But I myself couldn't do that—and if everyone were like me then it would be fine and there wouldn't be a problem in the world.

I don't dare make a conclusion about all this myself; I want to let historians consider it, since one can say that these are new questions worldwide. So many people have been shot in the Soviet Union. No one has been shot here—the situation is different. We have to await the verdict of historians. Take a careful look!

What is the verdict? It is that living people are more troublesome than dead people; it's better to shoot him and be done with it. [Otherwise] he will live for decades and you will have to be on guard all those years. I believe there are those who will seek revenge. Some say they want to kill thousands of Party members, tens of thousands. Of course, it is not necessarily because of the Campaign of Elimination of Counterrevolutionaries that they have enmity in their hearts. But why doesn't He Dongchang want to understand this situation? He has separated himself from the people! He has not investigated properly! Think about it—isn't it true?

Notes

1. The Campaign of Elimination of Counterrevolutionaries, the so-called *sufan* movement, began in 1955.
2. Lin Xiling was one of the most famous student victims of the anti-rightist campaign.
3. On February 27, 1957, Mao Zedong gave a speech at the Supreme State Conference entitled "On the Correct Handling of Contradictions Among the People." The speech was not published at the time and when it was, in June after the anti-rightist movement had begun, substantial revisions had been made changing its tone and content. In the original speech Mao spoke about two types of contradictions, "those between ourselves and the enemy" and "those among the people." He argued that these two types of contradictions would be resolved by different methods. While

the enemy would be suppressed and struggled against, one should instead use methods of persuasion and friendly criticism toward the people.

4. This parenthetical note was added by the editors of the reprinted Chinese text. The ellipses in this text were also in the original reprinted text.

5. The texts here says *xigua wanhui*, which literally translates as "watermelon party." This is probably another phrase for "struggle sessions" used at Qinghua University.

Further Reading

For primary sources in Chinese of the rightists' speeches and writings, see *Gaodeng xuexiao youpai yanlun xuanbian* [A Collection of Rightist Discussions from Schools of Higher Education] (Beijing: Zhonggong Zhongguo renmin daxue weiyuanhui shehui zhuyi sixiang jiaoyu bangongshi, 1958); and Niu Han and Deng Jiuping, eds., *Yuanshang cao: Yiyi zhong de fan youpai yundong* [Grass on the Plateau: Commemorating the Anti-Rightist Movement] (Beijing: Jingji ribao chubanshe, 1998).

For materials translated into English, see Dennis J. Doolin, *Communist China: The Politics of Student Opposition* (Stanford: Hoover Institution on War, Revolution, and Peace, Stanford University, 1964); and Roderick MacFarquhar, ed., *The Hundred Flowers Movement* (London: Stevens and Sons, 1960). The latter also contains useful information on both the rightists themselves and on the anti-rightist movement, as does MacFarquhar's *The Origins of the Cultural Revolution 1: Contradictions Among the People, 1956–1957* (London: Oxford University Press, 1974).

35
A Discussion of "Human Dignity" (1957)

Zuo Ai

"Lun 'ren de zunyan'" [A Discussion of 'Human Dignity'], *Zhongguo qingnian bao* [China Youth Daily], August 19, 1957.

The regime was quick to move against its critics when it became apparent that the critique was much more harsh and far-ranging than expected. The spring of 1957 thus turned out to be brief, and by early June the so-called anti-rightist movement was under way. The official backlash against the rightists began with the publishing of an editorial in the People's Daily *on June 8, 1957, followed by the publication of Mao's revised February speech, "On the Correct Handling of Contradictions Among the People." During the anti-rightist movement some 500,000 people were labeled rightists, expelled from their work units, and in many cases also sent to labor camps; for some, eventual rehabilitation took more than twenty years. The rightists were accused of various crimes, including having wanted to overthrow the socialist system and replace it with capitalism. Their views on democracy and rule of law were also criticized and vilified as bourgeois and reactionary. As this article reveals, beliefs in individualism, humanitarianism, and human rights were among the ideas singled out for criticism. The article incidentally also gives a good overview of the official position of the time on rights and human rights.*

The rightist gentlemen have begun to discuss "human dignity" [*ren de zunyan*].

"Human rights (*renquan*) have been violated and human dignity has been offended." This is the primary charge that the rightists make against the Party. For example, the rightist Liu Binyan[1] said: "After the new three-anti movement . . . human rights were violated and human dignity was offended; and in the campaign to eliminate counterrevolutionaries the mistakes made became even graver.[2] People were not respected and their dignity and rights were seen as insignificant." He also said: "Now it is really hard to blame anyone individually, as this is a problem of the whole country and an historical problem. It is a series of many small tragedies."

What a fine defender of human rights! But when all is said and done, is it still unclear whose human dignity and rights the rightist gentlemen wish to defend.

In our view, humans are marked by class. In a class society, because people's class positions and the interests they represent are different, their thinking, feelings, and opinions are also different. People will always have different positions and will protect and struggle for the interests, rights, and dignity of their own class. It may appear as if the rightists are struggling for the human rights and dignity of all people, but in reality they are deceiving both themselves and others.

In a class society, human dignity is also unequal. If there is human dignity of the exploiting class, then there is no dignity of the exploited classes. Although the population of the exploiting class is small, because it occupies the position of ruling power its members are a cut above all other people. The laboring people who make up the majority of the population find themselves in the position of being oppressed and insulted, economically and politically controlled, and fettered in their spiritual lives.

Today's youth are naturally not very familiar with the events of the past, but those in their sixties and seventies have seen and heard of these events. When government officials went out on the street, their arrival was announced with cries and the sound of gongs, attendants crowded around, and people were supposed to maintain a solemn silence and get out of their way: they did not just want dignity; they wanted to be awe-inspiring. Not only were the emperor and his relatives not like common people when they broke the law, but even the intellectuals were a cut above the working people in this respect. When they saw the country magistrate, ordinary people were supposed to kowtow, but intellectuals were exempt from the requirement to kneel. If a scholar broke the law, he had to have his scholarly rank changed, and only then could he be made to suffer the wearing of a cangue. At the same time, if a common person had offended [such a scholar], [the scholar] would send [the offending person's] name to the yamen, after which [the offender] would be in danger of being caught and brought to the yamen. "Evil tenants" (peasants) could be put to death if they were accused of cheating the landlord. But if landlords killed peasants or raped their daughters, it was not considered a crime.

In the Republic, things seemed to get a little better, but the laboring people still had no rights, to say nothing of dignity. Not only did people not have any dignity, but even the dignity of the Chinese nationality was violated. The imperialists could do as they liked in our motherland while the people were massacred and oppressed. The laboring people were on the verge of starvation and death, and the only rights they had were to be press-ganged, to have levies imposed on them, to be put in jail, and to be arrested, beaten, or sold. They were afraid of seeing a policeman; what kind of dignity did they have? Naturally, the intellectuals, being close to the ruling class, were still a cut above everybody else. One had only to be gilded by spending time abroad, join the GMD's Training Group, or study at Lu Shan—or else become a representative in the bogus parliament, of the committee which put down rebellions, or of the legislature—and one could obtain a high salary and favorable treatment. Not only would one be dignified, but even awe-inspiring. But no matter what, the common people never had a share of this good fortune.

Unlike the hypocrisy of the bourgeoisie, the working class openly proclaims the class nature of human rights. The constitution of the PRC states: "The PRC is a people's democracy led by the working class and based on the alliance of the workers and peasants." In our country, unlike in bourgeois countries, the majority of the population comprises the ruling class. They have rights, position, and dignity. They are the workers and peasants, as well as all those classes, strata, and social groups who support, defend, and take part in socialist construction. The rough fellows that the old men of the old society looked down upon, the farmers, herders, washerwomen, entertainers, incalculable numbers of workers, and intellectuals . . . now they are in charge of our great nation. The withered faces and drawn brows of old are no longer seen but have been replaced by smiling faces and the dignity and impressive bearing of masters. There are some groups of people who have no position and have lost their dignity; they are the imperialists, landlords, bourgeois bureaucrats, and counterrevolutionaries. They are the objects of the revolution and of the dictatorship [of the proletariat]. It is for such people that the rightists [express] sadness and compassion, and it is [for them they] struggle for rights, but in this [endeavor] they will never win the support of the people.

The rightists curse socialism as undemocratic, as not respecting people's rights and dignity, as if the capitalism they lean toward is the kingdom of freedom! This is an enormous lie! Look at the capitalist world of today: Britain's troops brutally repress the revolutionaries of Oman; French imperialists slaughter the freedom fighters of Algeria; and beneath the Stars and Stripes, Indians have been nearly wiped out and blacks are prevented from living in equality with whites. The dignity of all these people has been trampled underfoot. There are many people who like the Rosenbergs are upright, Communist Party members and peaceful activists, who have been arrested, imprisoned, restricted, or groundlessly labeled as criminals. All of these evils have been eradicated under socialism, which has promoted the dignity of the nationality and of people. Yet the rightists aren't satisfied. What kind of "human rights" do the rightists want?

The rightists have seized on the three-anti and the five-anti movements, the movement to reform the thinking of the intellectuals, and the campaign to eliminate counterrevolutionaries, in order to produce articles and shoot off their poisoned arrows. In fact, everyone knows that the three-anti and five-anti movements were a struggle between the working and the bourgeois classes. The bourgeoisie violated the promises laid down in the Common Program[3] and savagely attacked the Party and nation, making use of the five evils [of bribery, tax evasion, theft of state property, cheating on government contracts, and stealing of economic information]. The Party therefore led the working class in an offensive against the illegal activities of the bourgeoisie. This was a class struggle, a struggle that consolidated the leadership position of the Party and the working class. It caused the capitalist economy to come under the direction of the state-owned economy, which, on the one hand, increased its usefulness for the national economy and the people's live-lihood, and, on the other hand, overcame its passivity and laid a favor-able base for the socialist transformation of capitalism. The movement to reform thinking was a movement during which intellectuals used the methods of criticism and self-criticism to undergo self-transformation. It was a critique of the imperialist, capitalist, and feudal thinking of the intellectuals. This was a battle of the minds, which has been very effec-tive in strengthening patriotism and socialist consciousness among the intellectuals. The struggle to eliminate counterrevolutionaries took place during the period of China's socialist revolution because of the wanton attacks by the Hu Feng clique on the Party and the nation, and also because of the activities of counterrevolutionary elements hidden throughout the country.[4] This movement has been very useful in guar-anteeing China's peaceful completion of socialist transformation and construction. These movements were carried out using the method of the mass line and have therefore achieved great results, but have also resulted in some shortcomings and mistakes. Given the general nature of such movements, shortcomings were very hard to avoid, although at the top, all the way up to the central authorities, and at the bottom, all the way down through every grade of Party member and government official, every measure possible was taken to avoid errors and mistakes. After discovering errors and mistakes, the Party and people's govern-ment also immediately made serious efforts to handle and correct them. In this regard, one can praise the movements or not, but the violation of human rights and dignity is not an issue here. The rightists use the words "human rights" and "dignity" as part of the hidden tricks in their nega-tive articles: is this not plain for all the world to see? In their own eyes, these rightists are "national treasures," so no matter what crimes or atroci-ties they have committed, they remain untouchable. The three-anti and five-anti movements, the reform of [intellectuals'] thinking and the elimi-nation of counterrevolutionaries—all these movements unexpectedly broke out over their heads, and they must take responsibility for their own conduct. This [they felt] was defying the mighty, this was simply atrocious, and so they felt forced to [try to] reverse the verdict.

The rightists also say: "Does your nationwide struggle against the rightists show respect for human beings?" This time they are really making big fools of themselves. One can only say they are really asking for trouble. Your treatment by the people can hardly be said to have been poor. Among you are delegates to the People's Congresses, representatives of the Political Consultative Conference, members of the Standing Committee of the People's Congress, heads of ministries, provincial leaders, departmental leaders, heads of provincial offices, and so on. Was the trust and honor bestowed upon you by the people really so small? Did Mr. Luo Longji, minister of the fourth rank, not always sit on the rostrum at sports events?[5] If you had consciences you would at least admit that what you have gotten from the people far exceeds what you have given them. But you were not content with your lot! You wished to take paths which diverged from those of the people; you didn't want to have socialism, but rather to restore capitalism.

The Party wanted to give every member of the democratic parties the opportunity to take part in and aid the Rectification [Campaign of the Party], and so it everywhere held meetings, developed organizations, sent notices and journalists everywhere, and offered high posts, in order to ignite enthusiasm on all sides. But in one instant, the rightists changed their tunes and became endlessly excited and pleased with themselves. When the special moment came and the Hungarian incident took place, [the rightists tried to] follow the traditional script and replace the dynasty and don the emperor's clothes.[6] This kind of behavior from its beginning violated the morals of the Chinese people. If we are to discuss dignity, first we must tear off our own false masks. An old proverb says: "You must first insult yourself in order for others to insult you later." If you yourself first have done things to be ashamed of, can you complain later that others don't respect your dignity? They were thinking of driving out the laboring peasants and workers and reinstating capitalism when the people rose up and struck back to defend socialism. This is obviously a decisive intellectual and political struggle between socialism and capitalism—how can it be said that it harms the [rightist] gentlemen's dignity?

The high-sounding talk of the rightists naturally can momentarily hoodwink some people who don't have political experience and who didn't live through the old society and learn its lessons, or at least capture those who don't know how to use class analysis to analyse problems; there are still quite a few [people] who have a bourgeois or petty bourgeois outlook. However, life itself teaches us lessons, and history is a mirror of the truth. The people collectively remember things as if they were yesterday. Not long ago in the Kowloon Incident, the Taiwanese GMD member Liu was shot by an American soldier, who got off scott-free. The life of a Chinese is not worth a cent, and this knowledge weighs on the hearts of the Chinese people. On October 1, 1949, the spring of the Chinese people began. From that day on, the Chinese showed themselves to the world as an independent and strong people. Only then did the Chinese begin to live as human beings and enjoy the rights and dignity of human beings. The Chinese take this as an eternal truth: without the Party and socialism, the people would never have had either position or dignity. Socialism belongs to the people!

The rightists were right: the problem of human dignity is indeed an "historical problem," "a problem for the whole nation." Naturally it is also a "tragedy"—but in fact it is not a tragedy for the people but a tragedy for the rightists [who pose] as representatives of the people. For the people themselves, it is rather a very joyful drama.

Notes

1. Liu Binyan was at the time a journalist at *Zhongguo qingnian bao* and became one of its most prominent rightists. He was criticized not only for demanding human rights (a word which he later has said he never used at the time) but also for criticizing the bureaucratic style of Party cadres. Liu was sent down for labor reform in the countryside from 1958 to 1961, and again during the Cultural Revolution. He was only rehabilitated in 1979. After having earned a reputation as an investigative reporter for the *People's Daily* during the 1980s by writing critical articles on corruption and other themes, Liu was again targeted during the 1987 Anti-Bourgeois Liberalization campaign and expelled from the Party. Since 1988 he has lived in exile.

2. The 1950s saw several campaigns, beginning with the three-anti movement in 1951 against corruption, waste, and bureaucracy and the five-anti movement in 1952 directed against bribery, tax evasion, theft of state property, cheating on government contracts, and stealing of economic information. Whereas the target of the former was government and Party officials, the second campaign was directed against businessmen and entrepreneurs. In 1953, a new three-anti movement was launched. During the 1950s, intellectuals had to undergo ideological reform aimed at the eradication of feudal and bourgeois thinking; this ideological campaign is referred to below in the article. A campaign against counterrevolutionaries was carried out from 1950 to 1953, and in 1955 another campaign to eliminate counterrevolutionaries began, the so-called *sufan* movement, which is referred to in the article.

3. The Common Program for China, adopted by the People's Political Consultative Conference in September 1949, served as the constitution of the PRC until a constitution was promulgated in 1954.

4. Hu Feng was a literary critic and writer who became the main target of a campaign in 1955 in which his friends and other people who had been in touch with him also were implicated. Hu Feng spent twenty-five years in prison and was rehabilitated in 1980.

5. Luo Longji was at the time Minister of the Timber Industry as well as vice-chairman of the Democratic League. Together with another chairman, Zhang Bojun, Luo was accused of forming an alliance aimed at overthrowing the Party. The two of

them were the most high-ranking victims of the anti-rightist campaign and have to date not yet been officially rehabilitated. Luo Longji was a long-time advocate of human rights; see Text 22.

6. This refers first to the Party's encouragement of the democratic parties and other non-Party people to speak out, and then to the way this encouragement was "treacherously" turned against the Party. However, the Hungarian incident occurred in 1956, that is, before the Rectification campaign began, so this description is not historically correct.

Further Reading

See the previous text.

36
Do You Want to Be a Human Being? (1958)

Yin Haiguang

"Ni yao bu yao zuo ren?" [Do You Want to Be a Human Being?], *Ziyou Zhongguo* 19: 11 (December 5, 1958), reprinted in *Zhengzhi yu shehui: Yin Haiguang quanji* [Politics and Society: The Collected Works of Yin Haiguang] (Taipei: Guiguan tushu gongsi, 1990), vol. 12, pp. 749–62.

Beginning around 1945, the GMD stopped dismissing human rights as inappropriate to China and took an active part in international work on human rights in the UN. Despite this rhetorical support, however, human rights violations, including arrests of suspected Communist supporters and political opponents, and closures of journals and magazines critical of the regime, frequently occurred up to the lifting of martial law in 1987. But since human rights now was a legitimate idea—especially so since Taiwan identified itself with the so-called Free World—it became an effective political weapon that critics could wield against the regime. The magazine Ziyou Zhongguo (Free China Review), *founded by Hu Shi, Lei Zhen, Yin Haiguang, and others in 1949, is a good example of such an approach. The magazine was the main vehicle for liberal intellectual and political debate in Taiwan during the 1950s, but was forced to close down in 1960 when Lei Zhen was arrested and sentenced to ten years' imprisonment for having harbored plans to set up a political party. Articles touching upon the subject of human rights and individual freedom appeared from the start in the magazine. They include both theoretical and historical articles, as well as articles on more political and concrete issues. The* Free China *people criticized the GMD's sincerity about building democracy and respecting human rights, and argued that one could not fight dictatorship with dictatorship. In the struggle against communism, the regime should uphold freedom and democracy, since if this was its goal and what distinguished it from the Communists, it could not, as Yin Haiguang perceptively argues in the article translated here, violate its own goals and principles. The magazine was fiercely anti-Communist, but fighting communism was not its only goal: ultimately, it sought a democratic society in which people enjoyed extensive political and economic rights and freedoms.*

On December 10, 1948, the United Nations General Assembly passed and proclaimed the Universal Declaration of Human Rights (UDHR). In order to commemorate this proclamation and promote human rights, the UN designated this day as Human Rights Day. In all of human history, this holiday should be seen as humanity's greatest and most important day of celebration. Since the time when humankind first had letters to record events, there have been so many different civilizations which thrived and then disappeared, so many empires which arose and then fell, and so many brave heroes who performed on the stage of life and then quietly disappeared into the grave. These events have filled people with elation, inspiration, acclaim, and yearning, and have also brought people bitterness, grief, anger, and disappointment. But no matter what, the impressions produced by these events have been partial and temporary. Only the drafting of the UDHR has had implications for humanity's total freedom or enslavement, involving humanity's eternal fortune and misfortune. On this planet, under the sun's light, from the North Pole to the South Pole, from the Eastern to the Western Hemisphere, from the highest mountain to the deepest sea, as long as humans continue to live and multiply, there will be no human being who ought not enjoy the fundamental rights proclaimed in the UDHR, and as a result, not a day will pass without questions concerning the UDHR.

In reading the UDHR, we find the following significant ideas:

1. Its fundamental spirit is contained in the [ideas] of "liberty, equality, and fraternity." We may say that the UDHR grew directly out of this spirit. This world, which is full of enslavement, inequality, and murder, desperately needs liberty, equality, and fraternity to heal it; the UDHR is the recipe to heal the world. Only thus can humankind really move toward peace, prosperity, and happiness.

2. Fundamental human rights are something innate (*guyou de*) in each individual. That is to say, since we are born as humans, it is a priori that we possess human rights. Human rights are our possession from birth. This possession cannot be granted by any person, nor can it be transferred to another person. Merchants can produce wealth, but not human rights. Scientists can invent satellites, but they cannot invent human rights. If we necessarily want to say that human rights are given to hu-

mans, we can only say that they are given by God. In this world, except for God, no one can give us rights. A king is also a human being; he does not have the ability to grant us rights, nor can he create rights. . . .

3. Fundamental human rights are the essential conditions for being a human. Fundamental human rights are the innate rights of every individual; we should enjoy them fully and develop them. When we enjoy and develop our fundamental human rights, they should not be endangered in any way, nor can our rights be short-changed. If our fundamental human rights are jeopardized or violated, it is our humanity (*zuoren*) which is being violated. If our due, fundamental human rights are not fully respected, then our humanity is compromised. If we are completely deprived of our human rights, then our humanity is at an end. We all hear of "human rights" but we never hear of "cows' rights" or "horses' rights." If we are deprived of human rights, the necessary condition for our humanity, then what is left of us except dead men walking? If we are considered to be alive, what then separates us from cows and horses?

4. Fundamental human rights includes every part of life. We know that, whatever meaning or value we give to life, maintaining life is always the essential starting point for everything else in life. If we cannot maintain life, then the so-called meaning of life, morality and values, will all come to nothing. Therefore, our fundamental human rights must include the rights to maintain one's life. These include economic rights.[1] Ever since the dawn of time, though, maintaining one's life has been no easy task. In our own time, those who try to maintain their lives in the Communist world face a truly arduous task. If we wish to maintain life, we must not suffer from the control or restraints of any person, organization, or system. Thus, if we wish to enjoy the human right to maintain life, we must enjoy political rights. A human who merely survives and frequently is intimidated by others will never be able to feel secure, which is a very painful thing. In order to have our security protected, we need to enjoy the right to security. In the modern system of nation-states, we need to be able to participate in government and the drafting of laws if we want to enjoy the right to security, and so we must enjoy political rights as well. However, if a human only has enough to eat and drink and has no concerns about his safety, he still cannot be considered a person. In the pastures of America, sheep have enough to eat and drink, and the protection of their shepherds and sheepdogs for security. But we who are humans, would we be willing to spend our lifetime like the American flocks of sheep? Having come thus far in the discussion, the

question of the meaning and value of life forces itself upon us. We not only wish to live, but we also want to have meaningful and worthy lives. How is the meaning and value of human life expressed and developed? Only through freedom of expression, thought, assembly, and association. So we need to have all these freedoms. Each of these types of freedom is a type of human right. "All freedoms are human rights": unless there are human rights, there are no freedoms worth speaking of. And only when we have these freedoms will life be a complete and full life.

At this point in our discussion, we wish to pose a question: has humanity achieved these human rights?

When we view what has been said above from the perspective of logical order, human rights should be the most essential condition for humans, but from the point of view of the development of history, the formal declaration of human rights took place only in 1948. On this planet, the history of human existence is simply a history of struggle. Early in human history, humankind struggled against flood, drought, locusts, diseases, and various other dangers in nature. After progress was made in scientific discoveries, humankind more or less achieved a decisive victory over these dangers. Today, the greatest enemy of people are people themselves. Who are these great enemies? They are those who violate human rights.

Consciousness of human rights (*renquan de yishi*) is the result of the advance of civilization. It goes without saying that ancient chieftains had no sense of human rights. Under the power created by superstition, divine right of kings, and sorcery, people often unwittingly became the objects of sacrifice. Under the rule of despotic emperors, people were enslaved in droves to build the pyramids, construct the Great Wall, or dig canals, and often died in these ventures. In the age of emperors, we find examples of benevolent despots, but this was an extreme and rare good fortune. No matter what, given the influence of "under the wide heaven, all is the king's land; within the sea-boundaries of the land, all are the king's servants,"[2] the most that can emerge is "people-based" (*minben*) thought: the people, like flocks of sheep or herds of cattle, serve as the "capital" used by the emperor in his building schemes. The concept of democracy, not to mention human rights, had no way to develop. The concept of human rights arose in the modern West; people in the West by and large enjoy human rights. Nonetheless, all of today's dictators and totalitarian rulers see human rights as an expression of resistance to their repression. They have mobilized all the anti-human

rights ideas and theories they can find to eradicate human rights thinking, and they kill, arrest, and imprison with impunity in order to stifle
human rights. Why do they do this? It is because if one has human rights
there can be no power of dictatorship, and with freedom there can be no
totalitarianism. Between these two there is no space for compromise.

The Chinese people's struggle for human rights has a long and arduous history. Early on, in 1904, Sun Yatsen enumerated the ten great crimes
of the Manchu Qing dynasty.[3] Two of these stated that the Manchus
"have stifled the development of our people's consciousness, and they
have forbidden freedom of speech." This can be taken as the starting
point for the Chinese people's struggle for human rights in the modern
period. . . .

In 1924 the GMD convened a National Assembly in Guangzhou, where
they adopted the First Declaration of the National Assembly. The sixth
article on internal politics states: "It is determined that the people have
complete freedom of assembly, association, speech, publishing, residence, and religion." From this article we can tell that during the rule of
the Northern government, these freedoms were not complete.[4] The
GMD's power at that time was confined to Guangdong. The ideas that
the GMD promoted through its existence and development were what
China pinned its hopes on for a new life, as well as symbols of that for
which the broad masses of Chinese yearned. But after the success of the
Northern Expedition, the GMD extended its power over the whole country
and its arrogance grew; it founded a "revolutionary order" and installed
a one-party dictatorship. When the one-party dictatorship began, that
was when [hopes for] human rights were destroyed. In this period, labels like "counterrevolutionary," "reactionary," "evil gentry," and "running dog of the imperialists" were thrown around wildly; those stuck
with such a label had no hope of defending themselves, and those beaten
as a result were too numerous to count. An example will suffice to show
what kind of atmosphere the GMD's way of "realizing revolution" created. On March 16, 1929, the Shanghai newspapers carried a telegram
regarding the resolution which Chen Dezheng, a representative of the
Shanghai Special GMD Headquarters, had presented at the Party's Third
National Representatives' Congress.[5] The aim of the resolution was to
"deal harshly with counterrevolutionaries":

> Courts or other legal institutions permitted by law to hear cases should
> punish for counterrevolutionary offenses anyone who is certified as a

counterrevolutionary by documents from provincial or special municipal party branches. If [the courts] disagree, they can appeal [the matter to higher-level courts]. If higher-level courts or other legal institutions permitted by law to hear cases receive certificates [on the counterrevolutionary's status] from the Central Party Branch, they must squash the appeal.

This amounts to saying that if the Party office designates someone a "counterrevolutionary," then he is indeed a "counterrevolutionary." If the Party office orders the judicial organs to treat someone as [guilty of a] "counterrevolutionary offense," then the judicial organ must "act in compliance [with this order]." The Bolshevik spirit [of this thinking] leaps out at one! That atmosphere caused a general sense of insecurity and great dissatisfaction among scholars and educators. Concerns for the protection of human rights sprang up everywhere. Thereupon, on April 20, the same year, the Republican government issued an order on the protection of human rights, which read:

Human rights are protected by law in every country in the world. Now that our tutelage government is in existence, a foundation for the rule of law (fazhi) definitely needs to be established. All those entities within the Republic of China's legal jurisdiction, whether individuals or organizations, shall not engage in illegal behavior which harms the physical being, freedom, or property of others. Those who violate this order shall be harshly punished according to the law. Each department of the administrative and judicial organs are instructed to follow this order.

Although the wording of the order is convoluted—and the violation of human rights is forbidden by "individuals and organizations," but there is no mention of the government—still, for a "revolutionary government" to remember to invoke human rights is already a cause for false hopes in people's hearts.

Since 1929 thirty years have passed. Thirty years is quite some time. In these thirty years, the world has undergone unprecedented and exciting changes. Humankind has reached the nuclear age and is on the threshold of the space age. What progress have we then made in the field of the human rights movement? Just raising the question makes people feel ashamed. In these thirty years, we have been through two great wars. One was the war of resistance against the Japanese, and the other is the war against communism. From 1937 until today, the two wars have consumed twenty-one years of those thirty years. The wars were like giant wheels: the nascent human rights movement was all but ground to dust beneath them! On the mainland, the surging power of the Reds has been particularly lethal for the human rights movement. By the time the People's Communes were established, human rights simply had been completely negated. The Reds not only negated all political rights, but indeed all human rights whatsoever. They deprived the Chinese people of freedom of thought, speech, assembly and association, and making a living; in fact, of all freedoms. This is really a disaster unprecedented in Chinese history! . . .

The tactics used by international communism when in power are resilience and flexibility. When they feel it is necessary, they can make any kind of compromise domestically. Internationally, they display a particular ability at being bewilderingly changeable: they can appear strong one minute and weak the next, sometimes yielding and sometimes unyielding, first advancing and then retreating, sometimes being friends and sometimes foes. But on one point they never change: they cannot yield to human rights demands. If they did, then they would have to let all people enjoy the various freedoms of speech, thought, belief, education, assembly, association, choice of political system, and livelihood. The day that all people enjoy those freedoms, will the Communist system not begin to collapse from within? Which totalitarian ruler will willingly give up his own rule? Thus, for the sake of their own rule, they can give in on many fronts, but they cannot give in to human rights demands. Forty-eight countries signed the UDHR, but the USSR and its satellites did not dare to do so. From this can be gathered the depth of their fear of human rights. Although Achilles was strong, his heel was vulnerable, so when Paris struck him on his heel, he was brought down. When we oppose communism, why don't we strike at its weak point? During the period of "blooming and contending"[6] there was a lot of unease and commotion among the Reds; how weak they turn out to be, when their Achilles' heel is revealed under the attack of human rights demands! If those opposing communism don't seek out the enemy's weak point to attack, but consistently pursue an unrealistic military solution, or even admire his methods and strive to imitate or even surpass him—using these methods to oppose the Communists leaves one completely perplexed.

What, then, has the human rights situation been in Free China over the last eight or nine years? We cannot find the answer in propaganda but must seek for it in reality, and we especially will find it in the atmosphere created this year and spread all over the island from the center.

From the first article of the UDHR, we can see that [it] makes clear from the beginning the overwhelming importance of "human dignity" (*ren de zunyan*). In Taiwan, who enjoys "human dignity," apart from one tiny privileged group of people for whom it comes at a high price? Do we really enjoy the freedoms of speech, thought, assembly, association, and livelihood that are proclaimed in the UDHR? In Taiwan, is "anyone accused of a crime who has not yet been publicly sentenced according to law . . . seen as innocent," or are they falsely pronounced "already guilty?" When one is tried, does one have "all necessary protection to defend oneself?" Before being sentenced, are people subjected to torture? The second clause of article 20 of the UDHR reads: "No one may be compelled to belong to an association," but in Taiwan, how many thousands or tens of thousands of young people, when they are ready to enter high school, are not directed to fill out a form and then, without exception, compelled to belong to the National Salvation Youth Corps? This method of entering the Corps is said to be "voluntary." Those who organize the Youth Corps say that all patriotic youth who are conscientious, courageous, and righteous ought to join. This wording implies the hidden meaning that, "All those young people who do not join the Youth Corps are not conscientious, they are cowardly and unpatriotic." What youth would wish to be [regarded as] unconscientious, cowardly, and unpatriotic? Thus, unless one wishes to bear the stigma of being "unconscientious, cowardly, and unpatriotic," one has no choice but to join the Youth Corps. This verbal trickery is not difficult to understand. Of course a young person should be "conscientious," "courageous," and "patriotic," but this way of forcing young people to join the Youth Corps can only provoke their dislike. If a young person is "conscientious," "courageous," and "patriotic," he or she will have many opportunities to bring honor to the country; so why is joining the Youth Corps seen as the only test of one's patriotism? Why is it considered to be unconscientious, cowardly, and unpatriotic to study seriously instead of joining the Youth Corps? However one tries to defend it, this is "compelling someone to belong to an association," which violates clause 2 of article 20 of the UDHR. Also, article 26, clause 2, reads: "Education shall be directed to the full development of the human personality and to the strengthening of respect for human rights and fundamental

freedoms." Is the aim of education in Taiwan to make the next generation a tool of one party? Or is it "the full development of the human
personality"? The answer is plain for all to see.

I have discussed above [some] issues that can readily be connected to
various articles [of the UDHR] which have direct bearings [on our situ-
ation]. The most serious situation in Taiwan during the past eight or nine
years, however, is the abnormal, emergency ideology and atmosphere
of suspicion that have been created by the use of pretexts and unwarranted charges [against people]. People are exposed twenty-four hours a
day to the power of the police and the control of special forces. All kinds
of large and small, minor and major excuses and charges can at any time
bring about misfortunes or fortunes, safety or danger to anyone. This
kind of power resembles a hand from the nether world which rules over
the fate of the great majority of the people on the island, thereby threatening everybody's "life, freedom, and physical security." These days,
how many people don't consider one's own personal safety [first]? During the past eight or nine years a state of mind has been created where
everybody "hides at home." Everybody is cautious and refrains from
being enterprising. They only hope that disasters will not descend upon
them and that they will manage to survive in a troubled age. Our human
rights resemble the hibernating of insects during the severity of winter.
When we now are celebrating Human Rights Day it is really a day for
commemorating human rights victims.

It is easy for us to imagine that this fact-based report will be met with
a ready-made rebuttal which officials have fabricated to spread to educational institutions: "This is a time of war; if everyone has freedom of
thought, speech, assembly, and association, would this not result in the
breakdown of our [collective] will and the undermining of our [national]
strength? In order to carry on the battle against communism successfully, everyone must sacrifice these freedoms temporarily." Yes—in any
place, and at any time, those who are suppressing freedom can use "war"
as a convenient excuse. But we should not forget that this is a baseless
excuse. Now we would like to ask: Do we need to eat in a time of war?
Do we want to marry? Do we want to see movies? . . . If the answer is
yes, this proves that even in wartime, people cannot abandon human
rights. Human rights cannot be abandoned, no matter what the time,
place, situation, or reason, because if we abandon human rights, we will
not be complete human beings. As I said before, international communism is the sworn enemy of human rights. Thus, our struggle against

communism is being waged to protect human rights. If we say that we must abandon human rights in order to defend human rights, isn't this a contradiction? It is completely ironic that those who oppose communism should also violate human rights.

In this world of humankind, "human rights" is at the root of all questions. Without human rights, everything else loses its meaning and value. We can consider this truth from three perspectives: first, if we abandon human rights for nationalism, the result will be submissive people living under monarchs, dictators, and tyrants. What is there to be happy about in this situation? Hitler emphasized continually that the Germanic race and German willpower were superior, but held the lives of Germans in contempt and despised their human rights. He whipped up hatred for the French and British in order to make the German people into tools for his own power and will. Under this policy, the German race seemed to be lit up by fires of glory, but what was the result in the end? Second, if we abandon human rights and talk of "rule by the people" (*minzhi*), in the end we will have form without content. So-called public servants would be neither "public" nor "servants." Elections will become tricks played by monkeys. Words spoken by government officials will become edicts. Third, if we abandon human rights but talk of "rule for the people," the result will be that everyone becomes new slaves of the system. Over the last thirty to forty years, the Soviet Communist experiment has given us the best evidence of this. If there are no human rights, all talk is empty and all hopes are illusionary; our lives resemble those of pathetic insects. So whether or not we are whole people in the end depends on whether our human rights are protected. All those who want to be humans must struggle in order to promote their own human rights.

Notes

1. Here and below, we often render *renquan* simply as "rights" when it appears in compound expressions, like the present "economic rights" (*jingji renquan*), for expository convenience.

2. *Shijing* 205; translation from James Legge, trans., *The She Ching or the Book of Poetry* (Taipei: Southern Materials Center, 1985), p. 360.

3. In this article Sun Yatsen accused the Manchus of infringing upon the Chinese people's rights to life, liberty, and property. See "Zhongguo wenti zhen jie" [The True Solution of the Chinese Question], reprinted in *Sun Zhongshan quanji* [Sun Yatsen's Collected Works] (Beijing: Zhonghua shuju, 1981), vol. 1, pp. 243–55.

4. The GMD's "Northern Expedition" overthrew the warlord government in Beijing and reunified the country in 1927.

5. Hu Shi discusses this event and his own reaction to it in Text 21, above.

6. The period of blooming and contending refers to the Hundred Flowers Movement of 1957; for pro–human rights sentiments of the so-called "rightists," and the government's eventual response, see the previous two selections.

Further Reading

For a collection of Yin Haiguang's political works, see *Zhengzhi yu shehui: Yin Haiguang quanji* [Politics and Society: The Collected Works of Yin Haiguang], vols. 11 and 12 (Taipei: Guiguan tushu gongsi, 1990). On the *Free China Review* and liberals in Taiwan generally, see Zhang Zhongdong, *Hu Shi, Lei Zhen, Yin Haiguang: Ziyou zhuyi renwu huaxiang* [Hu Shi, Lei Zhen, and Yin Haiguang: Portraits of Liberals] (Taipei: Zili wanbao she wenhua chubanbu, 1990).

37

A Criticism of the Views of Bourgeois International Law on the Question of Population (1960)

Qian Si

"Pipan zichanjieji guojifa zai jumin wentishang de zhuzhang" [A Criticism of the Views of Bourgeois International Law on the Question of Population], *Guoji wenti yanjiu* [Studies in International Problems] 5:41–43 (1960). Translation from Jerome Alan Cohen and Hungdah Chiu, *People's China and International Law: A Documentary Study* (Princeton, NJ: Princeton University Press, 1974), vol. 1, pp. 607–10.

Qian Si's article was motivated by the international critique that China faced after its crushing of the uprising which broke out in Tibet in 1959. The background to this uprising is complex. The coexistence between Chinese and Tibetans under the so-called Seventeen-Point Agreement adopted in 1951 when Tibet was incorporated into the PRC was fraught with tension from the start. Mao Zedong's policy was initially one of moderation. Religious institutions were allowed to exist without interference and landowners continued to exercise hereditary authority over the peasant farmers who tilled their soil, but this policy met with opposition from within the CCP. When the tide of collectivization spread through the Chinese countryside in the mid-1950s, although political Tibet (what is today the Tibetan Autonomous Region) was exempt from this policy, it involved Tibetans living in other neighboring provinces such as Sichuan. As resentment against the policy spread among the Tibetans, uprisings broke out in many areas. Chinese hardliners were also beginning to advocate that "socialist transformation" reforms should be undertaken in political Tibet, while some Tibetans there began to organize an armed rebellion in support of the uprisings elsewhere. And in 1957 the CIA began to train and support Tibetan guer-

rillas. In March 1959 an uprising broke out in Lhasa which was harshly suppressed by PLA soldiers and led to the Dalai Lama's flight to India. After 1959, traditional Tibetan society was all but destroyed: monasteries were forced to close, monks and nuns were arrested, and Tibetan farmers and nomads had to give up their traditional way of living and were forced to live in communes. In the article translated here, Qian Si argues that foreign criticism and the UN resolution regarding the situation in Tibet constituted an interference in China's internal affairs. This line of argument has continued to play an important role in China's human rights diplomacy. But even despite this criticism of foreign interference, Chinese authorities and scholars have not hesitated to accuse others of violating human rights; we see here that Qian Si criticizes the United States for its treatment of Indians. Criticism of the human rights situation in the United States has likewise often been voiced in the post-1989 period. More surprising, in view of the CCP's critical view of the concept of human rights at this time, is Qian's portrayal of the PRC as the true defender of human rights. Qian thus tries to legitimize Chinese actions in 1959 by presenting them as constituting a defense of the human rights of the Tibetan people against local power holders and traditional customs. Qian, like many after him, speaks at length about the cruelty of what he describes as a feudal serf system under which the majority of Tibetans had been suffering until the PLA's "peaceful liberation" of Tibet in 1951 and its final destruction in 1959. Finally, Qian regards the use of and reference to human rights in the West as a sham, only serving to protect the rights of the bourgeoisie to exploit workers.

In international relations, imperialism frequently uses the pretext of "protecting human rights" to intervene in the internal affairs of socialist countries. The tunes of bourgeois international law scholars also serve this imperialist goal. Under the socialist system, the elimination of the system of private ownership of the means of production has led to the elimination of the economic basis that gives rise to political and legal inequality, and thereby guarantees the genuine realization of the human rights of the vast laboring people. The rights of landlords and bourgeoisie arbitrarily to oppress and enslave laboring people are eliminated; the privilege of imperialism and its agents to do mischief, kidnap, rob, rape, and massacre is also eliminated. To the vast masses of people, this is a wonderfully good thing; this is genuine protection of the human rights of the people. The bourgeoisie and the bourgeois international law scholars, however, consider this to be a bad thing, since it encroaches upon the "human rights" of the oppressors and exploiters. The socialist countries' suppression of counterrevolutionary criminals and rebellious elements supported and dispatched by imperialism in an attempt to sabotage the people's regime is a necessary measure adopted to protect the interests of the people. However, the bourgeoisie and the bourgeois international law scholars decry such measures as encroachments upon "human rights." In fact, they try to use the pretense of protecting "human rights" to slander socialist countries, and thus pave a legal way for their intervention. For instance, after our country pacified the rebellion of the upper-class reactionary clique of Tibet, in 1959 the imperialist-supported International Commission of Jurists slandered our country on the pretext of "human rights" and "freedom." In their so-called "Summary of the Report on the Question of Tibet" and "The Question of Tibet and the Rule of Law" and other reactionary documents, they increasingly cried that the Chinese government "deprived the Tibetan people of their fundamental human rights and freedoms" and that the Tibetan people have been subjected to "massacre, imprisonment, banishment, and forced labor." They demanded that the United Nations and other international organizations "assist the struggle of the people of Tibet to achieve justice and freedom" and "punish" the "crimes" committed by the Chinese government. They put on a false face of kindness and justice and dressed themselves up as the defenders of the human rights of the Tibetan people. This is indeed hypocrisy and shamelessness to the extreme. All people can see that when the vast masses of Tibetan people were serfs and were subject to oppression, being whipped, having their eyes gouged and their limbs cut off, and being killed at will by feudal serf owners, it [the International Commission of Jurists] did not consider these acts to be violations of human rights and did not come out with an appeal for the oppressed and the injured. Only when the Central People's Government with the support of the Tibetan people pacified the rebellion of the upper-class reactionary clique of Tibet and began to reform the Tibetan serf system so that the vast masses of Tibetan people might genuinely obtain freedom and liberation did it feel sorry and lose no time in accusing us of disrespect for "human rights," "humanity," and so forth. This is indeed a strange sense of "kindness." To put it bluntly, they do not want to protect human rights; they want to protect Tibetan serf owners' privileges of oppressing and massacring the vast masses of Tibetan people and to find an excuse to intervene in the internal affairs of China.

Imperialism often uses the pretext of respecting and protecting human rights to launch aggression and carry out intervention in the internal affairs of nationalist countries. For instance, when the revolutionary [courts] of Iraq and Cuba sentenced counterrevolutionaries and spies of imperialism to imprisonment, American imperialism and its agents all invoked the "abuse of human rights" and other arguments in their threats and provocations against Iraq and Cuba. During his visit to Brazil, Argentina, Chile, and Uruguay in early 1960, President Eisenhower further proposed to organize an "Inter-American Commission on Human Rights" to protect the "democratic freedoms" of the Latin American people.[1] As a matter of fact, this was an attempt by the United States to use the "Inter-American Commission for Human Rights" for further control over Latin American countries, since it may, at any time, intervene in the internal affairs of various American countries on the pretext of "protecting human rights."

In short, the "human rights" referred to by bourgeois international law and the "human rights" it intends to protect are the rights of the bourgeoisie to enslave and to oppress the laboring people, that is to say, the human rights of the bourgeoisie. Internally, they are used to conceal the real encroachment upon the rights and freedoms of the laboring people by the bourgeoisie; externally, they provide pretexts for imperialist opposition to socialist and nationalist countries. They are reactionary from head to toe.

Bourgeois international law's views of genocide are the same as those on the question of human rights, and are mainly used to malign and to oppose socialist countries.

The bourgeoisie have committed the crime of genocide many times in history. The American treatment of Indians is an example. According to statistics, there were as many as 14 million to 40 million Indians in Columbus's time. However, as a result of the policy of extermination carried out by the American bourgeoisie, there were only 400,000 Indians according to the 1957 statistics of the U.S. Bureau of the Census. Essentially, all Indians in the United States have been exterminated. During World War II, German Fascist bandits carried out the policy of exterminating all Poles, Czechs, Jews, and other nationalities, and killed millions of good people. This is another example of genocide that shocked the world. Under pressure from the people of the whole world who were angered by Fascist atrocities, the United States, the United Kingdom, and France were obliged to assume a hypocritical pose, and at the UN General Assembly in 1948 they reluctantly agreed to adopt the Genocide Convention. However, they smuggled something of their own into the Convention. They not only concealed the class origin of genocide, but also intentionally did not prescribe criminal responsibility for propagandizing about genocide, thereby providing an exit for future criminals to avoid responsibility. In fact, even though the Convention has been signed for more than ten years, the crime of genocide has never been stopped either in the United States or in the Union of South Africa. Bourgeois international law scholars have never forcefully accused or condemned those criminals. On the contrary, in order to meet the needs of imperialist opposition to socialist countries, they have fabricated some false accusations of genocide to slander and malign socialist countries. For instance, at the eleventh session of the UN General Assembly in 1956, the United States and the United Kingdom and other imperialist countries manipulated to submit an agenda item on the so-called "Question of Deportation of Hungarian Citizens," which fabricated the story that the Soviet Union engaged in genocide activities by large-scale massacre and exile of Hungarians. UN intervention was demanded. In 1959, after our country pacified the rebellion of the upper-class Tibetan reactionary clique, the so-called International Commission of Jurists mentioned above also groundlessly fabricated the story that "the Chinese even attempted to resort to massacring Tibetans, by means of serious physical and mental persecution, in order to exterminate the nation and religion of Tibet." It also stated that "such actions constitute the crime of genocide" and therefore the United Nations should intervene. Obviously, all this slander is designed to serve the ultimate object of an attempt by American imperialism and international reactionaries to use the question of Tibet to intervene in the internal affairs of our country. The foregoing further exposes the real face of bourgeois international law, which serves only the aggressive interests of imperialism.

Note

1. *Ch'ing-Li-pao*, Argentina, February 3, 1960. [We are unable to locate this source.]

Further Reading

For an additional text on the issue of Tibet from this period, see Zhou Gengsheng, "The United Nations' Intervention in the 'Question of Tibet' Is Illegal," reprinted in Cohen and Chiu, *People's China and International Law*, vol. 2, pp. 1329–32. For a contemporary official discussion on the human rights situation in Tibet, see the *White Paper on the Human Rights Situation in Tibet* (Beijing: State Council, 1991). A useful work on Tibetan history is Melvyn C. Goldstein, *A History of Modern Tibet, 1913–1951: The Demise of the Lamaist State* (Berkeley: University of California Press, 1989). For a discussion of the role of human rights in China's foreign policy, see Andrew J. Nathan, "Human Rights in Chinese Foreign Policy," *China Quarterly*, no. 139 (September 1994): 622–43.

Part VI

1976–1986,
Including the Democracy
Wall Movement

38
An Initial Inquiry into the Contemporary Theory of Human Rights and Fundamental Freedoms (1976)

Mab Huang

"Dangdai renquan yu jiben ziyou lilun chu tan" [An Initial Inquiry into the Contemporary Theory of Human Rights and Fundamental Freedoms]. *Si yu yan* 14:4 (1976).

Mab Huang (b. 1935), professor in the Department of Political Science at Soochow University on Taiwan, is a long-time advocate of human rights. The piece we have translated here dates from 1976 when martial law was still in effect on Taiwan and human rights violations frequent. It is, however, a more theoretical piece that does not touch upon concrete human rights issues on Taiwan. Huang calls attention to the drawbacks of the contemporary human rights theories and emphasizes that human rights need to encompass both civil and political rights as well as economic and social rights. It was not until the early 1980s that human rights organizations were established in Taiwan and work on concrete cases and issues was undertaken. During the past few years Huang has been deeply involved in the promotion of human rights education in primary schools, high schools, and universities. He is also active in the current work to establish a National Human Rights Commission. In addition to his human rights work on Taiwan, Huang also takes a strong interest in human rights on the mainland. He is a board member of Human Rights in China, an NGO based in New York that works to promote human rights in the PRC.

Since World War II, people the world over have universally emphasized the protection and promotion of human rights and fundamental freedoms. International organizations have also devoted great efforts to this kind of work, and an internationally acknowledged standard is gradually taking shape. But in the theoretical field there remain many questions that need to be explored.

Of the three most influential theories in the contemporary [debate], the first has its origin in the English liberalism of the seventeenth century, the second in Marxism, and the third in Rousseau's theory of "the general will." They all have different fundamental concepts, directions, and conclusions, and their influences with respect to practical policies are also quite different. If we could establish a new theory, one that would break through the present impasse of mutual conflicts and confrontations between different political ideologies and systems, and thus be universally acceptable to people the world over, it would be a great help to the promotion of human rights and fundamental freedoms.

Seventeenth-century English liberalism took the individual person as its subject and natural law and natural rights as its foundation. It assumes that society and government have come about through a [social] contract, and emphasizes that the citizens have certain rights and freedoms which, within a certain scope, the government cannot interfere with or infringe upon. This is what scholars call "innate human rights" (*tianfu renquan*), "political and civil rights," or "negative freedoms," such as freedom of religion, speech and assembly, and so on. Since the nineteenth century, when the industrial revolution gave rise to certain social problems and a gradual widening of the gap between rich and poor, liberalism has been revised so as to gradually allow the government to intervene, using its power and policies in order to alleviate the abuses of the capitalist system in Western Europe. This gave rise to the welfare state and has widened the scope of rights and freedoms to include the right to subsistence (*shengcun quan*), the right to work, the right to equal education, and so on. These are what scholars call "economic and social rights." Or to put it in a different way: in order [for people] to apply their human rights and freedoms, certain conditions have to be met. If the government or society cannot afford or is not willing to supply these conditions, human rights and freedoms inevitably become devoid of content and are of no use in the citizens' actual lives.

The above theory has been taken up by a majority of societies in Western Europe, and it also constitutes the foundation of the UN Charter and a number of covenants on human rights and fundamental freedoms; its influence and value cannot be overlooked. But it cannot be denied that the rise of seventeenth-century liberalism, and the theory of human rights and fundamental freedoms to which it gave rise, has been deeply influenced by the capitalist market economy system. It strongly emphasizes the individual's freedom in economic life, and in the end results in all kinds of exploitation in capitalist society. Although the policies of the welfare state try to remedy these abuses, contemporary scholars still dispute whether this will lead to a fundamental reform of the social system and to the complete protection of the human rights and freedoms of each member of society. To put it another way, the policies of contemporary welfare states have limited the [free] competition of capitalism and protected the classes that are in unfavorable positions [due to] this competition, so that the cruel, "survival of the fittest"–style exploitation of the early capitalist societies is now seldom seen. Still, so long as private property is concentrated in the hands of a few people and there is a close relation between [business] enterprises and the government, this will influence the formulation of government policies; won't a situation in which a minority exploits a majority continue to exist? The majority of people spend their lives working hard, exerting all their strength for the profits of the minority. Although [people's] material lives early on became quite prosperous, [their] lives and work are quite monotonous and dull and so their personalities (*gexing*) cannot develop. When there is an economic depression, there is general unemployment and [people's] lives are even less protected. In these circumstances, rights and freedoms also lose their practical meaning. Because of this, according to some scholars, seventeenth-century liberalism's excessive emphasis on freedom, especially economic freedom, needs to be corrected, and the concept of equality needs to be stressed. Only if freedom and equality are regarded as equally important, and cooperation replaces competition, can a new theory of human rights and fundamental freedoms be established. [We can also see this] from a different perspective. Contemporary science and technology are making giant strides, the power of government is expanding, and organizations are becoming increasingly bureaucratic; in addition, [we] also find [ourselves] in a period of chaos with a serious threat of war. [This induces] the government, either out of necessity or out of [a concern] with national safety, to restrict people's rights and freedoms so that the freedoms of speech and assembly, and the right to political participation, lose their traditional protection. If humankind cannot control the development of science and technology and use them to promote their happiness, then the threat of war will not diminish, the centralization of the power of government [will continue], and the social foundation of liberalism will crumble. All attempts to create a new [theory] of human rights and fundamental freedoms on such a foundation will meet with failure.

Marxism's scorn of bourgeois society's concept and realization of human rights and fundamental freedoms—its belief that these are illusions or fantasies—is well known. According to its view, only after humankind has grasped the knowledge and laws of historical development can it enjoy real freedom. Its starting point is the human collective, and it emphasizes the inexorable laws of history according to which society [develops] from primitive communist society, through slave society, feudal society, and bourgeois society into a socialist (communist) society. Humankind has to pass through a working-class revolution that overthrows the bourgeoisie's political power and establishes a temporary dictatorship of the proletariat in order to reach a classless society [in which the principle] "from each according to ability and to each according to needs" [is put into effect], wherein all productive forces are public and the system of human exploitation no longer exists. Only in this brand-new society will humankind enjoy real freedom, human nature be completely developed, and individual human lives be versatile and gifted. Scholars call this kind of theory "collective freedoms" or "positive freedoms" to differentiate it from [the theory of] "negative freedoms."

It cannot be denied that Marxism is one of the forces behind the contemporary communist revolution, but in the past few years communist theoreticians have done little to elaborate upon the Marxist [theory of] "collective freedoms" and "positive freedoms," which is probably owing to political restrictions [on their work]. In Communist countries, the Communist Party autocracy and their tight control of academic work makes theoretical innovation all but impossible. But Marxism is nonetheless not without influence on socialism and the policies of Communist states. According to the opinions of the political leadership of contemporary communist societies, their societies have still not reached the stage of "classless society." The "dictatorship of the proletariat" will still continue, and not only will the power of the state not be weakened, but it must on the contrary be strengthened. As a result, citizens' rights and freedoms must be identical with the policies [carried out] by the Party in these special historical circumstances. Consequently, although the constitution clearly stipulates a whole range of rights and freedoms, the traditional "civil and political rights" of Western European societies are not taken seriously, and freedom of religion, freedom of speech, and so on virtually do not exist. Comparatively speaking, socialist societies [instead] emphasize "work" and "from each according to ability and to each according to needs." They emphasize social and economic rights and the interests of workers and peasants, such as the right to receive education, free medical expenses, protection of the right to work, and so on.

It is not difficult to understand why the above mentioned Marxist theory of "positive freedoms" and "collective freedoms" and the policies of contemporary socialist states have met with critique and debate from many scholars. Some scholars have questioned whether "collective freedoms" is a meaningful concept; in other words, whether it is really meaningful to talk of human rights and freedom if one does not take the individual as the subject. In addition, there are some scholars who believe Marxism to be utopian, because on the basis of human nature and humankind's historical developments, the "classless society" which Marxism hopes to attain is [in fact] impossible. Conversely, they emphasize that "positive freedoms" will inevitably result in one class, one party, or one dictator using the slogan of sham freedoms to implement totalitarianism without any legal restraints, thereby infringing upon and violating people's rights and freedoms.

The view of citizens' rights and freedoms among the political leadership of contemporary Asian and African countries resembles Rousseau's theory of "the general will." They emphasize the idea of nationalism and the concepts of people's will and equality. Because of their historical past and their painful experience of imperialism, they reject the West's idea of liberalism, but neither do they completely accept Marxism. For example, some political leaders from Asian and African countries do not accept the Marxist theory of class struggle. In their opinion, their main task is to establish an independent and completely sovereign state, and on this foundation seek modernization and economic prosperity and development. Consequently, in order to lead people to contribute to the work of national construction and modernization, they emphasize national unity and equality and the innovation of moral concepts. They want to sweep away all old concepts, old privileges, and [old] differences between areas and tribes. The political leadership sees itself as the representative of "the people's will" and [so] does not permit divergent political opinions or political parties. In some of these societies it is felt that the demands of modernization conflict with citizens' rights and freedoms, and that in order to reach [the goal of] national modernization it is difficult to provide complete protection of citizens' rights and freedoms.

From the analysis above it is evident that there exist differences with respect to the concepts, directions, and concrete policies of the most influential contemporary theories regarding human rights and freedom, and that these [differences] involve conflicts of actual politics. In these circumstances, trying to develop a new theory that could be universally acceptable is of course extremely difficult. We will only attempt to raise some opinions to serve as points of reference for preliminary discussion.

Our fundamental view is that humankind cannot—or at the very least cannot now or in the foreseeable future—grasp the fundamental truths of the universe, life, and human society. With our existing knowledge we cannot predict the possible future development of human society. We have already revealed our skepticism regarding both the theory of "natural law" and "natural rights" upon which seventeenth-century Western European liberalism is based, and the Marxist idea of inevitable historical laws. We affirm that a new theory has to be built upon human needs and human capabilities. In order to completely satisfy humanity's needs (both physical and spiritual) and in order to develop our talent and intellect, humankind needs full opportunities to find out things and make experiments, discoveries, and choices, and thus human rights and freedoms need to receive complete protection. As science and technology develop and society changes, the content and scope of human rights and freedom will also naturally change. To be a bit more concrete, a new theory of human rights and freedom should include the following hypotheses and discussion-points:

1. One should give equal consideration to individual rights and freedoms and to collective interests. Humans are social beings who cannot live separated from the group. The collective includes the family, tribe, region, work organization, class, state, and international community. These collectives' interests should receive proper attention.

2. The individual's rights and freedoms should include "civil and political rights" and "social and economic rights." At the same time it must be stipulated that their scope should be widened as science and technology develop and society changes.

3. Any expansion of the government's power and functions must be confined to [better] protecting the human rights and freedoms of individuals and the interests of the collective. To give an example, the government may not use uniting the country or modernizing as an excuse to arbitrarily encroach upon the rights and freedoms of the individual, or upon the interests of a tribe, class, or work organization.

4. In the [realm] of economics, consideration must be given to protecting and effectively using natural resources, as well as to ensuring that the society's wealth is equitably shared. No government, political party, or class can monopolize the majority of the means or tools of production. Work must contribute to the development of [people's] personalities.

5. [People's] spiritual lives should be broadminded and lively. No government, political party, or class should be able to monopolize the educational system or the public media. Scientists, writers, artists, and

other members of society who engage in [deeply] felt and intellectually [challenging] work should receive the protection and encouragement of the government.

6. We must grant and keep pace with the internationally acknowledged standard of human rights and fundamental freedoms that is taking shape, as well as the gradually widening power of international institutions to restrict member countries, [so that] we can make ever more effective contributions to protecting and promoting human rights and fundamental freedoms.

The above hypotheses and views are only some suggestions with respect to principles; whether they are helpful in establishing a new theory, and whether they harbor contradictions and problems, can only be solved by a step-by-step discussion. We will have to await the study of specific cases before we can confirm which political, economic, and social systems and which concrete policies are helpful in protecting and promoting human rights and fundamental freedoms.

Further Reading

For an early piece by Mab Huang that deals with the PRC, see "Human Rights in a Revolutionary Society: The Case of the People's Republic of China," in Admantia Pollis and Peter Schwab, eds., *Human Rights: Cultural and Ideological Perspectives* (New York: Praeger, 1979). For a more recent work dealing with liberal human rights debates in China, see his "Universal Human Rights and Chinese Liberalism," in Michael Jacobsen and Ole Bruun, eds., *Human Rights and Asian Values: Contesting National Identities and Cultural Representations in Asia* (London: Curzon Press, 2000).

39
Human Rights, Equality, and Democracy (1979)

Wei Jingsheng

"Renquan, pingdeng yu minzhu," *Tansuo* 3 (1979). Reprinted in *Dalu dixia kanwu huibian* [A Collection of Underground Publications Circulated on the Chinese Mainland] (Taipei: Zhonggong yanjiu zazhi she bianyin, 1982), vol. 2, pp. 41–50. We have slightly modified the translation found in James D. Seymour, ed., *The Fifth Modernization: China's Human Rights Movement, 1978–1979* (Stanfordsville, NY: Human Rights Publishing Group, 1980), pp. 141–46.

During the autumn of 1978 a more relaxed and optimistic political atmosphere developed in China, culminating with the important Third Plenum of the Eleventh Central Committee held in December that year. The new political leadership was determined to restore law and order and rebuild the legal system, and to this end a new constitution was adopted in 1978 and a criminal code, China's first, promulgated the year after. Criticism of the excesses committed during the Cultural Revolution and in earlier political campaigns became accepted and widespread, and victims of these campaigns were now rehabilitated and restored to their positions. All these developments served to inspire and encourage Chinese citizens, who in November 1978 began to gather at a wall in Xidan in central Beijing, later to be known as the Democracy Wall, to put up big-character posters and debate the political issues of the day. The posters had a wide and varying content, ranging from accounts of personal grievances and persecutions, to more general demands for democracy, law and order, and respect for human rights. These writings were in many cases also gathered in more than one hundred different magazines that were put out around the country. During the democracy movement, human rights resurfaced as a powerful slogan and idea. The democracy activists were not an homogenous group of people, but took quite different views on a number of issues, including human rights, as we can see from the present text and the three following texts. Wei Jingsheng (b. 1950) was perhaps the most radical human rights advocate during this period. Apart from theoretical articles on the subject, Wei also published a critical article on the conditions in Qincheng Prison No. 1, which had housed many well-known political prisoners and where he himself would later be imprisoned. Wei's magazine also reprinted excerpts from Amnesty International's 1978 report, Political Imprisonment in the People's Republic of China. In the spring of 1979, Wei was arrested and a crackdown on the democracy movement began. In November of the same year, Wei was sentenced to fifteen years' imprisonment on charges of counterrevolutionary activities and leaking military secrets to foreigners; he was not released until 1993. What proved to be Wei's undoing was not so much his conception and discussion of human rights, nor his demand for a fifth modernization, that is, democracy, as his critique of Deng Xiaoping as a new despot and his all-out criticism of socialism.

More people today are discussing the issue of human rights (*renquan*) than that of equality. Actually, these issues are two aspects of the same question. We can practically say that the two are inseparable, because without equality human rights loses its real significance, and without human rights, equality is an empty expression. Because human rights and equality are two aspects of the same issue, I myself use the term "the equal human rights issue" (*pingdeng renquan de wenti*).

Human rights is an ancient concept. It was revived during the European Renaissance [under the influence of] more explicit humanist thinking. [People] reflected on human rights as a social issue, and early socialist trends of thought and socialist movements developed, based on the common desire to build a society that acknowledged equal human rights for all. The ability to respect and protect the equal human rights of every member of society became the premise of socialism. In the eighteenth and nineteenth centuries, when people were unable to satisfy their basic material needs, they naturally thought that the prerequisite of realizing equal human rights for all was for every member of society to be in control of economic power. Thus, at the time when the influence of mechanistic materialist philosophy was very strong, many people went a step further and assumed that the essence of social control was to be found in the economic realm, and that to establish full social control was equivalent to realizing equal human rights. Socialist trends of thought have developed along these historical lines, with economics as the starting point for achieving equal human rights. Marx's great contribution to this trend of thought was to build a comprehensive ideological system covering both philosophy and economics. His theory expounded economic socialism forcefully and in detail, separated socialism from the democracy movement, and gave rise to the "scientific socialism" movement.

Let us now turn the historical spotlight one hundred years ahead in time, and see what the results of Marxist socialist economics, that is, "scientific socialism," have been for humankind. We can see that people's hopes one hundred years ago have come to nothing. All the social systems set up according to Marxist principles—that is, the present socialist countries—almost without exception neither acknowledge nor protect the equal human rights of all the members of their societies. Even if these countries repeatedly and smugly proclaim themselves to be the "true democratic" societies, on what basis can they say that the people are their own masters if universal equal human rights are absent? The living reality is that these "true democracies" are built on the foundation of "the dictatorship of the proletariat," the vanguard of the proletariat—[that is,] the Communist Party and its centralizing leadership—and the autocracy of the Party's leaders. To put it simply, they are built on the foundation of dictatorship. What an absurd "truth" this is! We must begin to investigate this absurdity by starting with the theory's points of departure.

1. What Are Human Rights?

The fundamental definition of the concept of human rights is the rights (*quanli*) that humans have. What rights do humans have? From the moment one is born, one has the right to live and the right to fight for a better life. This is what people generally call "innate human rights" (*tianfu renquan*), for [they] are not bestowed on humans by some external entity, but, as in the case of all other things' rights to existence, come into being simply through [our] existence. This is just like the case of a stone, which, since it occupies a bit of space by virtue of its existence, has its right to existence vis-à-vis its surrounding objects. This is a kind of most natural right (*ziran quanli*), a right that does not need to be bestowed by any external entity. Since people do not live in a vacuum but are surrounded by other things, in their lives they relate, directly or indirectly, to their environment. We can therefore say that human rights exist relative to the rights to existence of all other things with which they come into contact. Thus, human rights are limited and relative rather than unlimited and absolute. This limitation constantly grows and changes with the development of the history of humankind and with man's quest to tame and control his surroundings. This explains why the main points of the concept of human rights constantly change and are constantly being improved. Human rights in everyday life have to be gradually achieved. There is no such thing as "ultimately achieving" human rights.

Man, like all else, exists in relation to things outside himself. Both in terms of time and of space, there are mutual influences between man and his surroundings. Thus, his existence will take the form of mutual struggle and mutual support. This struggle/support phenomenon between man and his environment can be divided into two main categories. One is the struggle between humankind and nature to obtain the necessities of life (what one generally calls production), including finding out about the natural world, that is, science. The other is the struggle among people themselves to obtain the rights to live (*shenghuo quanli*), what one generally calls politics, including the activity of finding out about mankind, that is, social science. So we can say that politics is the activity of obtaining or suppressing human rights. Through politics, people's rights to live are either realized or suppressed.

2. What Is Equality?

The struggle among people for their rights to live involves two basic types of activities. First, there is the question of how to distribute the fruits of material production and culture, commonly referred to as a struggle in the politico-economic realm. Through this struggle, each person receives a share to which he or she has a right. The second type involves each individual's vying for the rights and related activities involved in seeking one's fair share, which is commonly referred to as pure political struggle. One aim of this struggle is vying for distributive rights; the other is the [very] right to vie for things. In other words, [I am talking about] vying for one's equal right to the fruits of labor and for one's equal right to carry out political activities. The fundamental contents of this [second] type of right are fundamental political rights, such as freedom of speech, assembly, association, publication, belief, movement, and the right to strike.

Only when everyone has the above freedoms will the equality of political and economic rights be protected and become real. These freedoms are the conditions that protect the people when equal rights are endangered and that come to bear at any time to defend equal rights. Thus, fundamental political rights are the preconditions for equal human rights. It must be acknowledged in theory at least, that these freedoms should be unrestricted within their various spheres. After all, in an ever-changing world no one can possibly determine what ways and means could [in the future] be used to harm others' rights. Therefore, it is also impossible to [define] which ways and means would not harm human rights. One can only determine a few relatively safe and peaceful methods that avoid suppressing others' equal rights, which can be used as legal methods of struggle to protect equal human rights. Inasmuch as there are many people who abuse human rights to gain social power, and since those common people without rights find it relatively easy to use the above freedoms as methods of struggle, these freedoms must be unrestricted in theory and unregulated in reality in order to ensure that all people easily can make use of them. In this way, everyone is equal in respect to them.

Equality does not mean that if you eat an apple, I must also eat one. It means that both of us have the right to eat apples, but if I do not feel like eating one, I have the right not to do so. This is called freedom. Equality must encompass these two aspects of freedom to measure up to its name. Thus, equality in reality does not mean "averaging." Equality points to the similarity of opportunity and allows the same possibilities to be used for different purposes. The average points to the similarity of achievement, not to the use of opportunities for dissimilar aims. It restricts opportunities [of people with] dissimilar aims in order to achieve "sameness," and thus does not provide equality at all. Equality gives the same opportunities to the various disparate elements that make up an ever-changing world and gives every member of society the same chance to complete his life course. Inasmuch as the starting points are different, the results must necessarily also be different. The important thing is that these different results be obtained by different people under the same conditions, using the same opportunities. Thus, this result will be uniquely satisfying for the people taken as a whole; it is the result from which the people can gain the most satisfaction.

What are rights (*quanli*)? Rights are opportunities for recognition in the external world. These opportunities are unequal in a class-structured society. In modern times, politics has involved the struggle to achieve equality of opportunity, that is, equal rights. But this is certainly not the struggle for similar, or average, achievement. The absolute average, absolute sameness of achievement, is an unobtainable illusion. The equality of rights, or the similarity of opportunity, on the other hand, can and must be completely attained. Thus, it is realistic to struggle for equal rights; this is a struggle that is valuable and significant and has to be carried out. To struggle to achieve an average [achievement] is [a sign of] intellectualism, which is of no value or significance, and therefore has to be eschewed.

3. What Is Democracy?

Freedom is the right to use one's capabilities to satisfy one's desires, though not the right to satisfy any kind of desire one pleases. When people are born, they have the right to go on living, the premise for which is that once people are born they must struggle to go on living. There are two types of struggle. One type does not hinder the rights of others to live; the other rescinds or partly rescinds the rights of others. We believe the latter to be immoral and exploitative, while the former provides the opportunity for freedom of choice. Only when one's right to choose is not hindered can everyone's activities be protected and recognized. The freedom we recognize is the kind that provides opportunities for unlimited choices and possibilities; it is not the kind of freedom that results in everyone acting exactly as they wish to satisfy their desires. The latter would be premised on the denial of the freedom for the majority, with the inevitable result that a minority would be satisfying their desires [at the expense of the majority]. The first kind of freedom is established on the foundation of equal freedoms for all and it would by necessity imply the realization of fair opportunities for the majority.

Thus freedom can only be obtained if it is enjoyed by all humankind and can only be realized under conditions of mutual protection. It cannot be realized by some people depriving others of their freedom, nor can it be attained through the willful satisfaction of the desires [of a minority].

Equal human rights are humankind's individual and concrete rights to live, and they are premised upon some particular social preconditions. These preconditions consist of the freedom of each member of society to use his or her power to make decisions with respect to social institutions, and to use his or her equal rights to take part in political activities in order to protect his or her rights to live. [They also include] the freedom to put forward one's views on all aspects of social activities, and in this respect also be able to cooperate with other people. When these preconditions are [fulfilled] and become a part of the social system, that is called democracy.

Democracy in its original sense means letting people be masters of their own affairs. The concept of democracy covers a wide range. Briefly, it means that people have the right to follow their desires in exercising control over all things in human society, including control over economic, political, cultural, and social affairs. Since the desires of people are not completely identical, if we only emphasize control and neglect the aim of satisfying the desires of the majority, we will end up in the absurd state of "democratic dictatorship." The Marxist theory of "the dictatorship of the proletariat" was developed on the basis of analyzing and magnifying the aspect of control in democracy. When this theory was fully developed, it fundamentally negated the fact that the different members of society have the right to satisfy their different desires. In other words, it denied people's right to live as equals. By the time Marxism developed to the Leninist stage of "ruthless suppression of counterrevolutionaries," it fundamentally negated the fact that each person is free to carry out political activities to satisfy his or her personal desires in life and to fight for survival. This was an out-and-out negation of the most fundamental principle of democracy. As a result of this negation, democracy was cut off from reality and only its name was retained to adorn the ugly features of despotism. This explains why all social systems based on Marxist socialism are without exception undemocratic and even antidemocratic autocracies.

Democracy is not a goal in actual life. Instead, it is a social condition ensuring that all have equal opportunities to attain their goals in life. Thus, democracy is a social system. In the first place, it is a political system; in the second place, it is an economic system. It is not a subordinating or enslaving system designed to do away with people's freedom, but one that protects people's freedom and consequently provides them with a chance to work in cooperation with each other. In actual life, different people have different ideas. If people are not free to live and do things as they wish, it is impossible to have large-scale cooperation on a voluntary basis or to establish a cooperative social structure. Hence, to begin with, democracy must be a social system that protects freedom. On the basis of freedom, it must encourage voluntary cooperation and achieve unity of relatively unanimous interests. Democracy is not a means of centralism, nor is freedom a window dressing for discipline. Democracy is a means of protecting freedom, and discipline is the pillar of democracy. If we recklessly reverse the means and the end, we will only find ourselves sinking into the quagmire of Maoist dictatorship.

Does democracy exist in order to protect any and all desires of each individual? Or, to put it differently, does it exist in order to ensure the future realization of any and all desires? No, this is not at all the case. Democracy exists to protect the equal rights of each individual to satisfy his or her desires on the condition that the individual acknowledges other people's [similar rights] and that the realization of his or her own desires does not harm their rights. We believe that the realization of desires can only be relative and restricted and that there never will be such a situation as the complete satisfaction of all one's desires [as Marxism claims]. . . .

In a democracy, people work according to their wishes and ideals, and thus the best conditions and fairest treatment are ensured. All ideas and desires are treated equally, so democracy will not allow itself to be controlled by a single ideal, and in particular cannot coexist with idealism (*lixiang zhuyi*). The reason for this is that idealism not only rejects the rationality of alternative ideas, but rules out the right of other ideas to exist. It demands the merger of all ideas and declares that an ideology will only be realized to the extent that ideas have been forcefully unified. Hence, idealism is essentially despotic and undemocratic. Actually, all dictatorships have some kind of foundation in idealism. In the old days, the feudal dynasties used religion to dominate society ideologically. For modern socialism, it is Marxism that serves as the ideological prop. The promises given by these ideological props regarding the ideal state are utterly visionary and unverifiable. They may be a little better than the stuff sold by ordinary swindlers, but in terms of effect they are not only useless but harmful.

4. The Realization of Democracy Is the Precondition for Winning Human Rights

Some people say: We currently do not have human rights. I think that this saying needs to be supplemented: We currently do not have equal human rights. Do people living in despotic societies also have the right to live? Yes. Some people have the right to live by enslaving others, whereas the majority of people only have the right to live as slaves. In a despotic society, people do not enjoy equal rights of existence. Any social system that denies the equal rights of existence is despotic and totalitarian. Contrary to despotism, a democratic social system is established on the foundation of recognizing the equal human rights of all citizens. All social systems which acknowledge that everyone has an equal right to exist are democratic systems. Since, as we have said, democracy gives all people equal political rights to seek a livelihood, it follows that democracy is a precondition for gaining human rights.

As a result of years of absolutist politics based on Marxism and Mao [Zedong] thought, the workers, farmers, soldiers, and masses of our country do not enjoy political freedom. They are not in a position to affect the social system or their own lives. Seldom do their hopes and aspirations influence the government. This political powerlessness spells enslavement and economic exploitation. Contrary to what Marx asserted, politics is not always decided by economics. Nor will politics invariably determine economics, as Mao Zedong maintained. Politics and economics are two aspects of human society that influence each other while simultaneously governing each other. If either aspect fails to cope with the other, social development will be impeded. In a modern socialist society where the lure of idealism is combined with the coercion of dictatorship to exercise social control, the fact that people are powerless in political affairs, enslaved, and exploited will cause economic development to lose [its connection with] making people's lives easier, which in turn will hamper social development.

If we want to free ourselves from enslavement and have our lives keep up with modernization, we must first secure the [necessary] prerequisite: democratic politics. Reform of the political system and thorough practice of democracy are the first steps toward pushing the Chinese society forward and thoroughly improving the livelihood of the Chinese people. If this is not tackled, all other pending issues will remain pending forever.

Further Reading

For a useful introduction to the democracy movement as well as a representative selection of texts, including others by Wei Jingsheng, see James D. Seymour, ed., *The Fifth Modernization: China's Human Rights Movement, 1978–1979* (Stanfordsville, NY: Human Rights Publishing Group, 1980). For additional information on the background and political context of the movement, see Kjeld Erik Brodsgaard, "The Democracy Movement in China 1978–1979: Opposition Movements, Wall Poster Campaigns, and Underground Journals," *Asian Survey* 21:7 (July 1981); and Andrew J. Nathan, *Chinese Democracy: The Individual and the State in Twentieth Century China* (Berkeley: University of California Press, 1985).

40

A Chinese Declaration of Human Rights: Nineteen Points (1979)

China Human Rights League

"Zhongguo renquan xuanyan: Shijiu tiao" [A Chinese Declaration of Human Rights: Nineteen Points], *Zhongguo renquan,* no. 1 (1979). Reprinted in *Dalu dixia kanwu huibian* [A Collection of Underground Publications Circulated on the Chinese Mainland] (Taipei: Zhonggong yanjiu zazhi she bianyin, 1982), vol. 2, pp. 187–90. We have slightly modified and supplemented the translation found in James D. Seymour, ed., *The Fifth Modernization: China's Human Rights Movement, 1978–1979* (Stanfordsville, NY: Human Rights Publishing Group, 1980), pp. 83–86.

The China Human Rights League, as can be inferred from its name, took a particularly strong interest in the issue of human rights. The organization was established in order to promote the cause of human rights, and it put out a magazine that carried many articles on the subject. The League was to some extent inspired by the China League for the Protection of Civil Rights set up in the early 1930s (see Text 26). One of its central figures was Ren Wanding, later to become a prominent dissident. Like so many others, the organization suffered from internal strife that led to its splitting into two. The declaration translated here gives a good overview of the kind of rights for which these democracy activists yearned. They were predominantly civil and political rights, such as freedom of speech, the press, publication, assembly, association, and demonstration. But the League also attacked such typical Chinese organizations as the work unit (danwei), Party committee, and secret police, which all controlled people's lives, livelihood, and movement. Economic and social rights were also invoked: for example, the League called for improvement of the cramped living conditions of urban citizens and economic relief for the poor and unemployed. Many of the League's demands reflected the interests of young people who had been sent down to the countryside: they now demanded the right to be transferred back to their hometowns and the right to be accepted at university regardless of their political background. The League also spoke out in support of the right to autonomy for minorities; except in Wei Jingsheng's writings, minority issues did not otherwise figure prominently in the democracy movement.

The China Human Rights League was officially established in Beijing on 1 January 1979. The league discussed and approved [this] human rights declaration.

In the final analysis, the 1976 Tiananmen Incident was a human rights movement. The significance of human rights is more far-reaching, profound, and enduring than anything else. This is a new mark of the political consciousness of the Chinese people and the natural trend of contemporary history. With a new content and a unique spirit, our human rights movement this year has again won the support and approval of the whole world. This has hastened and promoted the establishment of relations between the Chinese and U.S. governments. To stimulate the development of our social productive forces and promote world peace and the progressive cause, we put forward the following nineteen points:

1. The citizens demand freedom of thought, freedom of speech, and the release of all prisoners of conscience and speech. It is as absurd to incorporate individual thinking in the Constitution as it is to have a successor listed in Party regulations and the Constitution. This is against the principle of freedom of speech and against the law of human thought. It is also against the materialistic principle of the "diversified nature of matter," is a manifestation of feudalism, and is regarded with great disgust by the people throughout the country. In the world there is nothing that is sacred, unchanging, or inviolable. The citizens demand the thorough elimination of superstition, deification, and personality cult, the removal of [Mao Zedong's] crystal coffin in favor of a memorial hall, the building of a memorial hall dedicated to Premier Zhou [Enlai], the commemoration of the May Fourth Movement every year, and the emancipation of faith from the confines of superstition.

2. The citizens demand that there be practical safeguards for their constitutional right to assess and criticize Party and state leaders. To save the present generation and all future generations from suffering, to protect truth and justice, and to develop productive forces, citizens demand that the feudal imperial criterion of equating opposition to an individual with opposition to the revolution (a criterion that is still being applied) be given up forever. They demand that our soci-

ety be built on the basis of the principles of people's democracy.

3. Give the minority nationalities sufficient autonomy. Our country is not only multinational but also has many political parties and factions. In our socialist development, we should take the existence of various political parties and factions into due consideration. Various parties and groups should be allowed to join the National People's Congress (NPC). It is most ridiculous that various parties and factions cannot join the NPC, which claims to be an organ with supreme power in the country. This is a manifestation of replacing the government with the Party and not separating the Party from the government. This is incompatible with democratic centralism. It will inevitably result in the continuous development of bureaucratism. Our country's citizens do not want a "showcase" constitution.

4. Citizens demand that a national referendum be held to elect state leaders and the leaders at all levels in various areas. Deputies to the Fourth and Fifth National People's Congresses were not elected in a general election involving all the people. This was not only a scathing lampoon of our socialist democracy but also made a mockery of the human rights of 970 million citizens. The citizens demand the establishment of a "citizens' committee" or "citizens' office" (*gongmin yuan*) through a direct vote of all the citizens. It would be a standing organ of the NPC and would be able to participate in discussing and voting on policy matters and to exercise supervision over the government. The citizens demand that the state uphold the law and punish those Party and state leaders who have violated the law, and also that the state use the law to supervise Party and state leaders.

5. Chinese citizens have the right to demand that the state make public the national budget, final financial statements, the gross national product, [and other important economic statistics].

6. The NPC can no longer convene in camera. The citizens demand the right to attend as observers and witness the proceedings of the NPC, its standing committee conferences, and its preparatory meetings.

7. State ownership of the means of production should be gradually abolished in a transition to social ownership. . . .

8. . . . Major changes in our domestic and foreign policies and guidelines in recent years have borne full testimony to the bankruptcy of "revisionism" in theory and practice. There is no objective basis for ideological differences and disputes to exist between China and the Soviet Union. The citizens demand détente. The Soviet people are a great

people. The people of China and the United States, China and Japan, China and the Soviet Union must be friends for all generations to come.

9. The citizens demand realization of the Marxist doctrine that a socialist society is one in which everyone can develop freely. Any socialist country's form of government is a continuation of the traditional form of capitalism. Without the material civilization of capitalism, socialist democracy and freedom cannot survive. The basic thinking of this classic doctrine is also an important lesson that the Chinese people have obtained after more than twenty years of groping in the dark. We must not only draw on Western science and technology but also on Western traditions, democracy, and culture. The citizens demand that the state continue to keep closed doors open. Let ideas smash through the confines of prisons. Let freedom spread far and near. Let the wise people of China share the treasure of the whole of mankind. Let the suffering generation enjoy freedom. Let the younger generation be spared suffering. Eliminate class prejudices and ban deceptive propaganda.

10. Citizens must have the freedom to go in and out of foreign embassies to obtain propaganda, the freedom to talk to foreign correspondents, and the freedom to publish works abroad. Make available all "internal reading matter" and "internal movies" and let everyone be equal in enjoying culture. The citizens must have the freedom to subscribe to and read foreign magazines and newspapers and listen to foreign television and radio stations. Citizens demand that the state grant publishing and printing rights that are true to the Constitution.

11. The system in which a citizen devotes his whole life to a work unit (*danwei*) must be abolished. Citizens demand the freedom to choose their own vocations, the freedom to dress as they like, and the freedom of movement. Abolish all regulations and systems that stand in the way of solving problems of husbands and wives being obliged to live in different parts of the country. Cadres demand the freedom to change [their work]. Personnel engaged in classified work should have the freedom of love and marriage. Middle school graduates should have the freedom not to be sent down to the countryside. We oppose the use of administrative measures to enforce family planning and other policies. Unemployed people demand the right to receive state relief.

12. Citizens demand that the state ensure basic food rations for peasants and eliminate [the phenomenon of] beggars.

13. Educated young people on state farms should enjoy reassignment rights. Educated young people in agriculture demand that the state abol-

ish inhuman treatment. [They demand] political equality, an improved standard of living, and a wage increase.

14. Citizens demand that the state ban the use of deceptive means to recruit various technical workers. Those cadres and units that practice deception should be punished by law. Those who give bribes, and especially those who receive bribes, should be punished.

15. While undivided attention is being paid to promoting modernization, no less attention should be given to the firm implementation of policy. Those who are victims of false, unjust, and misjudged cases demand that the state reform the system of appeal and give the organs handling the appeal the power to directly rectify [these cases]. The state law should punish those who [are responsible for] framing cases [against others]. The citizens demand that the state put into action the policy once applied to those GMD officers and soldiers along with their families who came over to our side in the early postliberation period.

16. Secret police and the Party committee of a work unit have no right to arrest citizens or investigate them. They have no right to use methods of reconnaissance against innocent people. The secret police system is incompatible with socialist democracy. Citizens demand its abolition.

17. Get rid of slum quarters and crowded living quarters where people of three generations or grown sons and daughters are packed close together in the same room. . . . Ensure the freedom to visit exhibitions inside and outside of the country. Abolish the system of censorship and allow artistic freedom and freedom of the media. Abolish the system of examining one's political record at college entrance examinations and ensure that all are [treated] equally with respect to grading.

18. We are "citizens of the world." Citizens demand that the borders be thrown open, trade be promoted, culture exchanged, and labor exported. They demand the freedom to work and study abroad and the freedom to make a living or travel abroad.

19. This league appeals to the governments of all countries in the world, to human rights organizations, and to the public for support.

China Human Rights League
Prepared 17 January 1979 in Beijing

Further Reading

See Text 39, above.

41
Problems in Chinese Society:
Questions and Answers (1979)

Yu Fan

Zhongguo renquan, no. 1 (1979). Reprinted in *Dalu dixia kanwu huibian* [A Collection of Underground Publications Circulated on the Chinese Mainland]. (Taipei: Zhonggong yanjiu zazhi she bianyin, 1982), vol. 2.

This article appeared in the magazine put out by the China Human Rights League, *and can be read as a theoretical sequel to the Nineteen-Points Declaration (see Text 40, above). Like the next selection, this article tries to defend human rights from a more Marxist point of view, in the process giving view to a more humanistic interpretation of Marxism. While the author does not reject the class character of man, he does not believe that this is all there is to human beings. He defends the view that there is such a thing as a human nature that transcends time and classes, and argues that human rights are those things that make us human beings and separates us from all other living beings.*

Q: What are human rights (*renquan*)?

. . . Human rights are the unique demands that distinguish the human race from all other living creatures (those tools that lack the power of speech, namely animals) and from those tools that have the power of speech but have either visible or invisible shackles (slaves and serfs). In other words, human rights are the rights uniquely possessed by human beings which cause them to be different from—higher than—all other animals and tools. In the final analysis, how different and how much higher are human beings? This is something that develops with the times. In different eras, [people's] levels, demands, and standards are also different. As with all concepts whose development reflects the development of objective conditions, so does the concept of human rights also develop following the progress of the objective conditions it reflects. If we consider the concrete situation in China at present, the concrete content of human rights, which we can also call its extension, is more or less reflected in the China [Human Rights League's] Human Rights Declaration.[1]

There are those who believe that human rights mean only the right to subsistence (*shengcun quan*). This is one-sided and mistaken. This kind of limited conception of human rights would, in the best of circumstances, be no more than the kind of rights a beloved pet has in a wealthy household.

Human rights include all legitimate rights that a social being ought to have; these rights would include, in addition to the right to subsistence, the rights to work, speech, publication, democracy, and so on.

Our way of posing and elaborating on the question [of human rights] may meet with censure from "theorists" who argue that proceeding from definitions is not the methodology of materialists. We feel that the distinction between materialism and idealism is not that simple. To proceed from a strictly scientific definition is not necessarily idealism. To elaborate on a problem by starting from a description of a concrete example is not necessarily materialism. If a definition is a scientific summary of a thing, then to elaborate on it starting from a definition is also materialism; if a discussion based on a concrete thing is subjective, superficial, and one-sided, then this kind of elaboration of a problem is still idealism.

Q: When was the question of human rights raised, and by whom?

The question of human rights was first raised during the late Middle Ages by the emerging bourgeoisie in Europe. The American War of Independence and Declaration of Independence, the French human rights revolution and Declaration of the Rights of Man: these were the first examples of human rights in both theoretical and practical forms, achieving brilliant victories of historical importance. Human rights could only have been discovered in the late Middle Ages, and at no other time, and only by the emerging bourgeoisie, and not by any other group; this was no coincidence but due to historical necessity.

The concept of human rights has three basic and distinctive features for which the fundamental possibility of realization came about only in the late Middle Ages. As part of the process during which humans evolved from apes, the first feature of human rights emerged, namely the idea that humans are "higher" than other animals; basically, this signified that in the face of the powers of nature, humans could attain freedom and "happiness," but other animals could not. The fact that humans could both manufacture and use tools can be taken as a symbol of this. Following on the development of both humans themselves, and the material means of production and reproduction they created, human society at the end of its primitive stage produced a new tool, a shackled tool that had the power of speech: the slave. At the same time, however, humankind created for itself a new task, the task of liberating slaves. Following the laws of history, as soon as this task was accomplished, human society produced a new tool, a tool that could speak yet was bound by invisible shackles: the serf. All the unfree peasants bound to the land were serfs, as were other members of feudal society who were fettered by feudalism. Humans are unwilling to be animals, slaves, or serfs; in other words, humans desire existence, freedom, happiness, and dignity. This is just a different way of referring to the same thing [we have been talking about], and human rights can thus be given a new definition: humans ought to have the rights to struggle for existence, freedom, happiness, and dignity.

In fact, human rights can be given other definitions as well. In science it is not unusual to use different words and ways of expression to describe the same thing or rule, or to give a [new] definition to a single concept. The second law of thermodynamics, for instance, can be expressed in different ways, and these different expressions can all be mutually derived from one another and they all confirm one another.

The law of dialectics will always tie together existence and death, freedom and bondage, happiness and unhappiness, dignity and abasement. This is because the law of any concept's dialectical unity of opposites is universal and absolute. The essence of human rights is therefore the *struggle for* existence, freedom, happiness, and dignity, rather than existence, freedom, happiness, and dignity in and of themselves. Should anyone invoke the dialectical nature of things (the unity of opposites) to deny that human rights are humankind's rights to struggle for existence, freedom, happiness, and dignity, even to the point of arguing that the struggle for human rights is for death, bondage, misery, and humiliation, then [we should] obviously label it completely absurd.

Q: What is humanism (*rendao*)?

Basically, if one clearly understands the concept of human rights, then humanism is not hard to clarify. Human rights are the due rights (*yingyou quanli*) of every member of human society. Humanism is to acknowledge and respect the human rights of every other member of human society.

Q: What is human nature (*renxing*)?

Human nature is the special characteristic of humankind not only to acknowledge and respect one's own human rights, but also to acknowledge and respect those of others. One could say that human nature is the unity of human rights and humanism. Humankind's human nature cannot be separated from our natural attributes, but human nature should not be summarized as man's natural attributes; human nature is the unity of humanity's natural attributes and our social attributes. If a person does not acknowledge and respect his or her own human rights, or acknowledges and respects his or her own rights but not those of others (which can be called lacking in humanism), then we can say that this person has lost his or her human nature or, using words to which philosophers are accustomed, that he or she is alienated and not a human person (*bushi ren de ren*).

Q: What is a human being (*ren*)?

A human being is a social animal who possesses thought and language, and can actively know and alter the world around him or her in order to satisfy his or her own needs. Thus a human being is a social animal who has ideals and can pursue them. A human being is a natural and social animal, with both natural and social attributes. If a human being only has natural attributes and not social ones, then that person is not complete and is only a human in the biological sense. This kind of "human being" can exist. A human being who does not have natural attributes but only social attributes, or in a different word, a creature who has transcended nature entirely, cannot possibly exist. A human who possesses human rights, humanism, and a human nature indicates a social creature who does not transcend the natural world, a person in whom natural and social attributes are unified.

Q: What is the class nature of a human being?

A human being's class nature is one of his or her social attributes, but it is not the entirety of a person's social attributes, nor is it a person's entire human nature, much less the entirety of a person him- or herself. A person's class nature reveals the nature of his economic position, which shows whether he is an exploiter or a laborer. The mutual relations between one's social and natural attributes are extremely complex; their gradual clarification can only be accomplished through research by natural and social scientists, or perhaps by scientists from some field which lies in between the two and is difficult to identify. Different kinds of concrete analyses must be carried out based on the real-life situations of different kinds of people, and one must avoid simplistic conclusions about someone's other attributes based on his or her class origin or position. This kind of metaphysical, subjective adherence to the theory of the unique importance of class-based and economically based identity has caused confusion in the minds of the Chinese people, and all kinds of real hardships which are still fresh in their memory. A person's class nature certainly has all kinds of deep linkages with all his or her other attributes, so it would be mistaken not to acknowledge them. To deny a person's class nature and reject class struggles would be mistaken, but to deny human rights, humanism, and human nature because one acknowledges class is an even greater absurdity.

Q: Are the struggle for human rights, the discussion of humanism, and the advocacy of human nature the monopoly of the bourgeoisie?

In theoretical terms, it would be absurd to confine the struggle for existence, freedom, happiness, and dignity, and all the key related concepts such as science, democracy, equality, and fraternity, to the bourgeoisie. In real life it would be a disaster for the nation and the people. (This is clearly revealed in the ideas and actions of the Gang of Four.)

Because the bourgeoisie early on experienced exploitation and stood in the position of the exploited, and because it was the most highly educated group among the exploited people of the Third Estate, it was the first class to discover and demand human rights, and to raise the calls for science, democracy, freedom, equality, and fraternity. These slogans not only represented the interests of the bourgeoisie but also the interests of all other oppressed and exploited classes. Precisely because [these latter groups] were the ones most in need of democracy, freedom, equality, and fraternity, they saw that they were not the monopoly of the bourgeoisie, and it was because of this that these slogans came to have a broadly appealing power and a vigorous life-force. History proves that science, democracy, freedom, equality, fraternity, happiness, dignity, and labor are the common treasures of progressive humankind; they constitute the superior tradition and pride of the human race and do not belong only to a single epoch or class. It is not contradictory to [simultaneously] acknowledge the existence of universal virtues that transcend epochs and classes, recognize the common desire of progressive humankind, and recognize the class nature of human beings in specific historical circumstances. Acknowledging only the existence of class nature and denying human nature and the existence of common demands among progressive humans fits neither reality nor the law of dialectics. From the point of view of philosophy, this is to make the mistakes of setting the individual against the general and of dividing the particular from the universal. Of course, historical periods and social classes differ, and understandings of human rights, humanism, human nature, science, democracy, freedom, equality, and fraternity as a consequence are not only not the same but can indeed differ greatly. Yet they have constantly been advanced by far-sighted individuals in society who sought to understand and realize the kingdom of the ideal (that is, the idealism of real life). People from different historical periods or classes have different understandings, but [this is no different] from anything else in the world: at different times and among different classes, and even between different individuals, identities in the understanding of any concept are only relative, while differences are absolute. But these absolutely different understandings exist in the context of relatively identical understandings; they cannot be severed from such identities and exist independently. So-called basically different or opposed understandings of things only have meaning and only are real when they acknowledge the existence of identical understandings.

We may well ask: at any time or among any class of people, could a person who has not entirely lost his powers of reason mistake the burning of incense and kowtowing for science? Could he take despotic rule for democracy? Could he take confinement for freedom, or hunger, cold, and ignorance for happiness? Could he call the launching of missiles peace, or murder and arson brotherhood?

To deny the existence of a thing because there exist different ways of understanding it, or for this reason to avoid contradictions, and to reject one's own rights—these are all absurd and laughable reactions.

Note

1. This is the so-called Nineteen-Point Declaration; see Text 40 above.

Further Reading

See Text 39.

42

A Rebuttal to the Critique of "Human Rights" (1979)

Du Guo

"Renqua[...]"], *Siwu luntan*, no. 13 (19[...] of Underground Publicatio[...]ng yanjiu zazhi she bianyi[...]

This and t[...]gh not sharing the official[...]f human rights from quite[...]luntan, a more moderate [...]t considered to be the extr[...] and the China Human Rig[...]d only a vague hint at suc[...]s from a Marxist perspec[...]f human rights that appea[...] point by point. The short-comings of the bourgeois concept of human rights are acknowledged, but the idea behind it, that people are born equal and enjoy equal rights, is defended as a pro-gressive and generally valid idea. The article argues that Marxism is not opposed to the idea of equal rights but that its concept of equality is different from that of the bourgeoisie, since it aims at the elimination of classes and the private ownership system. The article reveals a strong and uncompromising critique of the excesses committed during the Cultural Revolution, putting the blame squarely on the lack of respect for the constitution. It also describes the shortcomings of the current politi-cal system, and worries about the renewed critique against calls for democracy and rights from some within the political leadership.

Not long ago, under the influence of the spirit of the Third Plenum [of the Party's Eleventh] Central Committee, interest soared among the Chinese people in developing democracy and building the legal system. Some of them raised the slogan of and made demands for "human rights," which led to the appearance of some chaotic tendencies and deviations, including activities harmful to the nation. Because of this, some comrades within the Party whose thinking was rigid or semi-rigid availed themselves of the opportunity to make difficulties and set off an undercurrent of opposition to democracy and innovation. They berated and censured the masses' demands for democracy. For a period of time, [charges] such as "rightist," "deviationist," and "democracy extremist" were rampant, aimed at striking down those who dared to demand democratic rights. There were also some in ideological circles who were only too happy to suppress the mass movement; they claimed to be criticizing "human rights," but in reality they were always unsettled by demands from the masses for democracy and so leveled violent and unwarranted criticisms, "wielding a big stick" and "putting hats" on people. They twist the Marxist assessment of "human rights" and completely negate the historically progressive nature of bourgeois human rights. They also have set up all kinds of restrictions on, and impediments to, the liberation of thought which had been opened up by discussions of the standard for truth; this has caused some matters that had already been, or were in the process of being clarified, to once again sink into chaos and ambiguity; and thinking that had already been liberated once again faces the danger of ossification. Suspicion and apprehension are appearing again among the masses, the influences of which [unfortunately] will be very great. In order to clarify erroneous ideas, counter the cold wind that blows in opposition to the people and democracy, and follow the guiding principles of letting a hundred schools of thought contend, let us also discuss our views of "human rights."

The most potent argument of those who oppose "human rights" runs along the following lines: "human rights is a bourgeois slogan" that is "obsolete" and "in decline."

Quite right, "human rights" is a slogan used several hundred years ago by the bourgeoisie to oppose feudal autocracy. But should we oppose all "bourgeois slogans" without exception? Is not "class struggle" a bourgeois slogan? Was not "socialism" in 1847 also a bourgeois movement? (Cf. Engels's "Preface to the 1888 English edition of *The Communist Manifesto*.") If we must oppose something just because it is "bourgeois," then how are we to understand the [following] words in *The Communist Manifesto*: "The bourgeoisie has played a very revolutionary role in history"? Should the proletarian revolution really totally deny all that the bourgeoisie has accomplished and thus return to the dark Middle Ages?

It must be noted that it is not accidental that the slogan "human rights" has gained new life in contemporary China. It is not the malicious propaganda of a minority, nor the subjective product of a few people's minds; it is the reflection in people's minds of real-life social relations. [The reappearance of the slogan "human rights"] is an expression of the imperfection of legal institutions within the Chinese political system, of democracy's low level of development, of the remnants of feudalism, and of the appearance of rampant bureaucracy; it is the denunciation and rejection of the feudal, fascist tyranny created by Lin Biao and the Gang of Four. Thus, although this slogan has its class limits, includes some things proletarian socialist democracies should reject, and also easily can create some misunderstandings and produce harmful effects, these are all problems of [incorrect] understanding that can be [avoided] with proper guidance. We do not take up [the slogan of] "human rights," but we do not wish to go in the opposite direction. Nor do we wish to give up on something essential for fear of encountering problems and take this as an excuse to bring the development of democracy to a standstill. We should ask ourselves why, in the period of free capitalism, the most ringing call was for "the liberation of the proletariat" rather than for human rights. And why in the countries which today designate themselves as already having established socialist democracy, "human rights" has become the slogan that most inspires people to fight bureaucracy and totalitarianism. Unfortunately, this has happened in precisely those countries whose political systems are largely identical to ours. From this point of view, in order to really avoid the contradictions that have appeared in those countries, and to truly cause the slogan "human rights" to become "obsolete" and "in decline," so that it can be returned to the dustbin of history, we can only seek truth from facts and search for the causes that produce it. [Following on this,] we must engage in the necessary reforms and eliminate the relations and conditions on which [these calls for human rights] rely. If we do not do this, we can only go from one subjective method to the next, attempting to critique [human rights] by attacking it on all sides; can this method really lead to its complete refutation? Since this kind of critique by its nature does not imply seeking truth from facts, how will it be able to persuade people?

Another argument of those who oppose "human rights" is: "Human rights are not natural (*tianfu de*); rather, they are a product of history." They reprove those who raise the slogan of human rights by saying that they "do not grasp the meaning of human rights." Very well, let us see if these people themselves understand the meaning of "human rights."

Are there really any natural rights? If we answer this question without looking at it through the eyes of theologians, natural rights cannot possibly be said to exist. Marxists first of all do not believe in religion, nor do they believe in fate, so naturally they cannot believe in any "natural rights." Bourgeois thinkers derive the concept of "natural rights" from [their belief in] the "state of nature" (*ziran zhuangtai*). This is the distorted reflection of primitive communism in their thinking, but this is not to say that there never existed a period in history when people were born equal. The reason why Enlightenment thinkers conferred the idea of "natural" onto human rights was to raise the status of human rights— to make what was at the time still regarded as [simply] the rights of ordinary people into something sacred, so that it could be used to oppose the equally deified and sacred feudal privileges. Obviously, the important thing here is not [the word] "natural," but rather the principle behind it, that is, the concept of rights which implies that "all people are born equal." In fact, the criticisms in many articles have concentrated on this problem.

Are all people equal from birth? Or are they born unequal? Is inequality between people inborn or is it something acquired after birth? Many critics do not dare to face this question directly; they equivocate and beat around the bush and reach this conclusion: people ought to be unequal from birth. This resembles the idea that God made people unequal with respect to innocence—is this not the teaching of Christianity? According to Marxism, human inequality does not exist from the mother's womb but is determined by production and exchange relations in the real world. Apart from this [acquired inequality], there is no hereditary inequality! It was only in the feudal system of hereditary rank and wealth that a person immediately after birth was given unequal privileges. The bourgeoisie struck down these privileges and put all people into equal exchange relationships in the capitalist [system of] commodity production; this is the real meaning of bourgeois "human rights." It was from this point of view that Marx criticized bourgeois "human rights." He pointed out that these equal exchange relationships only constituted an equality of capitalist ownership rights and the equality to buy and sell labor. This, then, represented the true paradise of bourgeois "natural rights": freedom, equality, property rights, and. . . .[1] On the one hand, there is great wealth, and, on the other, deep poverty. This is the essence of "human rights"! For this reason, Marx rejected the bourgeois idea of equality. He pointed out that proletarian equality is the elimination of class, private ownership, and the relations of a capitalist commodity production system. Marx, however, did not deny the bourgeois slogan that everyone is "equal from birth." One should rather say that acknowledging that humans are equal from birth was exactly what Marx did: this is a common characteristic of proletarian democracy and bourgeois democracy. The only difference was that the bourgeoisie believed that only with the relationship of private ownership in a capitalist commodity production system could this kind of equality be realized and ensured, whereas Marx, on the other hand, believed that in order to realize true democracy and equality, the sources and conditions that give rise to class oppression must be eliminated. This is the fundamental difference between proletarian democracy and bourgeois democracy. It is in this sense that we claim that socialist democracy is higher, broader, and more mature and perfect than bourgeois democracy. Also, it is in this sense that we argue that Marxism does not oppose human rights but rather opposes and does not recognize a false and deceitful concept of human rights.

If we do not even acknowledge this point, would that not be the same as saying that people at birth exhibit differences that go beyond physiology and gender? What could these differences be? The only possibility would be to seek them in the noble blood of the past generations! If we want to reject even this most minimal kind of people's rights and reject such a simple view of equality, would this not be the same as to say that, among our revolutionaries, there also exist certain differences based on rank and honor? Then of what would proletarian comradely relationships consist? We had better fit them into the structure of feudal ranks! Some people play on the meaning of words and rack their brains to find a way to draw a sharp distinction between "people's democratic rights" and "human rights." Even though the cautious gentlemanly attitude of these people is noble and unsullied, this purifying of "people's democratic rights" and rejecting of the most minimal kind of equality between people means that "people's democracy" does not even measure up to bourgeois "human rights." Do we acknowledge that people have equal rights and that their relations are equal? Or do we acknowledge that people should be distinguished on the basis of wealth and social rank? Should we acknowledge the equality between revolutionary comrades—that no one is higher or more valuable than anyone else? Or should we acknowledge that a few people are higher than and superior to others, and therefore should ride roughshod over the rest? It is clear to what extent the poisonous traces of feudalism have taken hold of some people! In their understanding of "democracy," does there even exist a trace of the Marxist spirit?

Another critique of human rights is the following: from whom are human rights to be demanded? From the Communist Party? This is treason and heresy, desiring the overthrow of the Communist Party.

One who uses such a tone to pose the question harbors ulterior motives and sinister and vicious intentions from the outset. There is no point in conversing with Party leaders who exhibit such a barbaric and tyrannical style. We would like to ask, since the Communist Party is in power, of whom should rights be demanded, if not of the Party? Of the bourgeoisie? They were long ago beaten down and overthrown! But if not for that fact, would it not be hypocritical to ask the bourgeoisie for "human rights"? Would this not be a deception? Thus, real "human rights" and complete democracy can only be demanded of the Communist Party! They [can only] be demanded of the proletariat! Why is this so strange? Why is this so surprising and frightening? Does this not demonstrate the people's support for and trust in the rule of the Communist Party? The Gang of Four created so many disasters for us and left so many problems that since them the masses in one way or another have made various kinds of demands, even some which are not very reasonable, so that our Party has no choice but to face up to these problems and establish the greatest resolve to carry out all kinds of reforms in order to advance and ensure the smooth realization of the Four Modernizations. Is this not a major achievement? If some of us cannot get used to this—if some of us cannot comprehend this—it truly demonstrates that [those few] have put themselves into an inexpressibly regrettable position. If the masses have no rights whatsoever vis-à-vis these kind of people, I simply don't know how we can do what we want to do. We may say that this is how they reveal their secret terror of people's democratic rights.

Finally, those who oppose "human rights" also say the following: "Our country has already established the dictatorship of the proletariat and the rule of socialist democracy. Our country has for the first time resolved the problem of the people's democratic rights. Our country's citizens enjoy far-ranging democratic rights, etc." In order to ensure this judgment, they have removed the [Four] Great Freedoms, which early on had been enshrined in the constitution.[2]

Their rhetoric is compelling but hardly new. Didn't Lin Biao and the Gang of Four also use the same rhetoric? But the profound question is: at this moment in which they want to seize power and plunge the Chinese people back into crisis, will we again sincerely have faith in the use of this rhetoric to protect the people and the revolution? What would the result be? Quite right, we have already established the dictatorship of the proletariat, but the fact is that this dictatorship still is deeply unstable and imperfect. Yes, it is true that we have already established socialist democracy, but this democracy is far from perfect and hides many deep flaws, among which is that the question of people's democratic rights has not yet been resolved. The democracy is insufficient and people have no rights. This was [precisely] the situation in the past. If one does not even acknowledge this point, then the feudal fascist dictatorship established by the Gang of Four cannot be understood, and our current intense efforts to establish democracy and develop the legal system would be superfluous. But then, how could so many unjust, wrong, and misjudged cases have taken place? The days lost to the Gang of Four are too numerous to count. Should we not criticize and oppose [their] criminal acts of trampling on democracy? Should such fine offspring of the Party as Peng Dehuai and Zhang Zhixin really have been imprisoned and executed?[3] Is it inevitable and natural that a handful of privileged bureaucrats should ride roughshod over the people? Obviously, people who use such rhetoric are out of touch with the Third Plenum of the [Eleventh] Central Committee; they try to use this kind of sweeping affirmation to cover up the deficiencies in our system. Their intention is only to preserve by every possible means conditions that are advantageous for themselves. . . .

If we turn to the constitution, it is even more shameful. During the past ten years, has it not been a mere scrap of paper? How long ago was it that this sacred and inviolable thing in the minds of the Chinese people was overturned . . . and trampled to pieces? When Lin Biao and the Gang of Four used fabricated charges to one day label this person a traitor and secretly interrogate and injure him, and then the next day label that person a spy and illegally arrest him—if we may ask, were they aware of the constitution at all? When they created a literary inquisition, strangled people's freedom of thought, forbid their spiritual consciousness, and regarded speech as a crime, did they ever once ask about the constitution? When they violently suppressed the April Fifth Tiananmen [Movement of 1976] when people gathered to grieve over Zhou Enlai, did they inquire about the constitution? During those bitter days, if only the constitution had been of some use, it would have saved people many tears! Throughout these ten years, the constitution has stood disconsolately on the sidelines, [commenting on our plight] with biting irony. In comparison, saying that "people's democratic rights have already been resolved" [merely] seems remote and out of touch. Let me tell you something, though: the opportunity for this kind of rhetoric is over! The contradictions cannot be concealed. They cannot be whitewashed as a picture of peace and prosperity. China is on the eve of a great transformation. Although those who feel that their positions are not safe and that their empire is about to fall will try to use all kinds of clever methods, they cannot prevent this change from happening. History has its own inner logic; it doesn't pay attention to the noise and curses some people raise, but follows its own inevitable course. "The blue mountains cannot be hidden from view and the East China Sea will inevitably rise." The future belongs to the people!

Notes

1. Two characters are garbled in the original, as noted also by the Chinese editors of the reprinted edition.
2. The Four Great Freedoms refer to the freedoms to speak out freely, air one's views fully, hold great debates, and write big-character posters. These freedoms had been acknowledged and practiced during the Cultural Revolution and were then enshrined in the 1978 constitution. During the spring of 1979 they were seriously weakened as the government began to restrict putting up big-character posters, and in early 1980 they were removed from the constitution.
3. Peng Dehuai was China's Defense Minister when he in 1959 was dismissed from office for having criticized the Great Leap Forward. Zhang Zhixin was a cadre who was arrested in 1969 for opposing the Cultural Revolution and executed in 1975.

Further Reading

See Text 39.

43

How Marxism Views the Human Rights Question
(1979)

Xiao Weiyun, Luo Haocai, Wu Xieying

"Makesi zenmeyang kan 'renquan' wenti" [How Marxism Views the 'Human Rights' Question], *Hongqi,* no. 5 (1979).

The new attention to human rights among establishment intellectuals and official China after 1978 was primarily a reaction to the democracy activists' calls for human rights. As the article translated here reveals, it was generally held that discussions of human rights constituted a direct attack on the regime, and human rights were simply dismissed as a bourgeois slogan. Those who advocated human rights risked being charged with opposing socialism and wanting to restore capitalism. The democracy wall activists' open letters to the West, calling for Western leaders to show concern for the human rights situation in China, were strongly criticized as selling out to foreigners. "Human rights," according to the more conservative intellectuals, was not and could not be a dominant slogan in a socialist society. Some official writings, however, acknowledged that human rights talk at times could be useful to socialists as a weapon to oppose the bourgeoisie and obtain rights for themselves, but this constituted more of a tactical strategy than an affirmation of human rights as such. In these writers' analysis, based as it was on Marxist theories, there could be no such thing as universal and supra-class rights. Rights were not eternal, absolute, or universal, but reflected the productive forces in society and the interest of the class in power. In a class society, rights would thus reflect the interests of the bourgeoisie, whereas in a socialist society, the workers would enjoy extensive democratic and economic rights. This leads to the glorifying of the situation in socialist countries and a critique of the situation in the West. This article and the response from Lan Ying that follows illustrate how sensitive and problematic the topic of human rights was in the late 1970s.

The emphasis of the work of the Party has already been shifted to the construction of socialist modernization. In order to realize the Four Modernizations, we must work under the leadership of the Party to strengthen the dictatorship of the proletariat and develop socialist democracy so as to mobilize completely all positive factors [in society].

But with respect to developing democracy, there at present exist several different point of views. Some people are raising the slogan "struggle for human rights" (*zheng renquan*); this is one example. The majority of people who use this slogan do not understand clearly what "human rights" mean, but some are trying in vain to use it to confuse and poison people's minds and to plot for their own private interests. How one views the "human rights" question is related to the central issue of correctly understanding and differentiating between socialist democracy and capitalist democracy. It also relates to how one correctly exercises [one's] citizens' democratic rights in order to actively contribute to the Four Modernizations. We should use the viewpoint of Marxist thought to carry out a historical study and analysis of the "human rights" question.

Those who use the slogan "struggle for human rights" see "human rights" as the "spirit of humankind" and as a "universal truth" of boundless beauty, which is utterly absurd. Let us investigate the historical background and class nature of the birth of the "human rights" slogan. "Human rights" reflect the bourgeoisie's demands for economic and political power at the time of nascent capitalism. It was an intellectual weapon in the struggle of the bourgeoisie against feudal political power and the divine right of kings. . . . [Indeed,] it is not hard for us to see that "human rights" is always a bourgeois slogan. In society at present there are some with ulterior motives who energetically praise the bourgeois slogan of human rights; not only do they lack a Marxist spirit but their sense of patriotism has also disappeared into thin air. . . .

The nature of capitalist "human rights" is to confirm and protect the capitalists' right to private property and freedom to exploit [others]. Although the theorists of bourgeois "human rights" have different opinions about the substance of human rights, not only is there no argument regarding the protection of the right to private property, but they also all candidly admit as much. Locke believed that the most important "human right" was to property and that the government's main objective was to protect it. He also explicitly regarded the freedom to exploit hired labor as a component of "human rights." Rousseau also considered the right to private property as an important part of the protection of "human rights." He said: "Property is the true foundation of government and society; the citizens have agreed to its being truly safeguarded."[1] Bourgeois constitutions also take property as the nucleus of "human rights" and explicitly lay down its protection. The [French] Declaration of the Rights of Man, Article 17, says: "Property being an inviolable and sacred right, no one may be deprived of it except when public necessity, certified by law, obviously requires it, and on the condition of a just compensation in advance." In short, affirming and protecting the right to property is the heart of bourgeois "human rights." As Marx said:

"The practical application of the right of man to freedom is the right of man to private property. What does the right of man to property consist of? . . . The right of man to property is the right to enjoy his possessions and dispose of the same arbitrarily, without regard for other men and independently from society, the right of selfishness" ("On the Jewish Question," in *Collected Works of Marx and Engels*, vol. 1, p. 438). In a capitalist society, the great part of the means of production is in the hands of the capitalists; the protection of the so-called "right to private property" is no more than the protection of the system by which the capitalist exploits the laboring masses. The system of capitalist private ownership is the prerequisite for and foundation of the dictatorship of the capitalist class. If one starts from the premise of economic inequality, then the freedom and equality in politics and law for all people, proletariat and property-owners alike, will be nothing but a fraud.

If we look at the contemporary situation in capitalist societies, we can see that everywhere there is widespread unemployment, inflation, serious crime, racial discrimination, oppression of women, drug addiction and trafficking, etc. Where is human dignity? Where are the universal rights to freedom, equality, and happiness? According to statistics, in some capitalist-imperialist countries, those who wish to run for public office must spend more than $1 million; whereas those who wish to run for president must spend at least $50 million. This right can be enjoyed only by the wealthy and superwealthy who possess vast sums of U.S. dollars. In this kind of country, blacks and other people of color who are treated unequally cannot escape their lot even though the law affirms "human rights." Only those who close their eyes to reality and lack national self-respect can deliberately prettify capitalist-imperialist countries as being "human rights" paradises.

The Chinese people have already gained political power (*zhengquan*) and realized both the dictatorship of the proletariat and socialist democracy. But those who preach bourgeois "human rights" allege that in the new China there is neither a people's democracy nor any people's rights. Since this is a question that touches upon China's fundamental nature, we cannot help but make the necessary replies to these claims.

First of all, let us analyze what kind of "human rights" the people who raise the cry of "human rights" really want. They openly promote "the need for rational and conscientious guidance," "the abolition of class struggle, 'violent revolution' and all forms of 'dictatorship,'" and "reject the Party committee [system] in order to agitate for democracy."

This shows clearly that they do not desire socialism, the dictatorship of the proletariat, the leadership of the Party, or the guidance of Marxism, Leninism, and Maoist thought. They put themselves in opposition to the dictatorship of the proletariat and socialism and declare that the "human rights" they demand stand in absolute opposition to socialist democracy. They declare without reservation that "at present it is especially necessary to disseminate Rousseau's view of human rights" and "advocate the study of the culture and civilization which grew out of Christianity, and the establishment of democratic systems under the guidance of its teachings of peace, forgiveness, understanding, and brotherly love," and so on. These are the "human rights" they wish to promote. The Chinese people already have experience with the ideas and teachings for which they clamor: they are a hodgepodge of capitalism and imperialism. Naturally, the Chinese people reject this capitalist rubbish. The Chinese constitution sets forth clear guidelines for the upholding of the [four] cardinal principles of socialism, the dictatorship of the proletariat, the leadership of the Party, and Marxism, [Leninism, and Maoist] thought.[2] They represent the will and interests of the people of the entire nation. The people must abide by them, and if they deviate from them their democratic rights are out of the question. It is very clear that the "human rights" desired by those who loudly call for "human rights" really are nothing but the democracy and freedom of bourgeois individualism. In recent days as they loudly proclaimed their "struggle for human rights" slogan, they have ignored stability, unity, and the people's interests, disobeyed the advice of the Party and the government, raised all kinds of unreasonable demands, attacked government organs, criticized Party cadres, blocked traffic and railroads, and impeded production. These are the "human rights" they call for! If they were given these "human rights," our production, labor, and social order would be ruined, government assets would face losses, and the democracy and freedom of the majority of the people would be damaged. It goes without saying that the people would not give them the bourgeois "rights" for which they clamor.

Secondly, those who call for "human rights" talk nonsense, saying that China's socialist system lacks democracy and people's rights, and thus they claim to "struggle for human rights" as though they were the only "defenders of human rights" and "warriors for democracy." This is utterly ridiculous. In China, which has already achieved the victory of the socialist revolution and established the dictatorship of the proletariat and socialist democracy, the slogan "struggle for human rights" is an arrow without a target and indicates a desire to retrogress to a capitalist society. China is a socialist country; we do not endorse the slogan "struggle for human rights" that was raised by the bourgeoisie in the nascent capitalist period. Does this then mean that we do not talk about and even do not want people's democratic rights? Exactly the opposite. It is socialist countries that for the first time in human history have resolved the question of people's democratic rights; only in a socialist country will one have the most far-reaching democratic rights. This is something with which no capitalist country can compare. Lenin pointed out that: "Proletarian democracy is a thousand times better than any bourgeois democracy; the Soviet Union's political system is a thousand times more democratic than the most democratic capitalist country" (*The Proletarian Revolution and the Traitor Kautsky*).

In the economic sphere, Chinese socialist democracy manifests itself as the elimination of the private ownership of the means of production and thus also of the class root of man's exploitation by man. Our constitution protects the public ownership of the means of production and forbids exploitation. By implementing the principle of "he who does not labor shall not eat," we have fundamentally resolved the problem of people's democratic rights. By contrast, the essence of bourgeois "human rights" is the protection of the private ownership of the means of production, the defense of exploitation and oppression, and the use of the privilege of money to replace the old feudal privileges and hereditary rights. The claim that the proletariat and capitalists formally and before the law are equal is deceiving the proletariat and equating inequality with equality. It is a weapon of the bourgeoisie in their opposition to the liquidation of classes. In politics, our centralization of democratic rights is expressed in the fact that the people are the master of the nation; the people have the rights to manage the country, every kind of enterprise, and educational and cultural activities. These are the most important and fundamental rights of workers in a socialist system. China's constitution also fully protects all political rights and freedoms of the citizenry, such as the rights to vote and stand in election, the right to work and to receive education, and the freedoms of speech, correspondence, publication, assembly and association, demonstration, and strike. The constitution also guarantees equality between the sexes, equality of ethnic groups, and forbids ethnic discrimination and oppression. Step by step, China is developing social welfare, social relief, public and cooperative health care organizations, and steadily improving the material conditions in which workers can rest and recuperate. These activities and laws prove that Chinese citizens enjoy very wide-ranging democratic rights.

Furthermore, we also have strict laws and policies regarding criminals, counterrevolutionaries, and class enemies, including prisoners of war from the time of the civil war and the war against the Japanese. Extorting confessions by torture and corporal punishment are forbidden, and so are fascist methods of investigation. Chairman Mao pointed out that one should treat criminals as human beings: "As for reactionary classes and elements, after their political power has been overthrown, as long as they do not make trouble, cause harm, or create a disturbance, they should be given land and work and be allowed to live and reform themselves through labor, so that they can become new men" ("On the People's Democratic Dictatorship"). Our nation is led by the proletariat. The proletariat has the breadth of vision to transform humankind, and only the proletariat can treat such people [as those mentioned above] with revolutionary humanism. The last Qing emperor, Puyi, underwent reform through labor and thus became a new person. In his own words: "'Man' was the first character I learned in the *Three-Character Classic,* but in the first half of my life I did not really understand it. Only thanks to the Communists and the policy of reforming criminals can I understand today the meaning of this solemn word and become a true man." This is but one typical example. There are many similar examples to be found among those who have been granted amnesty by our government. Recently, China formulated a new policy regarding the rehabilitation of former landlords, rich peasants, counterrevolutionaries, and bad elements. Are these examples not sufficient to resolve the question under discussion?

But among those who advocate the slogan of bourgeois "human rights" there are those who openly request that the capitalist-imperialist countries show [us] kindness, calling on the bourgeois heads of state to show concern for the so-called "human rights question" in China. This is hardly surprising; it follows a certain logic, since this kind of people have pinned their hopes on bourgeois "democracy" and "human rights" and naturally can only run to the capitalist nations in search of it, begging their leaders for charity. But the Chinese people are deeply aware of the fact that our democratic rights have been received through a century of struggle in the course of which the three great oppressive forces of imperialism, feudalism, and capitalist bureaucracy have been overthrown.

They were not achieved through someone's charity. One hundred years ago, imperialism cruelly oppressed and invaded China; many Chinese died beneath its boot-heels and before its guns. In what way are they [i.e., imperialists] qualified to lecture us on "human rights"? In 1949, the new China was established; the Chinese people stood up and threw off their shackles. The advocates of "human rights" wish that imperialists would come and "show concern"—but this is not in keeping with China's sovereignty, her constitution, nor the dignity of the glorious Chinese people.

Of course, our opposition to bourgeois "democracy" and "human rights" does not mean that our current socialist system is already perfect. It is not that we do not wish to develop democracy; on the contrary, we believe it is not yet perfect. China's democratic system and laws are not yet perfect. The broad masses hope that the legal system will be strengthened and democracy perfected, and that all questions relating to political life will be resolved. We are struggling to accomplish this. We should also be aware of the fact that the damage done to the democratic dictatorship of the proletariat when Lin Biao and the Gang of Four ran amok was indeed very grave and needs to be remedied. But we must not lump together their feudalist fascist dictatorship with socialist democracy. After smashing the Gang of Four in order to address these questions, we thus began to develop democracy and liberate people's thoughts under the leadership of the Party. We then also began the discussion of practice as the sole criterion of truth. In order to solve the few remaining historical questions, many powerful measures were adopted with good results. Naturally, there are some problems whose resolution, due to the limitations of certain conditions, still will require [some time and effort]. But there are no grounds to conclude, based on the damage done by Lin Biao and the Gang of Four and some shortcomings in our work, that China has no democracy and people's rights.

It should be evident that the great majority of those who have been influenced by bourgeois "human rights" recognize the problems. But because they are young and have not experienced the oppression of imperialism and feudalism, or because they have not seriously studied Marxism-Leninism and Mao [Zedong] thought, they do not understand what bourgeois "human rights" really are all about. In the case of these people we must redouble our ideological work and make them understand capitalism and socialism, bourgeois democracy and socialist democracy. However, it must be understood as well that class struggle still exists in our country; there are many black sheep whom we must be on guard against. Stern measures must be taken against these black sheep who use democracy in order to seek their own personal gains, incite disturbances, and commit [other acts] with evil consequences.

History is a process of development and time marches forward. China is in the midst of advancing its socialist modernization; in order to realize the Four Modernizations we need to thoroughly develop democracy and protect people's democratic rights. Following the development of China's socialist modernization, our nation's democratic system will improve constantly and socialist democracy will bloom. Our great motherland will gain steadily in glory and thrive in prosperity.

Notes

1. The authors cite the *Social Contract*, but nothing like this appears there. The closest sentiment in Rousseau's writings is perhaps the following, from his *Discourse on Political Economy*: "It should be remembered here that the foundation of the social compact is property, together with its first condition that each person should be maintained in the peaceful enjoyment of what belongs to him." Donald A. Cress, trans., *Jean Jacques Rousseau: The Basic Political Writings* (Indianapolis: Hackett, 1987), p. 132.

2. These four cardinal principles were proclaimed in 1979 by Deng Xiaoping.

Further Reading

For a summary of the debates in 1978–79, see "Guonei baokan guanyu renquan wenti de taolun zongshu" [A Summary of the Debate on the Issue of Human Rights in Domestic Magazines], *Shehui kexue*, no. 3 (1979). For an example of another conservative article on human rights, written slightly later, see Gu Chunde, "Shilüe tianfu renquan shuo" [A Brief Outline of the Idea of "Natural Rights"], *Hongqi*, no. 7 (1982).

44

Is "Human Rights" Always a Bourgeois Slogan? A Discussion with Comrade Xiao Weiyun and Others (1979)

Lan Ying

"Renquan conglai jiu shi zichan jieji de kouhao ma?" [Is "Human Rights" Always a Bourgeois Slogan?], *Shehui kexue*, no. 3 (1979).

Despite the sensitivity of the human rights issue in the late 1970s, there nonetheless existed some important differences among establishment intellectuals. In the essay translated here, Lan Ying presents a relatively liberal, for want of a better word, view on human rights, and was even so bold as to openly criticize Xiao Weiyun and the others writing in the Party mouthpiece, Hongqi *[Red Flag], for which see the previous selection. Lan Ying argues that the historical origin of human rights should not be held against it and denies that the bourgeoisie has a monopoly on the idea. Nor does the fact that some people had used the slogan of human rights to attack the government undermine the value of human rights as such. Lan Ying argues that the proletariat can also make use of the language of human rights, claiming that it is possible to formulate a Marxist conception of human rights. But such a humanistic interpretation of Marxism was still very rare among intellectuals at the time. Lan Ying and other more liberal establishment intellectuals did not dispute that human rights problems had continued to exist in China after 1949. They emphasized, however, that it was the feudal tradition that was to blame, rather than socialism. The horrors of the Cultural Revolution were thus attributed to the feudal thinking of the Gang of Four. Lan Ying's article is a rather rare and early example of an affirmation of human rights and attempt to dress it in a socialist garb, but by 1982 the official discourse had generally begun to affirm and support human rights. By then, the previously ignored international human rights developments since 1948, and especially the fact that human rights included economic and social rights and the right to self-determination, came to be acknowledged and found to be acceptable to socialist China. As Lan here already suggests, human rights will come to be regarded as a useful tool in the struggle against colonialism, imperialism, and hegemonism.*

Xiao Weiyun and other comrades' "How Marxism Views the 'Human Rights' Question" (referred to below as Xiao's article) was published in issue no. 5 (1979) of *Red Flag*. It contains some very good views: for example, their emphasis that we must use a class analysis in order to reveal the hypocrisy of bourgeois "human rights," and their critique of the reactionary views of those who "openly request that the capitalist-imperialist countries show [us] kindness, calling on the bourgeois heads of state to show concern for the so-called human rights question in China." Another [constructive aspect of the article] is their stress that "how one views the 'human rights' question is related to the central issue of correctly understanding and differentiating between socialist and bourgeois democracy," among other things.

However, regarding how to treat the human rights slogan, and especially how to analyze and deal with the human rights question in a socialist society, Xiao's article contains some one-sided and simplistic views. For example, is it true that because the "human rights" slogan was raised by the bourgeoisie, we should conclude that "human rights is always a bourgeois slogan"? And is it true that because a handful of reactionary elements inside and outside China use "human rights" to attack the dictatorship of the proletariat and slander the socialist system, we should fundamentally deny that there are any "human rights problems" in a socialist society and rebuke those who raise the question of human rights by saying that they "desire the democracy and freedom of bourgeois individualism," and "want [China] to retrogress to a capitalist society"? These questions merit serious consideration and study. Following the guidance of Marxism and Mao Zedong Thought, [my] goal is to scientifically summarize our experience of the realization of the dictatorship of the proletariat, to correctly elucidate the human rights question, and to clarify all different mistaken ideas. This will have important, practical significance for advancing socialist democracy, strengthening the socialist legal system, protecting people's fundamental rights, consolidating the dictatorship of the proletariat, and realizing the economic construction [entailed by] the Four Modernizations.

After Xiao's article has investigated the historical background and class nature of the birth of the human rights slogan, he arrives at the following conclusion: "The 'human rights' slogan is always a bourgeois slogan." The fundamental thinking that is prominently expounded in the article is [the following]: the human rights slogan and [related] questions are always the product of bourgeois thinking, which is not in accordance with the interest of the proletariat and stands in opposition to socialism. Thus, Marxism should oppose the human rights slogan and the raising of human rights questions in each and every circumstance. . . .

We [will also] use the Marxist point of view to analyze the human rights question, [but we come to some different conclusions.] First of all, we must make an historical and class-based inquiry into the human rights slogan raised by the bourgeoisie. Although Xiao's article confirms the historical progressiveness of the human rights slogan raised by the bourgeois Enlightenment thinkers, it makes the sweeping generalization that "'human rights' is always a bourgeois slogan," and emphasizes that "China is a socialist country; we do not endorse the slogan 'struggle for human rights' that was raised by the bourgeoisie in the nascent capitalist period." This in fact is to lump together the bourgeois Enlightenment thinkers' human rights slogan, their human rights theory, and the bourgeois imperialist use of human rights to deceive people politically, which is not in accordance with an historical, class-based, and scientific analysis of the bourgeois human rights slogan.

Marx and Engels repeatedly proved that the bourgeoisie's raising of the human rights slogan took place in a new era, in order to break free from the fetters of feudal privileges and the divine right of kings. It was a manifestation in the intellectual and theoretical realm that aimed at sweeping away the obstacles to developing capitalism. [Human rights is] a product of capitalist production relations; the human rights proclaimed were prerequisites for defending capitalist private ownership. This was the historical limitation and class nature of bourgeois human rights theory. But from another point of view, since the rising bourgeoisie opposed feudalism, it also to some degree reflected the common desire of the majority of people. The human rights slogan and theory raised by early bourgeois Enlightenment thinkers thus also reflected the tradition of humankind's progressive thinking and we should take it as a precious spiritual legacy left to us by history. The human rights they raised stood in opposition to divine rights and privileges; this signified a great movement of the liberation of thought in human history. They advocated that everyone has the right to struggle for equality, liberty, and a happy life. Rousseau spent enormous energy discussing "the origin of inequality among people, its reasons, and the methods to conquer it." [Bourgeois Enlightenment thinkers] advocated ideas such as "people's sovereignty": if the ruler becomes a despot and violates people's rights, people have the right to overthrow the government and restore their "natural rights" (tianfu renquan). These [thinkers'] ideas had the notion of "natural rights" at their core, and even though this took a class-transcending, utopian form, those aspects of their thinking that put special emphasis on people's rights not only opened a new page in human history, but even today have their positive significance. We the proletariat uphold the historical materialist viewpoint; we do not exclude, and in fact even need to critically assimilate, any of humankind's progressive ideas. Just like the founder of Marxism assimilated the nucleus of Hegel's system of materialist philosophy, but added critical revisions: we should take a similarly scientific attitude toward bourgeois Enlightenment thinking about human rights, rather than a simplistic attitude of negation; still less should we conflate it with anti-socialist trends. We should "abandon the dross and select the essence," in order to critically carry on [the tradition of human rights].

Therefore, the bourgeoisie has its view of human rights, and the proletariat has its own view. We should rectify the monstrous lie of the bourgeoisie [which holds] that the bourgeoisie "shows concern" for human rights while we the proletariat, by contrast, do not raise the issue; that the bourgeoisie is "enthusiastic" about human rights but that the proletariat is afraid to speak of human rights. How can we accept this kind of distortion?

Looking back at the history of the proletariat's struggle against the bourgeoisie, we cannot confirm that "'human rights' is always a bourgeois slogan." It is exactly the opposite: we can only confirm that the proletariat has often raised the cry of "human rights" as a effective weapon in the struggle against imperialism and racism and against the landlord and bourgeois classes. During the period of democratic revolution led by the Communist Party—already in 1923 during the great strike of February 7—the slogans "struggle for freedom, struggle for human rights" were used. And during the second civil war of revolution, we also supported the China League for the Protection of Civil Rights organized by Cai Yuanpei, Song Qingling, Lu Xun, and others, which was very influential in advancing the uniting of progressive forces, both domestic and foreign, against Chiang Kai-shek. During the War of Resistance Against Japan, the famous "August Declaration" (1938) proclaimed by the Party also explicitly raised the slogan "fight for human rights and freedom." This was particularly true in the Party-led democratic base areas set up to fight Japan, wherein the "human rights" slogan served as an important guiding principle for the construction of the people's political power. Comrade Mao Zedong's 1940 article "On Policy" reads: "Concerning the rights of the people, it should be laid down that all landlords and capitalists not opposed to the War of Resistance shall enjoy the same human rights (renquan), property rights, and right to vote, and the same freedoms of speech, assembly, association, thought, and belief, as the workers and peasants" (Collected Works of Mao Zedong, vol. 2, p. 765).[1] In 1942, the government of the Shaanxi, Gansu, and Ningxia Border Region publicly announced that "Shaanxi, Gansu, and Ningxia will protect human rights and property rights" and clearly proclaimed that "the human rights and property rights of the people of the region will not be illegally violated."[2] . . .

Concrete analysis and research regarding the different human rights ideas and movements in the contemporary world is even more important [than these historical reflections]. Xiao's article says that the monopolistic bourgeoisie "at the same time as it continues to violently oppress [others], [nonetheless] wantonly proclaims 'human rights,' 'democracy,' and 'freedom' in order to deceive people, as a means to hegemony in the international arena, and in order to impede the Third World people's nationalist and revolutionary movements." This is not a complete description, however; it only reflects one facet of the larger picture. In reality, human rights has already become a universally valued political slogan of people the world over, and forms an important part of the content of the political struggle of every party and faction. We need to see that notwithstanding the imperialist nations' reactionary use of human rights to oppose the proletariat's revolution and the dictatorship of the proletariat, the proletariat is nonetheless struggling against the bourgeoisie in order to obtain more and complete human rights. In addition, there are the human rights for which Third World politicians and nationalists are struggling, which contain new contents informed by the opposition to imperialism, colonialism, and hegemonism. These developments are all in accordance with the historical tide of people of all nations fighting for social progress, political independence, economic development, and the protection of world peace. This tide of human rights has already broken through the narrow confines of the individualistic democracy and freedom of the bourgeoisie. It maintains that human rights are not only the rights and freedoms of individuals, but also include the rights and freedoms of classes and nationalities, which directly links the human rights question to struggles against class exploitation, national oppression, and racial discrimination, as well as against the growth, aggression, and economic exploitation of imperialism. We must, therefore, completely affirm that this [new] kind of human rights slogan has enormous progressive significance for the current struggle against hegemony and for the advancement of world peace. In 1955, Comrade Zhou Enlai attended the Bandung meeting [of the Non-Aligned Movement] as a representative of the Chinese government and people, and expressed his position in support of those nations' struggles for the realization of fundamental human rights. How can we say that human rights is only a slogan of the bourgeoisie?

If we say that in a capitalist system, the implementation of real human rights must give rise to irreconcilable contradictions within the system itself, and that in a socialist system, people's rights and personal freedoms receive complete protection, and [that socialism] also creates the conditions for further development and progress, then human rights are in complete conformity with the basic tasks of the proletarian construction of socialism and the consolidation of the dictatorship of the proletariat. Therefore, if we really believe in Marxism, we should also believe that paying attention to human rights, protecting human rights, and thoroughly realizing human rights are not things that can be accomplished by the bourgeois system, but [in fact] only by a socialist system. Does this mean that there are no human rights problems in a socialist society? Reality shows that we cannot say so.

Xiao's article starts from the premise that "human rights" is a bourgeois slogan, which [leads to its] treating [the above question] in a very one-sided way. The article emphasizes the fact that "the Chinese people already enjoy political power (*zhengquan*) and have realized both the dictatorship of the proletariat and socialist democracy." It then goes on to deny that human rights problems exist in a socialist society, and calls the invocation of human rights "an arrow without a target," without exception identifying [human rights] with the individualistic democracy and freedom of the bourgeoisie. This is detrimental to a genuine and thorough analysis of the problems and lessons that exist in our proletarian dictatorship.

We should be aware of the fact that the history of China's feudal society has been especially long; our transition to socialism took place on the foundation of a semi-feudal, semi-colonial system. Chinese society lacks a tradition of democracy, and although it has undergone a democratic revolutionary struggle under the leadership of the Party, the influence of many thousand years of feudalism cannot be totally erased. The effects are especially strong in thinking and ideology; they exist not only in society at large, but also in the inner circles of Party and state organs, reaching even some leading cadres. This is the case even after having entered the period of socialism. The bloody lessons of the ten-year, feudal, fascist dictatorship of the Gang of Four have made us realize that the effect on China of feudal despotism cannot be underestimated. The cancer of Lin Biao and the Gang of Four grew in this feudal soil. This kind of feudalistic and despotic thinking is even more backward and reactionary than bourgeois thinking. During the ten years when Lin Biao and the Gang of Four ran amok, the people's basic rights suffered serious damage. The Gang of Four has now been overthrown, but strengthening socialist democracy and the legal system and protecting people's rights in strict accordance with the constitution and the law will not be an easy task.

When raising the human rights question in a socialist society, we should not forget to criticize the individualistic democracy and freedom of the bourgeoisie, but even more important and basic is to root out the feudal, despotic ideas that "power makes the law" and "might makes right." We must thoroughly implement the important principle that "all people are equal before the law" and rule the nation by law; only then can we develop socialist democracy, defend the socialist legal system, and protect people's rights. . . .

Some comrades believe that the human rights slogan is "easily confused with bourgeois thought." This is completely unfounded. The bourgeoisie has raised many slogans and political concepts, such as democracy, freedom, and so on; can these not also be used by the proletariat after having been reformed and given a scientific meaning? Today, the human rights question has already become a political concept to which universal attention is paid; different international meetings and documents employ the "human rights" slogan with many different interpretations. We the proletariat ought to be especially concerned with human rights: we should research and boldly discuss human rights, use Marxism to elucidate every confusion and distortion, and clarify the proletariat's fundamental attitude toward and confirmation of human rights. Can this be called "confusing [human rights] with bourgeois thought"?

The proletariat is a thoroughgoing theorist of human rights. Its view of human rights is founded on the base of historically objective laws, which takes the reform of society as their goal and links social reform with the liberation of the individual. Marx and Engels, in *The Communist Manifesto*, countered the bourgeois attack on communism and criticized the false theory that equates eliminating class with eliminating "individual freedom" and "individuality," pointing out: "That which replaces the existing classes and the class antagonisms of the old bourgeois society should be a united structure where the development of freedom for one person is the condition for the development of the freedom of all" (*Collected Works of Marx and Engels*, vol. 1, p. 273). Marx and Engels both repeatedly commented on this important topic. In "Opposing Doolin," Engels wrote: "If all individuals do not achieve liberation, neither will society" (*Collected Works of Marx and Engels*, vol. 3, p. 333). In the first volume of *Das Kapital*, Marx said that the basic principle of the new society should be "the complete and free development of each individual" (People's Press, 1975, vol. 3, p. 649). But today there exists a one-sided understanding of Marxism, according to which communism opposes individual rights, the liberation of the individual, individual freedom, concern for human beings, and concern with material interests. This viewpoint takes the eliminating of class and the realization of human rights, which should be inseparably united, and puts them in opposition to one another. It was Lin Biao and the Gang of Four who spread this ultra-leftist view to create havoc and misrepresent and distort Marxism. . . .

As a new social order, socialism has gone through many twists and turns in its half-century of existence, but these were just interludes in the long process of historical development. It is an irrefutable law of history that socialism will triumph over capitalism; socialism represents the only hope for the liberation of humankind. The proletariat will shoulder the great historical task of eliminating classes and liberating humankind; it has as its major goal the development and construction of productive forces that will supersede those of the capitalist countries. It will step by step eliminate poverty, hunger, unemployment, national suppression, racial discrimination, wars of aggression, and all the other historical scourges of humankind. This is what Engels called making humankind "move from an animal to a real human existence," and "enter the new age in which humans will fulfill and create their own history." Are not Marxists armed with scientific communist thought the real, worthy, and thoroughgoing theoreticians of human rights? Therefore, on the great revolutionary banner of the elimination of class and the liberation of humankind, the words "implement genuine and complete human rights" should be written in large red letters.

Notes

1. For this article by Mao Zedong, see Text 29 in the present collection.
2. Other areas under the control of the CCP adopted similar regulations; see, for example, the regulations from the Shandong area, translated above as Text 28.

Further Reading

For another, more liberal article, see Xu Bing, "Lun renquan yu gongmin quan" [On Human Rights and Citizens' Rights], *Guangming ribao* (June 19, 1979).

45

Human Relationships, People's Rights, and Human Rights (1981)

Hang Liwu

"Renlun, minquan, yu renquan" [Human Relationships, People's Rights, and Human Rights], *Zhongyang ribao* (December 10, 1981). Reprinted in Chinese Association for Human Rights, ed., *Renquan lunwen xuanji* [Selected Essays on Human Rights] (Taipei, Chinese Association for Human Rights, 1982).

*Hang Liwu (1903–1991) studied at the University of Wisconsin and at the University of London. After returning to China, he spent some time teaching before becoming an official of the Nationalist government. In the 1940s, Hang served as a vice-minister of education and subsequently in the foreign service. When Taiwan in 1971 lost its position in the UN it became increasingly isolated internationally, which culminated with the American decision to establish diplomatic relations with the PRC and close its embassy in Taipei in 1979 . In the late 1970s, human rights became an important part of American foreign policy during the presidency of Jimmy Carter. To the GMD, the American human rights policy was at odds with its recognition of the PRC. These developments led Hang and others to establish, with government support, the Chinese Association for Human Rights in February 1979. One of the goals of the organization was to expose human rights violations on the mainland, but they also addressed domestic violations of human rights. Hang's piece translated here is certainly concerned with criticizing Communist excesses, but it also explores the compatibility between Confucian ideals and human rights. Even more striking is Hang's effort at reconciling Sun Yatsen's principle of people's rights (*minquan*) with the concept of human rights, an interpretation that is somewhat at odds with both Sun's own writings (see Text 18) and with the views of earlier GMD ideologists such as Zhou Fohai (see Text 20). This reveals that human rights, as Hang himself acknowledges, has become an idea which no society and no government can afford to ignore or dismiss.*

Human rights thinking (*renquan sixiang*) has existed in China since ancient times, but the term "human rights" came as a translation from the West. How is it that Chinese have taught of human relationships (*renlun*) and emphasized the way of humans (*rendao*) for thousands of years, but only in modern times have spoken of human rights? How is it that Chinese people believe that in the arena of human life, thinking about human relationships is at a higher level than the concept of human rights? How did the Father of our Nation [i.e., Sun Yatsen] assimilate human rights thinking into his principle of people's rights (*minquan zhuyi*)? In addition, how do people's rights and human rights differ from one another? If we have the principle of people's rights, do we still need to advocate human rights? Finally, what influence has the concept of human rights actually had in the international realm? Allow me to explain.

Human Relationships

Chinese culture has always put "humans" at its center, and it has always seen morality as of the first importance in [explaining] how to be a person (*zuo ren*) and how to regulate interpersonal relationships. Humans [follow] the "way of humans," and this way has its roots in human hearts, rather than being imposed from the outside. The three guiding principles of the *Great Learning* explain that the way to cultivate the self lies in manifesting bright virtue, in loving other people, and in stopping [only] at the highest goodness.[1] "Bright virtue" is something one finds within oneself and brings to light, starting with oneself and reaching out to others. A father's caring can make a son feel filial, just as a son's filiality can make a father feel caring. Mutual love leads to mutual caring, and mutual caring leads to even greater mutual love. When each person uses his or her virtue to engage in mutual love and mutual caring, this is the highest goodness. If human life can attain this highest goodness, what else is needed? As this principle is extended to the ordering of families, the governance of countries, and the pacifying of the world, it is natural to seek concord in society and Great Harmony (*datong*) in the world, with all following the way and coming together to form a unified whole; [in such circumstances,] there is certainly no need to rely on external coercion to force [people] to be this way.

Confucius said: "Lead them with virtue and regulate them by ritual, and they will acquire a sense of shame—and moreover, they will be orderly."[2] He also said: "In hearing lawsuits, I am no better than anybody else; what is required is to bring it about that there are no lawsuits."[3] When [his student] Zilu asked him about the gentleman (*junzi*), he responded: "He cultivates himself so as to produce assiduousness. [Zilu continued,] If he achieves this, is that all? [Confucius] said, He cultivates himself so as to ease the lot of others. [Zilu said, If he achieves this, is that all? [Confucius replied,] He cultivates himself so as to ease the lot of the Hundred Families."[4] The *Great Learning*'s "make the will sincere and correct the heart," "investigate things," and "extend knowledge" are all means to cultivate the self, order the family, govern the state, and bring bright virtue to all the world. The glorious developments that follow on cultivating the self—the so-called "inner sage and outer king" ideal—is the highest political philosophy of Confucianism.

Sun Yatsen[5] praised this, saying: "In ancient times, China had an excellent political philosophy. The passages in the *Great Learning* and the *Doctrine of the Mean* regarding investigating things, extending knowledge, making intentions sincere, rectifying knowledge, cultivating the person, ordering the family, governing the country, and pacifying the world: these had not yet been understood, nor expressed as clearly, by foreign political thinkers. This idea of beginning from an individual's inner [feelings] and extending them outward, of taking an individual's inner self as the starting point and ultimately reaching the pacification of the world: this is a unique treasure of our political philosophy and something that we should preserve."[6]

If we turn to the Confucian "Way of Kings" politics and look for its goal, we will find that it is gaining [the support] of people's hearts. Confucius said: "The people are the root of the state; when the root is secure, the state is at peace." The *Great Learning* explains the Way of governance: "That which the people like, like it; that which the people hate, hate it. This is called being a parent to the people."[7] It also says: "The Way: get the people, and this will get you the country. If you lose this Way, you will lose the country."[8] By the time this people-based (*min ben*) thought reached Mencius, it certainly had within it the lofty concept of human rights, as can be seen in his warning that: "The people are most valuable, after whom come the altars [of the gods]. Rulers matter least."[9]

The Chinese doctrine of the "people's hearts" has a fundamentally different starting point than the modern Western theory of human rights. Since Chinese thinking proceeds from inner to outer, extends the self to others, encourages voluntary benevolence, and seeks the well-being of the people, we can say that its goals are active. The principle of Western human rights lies rather in protecting and resisting, and its goals are thus passive. When human rights, which must rely on law and external coercion to achieve its goals, is compared to [Chinese] teachings about human relationships, which seek to regulate all inter personal relationships and seek a natural harmony, we can see that they even more [obviously] belong to two different realms.

Human Rights

Most people who discuss human rights take King John of England's being forced to sign the Magna Carta as the prelude [to the human rights era]. In fact, human rights thinking and terminology could already be found in the writings of the Greek philosopher Aristotle; it was in England, though, that the first efforts to actually institutionalize human rights took place. The Petition of Right of 1628 declared the importance of individual rights to freedom and recognized the inviolability of the people's right to private property; the Petition, together with the Bill of Rights of 1689, which prohibited the king from interfering in parliamentary legislation, were the harbingers of the right of today's legislators to speak with impunity. After this, in 1776 the American Declaration of Independence announced that "all men are created equal, [and] that they are endowed by their Creator with certain inalienable Rights"; together with the thirteen articles in France's 1789 Declaration of the Rights of Man, their mutual influence and successive impact ensured that the concept of human rights became deeply ingrained in people's hearts.

By the time of World War II, the many brutal atrocities committed by the Axis nations inspired the world's people to pay very serious attention to human rights. This led China, the United States, Britain, and the Soviet Union to jointly convene the Dumbarton Oaks Conference in 1944 in the outskirts of Washington D.C., where they drafted a plan for a future international organization and determined to protect human rights and fundamental freedoms. The next year, the San Francisco Conference passed the United Nations Charter, whose introduction said: "We the people of the United Nations [are] determined to save succeeding generations from the scourge of war, which twice in our lifetime has brought untold sorrow to mankind, and to reaffirm faith in fundamental human rights, in the dignity and worth of the human person, [and] in the equal rights of men and women and of nations large and small." On December 10, 1948, the UN passed the Universal Declaration of Human Rights, and in 1966 added the two human rights covenants. By 1976 enough countries had [officially] approved the two latter documents for them to go into force, from which we can see that there is an international consensus on the concept and substance of human rights.

If we ask where human rights comes from, [we will receive different answers.] The English philosopher Locke and the French philosopher Rousseau had their theories of innate (*tianfu*) or natural (*ziran*) human rights. On the other hand, utilitarians from Bentham to Mill believed that human rights were founded on utility, and modern idealists like Kant and Hegel thought that the origin of human rights lay in rationality (*lixing*). Contemporary sociologists, for the most part, hold that social needs are the cause of our promoting human rights. Although objectively speaking, these academic explanations are all different—even to the point of conflicting with one another—at one time or another, each has made a constructive contribution to the concept of human rights.

People's Rights

Sun Yatsen synthesized Chinese and Western cultures to create the principle of people's rights. On the one hand, he used the thinking about human relationships in Chinese traditional culture as his foundational understanding, and also added the spirits of the excellent examination and supervisory systems from China's past. On the other hand, he combined the best of Western democratic thinking and institutions, while simultaneously seeking to avoid those defects in freedom, democracy, and human rights. He used his keen intellect to create an original and complete political ideology and [corresponding] institutions: the Three Principles of the People and the Five Powers Constitution.

In Sun Yatsen's writings and lectures, he often raises human rights, even upon occasion quoting the saying "all people have innate human rights" (*tianfu renquan*), but he feels that they lack reliable grounds. Sun's characteristic way of distinguishing "people's rights" from "human rights" is that human rights emphasizes the protection of individuals, while people's rights emphasizes unifying the totality. As Sun was beginning to establish the Republic, he observed [the plight] of the people who were treated cruelly by warlords and Communists alike, which led him to raise the new slogan of "revolutionary rights." He said that, "The Nationalist Party's Principle of People's Rights is different from so-called 'innate human rights' . . . . The people who enjoy people's rights are only the citizens of the Republic; there is no need to extend this power (*quan*) to those who oppose the Republic, giving them the means to destroy it." Our former president Chiang [Kaishek] went a step further, maintaining that the Chinese Nationalist Party was a "revolutionary democratic party." President Chiang had a profound understanding of the view of life of the Three Principles of the People, which he summed up by writing: "The goal of life is to improve the lives of the totality of humanity. The meaning of life lies in creating life that can forever renew itself in the universe."

When Sun Yatsen and Chiang Kaishek took upon themselves the task of carrying on China's traditional culture while catching up with advanced civilizations, their commitment was to save the nation and benefit society, forgetting their smaller selves (*xiao wo*) to become their greater selves (*dawo*), and the scope of their "selves" broadened from the individual out to the collective, to the extent that the health and happiness of the country and nationality, and even the well-being of humanity, were all within the breadth of their vision. [This being the case,] one really cannot speak of them in the same breath with those whose starting point in struggling for human rights is seeking something for their own petty selves.

When we compare Sun's principle of people's rights with typical Western democratic politics, [we see that] naturally [the former] has some special traits. For instance, Sun recommends that power and ability (*neng*) be separated, so that the people have the power while the government has the ability. Where Western democracy has three simultaneous powers, Sun has a Five Powers Constitution: [Sun] does not accept the premise of mutual checks and balances, but rather has division of labor and cooperation as his goals. In addition, the principle of people's rights not only emphasizes the harmonization of individual and collective interests, but also pays heed to the appropriate coordination between freedom and safety and between democracy and efficacy. Finally, the principles of people's rights, nationality, and livelihood are genuinely interrelated; they need to be seen as a whole if we are to really appreciate the superiority of the Three Principles of the People.

Responding to Human Rights and Developing People's Rights

Given that we already have our unique principle of people's rights, do we really have a need to also advocate human rights? In today's world, as I have shown above, both the words "human rights" and its contents have been generally recognized the world over. Even Communist authorities, who [regularly] disregard or depreciate human rights as a pernicious vestige of the bourgeoisie, do not dare to completely ignore international censure concerning human rights; nor can they long ignore domestic demands from the people for human rights. Our principle of people's rights actually contains human rights consciousness (*renquan zhi yishi*), and we are in the midst of putting into effect democratic and constitutional politics. Despite the fact that we must continue to enforce martial law because of the need to defend against Communist invasion and to respond to various efforts at infiltration and subversion, we have already been able, over the last thirty years, to gradually expand and effectively carry out a variety of fundamental people's rights, including both public and private rights. It is obvious, therefore, that we do not have to avoid the subject of human rights.

In addition, our long-lived and profound Chinese culture has been able to absorb and assimilate many foreign ideas. For example, at one time the proselytizing of Buddhism [in China] was extremely vigorous, but after research and discussion by Chinese scholars, Indian Buddhism became sinified Buddhism, which not only did not cover over [the strengths of] Chinese culture, but actually increased the glory of Chinese culture. I deeply believe that Western democratic thought and its institutions, including the concept of human rights with its even more rich and beneficial contents, can serve as [examples] that we can use to improve the principle of people's rights. Their finest aspects can certainly be assimilated into our principle.

No democratic system in the world provides a perfect, flawless model [for others]. If we look at the famous British parliamentary system, [for instance,] we will see that it is in the last few decades [that] it has undergone an unprecedented test. Britain's Labour Party has very much been controlled by labor unions, and the legislation passed by the Labour governments have therefore for the most part been premised on [benefiting] the interests of workers, rather than reaching out to the wellbeing of all the people. Today a Conservative government wants to put restrictions on the power of labor unions. We have yet to see whether they will be successful, but even if they are temporarily successful, it will be difficult to ensure that the Labour Party does not regain political control in the future and reverse the current policies. From this example we can see that democratic institutions cannot be unalterable. At the same time, the future success of our Five Power Constitution will naturally provide an important point of reference for democratic institutions [around the world]. Its ideology and institutions combine the similarities and differences of people's rights with democracy, and people's rights with human rights, in ways that help to mutually inform and verify one another, and will certainly be of use [to others].

Still another [reason for taking human rights seriously] lies in our country's policy of opposing communism. The Chinese Communists are our great enemies with whom we cannot compromise, and they suppress human rights and have lost the hearts of their people. The core of our Three Principles of the People, by contrast, is developing people's rights and unifying the people's hearts. In order to oppose tyranny we should ever more strongly uphold people's rights, and we should happily accept and support the international consensus over the terminology and meaning of "human rights."

The UN has promoted human rights for several decades already; the International Bill of Rights has already gone into force; and the North Atlantic Treaty Organization (NATO), the European Community, and the Helsinki Conference [on Security and Cooperation in Europe] all without exception have made the development of human rights one of their central goals. In addition, the foreign policies of several important nations take the furtherance of human rights to be an important consideration—chief among these is the United States. Reagan's new government [wanted to] learn from the particular emphasis Carter placed on human rights while avoiding its excesses, and talked of making adjustments and adopting a more moderate approach, but this provoked criticism from the Congress and from media critics, and so [Reagan] is again putting emphasis on human rights. The meaning and significance of human rights has certainly penetrated deeply into the hearts of the world's people.

Given that we already have the principle of people's rights, do we need to also promote human rights? Our response to the international human rights movement, and the goal toward which we should diligently work, is the further development of people's rights!

Notes

1. *Great Learning* 1.
2. *Analects* 2:3; see E. Bruce Brooks and A. Taeko Brooks, trans., *The Original Analects* (New York: Columbia University Press, 1998), p. 110.
3. *Analects* 12:13; see Brooks and Brooks, trans., *The Original Analects*, p. 93.
4. *Analects* 14:42; see see Brooks and Brooks, trans., *The Original Analects*, p. 124.
5. Hang always refers to Sun as "Father of the Nation," but we now switch to "Sun Yatsen" for fluidity of translation.
6. *The Principle of Nationalism*, lecture 6.
7. *Great Learning* 10.
8. Ibid.
9. *Mencius* 14:14.

Part VII

The Late 1980s:
Before and After Tiananmen

46

The Origin and Historical Development of Human Rights Theory (1989)

Xu Bing

"Renquan lilun de chansheng he lishi fazhan" [The Origin and Historical Development of Human Rights Theory], *Faxue yanjiu* [Legal Research], no. 3 (1989).

In the late 1980s China entered a new stage in the debate on human rights. A more affirmative official position, as exemplified by official statements in support of the UDHR on the occasion of its fortieth anniversary, encouraged individual scholars who now dared to express more liberal and positive views of human rights. We here translate one of these relatively liberal articles, written by Xu Bing (b. 1951) of the Chinese Academy of Social Sciences. Xu Bing acknowledges that the issue of human rights has hitherto been taboo in China and that there are many misconceptions regarding the idea. He argues against those who see the concept of human rights as an exclusively bourgeois idea, lacking relevance and application to China. According to Xu, human rights refers to those rights that each human being ought to enjoy by virtue of his or her human nature. In contrast to the participants in the official debate of the late 1970s, Xu is prepared to acknowledge that human rights have a supra-class character. He also emphasizes that human rights are different from citizens' rights in that one cannot be deprived of them, as one could with citizens' rights.

Human rights (*renquan*) are rights (*quanli*) that each individual cannot do without for one moment; naturally, this is a most fundamental issue that concerns the whole of humankind. Although the theory of human rights was first raised by the bourgeoisie, the proposition in itself transcends the boundaries of class, nationality, race, and nation. Thus, as soon as human rights was raised, it became a common slogan of all of humanity, and a common banner under which all of humanity has called for subsistence (*shengcun*), development, and progress.

In the past, under the influence of extreme leftist ideas, we had great prejudices with respect to understanding the human rights question. On the one hand, as there had been great improvements of human rights since the founding of the new China, we unrealistically believed that there no longer existed any human rights problems, since the three great problems of imperialism, feudalism, and bureaucratic capitalism had been overcome and the Chinese people had become masters in their own home. On the other hand, since human rights was a slogan first raised by the bourgeoisie, we simply assumed without further analysis that it was a bourgeois slogan incompatible with proletarian revolutionary thinking. This kind of understanding led us to completely reject human rights. Enveloped as we were in extreme leftism, human rights became a taboo subject; no one dared to inquire into it, and violations of human rights repeatedly took place. During the Cultural Revolution, human rights were abused to an appalling degree. This could not help but cause people to reconsider human rights. After the overthrow of the Gang of Four, a few people again began to raise the slogan of the protection of human rights. Among these people there were of course quite a few who had a shallow or incomplete understanding of human rights, or even had a mistaken or confused understanding. What is regrettable is that at the time the official media did not undertake the necessary guidance, but [merely] issued a sharp warning against [human rights], describing it as a bourgeois slogan and not a slogan of the proletariat. To this day, our intellectual, legal, and political circles dodge this question or are coy about it, and do not dare to discuss it boldly and with confidence, so much so that when human rights are being discussed they become utterly uncomfortable. I believe that the banner of human rights belongs to all of humanity, and thus naturally to the Chinese people as well. Historically, the banner of human rights led humanity from barbarism to civilization, from a primitive level of civilization to a higher one, from autocracy to democracy, from the rule of man to the rule of law. We should continue to hold high the banner of human rights now and in the future, in order to march forward toward a better future for all of humanity. . . .

Human Rights and Citizens' Rights

The theory and realization of human rights already has seen a three-hundred-year-long history of development. By now the concept of human rights has a rich content. In order to precisely grasp human rights, we need first of all to analyze the content and precise meaning of human rights. Human rights first emerged [in the context of] single individuals —that is, humans in nature (*ziran ren*). In the beginning it referred to the individual rights of people. This kind of individual human rights can roughly be divided into three categories:

Rights of the Person (renshen quan)

The rights of the person are the most fundamental rights to be a person (*zuoren de zui jiben quanli*). The rights of the person are connected first of all with the rights to physical existence (*routi cunzai*), that is, the right to life (*shengming quan*). All people enjoy from birth the right to life, which is inviolable (the only exception being capital offenses laid down in the law and tried by the court). The right to health (*jiankang quan*), another fundamental right, is closely linked to the person; no person may suffer physical harm, and those who have been sentenced as criminals may not be corporally punished as a part of their penalty. Corporal punishment is a violation of human rights and should be forbidden by law. The right to freedom of the person is also inextricably linked with the physical body. No person may suffer arrest, detention, or restraint without due process of law. In order to protect the rights of the person, the criminal law lays down several important principles, for example the following: anything not expressly defined as a crime in the law may not be treated as a crime; retroactivity should not apply in criminal law; innocence is presumed; criminal penalties shall be regulated according to the law; the accused shall have the right to defend him- or herself and to receive the assistance of a lawyer; a distinction shall be made between accused and offenders; no one shall be compelled to confess or implicate him- or herself; no one may be sentenced for the same crime twice; children and minors may not be sentenced to death; and so on. Other examples include: humans may not be exposed to medical experiments without their consent; use of slave labor is forbidden; keeping people in bondage is forbidden; compulsory labor is forbidden, except in cases where people because of their crimes have been sentenced to compulsory labor. Another aspect of the rights of the person are the rights related to people's characters (*pinge*) and spirituality (*jingshen*). These include above all the right of personality (*renge quan*), which is the right of individuals not to have their personal dignity (*renge zunyan*) violated. Second are the rights to identity, to a name, to one's likeness, to one's reputation, to one's honor, to autonomy in marriage, and so on. The need to protect the rights of the person gives rise to the rights of personal security, which include the rights not to be illegally harassed, to freedom of correspondence, to privacy, to nonintrusion of one's home, and so on.

Political Rights and Freedoms

Political rights is another important category of fundamental human rights. They mainly refer to the right to participate in government and to vote and run for office; to the freedoms of speech, publishing, assembly, association, demonstration, religion and belief, and engagement in scientific and cultural activities; and to the rights to be informed about public and national affairs, to equality between the sexes, to broad equality before the law, and so on.

Economic, Social, and Cultural Rights

Economic, social, and cultural rights constitute the third category of fundamental human rights. They mainly refer to the rights to individual ownership of property, to employment, to unemployment insurance benefits, to equal pay for equal work, to education, to rest, to participate in labor unions, to receive social assistance in the event of injury, disability, sickness, or in old age, and so on.

The above three categories of rights are human rights that have the individual person as their basis; this is the traditional concept of human rights, which of course has been further developed in modern society. After World War II, collective rights were developed out of individual rights; they are "collective" as opposed to individual, since they indicate a type of right that is enjoyed by a certain category of people: they are rights that a group enjoys as a part of an entire collective. They mainly refer to the rights of women, children, the elderly, the handicapped, mothers (who have a right to special support from society during pregnancy and after birth), stateless people, refugees, children born out of wedlock, single mothers, minorities, and so on.

Human rights developed from individual rights to collective rights and subsequently to national rights (*minzu quan*). This was the result of the determined work of people in the Third World. The Third World believes that, although human rights are important, if national and state existence (*shengcun*) and development cannot be guaranteed, then human rights will come to nothing. Therefore, if we wish to affirm the protection of human rights, then we must first of all affirm and protect the rights of national and state existence and development.

For this reason, the Third World has used the form of international conventions to determine and standardize the rights to national self-determination (*minzu zijue quan*) and development as basic human rights. The two human rights covenants passed in 1966 guarantee the rights to national self-determination and development. This gave human rights a new life-force; it protected the rights to autonomy of weak and small nations and provided them with a weapon to oppose imperialism and colonialism. Human rights thus became a complete system of rights, consisting of the three parts of individual, collective, and national rights.

Another important change in the development of human rights is that in the early stage, their intrinsic (*guyou*) and inviolable (*buke qinfan*) nature was emphasized. Because violations of human rights were ubiquitous in feudal society and there was no protection of human rights, initial human rights demands concentrated on their inviolability and emphasized avoiding their external infringement. Then, as society developed, people gradually became aware that the realization of human rights requires certain social conditions, and especially material protection. For many human rights, emphasizing only their inviolability does not necessarily lead to their realization, especially where economic, social, and cultural rights are concerned. For example, how can one talk about the right to health if people do not even have food to eat? In order to truly realize human rights, people demanded that the state and society create the necessary conditions for people to enjoy the rights laid down in the law. People have labeled this effort a change from negative to positive human rights, and from passive to active human rights.

Above we have discussed the contents of human rights and their development. What is then the relationship between human rights and citizens' rights (*gongmin quan*)? The world today is a world with the individual country as its basic unit; the country is the fundamental organizational element. All people are subject to the restrictions of national boundaries; a true "citizen of the world" does not yet exist. In a world of many national borders, a person must first of all be a member of a given country, have the nationality of a given country, and be a citizen of a given country. (We will not discuss here either stateless people or refugees, who come into being due to special circumstances.) Humans in the abstract thus become specific people: Chinese, Americans, Japanese, and Koreans. Human rights is in itself first of all a legal concept; [it indicates] rights stipulated and protected by law. Human rights law refers in the first instance to domestic law—to the human rights stipulated and protected by the domestic laws of a certain country. Although internationally there are many international covenants that protect human rights, they must be concretely implemented by individual countries. The human rights that are stipulated by international law must be confirmed in domestic law by the states that are signatories to international covenants, otherwise they come to nothing. Human rights stipulated in domestic law take the concrete form of citizens' rights. Today, all civilized countries stipulate their respective citizens' rights in the form of constitutions and laws. Each state's citizens' rights are the human rights that its citizens may enjoy. Human rights take the form of citizens' rights; citizens' rights are the real form that human rights take.

However, human rights are not entirely the same as citizens' rights. Human rights refer to those rights that people should enjoy (*suo yingdang xiangshou de quanli*); citizens' rights refer to the rights that concrete people—citizens—enjoy in real life. Human rights are characterized by idealism. Citizens' rights are a concrete method to realize ideal human rights; they constitute the concretization, legalization, and realization of human rights. Human rights constitute the only basis for stipulating citizens' rights; citizens' rights should take the realization of human rights as their goal and human rights as a measure of their value. If they deviate from human rights, citizens' rights will inevitably become reactionary. For example, the principle of equal human rights is a fundamental principle of human rights, but South Africa's current laws mandate racial discrimination and unequal citizens' rights, which runs contrary to human rights.

There is often a gap between ideal and reality. There is also a gap between ideal human rights and real citizens' rights. Our elucidation above of the contents of human rights is based on the human rights defined according to the common standards of the UDHR and international conventions; they form humanity's common understanding of human rights. But if we say that internationally there are common standards for human rights, domestically citizens' rights differ from country to country. First of all, there are differences based on class. The ruling class which controls a state's organs of power always take as a priority the stipulation and protection of the citizens' rights of their own class, and they realize these rights at the cost of exploiting and limiting the citizens' rights of the ruled classes. Human rights should be equal, but real citizens' rights differ to the degree that classes are unequal. Furthermore, citizens' rights are subject to the restrictions of the economic, social, and cultural levels of society. People often cannot enjoy the human rights they ought to because of objective conditions. A country can only stipulate citizens' rights according to its concrete national situation (*guoqing*), so that differences between citizens' rights and the standards of human rights inevitably will result. If social, economic, and cultural levels of development are not taken into account and citizens' rights merely are copied from human rights, then citizens' rights will come to nothing and be as worthless as scrap-paper. For example, freedom of movement is an important human right, but China at its present stage does not yet have the conditions to make this right a reality. The constitution of 1954 stipulated this right, but the result was that [this commitment] could not be honored in reality. Of course, we should not deny the right itself just because we currently lack the conditions to fulfill it. On the contrary, we should affirm it, and actively create the conditions for its implementation.

Regarding the question of how to deal with foreigners or stateless people, there are obvious differences between human rights and citizens' rights. A state's citizens' rights only apply to its citizens, but naturally not to foreigners. For the latter we must reach beyond the confines of citizens' rights and directly apply the principle of human rights. Today people of different countries are coming into contact more and more often, so this question is being raised with increasing frequency. Wars between states have given rise to humanitarian concerns, such as the humane treatment of prisoners of war; in this context as well, it is not citizens' rights that set standards for their treatment but rather a direct application of human rights principles. From this it becomes obvious that human rights and citizens' rights are connected concepts that also have differences; they cannot be substituted one for the other, nor can they be set in direct opposition, but must be allowed to exist side by side.

The Class and Supra-class Nature of Human Rights

The world's different classes, political parties, nations, and individuals have somewhat different understandings of human rights, and their aims in discussing human rights are also not identical; each different view of human rights can bear the mark of a different class. But the human rights concept itself is a concept that transcends class. The "human" under discussion here is the abstract human being, which refers to all people, as characterized by their human physiology, without regard for differences of class, race, color, language, religion, property, educational level, or citizenship. In other words, the word "human" here refers to humans in their classless biological and social sense.

Human rights in its original sense refers to the affirmation of the rights of humans as defined above. Regardless of what their subjective motives were and of whether they intentionally were aiming at cheating people, the early bourgeois revolutionaries and thinkers, at least on paper, were very clear about one thing: human rights are rights to be enjoyed by all people. Human rights come with birth (*yu sheng julai*), and are not granted by any person, state, government, or law. Some went so far as to profess that human rights were not even given by God but were enjoyed by humans on the grounds of their characteristics as humans (*ren de zige*); they were purely a kind of natural (*tianran*) and inherent (*guyou*) right. It was precisely in light of this that [such thinkers] claimed that human rights were inviolable (*buke boduo*); since they were not granted by anyone, they could not be violated by anyone, not even by God. [The idea that everyone enjoyed human rights from birth] was also their basis for saying that human rights could not be given up by anyone: since human rights were not taken on by any individual of their own volition, they could not be thrown away. Human rights were also [claimed to be] inalienable (*buke rangdu*). No individual had taken them up by him/herself, so no individual could transfer them to another person. Human rights were [regarded as] attached to one's personality (*renge*).

It has been three hundred years since bourgeois thinkers first began to advocate human rights, and human rights theory and practice have been greatly developed. Today almost all civilized nations have laws which, at least on paper, guarantee the rights people have from birth until death, [including] equal rights, equality before the law, the inviolability of personal dignity, and protection from arrest and detention without due process of law. That is to say that the human rights demanded by the bourgeoisie in the early period have achieved affirmation and realization—at least verbally—in all countries, and are reflected in the laws of all countries.

China is no exception to this rule; especially after the painful lessons of the Cultural Revolution, our constitution and laws have solemnly guaranteed the fundamental standard of various human rights. The 1982 constitution stipulates: "All people who are nationals of the PRC are citizens of the PRC." The 1980 law on Chinese citizenship states that "if one or both of a person's parents are citizens of China, and the person is born in China, then that person is a Chinese national." That is to say, the characteristic of a Chinese citizen is chiefly based on the fact that he or she is of Chinese blood and was born in China. A child with Chinese blood naturally enjoys Chinese citizenship from birth and thus has the characteristics of a Chinese citizen, regardless of his or her class attributes or [subsequent] political behavior. China's civil law also stipulates that, "from birth to death, citizens have civil (*minshi*) rights" and "all citizens' civil rights are equal before the law." China's constitution also states that "the personal dignity of citizens shall not be violated." The conception of citizen and person indicated here clearly transcends class. In other words, even people who are class enemies (*jieji diren*) must be acknowledged as Chinese nationals; their characteristics as Chinese citizens and civil rights equal to other citizens must be acknowledged, and their personal dignity must be protected.

The principle of humanitarian treatment of prisoners of war is to an even greater degree based on the principle that human rights transcend class. A prisoner of war may well be the arch-criminal of an unjust war, a butcher who has killed people like flies, but as soon as he has surrendered or has been taken prisoner, he must receive humanitarian treatment based on human rights. There are two kinds of wars, civil wars and wars between states. Prisoners of war in wars between states are not citizens to be treated on the basis of citizens' rights: they are protected on the basis of human rights that transcend class and nationality. This kind of human rights has no class nature to speak of at all.

Humanitarian treatment of suspects and offenders is also a legal principle of every civilized nation, and reflects the level of every nation's legal culture and overall social civilization. After the damage of the Cultural Revolution, China's legal system once again reaffirmed the principle of legal humanitarianism. Whether a person is a great class enemy, or a criminal who murders without pity and deserves to be sentenced to death, we should still protect his or her personal dignity and treat him or her with basic humanitarianism, rather than with wanton cruelty, before the execution. Even if such a person is to be executed, only methods of execution stipulated by the law should be used. Some countries execute by hanging, others by electrocution, while China executes by shooting. We cannot use the methods of "a thousand knives and ten thousand dismemberments" for which the Gang of Four clamored. Even [the method of execution] should be subject to human rights considerations. The basic human rights of criminals whose crimes do not merit execution should be protected even more strongly.

The above analysis shows that the supra-class nature of human rights is very obvious. To deny the supra-class nature of human rights, to emphasize its class nature blindly, to grant human rights only to the people and not to the enemy: all this leads to the error of rejecting human rights altogether and results in the violation of human rights. Ever since the appearance of classes there has been class oppression and class differences. Humans then no longer existed in the abstract, but belonged to a certain class. Class differences and inequalities, and tensions between classes, have naturally left deep marks on human rights. The bourgeoisie early on had their fill of feudal oppression and began to call loudly for human rights; but as soon as they had seized the reins of power, the first thing they paid attention to was their own rights. Many of the human rights protected by law thus came to be the special privileges of the bourgeoisie. On paper, they stipulated that people enjoy rights equally, but because they held the reins of power and the means of production, in reality only the bourgeoisie could enjoy those rights to the fullest. Even the bourgeoisie themselves admitted that equal rights was only a slogan and an ideal, a goal which could never be reached. As to the class essence of human rights, it was early on unmasked by the great teachers Marx, Engels, Lenin, and Mao Zedong. We can say that in China this is all self-evident, and this author has nothing new to add to the discussion.

Generally speaking, in actual law human rights have a distinct class nature and an obvious supra-class nature. One cannot emphasize one and neglect the other. At the present, we must mainly guard against the leftist viewpoint and the leftist heritage with which the Cultural Revolution has left us. China is a country with a tradition of feudal autocracy. A prominent characteristic of autocracy is to ignore human rights and to act with utter disregard for human life. The victory of our revolution is only forty years old; the customs and evil legacy of feudalism still persist. If one stirs up "leftist" thinking, the dregs [of our feudal inheritance] can rapidly spread and human rights abuses become rampant.

The Cultural Revolution was a representative lesson. At that time, Lin Biao and the Gang of Four noisily advocated intense class struggle, calling for total dictatorship and labeling democracy, freedom, equality, fraternity, and human rights as "bourgeois." Again and again they called for ruthlessness against class enemies; the more ruthless one was, the more revolutionary. The more ruthless one's position was and the firmer one held it, the more clear one's purpose. Another reason for human rights violations was that mercy toward enemies was said to signify cruelty to the people, thus the greater the cruelty to an enemy, the better, and mercy was forbidden. The result was that barbaric behavior was rampant in the whole of China. The methods of abusing individuals and violating personal dignity became fiercer over time. Human nature (*renxing*) was ruined, morality retrogressed, violence was accepted, humanitarianism was criminalized, and human rights were [declared] reactionary. No matter how much hatred of class enemies was expressed, or how much savagery was used against them, it was not seen as excessive. In order to assuage the "people's wrath" [against class enemies], no matter what kind of torture, it was not seen as excessive! That was a dark page in humanity's history!

Recalling these painful experiences, we should reaffirm human rights and correct the mistaken idea that human rights is a slogan of the bourgeoisie and not of the proletariat. We cannot reject human rights because it was first raised as a slogan by the bourgeoisie. How many new slogans and concepts did the bourgeoisie initiate? Should we reject them all? Just because the bourgeoisie is hypocritical with regard to one aspect of human rights, we cannot write off the authentic nature of the bourgeois human rights movement, nor deny its great, historically progressive significance. We have already explained that human rights are the fruit of humanity's civilized development, which cannot be attributed solely to the bourgeoisie. In the same way, we should not totally deny human rights just because Marx, Lenin, and Mao Zedong criticized the theory and reality of bourgeois human rights. On the contrary, we should affirm human rights and express our own view of human rights. In fact, Marx himself did not completely deny human rights. He said that human rights is the most common form of rights. All of a person's rights can be described as human rights. Human rights is the most common name for rights; it has already become an established form of expression. Human rights should become the starting and reference point for all of humankind's activities.

We must also gauge the precise nature of China's human rights situation. Internationally, China has persistently respected human rights, and actively participated in all of the UN's activities to advance and protect human rights. During the period when China opposed the Americans and aided the Koreans [i.e., the Korean War], the war of self-defense against Vietnam, and the border war of self-defense against India, we were completely respectful of human rights, and waged war in a humanitarian way. We have always protected the human rights of foreign visitors, foreigners who live in China, and foreign investors in China. In order to protect the rights of international refugees, China has also done a great deal and made considerable sacrifices. This has all been commonly acknowledged and praised by the international community.

Domestically, China's human rights situation has been steadily improving. The citizens' rights which are guaranteed in the constitution and in the legal system basically meet the common standards of human rights of the UN. The human rights enjoyed by Chinese today cannot be compared with the situation before liberation. With the Third Plenum of the Eleventh Central Committee, Chinese citizens' rights developed considerably. For example, the inviolability of personal dignity was guaranteed for the first time in the 1982 constitution. However, we cannot overlook the divergence between laws and real life. Many citizens' rights that are guaranteed in laws and in the constitution remain on paper and are never fully enjoyed. The feudal tradition of ignoring human rights dies hard and violations of human rights still often occur; some of them truly shocking. In February 1989, the *People's Daily* had a story about a peasant who, because he suspected another peasant of stealing his horse, lost all sense of reason and killed the man he suspected with a knife. Before the murder he was cheered on by forty onlookers, both adults and children. There are some cadres who intentionally or unintentionally use or abuse their authority to violate human rights. One example is the case of the three lawyers in Liaoning who were held illegally for four years. We should consciously acknowledge that this kind of violation of human rights cannot be stamped out in a year or two. We should approach China's human rights problems with the attitude of "seeking truth from facts"; this is advantageous and cannot be harmful. Actually, any country, no matter how enlightened its government and how perfect its legal system, cannot at times avoid some violations of human rights; otherwise there would be no need to discuss human rights. For historical reasons, human rights is a rather foreign concept to the Chinese people; we need a broad, deep, and long-term movement for enlightenment about human rights, so that the Chinese people consciously can raise the banner of human rights together with the rest of humanity.

Further Reading

For another article representing the new, more liberal view of human rights in the late 1980s, see Yu Keping, "Renquan yinlun: jinian Faguo 'Ren yu gongmin quanli

xuanyan' xiang shi 200 zhounian" [An Introduction to Human Rights: Commemorating the 200th Anniversary of the French "Declaration of the Rights of Man and
the Citizen"], *Zhengzhixue yanjiu*, no. 3 (1989): 30–35.

47
Open Letter to Deng Xiaoping (1989)

Fang Lizhi

Originally sent on January 6, 1989, the letter is translated in Fang Lizhi, *Bringing
Down the Great Wall: Writings on Science, Culture, and Democracy in China* (New
York: Norton, 1990), pp. 242–43.

*Fang Lizhi (b. 1936) is a leading expert in astrophysics and cosmology, but along-
side his academic work he has throughout his life taken a strong interest in more
philosophical and political issues. Fang's first serious brush with the Chinese authorities came in 1957 during the anti-rightist movement, when he was criticized for
advocating reform of China's educational system and was expelled from the Party.
He was allowed to continue to work in his field, however, until the eruption of the
Cultural Revolution in 1966. Like so many other scientists and academics Fang was
then branded as reactionary, "struggled against," and "sent down" to the countryside to do manual work. Although he was allowed to resume teaching as early as
1969, when he was transferred to the University of Science and Technology in Hefei,
Anhui province, full rehabilitation did not come until 1978. In the 1980s Fang made
a name for himself as an outspoken critic of bureaucratism and lack of academic
freedom within the educational system. He did not confine himself to the educational field, but also addressed more political issues in speeches and lectures on
campuses around the country. The experiences of the Cultural Revolution served to
make Fang critical of the Party, and he was among the first in China to openly
question communism. When student demonstrations erupted in 1986, beginning at
Fang's university, it was inevitable that he would become a target in the campaign
against "bourgeois liberalization" that was launched in response. Fang lost his
position and was once again expelled from the Party. But far from being silenced,
Fang continued to discuss democracy and human rights in interviews with foreign
journalists. Fang strongly defends the idea that human rights are universal, and is
highly critical of any references to "China's unique characteristics" when it comes
to the implementation of human rights. In January 1989, Fang wrote an open letter
to Deng Xiaoping, reprinted here, in which he called for the release of Wei Jingsheng.
This was the first time a member of the intellectual establishment publicly demanded
the release of a political dissident. The letter created something of a stir and inspired other intellectuals and scientists to follow suit with open letters in support.
Although Fang and his wife Li Shuxian did not take active part in the 1989 democracy movement, they were later singled out as masterminds behind it. After having*

spent one year in the sanctuary of the American embassy in Beijing after the crackdown, they were allowed to leave the embassy and their country and are now living in exile in the United States.

Central Military Commission Chairman Deng Xiaoping:

This year is the fortieth anniversary of the founding of the People's Republic of China, and the seventieth anniversary of the May Fourth Movement. Surrounding these [events] there will no doubt be many commemorative activities. But beyond just remembering the past, the many of us even more concerned with the present and the future look to these commemorations to bring with them new hope.

In view of this, I would like to offer my sincere suggestion that on the occasion of these two anniversaries, a nationwide amnesty be declared, especially including the release of political prisoners such as Wei Jingsheng.

I believe that, regardless of how Wei Jingsheng is judged, his release after serving ten years of his sentence would be a humanitarian act that would improve the atmosphere of our society.

This year also happens to be the two-hundredth anniversary of the French Revolution. From any perspective, the ideas of liberty, equality, fraternity, and human rights (*renquan*) that the French Revolution symbolizes have won the respect of people all over the world. In this light, let me again express my earnest hope that you will consider this suggestion, and thus demonstrate even more concern for our future.

Sincerely, and with best wishes,
Fang Lizhi

Further Reading

For open letters sent off in support of Fang's appeal, see Fang Lizhi, *Bringing Down the Great Wall*, pp. 305–8. For Fang's view on human rights, see in particular "Patriotism and Global Citizenship," "China's Despair and China's Hope," and "Keeping the Faith," all translated in ibid.

48
Declaration of Human Rights (May 1989)

Chinese Human Rights Movement Committee, Beijing

Originally published around May 20, 1989. Reprinted in *Zhongguo minyun yuan ziliao jingxuan: dazibao, xiaozibao, chuandan, minkan* [Carefully Selected Original Documents from China's Democracy Movement: Large- and Small-Character Posters, Handbills, and Unofficial Publications] (Hong Kong: October Review Publishing House, November 1989), 2:92. Translated in Suzanne Ogden et al., *China's Search for Democracy: The Student and the Mass Movement of 1989* (Armonk, NY: M.E. Sharpe, 1992), pp. 280–81.

Despite Fang Lizhi's open letter demanding the release of Wei Jingsheng and respect for human rights (see Text 47 above), explicit human rights rhetoric did not figure much during the democracy movement that broke out in April 1989 after the death of Hu Yaobang, the disgraced former head of the CCP. This said, however, it is still true that demands for freedom of speech and publication constituted some of the central ideas of the movement. In some cases human rights ideas were also more explicitly discussed, as in the statement reprinted below. The drafters lamented the ignorance and neglect of human rights in Chinese society, a view shared by Xu Bing, writing around the same time in a more academic context (see Text 46 above). Many speakers and demonstrators made quite conscious references to the spirit of May Fourth and its ideals of human rights, democracy, and modernization. In the opening words of the statement below we thus hear a clear echo of Chen Duxiu's views from seven decades earlier (see Texts 10 and 11).

In view of the widespread ignorance and neglect of, or even apathy toward, human rights in Chinese society; in view of several thousand years of cruel interference in and infringement of human rights by our rulers; and in view of the need to create a new society, a new order, and a new morality, we hereby solemnly declare the following to be the inviolable and inalienable natural rights of human beings:

1. Everyone is born free and equal, regardless of origin, status, age, sex, professional level of schooling, religion, party affiliation, and ethnicity.
2. The rights to life and security, and to oppose oppression, are humankind's inalienable natural rights.
3. There are no crimes of conscience. Everyone has freedom of speech, writing, publication, and advocacy.

4. . . . Everyone has the freedom to believe or not believe in a religion or in various theories [such as Marxism].

5. . . . Everyone has the right to travel and to reside inside or outside the country.

6. Personal dignity shall not be infringed on because of criminal conviction.

7. The individual has the right to privacy. One's family, domicile, and correspondence are protected by law.

8. Everyone has the right to education. Higher education should be open to everyone based on achievement scores.

9. Private property acquired through one's [own] labor is sacred and inviolable.

10. Freedom of marriage between adult men and women shall not be interfered with by any outside force. Marriage must be voluntarily agreed upon by both parties.

11. Everyone has the right to assembly and association, whether openly or secretly.

12. The power of the government comes from the people. In the absence of free elections . . . , the people may rescind any power usurped either by force or under the guise of the will of the people by any individual or group (including any of the political parties).

13. Everyone has the right to either direct or indirect participation in government (through free elections of representatives).

14. The law is the embodiment of the popular will and cannot be changed arbitrarily by one individual or any one political party. Everyone is equal before the law.

15. The army is the defender of the interests of the people and of the state. It must strictly observe neutrality in political affairs and not [be subordinate to] an individual or a political party.

16. Democracy and freedom are the basic guarantees of social stability, people's well-being, and national prosperity. Therefore, each person has the right and the duty to establish and safeguard such a system and to oppose autocracy and tyranny.

Further Reading

For additional texts and documents by students and others from the movement, apart from Ogden et al., see Han Minzhu, ed., *Cries for Democracy: Writings and Speeches from the 1989 Chinese Democracy Movement* (Princeton, NJ: Princeton University Press, 1990). For a very useful and informative account of the movement, see Craig Calhoun, *Neither Gods nor Emperors: Students and the Struggle for Democracy in China* (Berkeley: University of California Press, 1994).

49
Who Are the True Defenders of Human Rights? (July 1989)

Shi Yun

"Shei shi renquan de zhenzheng hanweizhe?" [Who Are the True Defenders of Human Rights?], *Renmin ribao* (July 7, 1989).

In the immediate post–June Fourth period the Chinese leadership quickly voiced concerns about the use—or as they preferred to describe it, abuse—of human rights slogans during the democracy movement. At a national conference on propaganda in July 1989, President Jiang Zemin remarked that since young people were attracted to the concept of human rights, it was of vital importance to promote a Marxist analysis of human rights to counteract any bourgeois influences. The government's urgency to grasp the human rights issue was further underlined by the fact that human rights had now become an important and problematic issue in China's relations with the international community as China faced strong criticism for its suppression of the democracy movement. The Chinese authorities regarded the critique and sanctions imposed by Western governments as constituting interference in China's internal affairs. Human rights, they argued, was only being used by the West as a weapon in its strategy of "peaceful evolution": the policy of trying to subvert the socialist system in China. As the article translated here reveals, China no longer simply dismissed human rights as a bourgeois slogan, but instead tried to portray itself as the true defender of human rights. In this context it based its arguments on a selective reading and interpretation of international human rights standards.

The clamor of calls "demanding human rights" that once flooded the capital has grown quiet following the suppression of the rebellion [i.e., the events of June 4, 1989]. All fair-minded people can without doubt answer, based on their personal experiences, who really are the defenders of human rights and who are the violators. A major theoretical task today is to undertake an analysis of the human rights question based on reasoned thought and legal points of view, in order to reveal what the evil forces of those inside and outside China who hide beneath "human rights" are really all about.

Human rights arose from modern bourgeois enlightenment thinkers' critique of the medieval feudal system and its special privileges. These [thinkers] believed that people have certain "innate" (*tianfu*) fundamental rights. In the present century, especially after the experience of the two world wars, the international community has begun to pay special attention to human rights. In 1948, the United Nations General Assembly adopted the first international human rights legal document, the Universal Declaration of Human Rights. As a significant number of colonies gained independence, international human rights theory has continued to be imbued with new content. In 1966, the UN adopted the International Covenant on Civil and Political Rights and the International Covenant on Economic, Social, and Cultural Rights, which stipulated the rights of national self-determination and control over natural wealth and natural resources. This placed collective human rights (*jiti renquan*) in a [newly] important position and created a breakthrough in the traditional Western bourgeois human rights concept, which had the individual as its basic unit.

In 1986, thanks to the Third World nations' untiring efforts, the UN passed the Declaration on the Right to Development, which affirmed the rights of nations to use their own economic culture, wealth, and natural resources to develop without interference. The concept of collective rights then reached a new level of development. In addition, the UN has passed a number of resolutions, declarations, and conventions opposing colonialism, racism, and so on. Over the past forty years, the international human rights question has constantly changed and developed so that human rights is no longer a Western-patented product but rather reflects the demands and aspirations of a broad range of developing countries.

The Chinese government has consistently paid close attention to the question of human rights. Internationally, it has always affirmed and supported all the work and efforts done by the UN to protect human rights. China has signed seven international human rights conventions and has energetically performed its obligations. The Chinese government has always given distinctive moral support and all possible assistance to developing nations in their opposition to hegemony, colonialism, racism, foreign aggression and occupation, and the unjust economic order, in order to help Third World nations to develop their national economies; this has earned China high praise from the international community.

Domestically, the Chinese people, under the leadership of the Chinese Communist Party, have taken the road of socialism, which is the fundamental prerequisite for the realization of both individual and collective human rights. The constitution and laws that China has adopted thoroughly protect all the basic political, economic, cultural, educational, religious, and personal rights, as well as rights pertaining to women, children, the elderly, and social welfare. Already during the early days of its founding, our country eliminated the evils left by the old society, such as prostitution, drug addiction, trafficking in human beings, and arranged marriages. In 1959, the government thoroughly eliminated the barbaric and cruel system of peasant serfdom in Tibet, which enabled millions of serfs to throw off the shackles that bound them for life and obtain the right to be their own masters. China has also spared no efforts to develop the economy, culture, and education of every ethnic minority in order to raise their economic and cultural levels and make them equal members in the great family of the motherland. At the Third Plenum of the Eleventh Central Committee, China adopted the grand goal of realizing the Four Modernizations, and upheld the Four Cardinal Principles and the policies of reform and opening-up. The aim [of these several policies] is to more completely bring into play the intrinsic superiority of the socialist system, so as to develop the productive forces of society and raise the level of the people's material culture and standard of living. This, fundamentally speaking, is a sign of the further protection of the Chinese citizens' human rights.

Of course, the legal protection of the Chinese citizens' rights is still not perfect; a few problems remain with respect to the protection of human rights. Especially during the ten years of turmoil [i.e., the Cultural Revolution], everyone from the Party Chairman down to the common people suffered violations of their basic human rights; the laws of the nation ceased to exist and the national economy was on the verge of collapse. These [events] have given us some very painful lessons. After the Third Plenum of the Eleventh Central Committee, China has worked hard to develop socialist democracy and perfect the socialist legal system so that [these problems can be resolved].

Today, protection of human rights in China is still not completely satisfactory. Some evil habits that violate human rights, which had already disappeared, have now reappeared in a few regions; [these include] prostitution, marriages based on buying and selling, and the use of child labor. Thus, we need to further strengthen socialist democracy and the construction of a legal system, so that through democratic and legal methods, human rights will be even more conscientiously protected.

Human rights are concrete rather than abstract and relative rather than absolute. Both the concrete stipulations in each country's laws regarding citizens' rights (*gongmin quanli*), and the actual situation of citizens' rights in real life, are constrained by the country's political system, economic relations, cultural traditions, habits and customs, and many other factors. Thus, there is no and can be no universally applicable or abstract model of human rights for all of humanity; citizens' rights can only be concrete and real. At the same time, the legal protection of citizens' rights must also follow these general restrictions on rights. When realizing his or her rights, a citizen may not harm the interests of another person or of society. Thus, human rights can only be relative and restricted, and not absolute and unrestricted. To try to achieve rights without duties is an unrealistic fantasy.

During the [recent] counterrevolutionary rebellion, an extremely small minority of the people called for absolute, abstract human rights, and ignored the constitution and laws to incite illegal class boycotts, demonstrations, sit-downs, and hunger strikes, which seriously disturbed the normal studies, work, and lives of others. They furthermore used vicious methods, attacking and even killing members of the PLA and the Military Police. Where were democracy and human rights in all this? The handful of ruffians calling for "democracy" and "human rights" were in fact thoroughly opposing democracy and human rights. They raised a cry of "patriotism," but were in fact maintaining illicit relations with foreign countries. Their goal was to replace our socialist people's republic with a bourgeois republic.

The use of the banner of protecting human rights to pose as a "human rights defender" in order to interfere in other countries' internal affairs is a common tactic of some Western countries, especially the U.S.A. The American government and Congress's use of "defending human rights" as a pretext for interference in China's internal affairs during the whole process of suppressing the turmoil and rebellion is only the most recent example of this tactic. After the outbreak of the turmoil, the U.S. president pledged countless times "to support China's demonstrating students in their demands for freedom of speech and peaceful assembly, including the right to peaceful resistance and self-expression." [He also said that,] "the United States will do whatever it can to encourage people in China and other countries who are seeking democracy." The Congress passed a resolution in support of the so-called "democracy movement" and loudly called for China to "establish a political system that protects fundamental human rights, freedoms, and openness." On June 4, after China took decisive measures to suppress the counterrevolutionary rebellion, the American government, shamed into anger, was the first to call for sanctions to increase the pressure on China. After China, in accordance with the law, executed eleven of the worst thugs of the rebellion, the United States called for the "suspension" of exchanges of high-level officials between the two countries and wanted international financial institutions to "delay" loans to China. This was a thinly veiled effort to intimidate China and interfere in our internal affairs.

America's theoretical basis for interfering in China's internal affairs in the name of human rights is the idea of the "international protection" of human rights. Whether human rights is to be considered a subject for "international protection" or for "an individual country's jurisdiction" should be treated in accordance with specific situations and differences. All interference with other countries' rights to national self-determination, development, and individual human rights, based either on the new or the old imperialism and hegemonism, belong to the [realm] of international problems, and should be met with condemnation and opposition from the international community.

Whenever there are acts . . . of racial discrimination, apartheid, genocide, or slave-trafficking, or of the large-scale creation, expulsion or abuse of refugees, or whenever there are terrorist activities, they should be considered as international crimes of human rights violations that should be forbidden; for other countries to take measures to curb such acts is in accordance with international legal principles. However, when it comes to respect for citizens' rights, protection of minorities, women, and children, and punishment of criminal elements in accordance with the law, these all fall within the scope of domestic law of sovereign nations. As matters considered to be within domestic jurisdiction, no other country or international organization can formally interfere. Thus, no matter whether it is China's so-called "Tibet question," the legally passed sentence of the counterrevolutionary element Wei Jingsheng, or the suppression of the counterrevolutionary rebellion, they all fall clearly within the "realm of domestic jurisdiction," and the United States has no right to use the excuse of the human rights question to intervene.

America makes indiscriminate criticisms in the area of human rights everywhere as though it is the sole real defender of human rights. Thus, we might as well look at the reality [of these claims]. People all over the world still remember well the notorious anti-Communist and anti-Chinese bills of the McCarthy era. In the 100 years since the declaration of the emancipation of black slaves, serious discrimination against blacks and people of color has continued to exist in the United States. When American workers have exercised their rights and freedoms of speech, assembly, association, and demonstration and thereby threatened the monopoly of the capitalist system, the U.S. government has, in cases too numerous to mention, viciously repressed them with military troops and police forces.

In external affairs, in its self-appointed capacity as "world policeman," the United States has supported the apartheid regime in South Africa, outrageously sent troops to invade Korea, Vietnam, Grenada, and many other sovereign states, and has never ceased to carry out its violent interference and activities subversive of other countries' domestic affairs. This is the true face of America as "defender of human rights." What right does it have to lecture China on human rights?

What is America's real goal when showing such concern for China's "human rights problems"? The secret is revealed by Larry Diamond, one of the two editors-in-chief of the *Journal of Democracy*, published by the congressionally supported National Endowment for Democracy. He said that: "America's prime aim with respect to Communist countries in the movement to support human rights and democratization is to allow democratic elements in those countries to form networks in order to establish independent publications, labor unions, enterprise associations, and other organizations in order to break the Party and government's monopoly in the areas of news, organizations, and power, as well as to reduce the state's sphere of power so as to finally take political power." The plan revealed by this adviser matches closely the activities and program of the small minority involved in the counterrevolutionary rebellion in China. From this it is not hard to understand that America uses human rights as a pretext for interfering in China's internal affairs so as to pressure the Chinese government to recognize as legal such illegal organizations as the autonomous Federation of Students and the Autonomous Federation of Workers, with the malevolent aim of overthrowing the leadership of the Chinese Communist Party and changing our socialist system.

This effort, however, is completely futile. Nevertheless, from these negative examples from real life we can draw some profound lessons and inspiration.

Further Reading

For another example of the post–June Fourth official reaction to Western human rights criticism, see Yi Ding, "Opposing Interference in Other Countries' Internal Affairs Through Human Rights: 'Human Rights Have No Boundaries' Refuted," *Beijing Review* (November 6–12, 1989).

Part VIII

The 1990s

50
Human Rights: Three Existential Forms (1991)

Li Buyun

Li Buyun, "Lun renquan de sanzhong cunzai xingtai" [Human Rights: Three Existential Forms], in CASS Legal Institute, ed., *Dangdai renquan* [Contemporary Human Rights] (Beijing: Zhongguo shehui kexue chubanshe, 1992).

Beginning in the late 1980s and taking off in the early 1990s, academics in China began to explore human rights from a number of perspectives. Li Buyun (b. 1933), vice-director of the Human Rights Research Institute at the Chinese Academy of Social Sciences, has been one of the most influential voices in these discussions. Some of the academics come quite close to official government positions; indeed, some of them participated in the drafting of documents like the 1991 White Paper *(see Text 52). Others, like Li and the authors of Texts 54 and 55, push the discourse in new directions. Li's basic orientation is Marxist, but he develops out of Marx a quite robust doctrine of human rights. His main argument in the essay here translated, that prior to any legal rights people have "due rights," is quite important, since it seeks to establish a ground for human rights independent of the state, yet without falling back on earlier Western ideas about "natural" rights. Li argues that our due rights derive from a combination of our biological and social natures, and that far from being mere abstractions, they concretely exist in a variety of social practices and norms. Legal rights, to be sure, have various advantages over rights that are merely supported by (often implicit) social agreements, but Li stresses that legal rights are justified by their tie to due rights. In the essay's incisive final section, Li adds that in all countries, but especially those with weak democratic traditions (among other things), legal rights often fail to be translated into "real rights"—that is, rights that people enjoy in practice.*

Introduction

Human rights are the rights people should enjoy due to their basic natures; in other words, they are the "rights of humans" (*ren de quanli*). Today the contents of human rights are broad and varied, and can be divided into different categories when seen from different perspectives. For example, based on differing topologies of the contents of human rights, one can differentiate between rights of the person (*renshen quanli*), political rights, economic rights, cultural and educational rights, social rights, and so on. If one looks [instead] at the different subjects of human rights, they can be classified as individual rights, collective rights, and rights of nationalities. Or according to the different ways of defending human rights, they can be classified as domestic or international human rights. These are today's most commonly used methods of classification. In addition, this author believes that we may differentiate human rights from the perspective of the forms in which they are realized and exist, and so distinguish them as due rights (*yingyou quanli*), legal rights (*fading quanli*), and real rights (*shiyou quanli*). The following essay is an effort to expound on these questions. . . .

Section Two

Some comrades state in their works that human rights are "the rights of human beings," "the rights that people enjoy or should enjoy because they are human beings";[1] "human rights are the rights a person enjoys or should enjoy."[2] But of the comrades who have this point of view, some believe that the "rights" they refer to are only legal rights; some do not discuss or analyze the concept of "rights which people ought to have," or deliberately avoid doing so. In the end, in life in modern society, are there due rights? What is the nature and condition of these rights? What are the differences between [due rights] and what in the West are referred to as "natural rights" (*ziran quanli*)? This author will try in the following section to explore these questions.

If we take the original definition as a starting point, the term human rights indicates those rights that a human being ought to have. Legal rights are simply due rights that people have used the tool of law to legalize and institutionalize, in order to provide the most effective protection of those rights. Therefore, legal rights are legalized human rights. Although legal rights are standardized human rights that are more concrete, precise, and reliable [than due rights], we cannot say that the two are identical, nor that there are no due rights outside legal rights. Because of the limits of objective and subjective conditions, the legal systems of all countries must undergo processes of development. Thanks to various conditions and restrictions, it is not a foregone conclusion that legislators will be willing to take legal measures to confirm and standardize due rights, and so these rights may not be rationally and thoroughly protected. Only if people's due rights exist can the question of whether and how to protect due rights come up. If one denies the existence of due rights, then the concept of legal rights can be compared to "a body of water that lacks a source" or "a tree that has no roots."

In fact, the existence of due rights is not and should not be equated with the existence of legal rights. Two examples may serve to clarify this point. The first written constitution in the world was the U.S. Constitution of 1787. At that time, because of [its authors'] differing opinions, the Constitution did not include any concrete provisions for the protection of human rights. Only in 1791, due to the energetic attempts of such democrats as Thomas Jefferson, were citizens assured the enjoyment of some basic human rights through the first ten amendments to the Constitution, the Bill of Rights. Can it be said that, prior to 1791, Americans should not have enjoyed the rights granted protection under the Bill of Rights? Of course not. China's current constitution dates from 1982. Article 38 reads: "The personal dignity (*renge zunyan*) of citizens of the PRC is inviolable. Insult, libel, false charges, or frame-up directed against citizens by any means is prohibited." This is the first time in China that such rights were assured in the constitution. Can we say that, prior to the promulgation of the 1982 Constitution, the Chinese people did not have the right not to have their personal dignity violated? Of course not. Laws are tools for the adjustment of social relations, and in any country it is necessary that their application as a means of affirming and protecting due rights requires a process [over time]. Nonetheless, some processes are rational and some are not. If one believes that human rights are only those rights stipulated by the law and that there exist no "due rights," isn't that the same as acknowledging that those dictatorships that disdain human rights and refuse to use legal measures to affirm or protect them are correct and rational?

Before due rights are affirmed and protected by law, they [nonetheless] exist objectively in real social life. In essence, the relationship between rights and duties is a social relationship. Rights and duties in law exist in legal relationships (including abstract and concrete legal relationships). Legal relationships have the existence of law as a precondition, and are their own special type of social relationship. After some [significant] portion of due rights and their correlated duties are legalized and institutionalized, they are transformed into legal rights and duties. At the same time, it is not difficult to see and understand another group of [due rights and duties], which exist in a variety of other kinds of social relationship. For example, in March 1949 the Central Committee of the CCP proclaimed the "Instructions regarding the annulment of the GMD's six laws and the affirmation of the legal principles in the liberated areas." After this, the old legally constituted authority on the

Chinese mainland ceased to exist. In April 1950, the first marriage law in the new China was proclaimed. Although this law was rapidly institutionalized, for a short period of time the rights and duties inherent in domestic marital relations in China did not have a law to confirm and protect them. Yet during that time, all kinds of rights and duties existed between husbands and wives and parents and children. In countless numbers of homes, parents educated and protected the rights of their minor children, and children fulfilled their duties to provide for their aged parents.

Even in circumstances in which people's "due rights" are not legally confirmed and protected, [these rights] are still acknowledged and protected in differing ways and to differing degrees by a variety of social forces. One way is through social organizations, including the programs and rules of political parties and social groups. Another is through various local rules and regulations in villages. A third way is through social customs and traditions. A fourth way is through people's moral principles and social and political consciousness. All these social forces and factors which affirm and protect "due rights" are less concrete and clear than legal methods, and have neither the qualities of universal applicability and standardization, nor the compulsory force at the level of the state to support them. But these [nonlegal kinds of] acknowledgment and protection can be seen and felt; they prove that, in real life as it is lived in society, "due rights" exist objectively in real social relations and are not at all imaginary or illusionary.

Many people believe that rights is a legal concept only appropriate in the legal sphere, and thus deny or doubt the scientific nature of "due rights." This viewpoint is not correct. Rights and duties are concepts with broad scopes. They include not only the rights and duties enshrined in national law but also the rights and duties in the regulations of political parties, social groups, and enterprise organizations, as well as the duties implied in moral and religious spheres. The differences between the rights and duties acknowledged under national law and those spelled out by the regulations of social organizations lie only in the specific contents and particular ways they are implemented. They all have the forms and characteristics common to rights and duties. One portion of "due rights" and of the duties that go along with them is concretely reflected in legal principles and documents or in the rules of social organizations; another part is manifested through human morals, social and political concepts, and other traditions and customs that approve and support social relations. For instance, in a certain country at a certain time, there may be no law or regulation forbidding the violation of personal dignity, yet one's rights of personality (including the right not to be insulted, not to have one's name slandered, not to have one's honor disgraced, and so on), although sometimes violated and trampled upon, are adequately reflected and manifested in social relations and can receive the affirmation and respect of at least some part of the members of the society.

Although the "due rights" that we are discussing resemble the innate rights (*tianfu renquan*) which Western theorists call "natural rights" (*ziran quanli*), in some fundamental respects principled distinctions can be made between the two. The theory of innate rights opposes natural rights to monarchical and divine rights, which had great significance for historical progress. The theoretical basis for this concept of "natural rights" includes several rational elements: it raises the concepts of "ought to be" as versus "existing in reality," and suggests that prior to legal rights, there exists a type of rights that people ought to enjoy. However, the entire idea of innate rights and their theoretical basis in "natural rights" is constructed on a foundation of historical idealism. A concrete analysis reveals that the differences between these conceptions of rights lie in the following essential problems.

The first is the problem of the source of rights. "Natural rights" implies that before the formation of the state, man was in a state of nature. At that time the relations between people were regulated by "natural law"; "natural rights" were bestowed by natural law and were innate. As states were produced and sought to issue man-made laws, these laws were subject to "natural law." Natural laws and rights are all given to humankind at birth. Their origins are "nature," human "reason" (*lixing*), and human nature (*renxing*). By human nature, [advocates of natural rights] mean man's original nature—the abstract nature of people separate from society. In reality, this refers to man's natural properties, not his social characteristics. Although several rational elements are included in this theory, overall this discussion suffers from idealism, and its historical viewpoint is complete idealism.

The "due rights" that we have been discussing differ sharply from these kind of theories. The production and source of "due rights" have two aspects, namely their inner and outer causes. The inner cause refers to man's original nature or essence, which itself includes both his natural and social characteristics. Man's original nature is the unity of his natural and social characteristics. This is the intrinsic foundation of the production and development of "due rights." The outer cause refers to the level of development of human society's material and spiritual culture. They are the external conditions for the development of "due rights" from lower to higher levels. Marx pointed out that man's original nature "is the sum total of all social relations." His thesis is a historic contribution to the theory of human nature, and his point of view gives a scientific basis on which to ground the theoretical study of human nature. All people want to exist (*shengcun*), to develop, to reason, and to lead a happy life. These are determined by the natural characteristics of human physiology and psychology; they are for humans a kind of instinct. Classical Marxist writers have also discussed in depth the fact that freedom and equality are basic to human nature. The foundation of rights are interests (*liyi*). The relation of rights and duties among people are in essence relations based on interests. Marx said, "What men seek is inextricably connected to their interests." In the final analysis, humans take the struggle for human rights as a basic goal in order to fulfill all of their own needs and interests. This is the inexhaustible impetus behind the development of human rights.

However, pure interest and aspiration do not constitute human rights, because people do not live in the world in a complete state of isolation. Between individuals, between groups, and between individuals, groups, and society exist many intricate and different social relationships. Among them, property and economic relationships are essential and fundamental. All of human society has been carried forward by the contradictions of production power versus production relations, and of production relations versus the superstructure. Fixed production power and production relations constitute the pattern of social production. The essence and circumstances of social relations between individuals in various historical stages in human societies, in turn, are all decided by society's patterns of production. The social relations between people are the origin of due rights; the intrinsic basis of the production and development of human rights emerges concretely in three dimensions, [which are set forth below]:

(1) The existence of social relations is the precondition for the existence of human rights. If man existed in complete isolation, there would be no need for rights and duties to regulate the clash of contradictory interests between people. (2) In the fixed historical stages in human society (for example, slave, feudal, capitalist), the essence and condi-

tions of all kinds of social relations between people determine the essence and conditions of human rights. (3) Human rights and the consciousness of human rights mutually depend on each other. The different positions people occupy in different social relations determine their consciousness of human rights. But this kind of consciousness of human rights also affects human rights and human rights institutions. From all this we can see that with its doctrine of human nature and the principles of historical idealism, Marxism created a truly scientific foundation for the theory of the origin of human rights. Only thus could the laws of the production and development of human rights be thoroughly and comprehensively clarified.

The second [essential problem] is the condition in which [the different types of rights] exist. According to the theory of "innate rights," natural law and natural rights exist in human thought and consciousness. Kant called these natural rights "moral rights" (*daode quanli*). [Advocates of natural rights] believe that in actual social life, [as opposed to in people's consciousness,] there are only man-made laws and legal rights. To [most] people, therefore, natural rights in the end have a sort of mystical essence. The rights we are speaking of, due rights, are completely different. They exist within actual social relationships. Here we must strictly distinguish "human rights" from the consciousness of human rights. Before due rights are legalized or institutionalized, despite the facts that their exact conditions are sometimes in flux and their existence and conditions are influenced and constrained by certain moral concepts, rights exist in actual social life. If we compare these "rights" to the [mere] consciousness of human rights, we see that the former belong in the category of "social existence": they are not created simply by people willing their existence.

The third [main problem] relates to the question of the essence of rights. From the point of view of innate rights, natural rights are a kind of pure abstraction. They apply to all people without discrimination. Thus, they have no class nature. This causes some (such as some capitalist scholars) to maintain that in a class-based society, class divisions and contradictions exist objectively, but since natural rights have only an abstract essence, they thus transcend class contradictions and oppositions and do not have a class nature. In actual life, [in contrast,] the "due rights" we are speaking of are concrete; each and every concrete right exists within all kinds of economic, political, cultural, and other social relationships. The concept of due rights is an abstraction from many concrete rights; yet if all kinds of concrete rights did not exist in actual life, this kind of abstraction becomes an abstraction without contents and hence loses its basis and meaning. In a class-based society, the concrete nature of rights must lead to their having a class nature. After due rights are affirmed by law and become legal rights, they no doubt have a class nature (since "law embodies the will of the ruling class"). In addition, even when they do not have the affirmation and protection of laws, due rights still have a class nature. The amount of rights an individual can enjoy is determined by his or her position in social relations. At the same time, the enjoyment of due rights is subject to the influence and constraints of the points of view of others. Because individuals' class positions differ, some people feel that a given right "ought" to be enjoyed, while others feel that it "ought not" be enjoyed.

The fourth question concerns the evolution of rights. From the point of view of innate rights, natural rights are unchanging, no matter what the past was like and no matter what the present is or the future may be. Since natural rights are said to be produced by man's "natural properties," are the manifestation of "rationality," and are a pure abstraction, it is logical that they have an unchanging nature. Due rights, which we have been discussing, are quite different. They change and develop constantly. On the one hand, their essence and condition are determined by social relations within a definite historical period, while on the other hand, their actual level of realization is subject to the influence and constraints of the developmental state of the entire society's material and spiritual culture (which includes education, science, and the arts, as well as the people's level of morality, and so on).

Section Three

Providing for human rights the most complete and practical protection is a basic goal—indeed, one of the fundamental signs—of modern legal societies. Today law is increasingly becoming human society's most universal, authoritative, and effective means of social regulation. The arm of the law reaches into almost every sphere of social life; all of people's behavioral choices come under the regulation and control of the law. In capitalist countries, the capitalist class has paid great attention to the use of legal measures to protect capitalist human rights. The classical Marxist authors also emphasized the use of the law to affirm and protect the people's due rights. Marx said, "Legal codes are the holy scriptures of the people's freedom."[3] Lenin also said, "The constitution is a document in which the people's rights are written down."[4]

Why do people thus take legal measures that protect human rights so seriously, and turn due rights into "legal rights"? The fundamental reason is that law has a great instrumental value, and at the same time has a unique moral value. As a tool, law has fundamental characteristics like representing the will of the state, setting behavioral standards, enjoying universal effectiveness, and allowing coercive implementation. The source of the law's social potential is in these fundamental characteristics. After due rights have been confirmed and have become "legal rights," this kind of right can change and become extremely precise and concrete; it can be raised to the level of an expression of the will of the state and exert a universal binding force on all the citizens. A state can use its compulsory force to protect the realization of such rights. The usefulness of law to protect human rights cannot be compared to that of any social organization's regulations, the local rules and regulations in villages, or any other methods of protection.

In addition, the law is the manifestation of fairness and justice; its basic nature is to seek equality for all before it. Although in a society where there are class antagonisms, laws do not really achieve this level of fairness, nonetheless their unique moral value in protecting the basic value and dignity of the individual has been and continues to be of enormous importance, both in China and in other countries. Thanks both to the law's instrumental and moral value, in the current era when human civilization has developed to this high point, we can even say that where there is no law, there are no human rights; where the law is trampled upon, human rights vanish into thin air.

Of course, we should not advocate the omnipotence of law. In fact, the question of human rights is not purely a legal question. While the transformation of due rights into legal rights is of great significance, we should not view the law as the only way to protect human rights. One of our aims in raising the question of due rights has been to clarify the other social forces and elements that are of definite use in the protection of human rights. If the concept of due rights is rejected and an equation drawn between "legal rights" and "human rights," then the question of human rights appears to be a legal question only.

Paying attention to the concept of "real rights" (*shiyou quanli*) is also not without significance. So-called "real rights" are the rights that people really enjoy. In a certain country, due rights may be completely provided for according to the law, but the human rights situation in that country can still have problems. There is often an enormous distance between legal rights and real rights. Today it is not difficult to stipulate complete protection for human rights by passing laws, but it is not easy to ensure that these legal rights will achieve complete and practical realization. No matter what a country's human rights situation, it will to a great degree be subject to this limitation.

In general, the elements that prevent legal rights in a given country from becoming real rights are the following: (1) The conception of legal institutions and the human rights consciousness of the country's leaders at all levels. This is the main obstacle to the real enjoyment of human rights in countries that lack a tradition of legal and democratic systems. (2) The level of development of political democratization in a given country. A country may have comparatively effective laws, but this is not the equivalent of the rule of law. The fundamental sign of the rule of law is that the law has paramount power. Countries with the rule of law can only be built on strong democratic foundations. (3) The level of development of a commodities economy. Marx, in his incisive analysis, noted that the concepts of freedom and equality have an inseparable relationship to the commodities economy. Under socialism, with its planned development of the commodities economy, the popularization and promotion of the consciousness of human rights rests on a reliable economic base. (4) The level of development of society, the economy, and culture are all closely related to the complete enjoyment of labor rights and the rights to leisure, education, and so on.

From due rights to legal rights, from legal rights to real rights—this is the fundamental form that the realization of human rights takes in social life. This is not the only form, however; other social factors have roles in the process by which human rights are realized. The relations between these three types of rights are not parallel but successive, though their contents overlap to a great degree. Following the continual forward development of human civilization, they have gradually grown closer and their overlap has grown wider. There will always be contradictions, however: due rights will always be broader [in scope] than legal rights, and legal rights will always be broader than real rights. It is these contradictions that constantly drive people to struggle for the realization of human rights.

Notes

1. Dong Yunhu and Liu Wuping, eds., *Shijie renquan yuefa zonglan* [A Glance at World-wide Human Rights Agreements] (Chengdu: Sichuan renmin chubanshe, 1991), p. 75.
2. He Huahui, *Bijiao xianfaxue* [Comparative Constitutional Studies] (Wuhan: Wuhan daxue chubanshe, 1988), p. 60.
3. *Makesi Engesi quanji* [Collected Works of Marx and Engels] (Beijing: Renmin chubanshe, 1973), vol. 1, p. 71.
4. *Liening quanji* [Collected Works of Lenin] (Beijing: Renmin chubanshe, 1955), p. 448.

Further Reading

Another important essay by Li is "On Individual Rights and Collective Rights," in Peter R. Baehr, Fried van Hoof, Liu Nanlai, Tao Zhenghua, editors in chief; Jacqueline Smith, ed., *Human Rights: Chinese and Dutch Perspectives* (The Hague: Martinus Nijhoff, 1996), pp. 119–32.

51
Prison Letter (1991)

Wei Jingsheng

The Courage to Stand Alone: Letters from Prison and Other Writings, ed. and trans. Kristina Torgenson (New York: Viking, 1997), pp. 164–76.

For details on Wei's life and activities leading up to the 1978–79 Democracy Wall movement, see the introduction to Text 39, above. As there noted, Wei was arrested in 1979. He spent fourteen years in jail and was paroled on September 14, 1993—a few days before the International Olympic Committee's decision on whether to award the 2000 Summer Olympics to Beijing. If Wei's release was an attempt to influence the IOC decision, it failed, with the games going to Sydney. Wei spent a brief time out of custody, endeavoring to write, publish, and meet with fellow countrymen and foreign journalists, before he was seized and held incommunicado for more than a year, the government denying knowledge of his whereabouts. After a show trial, Wei was ultimately sentenced to fourteen years in prison, plus three more years' deprivation of political rights, in December of 1995. In November 1997, however, on the heels of a state visit by Jiang Zemin to the United States, Wei was released on medical parole and left China for the United States, where he now lives in exile. The letter that we reprint here is one of a large number that Wei wrote to high government officials while serving his first prison term. Wei is sharply critical of the Chinese government's position on human rights—soon to be formalized, at the time Wei wrote this letter, in the first White Paper on Human Rights *(see Text 52). He force-fully rebuts a number of arguments used by the government, including the views that human rights is an internal affair, that different cultures and societies have different human rights conceptions, and that economic rights supersede all other rights.*

June 15, 1991

Dear Jiang Zemin and Li Peng:

Human rights have become a popular topic of conversation lately and even the Party line on the issue seems to have softened somewhat. It has declared that it intends to "study human rights theories and questions in order to deal with the peaceful evolution of hostile forces," and so on. These very words prove that the basic theories of the Communist Party as they currently exist do not cover the issue of human rights, and that people are no more than tools for production and struggle within its theoretical framework. Tools, naturally, do not have any rights All they have is the "right" to be submissive and to be used. When "peaceful evolution of hostile forces" comes into the picture, and the tools are no longer as docile and useful, then it becomes necessary to find out what to do to make them docile once again. At least, this is the stand and attitude revealed in your Party's newspaper. As for the many proc-lamations you have made during international diplomatic occasions, based on experience and your Party's own views, they cannot be taken at face value.

You may consider my views to be the futile and worthless thoughts of a heretic. After all, I am a former tool whom you now regard as no longer docile, and a leading dissident who has been falsely branded as part of the "human rights vanguard." But I have never been incited or instigated by "human rights diplomacy employed by hostile countries or hostile forces" and have not been influenced by theories of modern human rights in the West. The only information on human rights that I have access to comes from your Party's own publications. One thing I do know for sure, however, is that your Party unyieldingly holds the same view of human rights that the Nazis did, which helps to explain why you gnash your teeth at the mere mention of human rights and are so eager to get rid of them.

The Tibet problem (since the founding of the People's Republic), for example, did not stem from the "ambitions of imperialist forces" and human rights diplomacy. It is true that serious human rights problems, and even racial discrimination, have occurred in that region during the past forty years and imperialist aggression did indeed take place (several decades ago), but this all happened before human rights diplomacy came onto the scene. The imperialists had left India long before, and besides, what ambitions would they have for Tibet, a region which they had never even colonized in the first place? The root causes of the problems in Tibet are all internal and lie in the theories and practices of your Party. Do not call the crow black, when you yourself are blacker. Neither the existence of South African racists, nor the Ku Klux Klan, nor feudal serfdom in old Tibet gives you the right to ignore human rights, or proves that you have a good human rights record.

But what is the use of saying all this nonsense anyway? Let us take a serious look at human rights theories and practices, how they stand in relation to socialism, and in particular why Marxist societies often turn out to be political structures that do not respect human rights. These questions are matters of primary importance for modern China. They may seem very far removed from us, but actually they are very close to home; they might appear as merely abstract concepts, but they are, in fact, very concrete. The lack of human rights is the principal cause for many of the concrete problems confronting Chinese society. Human rights are also a problem about which fallacies and confusion abound. It will take concerted efforts by all to clarify these human rights theories and activities. I can only talk on the basis of some of the precise information gleaned from your Party publications, so my lack of thoroughness is inevitable.

FALLACY ONE: Human rights are the internal affairs of a country, and foreign governments and organizations have no right to interfere.

Internal affairs are matters decided on by the government of each country. If human rights issues are the internal affairs of a country and the government decides not to respect human rights, do human rights simply cease to exist as a problem? Rights that a government does not recognize as human rights naturally cannot be considered human rights issues. In other words, they become merely questions of internal legislation and jurisdiction, and problems not stipulated by the law are problems that do not exist. Your Party obviously adheres to such logic, which also happens to be the sort of thinking upheld by Hitler, the South African racists, and ancient Chinese emperors. According to such logic, it is both legal

and reasonable to ignore and infringe upon human rights, and democratic revolutions, socialist revolutions, and revolutions for national independence in various countries are thereby all considered illegal and
unreasonable.

FALLACY TWO: There are different standards of human rights. Differ-
ent standards apply to different countries, nations, cultural traditions,
and social systems, and people should be content with the human rights
standards stipulated in the laws of their country.

If such a theory were tenable then all human rights conditions would be
reasonable and there would be no such thing as "human rights problems." What, then, is the use of talking about "international cooperation
on human rights," "condemning so-and-so for gross human rights violations," "resolutely imposing sanctions against so-and-so's apartheid,"
and such? Yours is a sovereign state, but so are other states; your human
rights standards are "stipulated by law and represent the will of the government," but is this not also true of other countries? In your country,
you say, human rights conditions are the consequences of "cultural traditions, the social system, and historical changes." Did you think that in
other countries they just fell out of the sky? Your "internal affairs" will
bear no interference, but do you think other countries welcome your
interference in their "internal affairs"? All this goes to show that the
"theory of different standards" does not hold water because you have no
way of proving that your laws and policies are of a reasonable standard
while those of others are not. In order to prove that yours are reasonable,
you would have to cite more objective standards.

We can also see that, although the safeguarding of human rights and
basic freedoms depends on legislation and policy enforcement on the
part of sovereign states, human rights themselves have objective standards that cannot be modified by legislation and cannot be changed by
the will of the government. "Human rights issues" pertain to how a government protects and respects the rights of its individual citizens, not how
reasonable the government is in its actions. These "issues" have to do with
how to protect the relatively weak rights of individuals under the relatively strong organs of power. They are common objective standards
that apply to all governments and all individuals and no one is entitled
to special standards. Like objective existence and objective laws, they
are objective truths. That was why Rousseau called them "natural rights."

These "natural rights" are not "protected by heaven" as your bootlicking hack propagandists try to argue, but are "rights with which every person is born." They are things that we fight for as a matter of course and we don't need to be taught by "hostile countries and hostile forces" to do so. They are the natural laws and rights of life—just like eating or having sex. In other words, they are instinctive and that is why they are called "natural." It is abominable sophistry to try to argue that people can do without food because there are some people who have nothing to eat; or that people can do without sex because there are widows and bachelors around. It is similarly abominable to argue that people do not need human rights because they are able to adapt to an animal-like existence or because there are people who consciously act in a servile manner; or that there is no such thing as objective human rights standards simply because dictatorial slave societies still exist.

It is precisely because human rights are independent of the will of the government, and even independent of the will of all mankind, that people fight for the realization and expansion of human rights as a natural and unprovoked matter of course. They gradually come to the realization that the more widespread and reliable the protection of human rights is, the more their own human rights are protected. Just as man's understanding of objective truths and objective laws is a gradual process, man's understanding and comprehension of human rights is a gradual process. Just as man's grasp and utilization of objectives laws is a progressive process, man's protection of the theory and practice of human rights is a progressive process. Thus, it is a plausible excuse to say that our theories and practices in this regard are still backward and that human rights conditions differ in different countries and nations under different cultural conditions and social systems.

However, the presence of different conditions and views cannot be taken as an excuse to violate and disregard human rights or to demonstrate that laws enacted by individuals can override objective truths or to argue that laws that violate human rights are justified. Any doctrine that preaches the supremacy of law is just another form of fascism. To them, the law is not the servant of the people's will or the embodiment of objective truths, but quite the other way around: The people and truths become the servants of the absolute law and its enforcing agents. Not only the people but also objective truths become subordinate to the ruler's will as expressed in the name of the law and the state.

Chinese people as a whole find the fascist soil of this "doctrine of the supremacy of law" quite unacceptable. Most Chinese people judge whether a person is right or wrong based on whether or not he or she abides by the law. However, they also look at whether or not the law protects and serves the people in judging whether the law is right. They take particular care in judging the law enforcement agents. There is no place for the "doctrine of the supremacy of the law." When there is a conflict between the people and the law, they favor putting the people first.

This may sound like the "human rights theory" handed down since the time of Rousseau, but it is also the essence of the humanistic, or democratic, tradition found in traditional Chinese culture. This tradition has been deeply rooted in people's hearts for over two thousand years and there is no way it can be pushed aside for the feudal or prefeudal ideology of the "doctrine of the supremacy of law." What is really important now is not so much counteracting the effects of this doctrine as finding out how political and administrative organs can be made to show more respect and provide more protection for human rights. This is in keeping with the wishes of the times and of the people and will save your Party and you yourselves from being wiped out. In the face of the crushing tide of history, one must go along with it or perish. This is true at all times and in all countries.

FALLACY THREE: It is permissible to discuss the issue of human rights and carry out international cooperation on human rights, but it is an "abnormal phenomenon" to preach specific values, ideologies, and models.

The difference between a democratic system that respects and protects human rights and basic freedoms and a totalitarian system that does not lies in their different "social models." It also lies in a difference in ideologies—the theories on the basis of which social models are established and exist. There is also a difference in values—the basis for these ideologies.

The values of Hitler and all totalitarian rulers can only produce fascism, or "national socialism," an ideology that takes away or suppresses individual rights and freedoms in the name of the state or the society. A social system established on the basis of such an ideology can only be a Nazi or totalitarian social model. Whether or not a system respects and protects human rights is what basically distinguishes the values of democracy and freedom from those of totalitarianism and enslavement.

If people are allowed to "discuss human rights and carry out international cooperation on human rights," they will naturally try to interfere with, stop, and change those systems or institutions that do not respect and protect human rights. Opposition to, and sanctions against, South African apartheid, for instance, is large-scale "international cooperation on human rights." If, in this exercise, people are not allowed to promote values based on the basic human right of equality for all, or to rely on the ideology of "democracy based on individuals" in trying to promote a social model of "democracy and freedom," and can speak only "within the limits prescribed by law," can this cooperation on human rights be effective? It is nothing more than a fig leaf covering the ugly features of the anti–human rights social model of enslavement; it is merely a clever trick to oppose social progress.

FALLACY FOUR: It is permissible to discuss and even protect human rights, but no international pressure will be tolerated. Emancipation of human rights under a dictatorship can only come about through the dictatorship's "own choice."

Without exception, any social model based on dictatorship and enslavement that does not respect human rights is held together by force and defiance of reason. However, if it is reasonable and can accept reasonable exchanges, it can become a democratic social model that respects human rights. It is only under this precondition that inadequate protection of human rights can be rectified and remedied through discussion and cooperation. Even then, the governments of these countries may not take the initiative to make major moves to improve their human rights conditions unless they are subjected to pressures from within and without. The civil rights movement that took place in the United States not long ago is an obvious case in point.

A social model that must be held together by deception and violence can only give rise to a society of enslavement where human rights are not respected. The most obvious trait of such regimes is that they only recognize authority based on violence and strength (the threat of violence), but do not recognize rights that should be respected and protected. Their maxim is that political power grows out of the barrel of a gun; in other words, if you win a country on horseback, you must rule it on horseback. It is brute force rather than the people's will that constitutes the cornerstone of these regimes. Such is the essence of dictatorship.

Under the circumstances, there are only two ways to bring about change: either use violence to counter violence and topple the government through revolution, or force it to change gradually, that is, to reform, through the exertion of pressure from within and without, but mainly from without. Of the two, reform seems more desirable because it is less destructive. Although it implies greater difficulty and complexity, it ensures a more stable and predictable situation. It will also be socially, politically, economically, and culturally less damaging to the country itself and countries with related interests. One way to minimize losses and setbacks for all sides is for countries with related interests to exert pressure and help bring about internal progress and reform. If other countries are not allowed to exert pressure, and the forces of reform are left to fight the bloody and powerful apparatus of violence alone, they will be left with only one choice: violent revolution entailing numerous setbacks, huge losses, and an uncertain future.

If I remember an official statement by your Party correctly, the fascist regimes of Hitler and Mussolini owed their expansion to the fact that the international community "did not exert any pressure or intervene in their internal affairs." Your Party called this a "policy of appeasement" in various official documents and said that "the stupid imperialist governments and profit-seeking bourgeoisie" were partly to blame for the outbreak of World War II, which I think is a correct historical conclusion. But why are you taking an opposite stance now? The reason is not difficult to see! It is because you have identified your values, ideology, and social model with Hitler and present-day South Africa.

FALLACY FIVE: "We have managed to feed and meet the subsistence needs of over one billion people" and "this is the greatest human right."

If feeding the people and keeping them from starving or freezing to death constitutes the greatest respect for human rights, then consider the feudal lords and slave owners. The fact that slaves and serfs were kept from starving or freezing to death could prove that the slave owners had protected "the greatest human right" as you have done. The Nazi concentration camps were also responsible for feeding the Jews and other "inferior races" in captivity and keeping them from starving or freezing to death. Following this reasoning, are not the survivors of the Holocaust, like the ordinary Chinese people who survived numerous brutal and barbaric movements and "mistakes" by the Communist Party, proof that Nazi racism was one of "the greatest human rights" doctrines? If this is in fact your concept of human rights, then it is an anti–human rights concept similar to that held by the slave owners and Nazis and is something that goes against a perception of value that respects the dignity and rights of every individual.

Is this the concept of human rights held under communism and its manifestation in Marxism? In my opinion, no Marxist since the time of Marx would openly admit that it is. With the exception of a small number of foolish pigs who've left their sties and do not really know what they are talking about, the majority of genuine or self-proclaimed Marxists would, either sincerely or out of their need to hide, deny that they believe in an anti–human rights concept that goes against the interests of mankind. The thing is, not only Marxism but every ideology that advocates "reliance on violence and all means both fair or foul" when the "interests of all mankind or of all the people within a certain scope" are at stake, turns a blind eye to human beings and believes in doctrines that go against human rights and values. Nazism, fascism, anarchism, and all brands of modern terrorism have basic principles that go against human rights incorporated in their theories and practices.

You claim that "we have managed to feed one billion people" when it is actually you who are living off the labor of the people, and you claim that "we have met their subsistence needs" when it is the people who have solved the problem of food and clothing themselves through their own wisdom, resourcefulness, and arduous labor under extremely difficult conditions that have been compounded by exploitation and oppression carried out by Party ruffians and bureaucrats. Doesn't your rhetoric sound like that of a slave owner? Somewhere between the anarchist slogan inviting workers and peasants to "take back the fruits of your labor" and the tune of the slave owner, there is "a red thread that runs through all" and that serves as a balance and link. This thread is your Maoist doctrines, "Once one has power, one has everything" and "Political power grows out of the barrel of a gun," together with Marxism and the doctrine of the supremacy of violence that preaches the seizure and maintenance of a totalitarian regime through violence.

At a time when China is moving from an agricultural and pastoral economy into the modern industrial and information age, its traditional moral basis in "benevolence, righteousness, and propriety" has been destroyed, but it has not yet accepted "human rights, freedom, and equality" as the moral basis of the age of industrial democracy. China's wise ideological and cultural traditions likewise have no way to accept any moral basis of "universal fraternity and equality" as it is religious and based on superstition. Society is thus left in a nihilist and chaotic state. By opposing tradition and making violence supreme, your doctrine of general hatred can only add fuel to the fire and bring greater chaos and suffering to society. It is because of this that I say that the human rights issue is truly one of the basic issues in determining whether or not a country can enjoy long-lasting peace and prosperity.

FALLACY SIX: "Looking after the interests of the majority of people is our major point of departure on the issue of human rights."

On the surface, these words sound fine, but in fact there are often things that need to be examined beneath the surface. When talking about the rights that every person should enjoy, the claim that "the majority is the point of departure" is an act of deceptive sophistry and excuse-making. It occurs when faced with a situation that one cannot deny but in which one is unwilling to admit fault. This is because even if we talk about "gross violations of human rights," the phrase still refers to the violation of the rights belonging to every individual—in other words, the violation of an individual's internal affairs. It does not refer to a matter of contention that may or may not belong to a particular individual, and does not refer to public matters in the political, economic, or environmental domains. These are expressed by other concepts. Rather, it refers to rights that should belong to every individual. This has nothing to do with "the majority," and the majority has no right to curtail the basic right to freedom of even a small minority. Although parts of their concepts can be duplicated and may overlap, we cannot thus say that chemistry equals physics, that energy equals transport, that grain equals smelly night soil, and so on. This is the same sort of sophistry as using the majority as an excuse to confuse the issue of the human rights that belong to every individual.

Perhaps these words indicate that in our country's society, there exists a majority that enjoys rights and a small minority that does not enjoy basic rights. Who, then, is this majority, and who is the small minority? Do we need to redraw class divisions? Or are some minority nationalities going to serve as the antithesis, as was the case in the 1950s and 1960s? Regardless, juggling with terms such as "the majority" on the question of basic human rights proves that this society is an unequal one and that the Constitution and laws that talk of "all persons being equal" are nothing more than wastepaper. This, then, produces a dilemma. Either the Constitution and the laws have been cleverly juggled by people so that some enjoy full rights and others enjoy fewer rights or none at all, and the surface and content of the laws and the Constitution are different or even meaningless; or else some people have usurped the rights that should belong to every person rather than to only some of the people and therefore there has been a large-scale violation of human rights. Which of the two situations do you think is the most likely? Or do both exist simultaneously?

South Africa is a country in which a small number of white people violate the rights of the majority of the people, including some white people. This certainly cannot be tolerated and it is certainly valid to openly attack such abuses. However, people of your age should remember that the Nazis and some "socialist comrades" who were not Nazis used the pretext of "the majority" to eliminate the "inferior races"—the Jews, the Tatars, and the blacks. Is it the case that because some persons constituted "the majority" in Germany, the Soviet Union, and the United States they had the right to violate the rights and freedoms of other people? Was it the case that because such violations did not violate the laws of these countries at that time, and were tolerated, supported, and implemented by the governments, that they were reasonable and should not have been denounced, since as you say, "interference in internal affairs is impermissible"? While the violation of human rights based on race and national differences is obviously a barbarous act, is not the violation of human rights within a single race or nation, based on artificial differences or even with no basis at all, even more barbarous and intolerable? If the people allow those who hold power in the people's name to violate and ignore the rights of some of the people, then at the same time they are giving them the power to violate the rights of all the people. This is especially so in a society where there are no racial or cultural differences.

FALLACY SEVEN: Marx had a famous popular definition: "Man's nature is the sum of his social relations." Some people, on this basis, infer that as different societies have different social relations and the sums of such relations are different, there are also different human natures. Thus, the different views on and practices of human rights are suited to different types of human natures and the rationality of all of these should be fully recognized. It would be an abnormal phenomenon to have uniform requirements.

Man is not a product of his social relations, nor indeed of any relations. He is not a robot, nor is he a product created by other people based on a pattern for man. Rather, he is a product of nature. Thus, his essential qualities are likewise a product of nature. These are "instinctive" and very basic and they constitute a human "commonality" that is inborn and possessed by all and on which all other human natures and social relations are based. Human rights and basic freedoms refer to the satisfying or realizing of this part of human nature. They are the sum of hopes and aspirations that emerge naturally and do not need to be taught.

Human rights are themselves a type of social relation. The respect and protection of human rights and basic freedoms is in itself a social institution, a social system, and a mechanism to ensure its own effectiveness. However, this refers to primary-level social relations, which emerge from man's basic nature or, put another way, are the foundation of all social relations. These are basically different from those social relations that are derived and that are stipulated or manufactured by man.

Wherever a great amount of social injustice is enshrined in law, that is to say, where the cornerstone of a legal system is social injustice maintained through violence, the social models are societies of enslavement such as slavery and fascism. These societies can be distinguished by determining the degree of human rights existing in them. We need to look at whether or not within these societies the basic freedoms and rights of a part or the majority of the people have actually been expropriated "by law." Law is people's social nature and is not the sole or most basic standard for social relations. Human rights are a more basic standard.

In order to have progressed to its present stage, Western civilization has had to safeguard outstanding elements of its culture and tradition and learn many things from the remarkable achievements of the civilizations of China and elsewhere. This has enabled it to maintain appropriate development for itself at pace with an increasingly rapid global development. Chinese civilization has begun a similar process of study and assimilation. At the present time, is it really necessary that we continue to enshrine and worship "isms" that Western civilization has already spit out?

Further Reading

For Wei's 1978–79 writings, see Text 39. The balance of the text from which we have drawn the current selection is also well worth reading, both for biography and commentary; see especially "My Opinions of the 'Draft Revision of the Constitution,'" *The Courage to Stand Alone*, pp. 37–49. The same volume contains an account of Wei's struggles by Sophia Woodman, which details the events surrounding his second trial. For an important study of China's prisons and labor reform camps—the sites in which Wei wrote the current selection—see James D. Seymour and Richard Anderson, *New Ghosts, Old Ghosts: Prisons and Labor Reform Camps in China* (Armonk, NY: M.E. Sharpe, 1998).

52
White Paper on Human Rights in China (1991)

Information Office of the State Council

Original version: Zhonghua renmin gongheguo guowuyuan xinwen bangongshi, *Zhongguo de renquan zhuangkuang* [Human Rights in China] (Beijing: Zhongyang wenxian chubanshe, October 1991). Translated as Information Office of the State Council of the PRC, *Human Rights in China* (Beijing, November 1991). Subsequent sections in the *White Paper* include: 2. The Chinese People Have Gained Extensive Political Rights; 3. Citizens Enjoy Economic, Cultural, and Social Rights; 4. Guarantee of Human Rights in China's Judicial Work; 5. Guarantee of the Right to Work; 6. Citizens Enjoy Freedom of Religious Belief; 7. Guarantee of the Rights of the Minority Nationalities; 8. Family Planning and Protection of Human Rights; 9. Guarantee of Human Rights for the Disabled; 10. Active Participation in International Human Rights Activities.

Soon after the crackdown on the Democracy Movement in June 1989, the Chinese government began to sponsor academic research into the subject of human rights. Some of the fruits of this research are essays that appear elsewhere in this Reader. *In November 1991, the official view of human rights was summarized and presented in the* White Paper on Human Rights in China, *soon to be followed by other White Papers addressing more specific issues, such as prison conditions, the situation in Tibet, religious freedom, and so on. In the 1991* White Paper *China officially and unambiguously endorsed the language of human rights and praised the development of the international human rights regime. At the same time, though, the document argues that the specific contents of human rights vary with "differences in historical background, social system, cultural tradition, and economic development." In addition to making this relativist argument, the* White Paper *also dwells at length on the priority of the "right to subsistence" (shengcun quan) over other human rights, and furthermore argues that said right cannot be secured except by indepen-*

dent, sovereign nations. China's most important goals, then, are the collective goals of national strength and independence, followed closely by national economic development. One explicit aim of the White Paper *was to refute foreign criticism and present an alternative and more rosy picture of the situation in China. And to this end, it presents a detailed overview of the atrocities committed by the imperialists in China before 1949, while keeping silent on disasters since then, such as the great famine of 1960–61 and various political campaigns that have also resulted in the deaths of millions of people. We reprint here the preface and first section of the* White Paper.

Preface

It has been a long-cherished ideal of mankind to enjoy human rights in the full sense of the term. Since this great term—human rights—was coined centuries ago, people of all nations have achieved great results in their unremitting struggle for human rights. However, on a global scale, modern society has fallen far short of the lofty goal of securing the full range of human rights for people the world over. And this is why numerous people with lofty ideals are still working determinedly for this cause.

Under long years of oppression by the "three big mountains"—imperialism, feudalism, and bureaucrat-capitalism—people in old China did not have any human rights to speak of. Suffering bitterly from this, the Chinese people fought for more than a century, defying death and personal sacrifices and advancing wave upon wave, in an arduous struggle to overthrow the "three big mountains" and gain their human rights. The situation with respect to human rights in China took a basic turn for the better after the founding of the People's Republic of China. Greatly treasuring this hard-won achievement, the Chinese government and people have spared no effort to safeguard human rights and steadily improve their human rights situation, and have achieved remarkable results. This has won full confirmation and fair appraisal from all people who have a real understanding of Chinese conditions and who are not prejudiced.

The issue of human rights has become one of great significance and common concern in the world community. The series of declarations and conventions adopted by the United Nations have won the support and respect of many countries. The Chinese government has also highly appraised the Universal Declaration of Human Rights, considering it the first international human rights document that has laid the foundation for the practice of human rights in the world arena. However, the evolution of the situation in regard to human rights is circumscribed by the historical, social, economic, and cultural conditions of various nations, and involves a process of historical development. Owing to tremendous differences in historical background, social system, cultural tradition, and economic development, countries differ in their understanding and practice of human rights. From their different situations, they have taken different attitudes toward the relevant UN conventions. Despite its international aspect, the issue of human rights falls by and large within the sovereignty of each country. Therefore, a country's human rights situation should not be judged in total disregard of its history and national conditions, nor can it be evaluated according to a preconceived model or the conditions of another country or region. Such is the practical attitude, the attitude of seeking truth from facts.

From their own historical conditions, the realities of their own country and their long practical experience, the Chinese people have derived their own viewpoints on the human rights issue and formulated relevant laws and policies. It is stipulated in the Constitution of the People's Republic of China that all power in the People's Republic of China belongs to the people. Chinese human rights have three salient characteristics. First, extensiveness. It is not a minority of the people or part of a class or social stratum but the entire Chinese citizenry who constitutes the subject enjoying human rights. The human rights enjoyed by the Chinese citizenry encompass an extensive scope, including not only survival, personal, and political rights, but also economic, cultural, and social rights. The state pays full attention to safeguarding both individual and collective rights. Second, equality. China has adopted the socialist system after abolishing the system of exploitation and eliminating the exploiting classes. The Chinese citizenry enjoys all civic rights equally irrespective of money and property status as well as of nationality, race, sex, occupation, family background, religion, level of education, and duration of residence. Third, authenticity. The state provides guarantees in terms of system, laws, and material means for the realization of human rights. The various civic rights prescribed in the Constitution and other state laws are in accord with what people enjoy in real life. China's human rights legislation and policies are endorsed and supported by the people of all nationalities and social strata and by all the political parties, social organizations, and all walks of life.

As a developing country, China has suffered from setbacks while safeguarding and developing human rights. Although much has been achieved in this regard, there is still much room for improvement. It remains a long-term historical task for the Chinese people and government to continue to promote human rights and strive for the noble goal of full implementation of human rights as required by China's socialism.

In order to help the international community understand the human rights situation as it is in China, we present the following brief account of China's basic position on and practice of human rights.

I. The Right to Subsistence—The Foremost Human Right the Chinese People Long Fight For

It is a simple truth that, for any country or nation, the right to subsistence (*shengcun quan*) is the most important of all human rights, without which the other rights are out of the question. The Universal Declaration of Human Rights affirms that everyone has the right to life, liberty, and the security of person. In old China, aggression by imperialism and oppression by feudalism and bureaucrat-capitalism deprived the people of all guarantees for their lives, and an uncountable number of them perished in war and famine. To solve their human rights problems, the first thing for the Chinese people to do is, for historical reasons, to secure the right to subsistence.

Without national independence, there would be no guarantee for the people's lives. When imperialist aggression became the major threat to their lives, the Chinese people had to win national independence before they could gain the right to subsistence. After the Opium War of 1840, China, hitherto a big feudal kingdom, was gradually turned into a semi-colonial, semi-feudal country. During the 110 years from 1840 to 1949, the British, French, Japanese, U.S., and Russian imperialist powers waged hundreds of wars on varying scales against China, causing immeasurable losses to the lives and property of the Chinese people.

The imperialists massacred Chinese people in untold numbers during their aggressive wars. In 1900, the troops of the Eight Allied Powers—Germany, Japan, Britain, Russia, France, the United States, Italy, and Austria—killed, burned, and looted, razing Tanggu, a town of 50,000 residents, to utter ruins, reducing Tianjin's population from one million to 100,000, killing countless people when they entered Beijing, where more than 1,700 were slaughtered at Zhuangwangfu alone. During Japan's full-scale invasion of China, which began in 1937, more than 21 million people were killed or wounded and 10 million people mutilated to death. In the six weeks beginning from December 13, 1937, the Japanese invaders killed 300,000 people in Nanjing.

The imperialists sold, maltreated, and caused the death of numerous Chinese laborers, plunging countless people in old China into an abyss of misery. According to incomplete statistics, more than 12 million indentured Chinese laborers were sold to various parts of the world from the mid-nineteenth century through the 1920s. Coaxed and abducted, these laborers were thrown into lockups known as "pigsties," where they were branded with the names of their would-be destinations. During the 1852–58 period, 40,000 people were put in such "pigsties" in Shantou alone, and more than 8,000 of them were done to death there. Equally horrifying was the death toll of ill-treated laborers in factories and mines run by imperialists across China. During the Japanese occupation, no less than 2 million laborers perished from maltreatment and exhaustion in Northeast China. Once the laborers died, their remains were thrown into mountain gullies or pits dug into bare hillsides. So far more than 80 such massive pits have been found, with over 700,000 skeletons of the victims in them.

Under the imperialists' colonial rule, the Chinese people had their fill of humiliation and there was no personal dignity (*renge zunyan*) to speak of. The foreign aggressors enjoyed "extraterritoriality" in those days. On December 24, 1946, Peking University student Shen Chong was raped by William Pierson, an American GI, but, to the great indignation of the Chinese people, the criminal, handled unilaterally by the American side, was acquitted and released. Imperialist powers exercised administrative, legislative, judicial, police, and financial powers in the "concessions" they had set up in China, turning them into "states within a state" that were thoroughly independent of the Chinese administrative and legal systems. In 1885, foreign aggressors put up a signboard at the entrance of a park in the French concession; in a blatant insult to the Chinese people, it read, "Chinese and dogs not admitted."

Forcing more than 1,100 unequal treaties on China, the imperialists plundered Chinese wealth on a large scale. Statistics show that, by way of these unequal treaties, the foreign aggressors made away with more than 100 billion taels of silver as war indemnities and other payments in the past century. Through the Sino-British Treaty of Nanking, the Sino-Japanese Treaty of Shimonoseki, the International Protocol of 1901, and five other such treaties alone, 1,953 million taels of silver in indemnity were extorted, 16 times the 1901 revenue of the Qing government. The

Treaty of Shimonoseki alone earned Japan 230 million taels of silver in extortion money, about four and a half times its annual national revenue. The losses resulting from the destruction and looting by the invaders in wars against China were even more incalculable. During Japan's full-scale war of aggression against China (1937–45), 930 Chinese cities were occupied, causing US$62 billion in direct losses and US$500 billion in indirect losses. With their state sovereignty impaired and their social wealth plundered or destroyed, the Chinese people were deprived of the basic conditions for survival.

In face of the crumbling state sovereignty and the calamities wrought upon their lives, for over a century the Chinese people fought the foreign aggressors in an indomitable struggle for national salvation and independence. The Taiping Heavenly Kingdom Movement, the Boxer Movement, and the Revolution of 1911, which overthrew the Qing dynasty, broke out during this period. These revolutionary movements dealt heavy blows to imperialist influences in China, but they failed to deliver the nation from semi-colonialism. A fundamental change took place only after the Chinese people, under the leadership of the Chinese Communist Party, overthrew the Guomindang reactionary rule and founded the People's Republic of China. After its birth in 1921, the Communist Party of China set the clear-cut goal in its political program to "overthrow the oppression by international imperialism and achieve the complete independence of the Chinese nation" and to "overthrow the warlords and unite China into a real democratic republic"; it led the people in an arduous struggle culminating in victory in the national democratic revolution.

The founding of the People's Republic of China eradicated the forces of imperialism, feudalism, and bureaucrat-capitalism in the Chinese mainland, put an end to the nation's history of dismemberment, oppression, and humiliation at the hands of alien powers for well over a century and to long years of turbulence characterized by incessant war and social disunity, and realized the people's cherished dream of national independence and unification. The Chinese nation, which makes up one-fourth of the world's population, is no longer one that the aggressors could kill and insult at will. The Chinese people have stood up as the masters of their own country; for the first time they have won real human dignity and the respect of the whole world. The Chinese people have won the basic guarantee for their life and security.

National independence has protected the Chinese people from being trodden under the heels of foreign invaders. However, the problem of the people's right to subsistence can be truly solved only when their basic means of livelihood are guaranteed.

To eat their fill and dress warmly were the fundamental demand of the Chinese people who had long suffered cold and hunger. Far from meeting this demand, successive regimes in old China brought even more disasters to the people. In those days, landlords and rich peasants who accounted for 10 percent of the rural population held 70 percent of the land, while the poor peasants and farm laborers who accounted for 70 percent of the rural population owned only 10 percent of the land. The bureaucrat-comprador bourgeoisie who accounted for only a small fraction of the population monopolized 80 percent of the industrial capital and controlled the economic lifelines of the country. The Chinese people were repeatedly exploited by land rent, taxes, usury, and industrial and commercial capital. The exploitation and poverty they suffered were of a degree rarely seen in other parts of the world. According to 1932 statistics, the Chinese peasants were subjected to 1,656 kinds of exorbitant taxes and levies, which took away 60–90 percent of their harvests. The people's miseries were exacerbated and their lives made all the harsher by the reactionary governments who, politically corrupt and impotent, surrendered China's sovereign rights under humiliating terms and served as tools of foreign imperialist rule, and by the separatist regime of warlords who were embroiled in endless wars. It was estimated that 80 percent of the populace in old China suffered to varying degrees of starvation and tens of thousands—hundreds of thousands in some cases—died of it every year. A major natural disaster invariably left the land strewn with corpses of hunger victims. More than 3.7 million lives were lost when floods hit east China in 1931. In 1943, a crop failure in Henan province took the lives of 3 million people and left 15 million subsisting on grass and bark and struggling on the verge of death. After the victory of the War of Resistance against Japan, the reactionary Guomindang government launched a civil war, fed on the flesh and blood of the people, and caused total economic collapse. In 1946, 10 million people died of hunger countrywide. In 1947, 100 million, or 22 percent of the national population then, were under the constant threat of hunger.

Ever since the founding of the People's Republic of China in 1949, the Communist Party of China and the Chinese government have always placed the task of helping the people get enough to wear and eat on the top of the agenda. For the first three years of the People's Republic, the Chinese people, led by their government, concentrated their efforts on healing the wounds of war and quickly restored the national economy to the record level in history. On this basis, China lost no time to complete the socialist transformation of agriculture, handicraft industry, and capitalist industry and commerce, thus uprooting the system of exploitation, instituting the system of socialism and, for the first time in history, turning the people into masters of the means of production and beneficiaries of social wealth. This fired the people with soaring enthusiasm for building a new China and a new life, emancipated the social productive forces, and set the economy on the track of unprecedented growth. Since 1979, China has switched the focus of its work to economic construction, begun reform and opening to the outside world, and set the goal of building socialism with Chinese characteristics. This has further expanded the social productive forces and enabled the nation to basically solve the problem of feeding and clothing its 1.1 billion people.

Tilling 7 percent of the world's total cultivated land averaging only 1.3 *mu* (one *mu* equals one-fifteenth of one hectare) per capita as against 12.16 *mu* in the United States and the world's average of 4.52 *mu*—China has nevertheless succeeded in feeding a population that makes up 22 percent of the world's total. Contrary to some Western politicians' prediction that no Chinese government could solve the problem of feeding its people, socialist China has done it by its own efforts. The past forty-odd years have witnessed a marked increase in the average annual per-capita consumption of major consumer goods despite a yearly average population increase of 14 million. A survey shows that the daily caloric intake per resident in China was 2,270 in 1952, 2,311 in 1978, and 2,630 in 1990, approaching the world's average.

The life-span of the Chinese people has lengthened and their health improved considerably. According to statistics, the population's average life expectancy increased from 35 years before liberation to 70 years in 1988, higher than the average level in the world's medium-income countries, while the death rate dropped from 33 per thousand before liberation to 6.67 per thousand in 1990, which was one of the lowest death rates in the world. China's 1987 infant mortality of 31 per thousand approached the level of high-income countries. The health of the Chinese people, especially the physical development of youngsters, has greatly improved as compared with the situation in old China. An average fifteen-year-old boy in 1979 was 1.8 centimeters taller and 2.1 kilograms heavier than his counterparts living during the 1937–41 period; and an average girl of the same age in 1979 was 1.3 centimeters taller and 1 kilogram heavier. Since 1979, the health of the Chinese people has improved further. The label on old China, "sick man of East Asia," has long been consigned to the dustbin of history.

The problem of food and clothing having been basically solved, the people have been guaranteed with the basic right to subsistence. This is a historical achievement made by the Chinese people and government in seeking and protecting human rights.

However, to protect the people's right to subsistence and improve their living conditions remains an issue of paramount importance in China today. China has gained independence, but it is still a developing country with limited national strength. The preservation of national independence and state sovereignty and the freedom from imperialist subjugation are, therefore, the very fundamental conditions for the survival and development of the Chinese people. Although China has basically solved the problem of food and clothing, its economy is still at a fairly low level, its standard of living falls considerably short of that in developed countries, and the pressure of a huge population and relative per-capita paucity of resources will continue to restrict the socioeconomic development and the improvement of the people's lives. The people's right to subsistence will still be threatened in the event of a social turmoil or other disasters. Therefore it is the fundamental wish and demand of the Chinese people and a long-term, urgent task of the Chinese government to maintain national stability, concentrate their effort on developing the productive forces along the line that has proved to be successful, persist in reform and opening to the outside world, strive to rejuvenate the national economy and boost the national strength, and, on the basis of having solved the problem of food and clothing, secure a well-off livelihood for the people throughout the country so that their right to subsistence will no longer be threatened.

Further Reading

Translated full texts of several White Papers on Human Rights can be found on the Internet at http://www.chinaguide.org/e-white/.

For a detailed analysis of the context in which the *White Paper* was produced, see Ann Kent, *China, the United Nations, and Human Rights: The Limits of Compliance* (Philadelphia: University of Pennsylvania Press, 1999).

53

Statement on the Issue of Human Rights in China (1991)

Liberal Democratic Party of China

Translation reprinted from Foreign Broadcast Information Service Daily Report: China, FBIS-CHI-91–222 (November 18, 1991), pp. 22–23. Text originally published in *Ming pao* (November 16, 1991).

In 1991, sentences still continued to be meted out against those who had taken part in the 1989 Democracy Movement, but this did not stop others from engaging in dissident activities. In 1990–91 there were several attempts in Beijing and other places to establish labor unions and political parties. In Beijing, one of the organizations established was the Liberal Democratic Party of China. The publication in 1991 of what was to become the first of a series of White Papers on Human Rights (see previous text) provoked reactions from dissidents at home and abroad. Since the government accepted and itself made use of the language of human rights, it was inevitable that dissidents also increasingly would come to refer to human rights and China's international obligations in their statements and open letters. Members of the Liberal Democratic Party of China thus promptly wrote a statement demanding the release of political prisoners and respect for the UDHR. It is also symptomatic that it was issued on the eve of U.S. Secretary of State Baker's visit to China, as dissident activities have come to feed on foreign visits and foreign media attention. The statement was posted at Beijing University and one hundred copies were printed and distributed to other places around the country. The members of the Liberal Democratic Party of China were all arrested in 1992. They spent two years in incommunicado detention prior to their trial in July 1994, when they received some of the harshest sentences meted out in the post-1989 period. Hu Shigen, who allegedly drafted the statement, was sentenced to twenty years' imprisonment for counterrevolutionary crimes, Kang Yuchun got seventeen years, and Liu Jingsheng, who helped distribute the statement, received fifteen years. As of this Reader's *publication, they are all still in prison.*

Amid a wave of condemnation both at home and abroad, the CCP authorities were compelled to issue a "White Paper on Human Rights" in China. It is not difficult for those who know the real facts to expose the lies and quibbles in the "White Paper." Nevertheless, this is still a great victory of the people in the international community and at home who work for the democratic cause in China. We hereby express our sincere gratitude and extend our respects to friends who show concern for the human rights situation in China. In the meantime, we also hope that the

"White Paper" is a positive posture of the CCP authorities for improving the human rights situation at home and that this is a turning point for continuing to improve the human rights situation in China as a result of the concern and pressure exerted at home and abroad. For this reason, we hereby issue the following statement:

1. The CCP authorities must strictly abide by the "UN Charter" and the "International Human Rights Convention," and truly assume their responsibility as a signatory. As a step toward observing the "International Human Rights Convention," the CCP authorities must, first, truly protect human rights at home. Political freedoms of citizens, such as freedom of thought, speech, religious belief, assembly, press, publication, demonstration, and meeting and freedom to strike are basic human rights. If such freedoms of citizens are not protected, human rights are out of the question. Over the past forty years since the CCP has imposed its rule on the country, freedom has never been truly respected and protected. The horrifying "June 4" massacre occurred because of this. Nobody can tamper with history. If the CCP authorities intend to change the isolated situation of being spurned by the whole world, they must take the practical action of improving the human rights situation. Any attempt to deceive public opinion both at home and abroad with lies and quibbles can only excite stronger condemnation both at home and abroad.

The pro-democracy movement in China is an important component part of international human rights activities. The existence of the one-party autocracy of the CCP is a severe threat to the international human rights movement. The autocratic iron curtain in East Europe and the Soviet Union has been smashed. The Chinese people, who account for nearly one-fourth of the world's population, are still enduring the great suffering of having no freedom. This is a grim reality facing the present international human rights movement.

We call on the United Nations, various international organizations, governments in various countries, political parties, groups, and personages to show their concern for the human rights situation in China, and put necessary pressure on the CCP authorities unceasingly to compel them to respond and make concessions to the unanimous demand of the international community. We also call on the international community to provide support for the pro-democracy movement in China in terms of morality and materials. In particular, they should express humanitarian support and rescue those pro-democracy activists who are jailed and persecuted.

2. Since the CCP became a ruling party, it has imposed a bureaucratic-monopoly, military, and police rule on China to exercise comprehensive autocracy over the Chinese people politically, economically, and culturally, and deprive the Chinese people of the basic human rights that they should have enjoyed a long time ago. From the large-scale persecution of the intellectuals in 1957 to the ten-year catastrophe of the Great Cultural Revolution, which started in 1966, and to the massive massacre and persecution of the pro-democracy activists in 1989, the crime of the CCP authorities of exercising autocracy has triggered the hatred of all Chinese people, including the majority of those fair-minded Communist Party members with a conscience. The perverse acts of the CCP authorities have brought poverty and suffering to the Chinese nation. Only by awakening promptly, proceeding from national righteousness, conforming to popular will and historical trend, giving up its one-party private gains, and practicing democratic politics can the CCP authorities free themselves from the hopeless situation. Only thus can our national invigoration stand a chance of success.

As the first step of national political reconciliation, we call on the CCP authorities to:

- release as early as possible all political and religious prisoners, and not impose cruel torture and inhumane treatment on them;
- stop all political persecution of pro-democracy organizations and activists and rehabilitate their reputation;
- acknowledge citizens' political rights and the existence and rights of all persecuted underground dissidents and organizations and convene at an early date a national meeting extensively attended by various political parties and people's representatives to commonly discuss a series of important issues connected with the future and destiny of the state, and hold a referendum when necessary.

We call on democratic political parties, pro-democracy organizations, and activists both at home and abroad to unite and coordinate their actions to force the CCP authorities to follow the track of rationality and rule by law. Let us work as one and make contributions to democracy, unification, and development in China!

Liberal Democratic Party of China
November 12, 1991

Further Reading

For additional information on the people behind the statement and the verdict against them, see Amnesty International, *Six Years After Tiananmen: Human Rights Violations Continue* (AI Index: ASA 17/28/95, London, June 1995). Many other statements on human rights have appeared since 1991; for a representative selection, see "Letters from Citizens: China's Human Rights Movement," *China Rights Forum* (Summer 1995): 10–14. For a statement from 1998, see Text 59 below.

54

Human Rights, Rights, and Collective Rights: An Answer to Comrade Lu Deshan (1992)

Zhang Wenxian

"Renquan, quanli, jiti renquan: da Lu Deshan tongzhi" [Human Rights, Rights, and Collective Rights: An Answer to Comrade Lu Deshan], *Zhongguo faxue* [Chinese Legal Studies], no. 3 (1992): 116–18.

Zhang Wenxian, a legal scholar at Jilin University, has been an important contributor to academic discussion of human rights throughout the 1990s. His 1991 article "On the Subjects of Human Rights and the Human Rights of Subjects" generated considerable controversy by downplaying the importance of collective rights and stressing that individuals were the proper subjects of human rights. The official stance on these issues, as seen for instance in Texts 52 and 56, is that collective rights (such as the nation's right to development and self-determination) are human rights that actually have priority over individual human rights. It should be noted, as indeed Zhang takes pains to point out in the present article, that Zhang never denied the existence of collective human rights in the realm of international law. Be that as it may, several articles were published criticizing Zhang on these counts, one of which Zhang replies to in the article we have translated here. Zhang's views, like those of Li Buyun and Xia Yong, represent the development of a cautiously independent scholarship on human rights during the 1990s.

In *Chinese Legal Studies* (1992, no. 2), Comrade Lu Deshan's article "Another Discussion of the Subject of Human Rights" (referred to below as Lu's article) appeared. This article was partially a debate with my own earlier article "On the Subjects of Human Rights and the Human Rights of Subjects" (published in *Chinese Legal Studies* [1991, no. 5]). What follows is an answer to and a dialectic with parts of Lu's article.

Part I: Did I Really Deny the Existence of Collective Human Rights?

Lu's article concludes that I denied the existence of collective human rights (*jiti renquan*): "Zhang clearly denies the existence of collective human rights." After this, he begins a polemic against the viewpoint that there are no collective human rights. This is clearly a misinterpretation of my article. In fact, my viewpoint is the following: in the area of domestic law, the concept of "collective human rights" has not yet been publicly introduced, but in international law, "collective human rights" is an indispensable concept. My article clearly and definitely points out: "The concept of collective human rights first appeared in international law as a weapon for Third World nations in the battle against imperialism, colonialism, and hegemonism for the rights to racial equality, national self-determination (*minzu zijue quan*), control of natural resources, development, and peace. In the international struggle, this concept is undeniably useful; in the current and future struggle for international human rights, we should continue to raise the call for 'collective human rights,' guard the right to national sovereignty and the right of national groups to develop, and resist some imperialist nations' 'human rights offensive.'" It is clear that the viewpoint denying collective human rights which Lu ascribes to me has nothing to do with my article.

In order to prove that I "obviously deny the existence of collective human rights," Lu quotes the following from my article: "In this kind of legal structure, there is no need whatsoever to bring in the concept of 'collective human rights.'" It is regrettable that Lu's critical discussion of this phrase does not explain the argument on which my conclusion is based, nor does it explain the meaning of "this kind of legal structure." My space here is limited, so I cannot cite much more from the original article, but will just point out the following. First of all, the "kind of legal structure" I mentioned refers to the rights of nationalities (*minzu*), classes, political parties, and other collectives in domestic legislation. Secondly, if Lu does not agree with my viewpoint, does this mean that he considers it necessary to change the rights of nationalities, classes, political parties, and mass organizations that are contained in our Constitution and laws into "collective human rights of nationalities," "class collective human rights," "political party collective human rights," and "mass organization collective human rights"?

Thirdly, the fact that we do not use the concept of "collective human rights" in domestic legal structures does not prevent people from using this concept in the moral, political, and ideological senses. It also does not prevent any scholar from using and transforming concepts like "rights of nationalities" or "political party rights" in his or her own work to mean "collective human rights of nationalities" or "political party collective human rights," if he or she feels this makes the concepts more scientific, simple, and able to meet the standards of legal scholarly language. Thus I have not rejected collective human rights and their great importance, but rather have limited the scope and object of their usage.

Part II: Why Have I Taken the Subject of Domestic Human Rights and Primarily Limited It to the Individual?

Lu believes that the reason I have emphasized that the subject of human rights *can only be* the individual is because while individual and collective rights are in fact equally dependent on one another, I believe collective rights to be contained within the category of individual rights.[1] This shows that Lu does not grasp my viewpoint. The reason I have largely limited the subject of domestic human rights to the individual is because of linguistic analyses and legal investigations of "rights" (*quanli*), "the subject of rights," "human rights," and "the subject of human rights." I believe that "human rights" and "rights" are not equivalent concepts. "Rights" is a general designation and a covering term which refers to all legally confirmed and protected rights and interests (*quanyi*) that people have and ought to have. "Human rights" is a concept derived from "rights," and refers to the fundamental rights one enjoys, or ought to enjoy, from birth, as well as any essential extensions of these rights. Human rights are a part of the system of rights.

Correspondingly, the scope of the subjects of human rights is not the same as the scope of the subjects of rights. The subjects of rights range widely, including all who enjoy rights (including human rights), assume rights, and exercise rights, such as individuals, organizations, national groups, classes, political parties, nations, international organizations, and so on. The subjects of human rights are only one portion of the subjects of rights; they mainly refer to conscious, actually existing individuals. It is very clear that if you take "the subjects of human rights" to be primarily limited to individuals, not only does this not deny that collectives are the subjects of rights, but on the contrary, it alerts people to the limitations of "human rights" and "the subjects of human rights." Human rights as individual rights are only one of many kinds of rights, and can in no way imply or represent all the other subjects of rights. My essay was very clear on this point.

According to the logic of Lu's article, if we try to make human rights and the subject of human rights the same as rights and the subject of rights, this will make human rights into an all-purpose concept capable of covering [the same range as] rights. This is a manifestation of the generalization of human rights that I criticize in my article. In fact, the difference between Lu and me does not lie in whether we acknowledge the existence and importance of collective rights, but rather in whether we want to make "collective rights" into "collective human rights." I must point out that in the past, human rights was forbidden territory; no one dared to label as "human rights" those rights which were originally considered to be within the scope of human rights. Now, however, human rights is a popular topic. Today everyone sticks the label of "human rights" on rights that were not originally considered within the scope of human rights or on rights which there is no need to call "human rights"; it seems that without this label, rights will not be seen as having any important meaning. This is hardly a desirable development.

Part III: What Are "Collective Human Rights"?

"Collective human rights" is a new concept that appeared in the 1970s. It represents an enrichment, development, and breakthrough in the traditional human rights concept. The 1979 Resolution on the Right to Development of the Twenty-Third UN General Assembly (Res. 34/46) and the 1986 Declaration on the Right to Development of the Forty-First UN General Assembly (Res. 41/128) stated that there is an inalienable human right to development; not only is the equal right to development a privilege (*tequan*) (an alternate translation would be innate right [*tianfu quanli*]) of individuals, but also of nations.[2] These two resolutions confirmed that each nation and nationality has the right to self-determination, and that every nation's people have the right to dispose of their nation's natural resources and wealth according to the models of economic, social, and cultural development established by their national conditions. Against the background of this kind of international struggle and international legislation, "collective human rights" took shape as a generalization of these founding rights. In order to distinguish them from traditional "individual human rights," the concept has its own specific terminology. (Of course, whether or not the expression "collective human rights" is [adequately] precise still needs deliberation.)

The origins of "collective human rights" as a concept determines its meaning. Collective human rights primarily takes as its nucleus the rights to development of nations and nationalities, including any other related systems of rights. The subjects of collective human rights are primarily sovereign states, nationalities (in the political, rather than in the socio-cultural or anthropological senses), and a people considered as a whole. Most scholars inside and outside China use the concept of "collective human rights" in this way. We cannot simply rely on our own, subjective ideas and arbitrarily generalize the subject of collective human rights to include every collective and mass organization within the scope of domestic law. In Lu's essay, collective human rights refers to two different situations, both the rights enjoyed by collectives and the rights arising from collective movements. He also includes the organizations, political parties, and classes that fall within domestic law together under the name of "collective human rights." [If we follow this example,] the term "collective human rights" will lose its original relevance to our current era and its progressive meaning.

The aim of developing nations in raising the call for "collective human rights" was to oppose the unequal international political and economic order, the hegemonic and monopolistic capitalist political extortion and economic exploitation, and the policy of interfering in other nations' internal affairs under the pretext of "human rights diplomacy." But if the rights of domestic mass organizations, classes, and political parties also become "collective human rights," then the bourgeois class will have bourgeois "collective human rights" and the proletariat class will have its proletariat "collective human rights." Will "collective human rights" then not become a value-neutral concept? It could be used by the broad masses of laboring peoples on behalf of the workers, or by the minority of exploiters on their own behalf. In every historical period, haven't exploiters and reactionaries used the so-called "collective human rights" they enjoyed and exercised in order to exploit and oppress the broad laboring masses? Is it really necessary to emphasize such neutral "collective human rights"?

Notes

1. I have substituted the italicized words for Lu's original "is primarily" [author's note].
2. Article 1, paragraph 1 of the Declaration reads: "The right to development is an inalienable human right by virtue of which every human person and all peoples are entitled to participate in, contribute to, and enjoy economic, social, cultural, and political development, in which all human rights and fundamental freedoms can be fully realized." *Declaration on the Right to Development*, G.A. res. 41/128, annex, 41 U.N. GAOR Supp. (No. 53) at 186, U.N. Doc. A/41/53 (1986).

Further Reading

Zhang's original "The Subjects of Human Rights and the Human Rights of Subjects" also appeared in the well-known collection, *Dangdai renquan* [Contemporary Human Rights], ed. CASS Legal Institute (Beijing: Zhongguo shehui kexue chubanshe, 1992). Another article that argues for the individual's being the fundamental subject of human rights is Luo Mingda and He Hangzhou, "Lun renquan de geti shuxing" [On the Individual-based Characteristics of Human Rights], *Zhengfa luntan*, no. 1 (1993).

55
Human Rights and Chinese Tradition (1992)

Xia Yong

"Renquan yu Zhongguo chuantong" [Human Rights and the Chinese Tradition]. This selection originally appeared in the epilogue of Xia Yong, *Renquan gainian qiyuan* [The Origin of the Concept of Human Rights: A Chinese Interpretation] (Beijing: Zhongguo zhengfa daxue chubanshe, 1992). It was reprinted in Liu Nanlai et al., eds., *Renquan de pubianxing he teshuxing* [The Universality and Particularity of Human Rights] (Beijing: Shehui kexue wenxian chubanshe, 1996), pp. 64–77. The translation comes from Peter R. Baehr, Fried van Hoof, Liu Nanlai, Tao Zhenghua, editors in chief; Jacqueline Smith, ed., *Human Rights: Chinese and Dutch Perspectives* (The Hague: Martinus Nijhoff, 1996), pp. 77–90, slightly modified.

Xia Yong (b. 1961) is a professor at the Chinese Academy of Social Sciences, and has been an active participant in discussions of human rights through the 1990s. Xia wrote the first dissertation in China to deal with human rights, from which the following piece is taken. He has written on the history of and current debates in Western rights theory, on rights in Chinese law, as well as on the complex relations between Chinese tradition and Chinese rights discourse. He was also the lead editor of a multifaceted study of the contemporary consciousness and practice of rights in many different aspects of Chinese society. The essay we present here is one of the few Chinese contributions to the recent literature on human rights to deal extensively with the question of human rights and China's cultural tradition. Xia's sympathetic account of Confucian ideas, and his criticisms of Western excesses, bears a resemblance to Liang Shuming from seventy-one years earlier (see Text 17), although unlike Liang, Xia consciously sets out to relate Confucian concepts to the concept of human rights. In this respect at least, he has more in common with Hang Liwu (see Text 45). Xia asks whether there are fundamental conflicts between traditional Chinese thought and human rights, and answers that there are not. Indeed, he goes on to argue that far from conflicting with human rights, the central Chinese commitment to harmony can make constructive contributions to international human rights discourse. He does recognize that human rights were not developed in traditional China, which he explains in part by suggesting that they were not needed to the same degree as they were in Western society.

Introduction

Human rights are usually referred to as universal rights, because their subject consists of all human beings and their contents include stipulations common [to all people], without regard for differences between human beings of race, class, nationality, religion, color, status, property, position, and so on. However, in fact, such differences not only exist in human society but also have a very strong influence upon the understanding, enjoyment, and implementation of human rights. Viewed from the standpoint of contemporary human rights theory and practice, these differences among traditions of culture and civilization have had the most profound, broad, and serious effects. We therefore are faced with a difficult task, which on the one hand asks us to put the concept of human rights in the context of different traditions and to reconsider and improve it, in order that the concept of human rights will be compatible with different traditions of culture and civilization, rather than only with the Western tradition, and become truly universal rights. On the other hand, in the process of the contextual interpretation of human rights, [our task requires us] to test and reform the traditions concerned and make them compatible with the spirit of human rights.

In recent years, human rights has no longer been seen on the Chinese mainland as a slogan of the bourgeoisie. However, some deeper cultural problems have not yet been solved. For example, can only Western culture give rise to the concept of human rights? Are Chinese traditions incompatible with human rights? Does acknowledgment and implementation of human rights inevitably take Western culture as its standard? Here I will deal with three issues.

1. There Exist No Vital Conflicts Between Human Rights and Chinese Traditions

The concept of human rights does not originate from China. There are two [common] explanations for this. One explanation is that extremely severe political, spiritual, and economic oppression existed in traditional Chinese society. Chinese culture was a backward farming culture, and the basic spirits of this culture were autocracy and collectivism (*tuanti zhuyi*), so it was bound to trample on human nature and destroy individuality and even do people great harm. In this case it was absolutely impossible to advocate and practice human rights.[1] Another explanation is that political, spiritual, and economic oppression in Chinese traditional society was not as severe as in ancient Western society, Chinese culture was the most advanced and most vital culture of humankind, it had the greatest regard for humanism, and pursued the great harmony of all humankind. This [latter] reason why the concept of human rights does not originate from China is that Chinese ancestors lived a more peaceful and harmonious life than Western barbarians. They disdained the scramble for power and profit and could, with no need to resort to rights and the rule of law, enjoy the equality, freedom, security, and social welfare pursued by Western human rights and the rule of law.[2]

Both these explanations have some justification but both are oversimplified and one-sided. We can cite numerous facts to refute the first explanation. For instance, the economic exploitation in ancient China was not so severe as in ancient Western society and extra economic coercion by the landlord class was far less cruel than that of slavery in ancient Greece and Rome. Politics in ancient China put great emphasis on appointing people on their merits and through imperial examinations; this was at least not inferior to the aristocracy in ancient Western society which paid attention to property qualification and class status. It is difficult to say that the ideas of "harmony," "the golden mean," and "all things as an organic whole" are not more profound than the ideas of dualism and creation of the world by God. The rules of "the benevolent loving people," "people being more precious than the monarchs," "saving all beings," and "back to nature and simplicity" do no harm to people and are not cannibalistic.

Likewise, we can also cite a number of facts to refute the second explanation. For example, the productive forces of ancient Chinese society were long shackled by autocracy and a small-scale peasant economy with the result that many people lacked enough food and clothing. Corruption, partisan struggles, disastrous warfare, literary inquisitions, torture, and even eating of "two-legged lambs" occurred incessantly. [Consider the Three Bonds:] "ruler guides subject, father guides son, and husband guides wife." Not a bit of the spirit of democracy, freedom, and harmony can be found here. It is difficult to sustain and develop equality, freedom, security, and social welfare that are not based on human rights and the rule of law.

We can see that the above-mentioned two explanations cannot really tell us why the concept of human rights did not emerge in ancient Chinese society. What they represent are two kinds of cultural sentiments among Chinese scholars since the May Fourth [Movement in 1919], rather than two explanatory theories. The former expresses the mood of abandoning [our] traditions and worshipping Western ones, and the latter reveals the sincere and anxious feeling of rejuvenating [our] traditions and creating new ones.

Nevertheless, these two explanations are instructive. Although the first explanation denies the compatibility of human rights with Chinese traditions, it does not deny the existence of demands for human rights in Chinese traditional society; although the second explanation denies the existence of demands for human rights or the existence of the question of human rights, it does not deny the compatibility of human rights with Chinese traditions. This calls for further study. In my opinion, there are three spirits in the concept of human rights, which are humanism, the rule of law, and great harmony.[3] The spirits of humanism and great harmony contained in human rights not only existed but were also quite widespread in ancient Chinese society. What China lacked was primarily the spirit of the rule of law. Humanism can be said to be the basic characteristic of Chinese traditional culture. Numerous popular expressions with which ordinary people are familiar can be cited here, not to mention discussions by the sages of ancient China; for instance, "the benevolent love the people," "dying for a just cause," "human beings are the most valuable on earth," . . . and so on.

Judging from the logical structure of the idea of human rights, the idea of human rights in ancient Western philosophy logically consisted of the concepts of ultimate authority, equal personality (*renge*), and freedom of essential nature (*benxing*).[4] Although no idea of human rights emerged in Chinese history, notions of moral law and of equal personality that transcend positive laws did exist beyond doubt in the ancient philosophy of China. Confucianism, Daoism, and Buddhism are also full of the idea of freedom. It did not evolve into the concept of a right only because it was inward-looking, self-sustaining, and detached; rarely [was this idea of freedom] connected with self-interest, independence, self-defense, and confrontation in social relations. Therefore, we cannot draw the conclusion that the principles of human rights are absolutely incompatible with Chinese traditions on the ground that Chinese traditional society did not discuss human rights.

Chinese traditions of civilization are not as distinctly different from Western ones as they are described by those engaged in comparative studies of culture. In fact, there are more common grounds than differences between the two. The key reason for the failure of the concept of human rights to emerge in Chinese history is that according to Chinese traditions, humanism is practiced and great harmony pursued not by means of emphasizing the rights of individuals but through their duties, and not by means of emphasizing the rule of law but through the rule of virtue. Chinese traditional society did not have a total disregard for the rights of individuals and the rule of law. For instance, so-called "engaging in a lawsuit" among the people is to settle disputes over rights and duties; "paying with one's life for a murder" and "repaying a debt for the money borrowed" are undoubtedly based on the rights of one party concerned; such rights of demanding justice enjoyed by ordinary people as beating the drums at the gates of feudal government offices and blocking the way of officials' sedans . . . were at least recognized by customary laws in ancient China; "being prompted by sentiments but controlled by rites," "giving everyone his due and preventing disputes," and "observing rites and duties" contain some flavor of the rule of law. Of course, this kind of rule is rule by law rather than rule of law. In the final analysis, [ruling] by means of emphasizing the duties of individuals and morals means to practice humanism and to achieve great harmony by relying on positive mutual love and concessions between man and man, rather than by passive mutual constraint. Therefore, sages in ancient China could speak strongly about human nature and humanism and about the benevolent loving the people and the people being more precious than the monarchs, but never about human rights and winning rights for the people. In this sense, the difference between Chinese and Western traditions lies in means only. What is more important is that the concept of harmony in Chinese tradition is not only compatible with human rights, but could also govern and improve traditional Western human rights. This will be addressed later.

2. Why Did Chinese Traditional Society Not Discuss Human Rights?

From the perspective of administering a country, what Chinese traditional politics pursued was the politics of ritual laws (*lifa*) rather than the politics of contract laws (*yuefa*). Three points are worth noticing about the politics of ritual laws. The first is [the idea of] inner sage and outer king; the second, the observance of rites and righteousness; and the third, the cultivation of benevolent and wise men. The questions which these three points were designed to address were: what is the foundation of the political order, on what basis is it used, and why. Confucianism stands for "rule of man," but its essence is rule by sages and men of virtue. That means "it is appropriate for the benevolent to hold high positions," as stated by Mencius. This is not an arbitrary rule as is generally known. It is quite similar to Plato's ideal that the "philosopher is king." However, the personality of Chinese sages is supposed to unite [all of the following:] inner sage and outer king; leaving and entering the world; and cultivating virtues, leaving worthy writings to posterity, and rendering distinguished service. Cultivating moral character, governing the family, administering the country, and establishing peace and order throughout the world are a comprehensive process. If sages are not emperors, the monarch should cultivate and develop his own benevolence so as to match his position with virtues and to carry out a policy of benevolence. Only in this way can a fairly sound social-political order be established and lasting peace and stability be achieved. Here lies the truth that "government as administration depends on man." This proposition concerning the administration of a country stresses the duties of those in power to society and to the people. To perform these duties is not required by law, but relies on the spontaneous feeling or self-perfection of those in power. If "duty as basis" (*yiwu benwei*) is said to be a major characteristic of Chinese traditional political and legal culture, the genuine spirit of "duty as basis" puts special emphasis on the moral duties of those in power and makes this the starting point of administering a country and establishing peace and stability across the land. This kind of "duty as basis" is not identical with the "right as basis" contained in Western political and legal culture on a moral and logical level. It is also entirely different from the duty as basis approach of the Legalists, which [applies only] to the people and corresponds with power as basis [for the rulers]. However, the duty as basis advocated by the politics of sages presupposes the established ownership of political power. In other words, it is an established fact that political power is in the hands of a handful of people, and under the premise that this fact will not be altered, efforts are made to demand that those in power work selflessly for the public interest, defend the country, and cherish the people.

Of course, a sound social-political order is not the outward manifestation of the intrinsic virtues of sages and men of virtue. It relies on a set of social norms called rites (*li*). Rites are both customary laws for daily use by the ordinary people, and moral laws sorted out and developed by sages and men of virtue. They are part of actual law, too, but are by no means [the same as] contract laws, [which are] formulated by all strata and interests in society through struggle and compromise. Rites are a kind of immanent law. They are applied to all members of society and no Western-style churches are needed to be in charge of their implementation. Rites are not the basis of scrambling for power and profit and carrying out mutual confrontation, but the foundation for the people to seek a harmonious world in which no disputes and lawsuits exist. Morals, religion, law, politics, and society are integrated. The function of rites is not merely to develop a specific social political order . . . ; their more important function is to encourage "all to return to benevolence," which is to say that the demands set by Confucianism on all people to observe rites were designed to ultimately cultivate a complete moral personality for everybody through the imperceptible influence of rites. This is the well-calculated reason why Confucius stood for rule by rites and opposed rule by penalty. According to the Confucianism ideal, observing rites (*li*) and practicing righteousness (*yi*) are synchronized. Righteousness is identical with self-cultivation but is opposed to selfish interests of individuals. Accordingly, the relations between people should not be relations of interest which all contend for, but should be moral relations of loving and helping each other. People should reciprocate sincerity with sincerity and treat one another with virtue, rather than exchange interests for interests and pay too much attention to gains. Therefore, the most important social-political principles in ancient China were the benevolent person's righteousness, the golden mean, and harmony, rather than Western-style fairness and justice connected with disputes over rights and duties. Furthermore, unlike the Western outlook on justice which emphasizes rights, the Chinese outlook on justice stresses duties.[5]

The reason why Chinese traditional society did not discuss human rights can also be found in the subject of rights. The subject of rights is human beings, and the emergence of human rights is the result of the continuous growth of demands for rights and accumulation of rights of human beings. This growth depends on the development of human beings in specific societies, which, in turn, depends on specific economic, political, and cultural developments. Specifically, a right is a relational concept. It indicates a kind of social tie between people, and such ties presuppose the relative separation from, and independence of, the subjects of rights. Certainly, rights and duties show not only the existence of individuals and their mutual relations, but also, more importantly, the social relations of "taking" and "giving" among individuals. "Taking" and "giving" are concepts that are opposed to each other. In Western history, the development of the system of rights presupposed not only a boundary between people in a general sense, but also divisions and confrontations among individuals and between classes. The greater the independence and confrontation between the subjects of rights, the stronger the demands for rights and the more advanced the legal systems. The situation in Chinese traditional society was quite different. We might as well examine the question of the subject of rights in ancient China in economic, political, and cultural terms.

In economic terms, a self-supporting and small-scale peasant economy was the basic mode of ancient Chinese economy. Individuals were subordinate to families. They were not independent producers and managers, nor were they independent subjects of economic interests. Family heads enjoyed privileges (*tequan*) over family members and undertook duties to the latter. Natural blood relationships were the key foundation on which people coordinated their labor and carried out social cooperation. Such a natural economy and "natural" relationships were different from those in ancient Western society, which gradually disintegrated and even left individuals at the mercy of the society, foreign nations, and the market, as the result of the mixing of races, slave wars, and the commodity economy. Families provide individuals with tender shelter. Therefore, in Chinese traditional society, the separation and confrontation of individuals as the subjects of interests, and their independence in production, exchange, distribution, and consumption, were extremely limited. The "relations of dependence of human beings" played a predominant role. As this was the case for human beings, so was it in their doctrines. If strong emphasis had been laid in this economic mode on the rights of individuals, and too many boundary lines had been delimited between people, nothing would have been achieved and even the most fundamental needs of subsistence and social order could not have been guaranteed. As we know, in the course of the disintegration of Western feudal economy, the demands for and accumulation of rights by foreigners, urban residents, and the bourgeoisie directly promoted the emergence of modern human rights, but these three kinds of subjects of rights, especially the bourgeoisie, did not really exist in Chinese traditional society.

In political terms, individuals did not have an independent social political status as "citizens" (*gongmin*). The status of each individual was first determined by his or her ethical status and status in blood relations such as father and son, older and younger brothers, and husband and wife. Since the family was integrated with the State, the status of blood relations was interlinked with social status, such as that between ruler and subject, officials and common people, and people of high and low status. Such statuses became the basis of the relations of rights and duties. In Western history, in addition to the impacts produced by the commodity economy and racial wars on blood ties, the status of citizens and religious believers successively eroded the status of family members. Moreover, no political entity that could be used as the subject of legal rights existed in ancient China. Holding sway over a region and setting up separationist rule occurred frequently, but this was quite different from disputes over rights and duties between ordinary people and aristocrats, between kings and feudal lords, between the king and the Pope, and between king, Pope, and the bourgeoisie. After the system of imperial examination was carried out vigorously and "a good scholar makes an official," this flow of social strata alleviated to a certain degree the tense antagonistic relations between hereditary imperial power and society, and reduced the possibility and necessity of the existence of the intelligentsia as an independent social-political entity and an advocate of the rights of spiritual freedom and freedom of speech and the press. Furthermore, in Western history human rights were often synonymous with "freedom" and "emancipation," and they derived from the direct resistance to the authority of God, the spiritual control of the church, and the cruel rule of kings and feudal lords. In ancient China, there existed no Western-type God, church, or feudal lords, and the rule of emperors relied on the tender ties of family blood relations and the enormous power of family heads as well as the ethics, the cardinal guides, and the constant virtues of Confucianism. Therefore, the external incentives for our Chinese ancestors to oppose political and spiritual oppression and particularly to oppose government control and seek independence and freedom of individuals was not as strong as in ancient Western society.

In cultural terms, ancient Chinese culture lacked the absolute concept of individuals separated from and opposed to others that existed in the West. The "heaven" referred to by Confucianism was the heaven of righteousness and principles, and the "people" referred to by Confucianism were people of righteousness and principles. The characteristics of each individual were defined by his or her social relations. Furthermore, individuals were subordinated to the collective and in the first instance had to serve the collective. [Relations] between individuals, between human beings and society, and between human beings and nature were all understood to be unified on an ontological level. Unlike in the West, there were no tense relations between human beings and God in China. In Chinese traditional culture, relations between mankind and supernatural authority have never occupied a predominant position. The mainstream of Chinese ideological traditions take humans as the basis and have [primary] regard for practical, daily utility. It rarely talks about principles deviating from facts. However, in Western history, apart from the tense relations between people in economic and political life, there also existed the tense cultural relations of dualistic antagonism between human beings and nature, individuals and society, human beings and God, empiricism and transcendence, and social justice and natural justice. It was in these antagonistic relations that individuals were able to achieve certain absolute and isolated abstract stipulations with the aid of transcendent authority, and in order to safeguard their own abstract existence, these absolute a priori individuals must enjoy the same absolute, a priori, and abstract rights. Such rights were regarded as innate qualifications, powers, and endowments. These are the so-called natural rights or human rights. They are the basis on which people rely to resist reality. The more isolated people are and the more they resist society and are antagonistic to others, the more absolute their rights, the more they are guaranteed, and the more they discuss human rights. Rights are things-in-themselves, while duties are derived from rights. Defining duties is aimed at protecting rights. Fulfilling duties does not rely on spontaneous kindheartedness, but is compelled by the demands of the objects that are supported by transcendent authority and confirmed by law.

This was indeed inconceivable to our Chinese ancestors. Of course, this does not mean that Chinese culture does not recognize individuals and the dignity and value of individuals. This author is of the opinion that Chinese culture develops the individual's subjective spirit in its own unique way. For instance, to achieve merits and virtues, to transcend worldliness and attain holiness, and to reach the level of nirvana, all rely entirely on the moral efforts of individuals; such efforts themselves embody the dignity and value of human beings as such. Moreover, this outlook on dignity and value is superior to the outlook deriving from the holy character of Christianity, because it is not transcendent, a priori, and hypothetical, but can only be displayed through a posteriori arduous efforts and self-sublimation. From this we can see that individuals in Chinese culture are introspective, yielding, altruistic, and harmonious subjects of morals instead of extroverted, demanding, egoistic, and contending subjects of interests. Such individuals are apt to become the subjects of universal duties rather than the subjects of universal rights.

However, individuals' lacking the spirit [associated with] being the subject of rights does not mean that individuals in Chinese culture lack the spirit to reform society and resist evils. Max Weber held that Confucianism advocates self-restraint and observance of rites and customs, and when dominated by such a state of mind, "Not reaching beyond this world, the individual necessarily lacked an autonomous counterweight in confronting this world. . . . Such a way of life could not allow man an inward aspiration toward a 'unified personality.' . . . Hence, there was no leverage for influencing conduct through inner forces freed of tradition and convention."[6] This view has become fashionable among Western sinologists. I think that this view only casts an eye at the restraining role of rites and customs and fails to see the stimulating role of another more important concept—"benevolence." Benevolence indicates an entirely independent moral personality. Benevolence, though closely related to rites, was, after all, placed above rites. The philosophy of benevolence was more complete and more profound than rites, and the learning of benevolence, when developed to the highest level, had the tendency to oppose feudal ethical codes, authority, and traditions. It was precisely because of the intrinsic motive force of benevolence that a tradition of resisting the politics of the time existed in ancient China all along.[7] Many intellectuals gave their life for righteousness and for just causes, assailed dark and corrupt politics, and even laid claims to the right of "wiping out tyrants." This power [directed at] saving the country and helping the people did not come from God but from individuals' states of mind of no longer being able to bear [wrongdoing]. The intrinsic motive force of benevolence was not only noble but also powerful. The sole regret is that in social life there was, after all, only a handful of people who understood benevolence and practiced righteousness. Benevolence was not like the spiritualism or selfish desire of the West which could cover all the people, thus becoming the internal force behind their struggles for rights and profits and the basis for their legitimization. Therefore, the traditional learning of benevolence could not possibly become a secular learning of rights; human rights could not be derived directly from the Chinese traditional principles of benevolence.

3. Human Rights and Harmony

A number of foreign scholars have attributed the lack of discussions of human rights in Chinese traditional society to the concept of harmony.[8] ... The failure of the emergence of the Western concept of human rights in Chinese traditional culture was certainly related to the concept of harmony. However, we should never put the blame on the concept of harmony itself and mistake the concept of human rights as being incompatible with the concept of harmony, and human rights as being incompatible with the spirit of Chinese culture, thereby leading to the abandonment of harmony and the arbitrary advocacy of human rights. If we do not confine ourselves to one thing at a time, but instead widen our vision to consider some truths about the evolution of the universe, nature, and human society, it will not be difficult to find that harmony is an extremely profound and great concept with eternal vitality. We are able to see by perceiving directly through the senses alone that in the universe, celestial bodies move in an orderly way, the four seasons change alternately, warm and cold weather succeed one another, trees, flowers, and plants add radiance and beauty to one another, the sounds of singing birds, howling animals, and the flowing water of brooks are in great harmony; even in the human body, main and collateral channels and internal organs are in a harmonious mix. These phenomena are harmony. Harmony is the essence of the universe. It exists in the natural universe and in the human world; it requires neither premises from physics nor transcendental methods to prove its existence. In Chinese traditional thinking, harmony is interlinked with nature. Nature is harmony and vice versa. The nature referred to here is not "nature" in the Western sense of transcendentally existing natural law, nor is it the natural world as opposed to the human world. Rather, it is nature which emerges spontaneously. This spontaneity is considered as the ultimate essence of the universe. Nature and harmony in this sense are inherent, universal, and immediate, and are not necessary for people to "seek" outside the human world. This is because humanities and nature, as well as humanism, the moral way, and the principles of all things, are all integrated. "The essential principle is the principle of human relations in daily affairs. In humans this is nature (*xing*), in things it is principle [*li*], and in affairs it is righteousness (*yi*); they are all manifestations of the essence of the universe."[9] People must understand, realize, and apply it. Development of rites and music by the sages were applications of this essential principle. As was mentioned earlier, rites have the triple character of customary law, moral law, and actual law. They are not Western-style contract-laws. Moreover, rites are not Western-style natural law, either. They are not a set of sacred laws, supported by transcendent authority, which dualistically oppose actual law. Rites are the unity of metaphysics and concrete science, natural law and humanism, and morals and law.[10] The cultural character of rites lies in this spirit of integral and natural harmony. We can say that rites embodied the law of harmony of our Chinese ancestors and were the best system of norms with the greatest vitality in Chinese traditional society. Without the culture of rites there would not have been a "state of rites" and the continuity of the lifeblood of the Chinese nation. Chinese traditional society did not discuss human rights not mainly because of the rites, but because of traditional society itself, as society does not originate from rites, but rites originate from society. It is not the spirit of seeking harmony in rites, but the concrete contents of rites that contradict human rights and the rule of law. Just as the formulation of rites and music gave relief [to those] in distress and help to those in danger in ancient times, when promoting human rights and rule of law today, we should understand the national conditions (*guoqing*) and the character of the people (*minxing*), grasp the "essential principle," develop the spirit of integral and natural harmony, and be adept in reasoning out practical principles from within real life—all without the need to borrow dualism, ultra-individualism, and egoism from the Western God.

Harmony is both essence (*ti*) and application (*yong*). The above was with respect to [harmony] as essence. In the sense of application, human rights not only are compatible with harmony, but they also promote each other. We may make human beings the core and divide actual harmony into three categories, namely, the harmony between human beings and nature, the harmony between people, and the harmony between physical and mental aspects of human beings. I would like to discuss here mainly the relations between human rights and the harmony of the second category (although human rights have a bearing on the harmony of the other two categories, too). The achievement of harmony between things requires both separation and connection. However, the separation must have a certain limit and the connection must be organic. A harmonious society should be a mixture of division and merger, individual and collective, and part and whole. Being partial to any one aspect would cause disharmony. The above-mentioned three major spirits of human rights—humanism, rule of law, and great harmony—are precisely the embodiment of the way of harmony of humankind. Besides, historically, any kind of established social tradition contains certain elements of harmony, their differences mainly lie in ways of seeking harmony, degrees of harmony, and value orientations. As described earlier, in Western cultural history, human beings and nature, person and person, and human souls and bodies were divided and antagonistic to each other. The essence of the system of rights and the concept of human rights is, among the divided and antagonistic people, putting emphasis on the power enjoyed by individuals over themselves and their possessions, thus leading to the establishment of a number of rules of rights and duties, and to stable social relations. It was precisely because the point of departure of the system of rights and the concept of human rights in the early period of Western history was division and opposition that they had a strong flavor of individualism and antagonism. Furthermore, as the superior was selected and the inferior was eliminated, the state and laws were controlled by the ruling classes and human rights usually served only the strong, so that the rich and the officials were given special treatment, and division and antagonism among the people accelerated on some occasions. Nevertheless, we must see that the Western system of rights and of the concept of human rights were measures taken against the background of the West's divided and antagonistic economic, political, and cultural [world,] with a view to solving Western social problems and establishing a minimum human order. Without these measures, the [subsequent] destiny of Western society would have been inconceivable. In that case, people would have killed one another and perished together. Therefore, no matter whether Westerners have an awareness of harmony, the system of rights and the concept of human rights have performed the function of harmony in practice.

The case in China was different. As described earlier, in Chinese cultural traditions there existed no such division and antagonism between human beings and nature, between people, and between human beings and God. Our Chinese ancestors pursued the integration of heaven and human beings, filial piety, fraternal duty, loyalty, and righteousness and laid emphasis on the "preciousness of harmony" without advocating contention. Under the economic, political, and cultural conditions at that time, the application of the concept of harmony inclined toward linkages and integration and emphasized ritualized yielding and making offerings [to others], thereby failing to create a set of developed systems of rights and concepts of human rights. Consequently, the principles of humanism and great harmony could not be embodied and practiced by means of the rule of law. This was inevitable, because at that time human rights and the rule of law were not the best means for the Chinese to solve their social problems; they were not essential to their survival and development. However, we should also pay attention to the shortcomings of the doctrine of harmony in Chinese traditional society. First of all, the independence and freedom of individuals were at very low levels in social life, and the social ties between people were in many aspects predetermined, passive, and subordinate rather than independent, active, and equal, thus directly impeding the improvement of the level of social harmony. In daily life, people often attempted to eliminate conflicts and seek harmony between people by melting [away] private interests and eliminating individuality. [They also] simultaneously followed nature, were unfettered and nonstriving (*xiaoyao wuwei*), and made physical and mental adjustments to enhance their sense of superficial harmony. The problem was that although traditional Chinese culture lacked the Western sense of divisions and antagonisms between human beings and nature, between humans, and between human beings and God, nevertheless, as in any human society, contradictions and conflicts between human beings and nature, between individuals, between individuals and organizations, between classes, between human beings and God, and between body and mind actually did exist in Chinese traditional society. In other words, in traditional culture there were no antagonistic concepts, but in traditional society there were adversarial relations. Although Western prescriptions could not necessarily cure China's disease and although it was impossible and all the more unnecessary for our Chinese ancestors to hanker for Western-style human rights and rule of law, it is worthwhile to reconsider how the doctrine of harmony actually applied in Chinese traditional society. For instance, social productive forces failed to be emancipated; science and technology failed to be fully developed; benevolence, righteousness, rites, wisdom, and faith failed to check the rampage of autocracy and the endless cycling of order and disorder. Confucianism never succeeded in establishing an inner sage as an outer king, so it was often the power doctrine of the Legalists that dominated actual political life. Therefore, if we transcend historical possibilities and necessities by basing our analysis on the instrumental point of view of pure reason, it can then be said that in terms of social harmony, what is lacking in the Chinese traditional doctrine of harmony is precisely the system of rights and the concept of human rights, and only when the spirit of humanism and great harmony in the Chinese traditions are accompanied by the spirit of the rule of law, can the harmony of humankind be better promoted.

History is already in the past, and the present is becoming history. Chinese culture has existed and developed and is being continuously created. Over the past one hundred years, great changes have taken place in the various factors which determined the lack of discussion of human rights in Chinese traditional society. Social harmony cannot be achieved and promoted by relying on rites, religion, and power alone. Together with people all over the world, Chinese people are advocating and promoting human rights. At this juncture, we should develop all the more the spirit of harmony. On the one hand, this will counteract the weaknesses of the traditions of human rights and the rule of law, and on the other hand, it will make use of the concept of harmony to lead to new theories and systems of human rights. Only in this way can we overcome the tendency of ultra-individualism, egoism, and antagonism contained in Western traditional human rights and eradicate the roots of accumulated poverty, weakness, and disorder in Chinese traditional society.

When making use of the concept of harmony to interpret and promote human rights, there are two points to which we should pay attention. The first point is the status and value of individuals. The independence and freedom of individuals are essential conditions for the harmony of the whole. Harmony is not unification (*heyi*); instead, "all things on earth contend for their freedom." Independence and freedom are inherent requirements of harmony. Furthermore, everybody is a relatively self-supporting harmonious subject; the existence of human beings has its dignity and value. Such dignity and value do not come from God, but from human beings themselves and from the universe and nature, so they are possessed by all human beings. Thus, in social life, everyone has or should have some interests, demands, qualifications, powers, functions, and freedoms—and that means some rights. These rights are essential to the survival and development of everyone and to the achievement of social harmony as well. Accordingly, enjoying rights itself should also become a right. The second point is the coordination of various contradictions and conflicts. When giving consideration to human rights from the concept of harmony, we should no longer proceed from absolute rights of abstract individuals to establish relations of rights and duties. Rather, we should study and practice human rights in the context of particular social relations. Here, special attention should be paid to efforts to seek coordination among various individuals and between various nations and cultures. Only in this way will it be possible to harmoniously blend East and West, link together ancient and modern, and open up new possibilities.

Notes

1. This view has been popular in China since the May Fourth Movement and particularly over the past decade. See the speech of the author at the forum held on the fifth anniversary of the first publication of *The Study of Comparative Law* in the first issue of that periodical in 1991.

2. "Western democratic revolution was a revolt against the brutality experienced from absolute monarchism; there was no comparable cause against which the Chinese were impelled to revolt. Kinship-sheltered individuals did not similarly feel the brutality of the Chinese imperial State." "I am not arguing that there is no room for human rights in East Asia, but merely that the quest for human rights has not been a preoccupation. No perceived deprivation; no perceived need for eman-

cipation." "If Westerners sought the enforcement of their rights by placing themselves in an adversarial relationship with the State, the Chinese secured their rights by applying the same rules of conduct to the sovereign and the people." See James C. Hsiung, ed., *Human Rights in East Asia: A Cultural Perspective* (New York: Paragon House, 1985), pp. 10–12, 90.

3. See Xia Yong, *Renquan gainian qiyuan* [The Origin of the Concept of Human Rights: A Chinese Interpretation] (Beijing: Zhongguo zhengfa daxue chubanshe, 1992), pp. 169, 173.

4. See ibid., pp. 86–114.

5. See Xia Yong, "Renquan daode jichu chulun" [On the Moral Foundations of Human Rights], *Dangdai renquan* [Contemporary Human Rights] (Beijing: Zhongguo shehui kexue chubanshe, 1992).

6. Max Weber, *The Religion of China* (New York: Free Press, 1951), pp. 235–36. Jin Yaoji, *Zhongguo fazhan cheng xiandaixing guojiade kunjing: Weibo xueshuo de yimian* [The Predicament of China's Development Into a Modern Country: One aspect of the Doctrine of Weber].

7. See Zhang Duangshui, "Benevolence and Rites—Moral Independence and Social Constraint," in Huang Chun-chieh and Liu Tai, eds., *Tiandao yu rendao* [The Law of Nature and Humanism] (Taipei: Lianjing, 1982).

8. See Peter K.Y. Woo, "A Metaphysical Approach to Human Rights from a Chinese Point of View," in A.S. Rosenbaum, ed., *The Philosophy of Human Rights* (Westport, CT: Greenwood Press, 1980), pp. 118–20; Joseph Needham, *Zhongguo kexue jishu shi* [History of Chinese Science and Technology] (Shanghai: Shanghai guji chubanshe, 1990), vol. 2, p. 566; and several of the articles in J.C. Hsiung, ed., *Human Rights in East Asia: A Cultural Perspective* (New York: Paragon House, 1985).

9. Zhang Dainian, *Zhongguo zhexue dagang* [Outline of Chinese Philosophy] (Beijing: Zhongguo shehui kexue chubanshe, 1982), p. 177.

10. "Rites are the law of the heaven, the principle of the earth, and the norm of behavior of human beings," in *Zuo Commentary on the Spring and Autumn Annals*, 25th year of Duke Zhao.

Further Reading

Other works by Xia Yong on human rights include *Renquan gainian qiyuan* [The Origin of the Concept of Human Rights: A Chinese Interpretation] (Beijing: Zhongguo zhengfa daxue chubanshe, 1992); "Renquan daode jichu chulun" [On the Moral Foundations of Human Rights], in *Dangdai renquan* [Contemporary Human Rights] (Beijing: Zhongguo shehui kexue chubanshe, 1992); and "Xiangmin gongfa quanli de shengcheng" [The Formation of Chinese Rural Citizens' Rights in Public Law], in Xia Yong, ed., *Zouxiang quanli de shidai* [Toward an Age of Rights], 2nd ed. (Beijing: Zhongguo zhengfa daxue chubanshe, 1999). For another example of mainland scholars trying to relate Confucian ideals and human rights, see Du Gangjian and Song Gang, "Relating Human Rights to Chinese Culture: The Four Paths of the Confucian Analects and the Four Principles of a New Theory of Benevolence," in Michael C. Davis, ed., *Human Rights and Chinese Values: Legal, Philosophical, and Political Perspectives* (Hong Kong: Oxford University Press, 1995).

56
Vienna Conference Statement (1993)

Liu Huaqiu

"Statement by Liu Huaqiu, Head of the Chinese Delegation," reprinted in James T.H. Tang, ed., *Human Rights and International Relations in the Asia-Pacific Region* (London: Pinter, 1995), pp. 213–17.

The United Nations World Conference on Human Rights was held in June 1993 in Vienna. Prior to this conference, regional preparatory conferences were held in Tunis, San José, and Bangkok, with the goals of analyzing past achievements and failures in the international human rights regime, and making recommendations for improved mechanisms of implementation. The Bangkok conference became a forum for newly confident Asian regimes to attempt to put their own stamp on an international human rights process that they viewed as dominated by Western interests and conceptions of rights. The resulting Bangkok Declaration *is a complex—some would say contradictory—document that endorses the universality of human rights but qualifies this at the same time, most famously in its Article 8: "[The signatories] recognize that while human rights are universal in nature, they must be considered in the context of a dynamic and evolving process of international norm-setting, bearing in mind the significance of national and regional particularities and various historical, cultural, and religious backgrounds." Many of the signatories to the* Declaration *became involved in promoting what came to be called "Asian values," an idea that is harshly criticized by Liu Junning in our Text 58, below. The present selection is the speech made at the subsequent Vienna conference itself by China's representative Liu Huaqiu. While endorsing international human rights work, Liu echoes the sentiments prominent in the* Bangkok Declaration, *and reiterates China's official position that no country can use human rights concerns as a pretext to interfere with other countries' internal affairs. He also puts forward the view that an individual must not "place his own rights and interests above those of the state and society" and stresses the centrality of the right to economic development.*

The World Conference on Human Rights is convened on the occasion of the forty-fifth anniversary of the Universal Declaration of Human Rights. This is a noteworthy event in the international community today. We hope that this Conference will contribute positively to strengthening international cooperation in the field of human rights and to promoting full enjoyment of human rights and fundamental freedoms of people of all countries. Please allow me to take this opportunity to offer, on behalf of the Chinese government and people, our warm congratulations to the Conference, and wish the Conference a success.

In the wake of World War II and victory over the brutal fascist forces, the United Nations worked out the Charter of the United Nations and the Universal Declaration of Human Rights which give expression to the long desire of people across the world for the respect and protection of human rights and fundamental freedoms. It has, through relentless efforts, scored many achievements in safeguarding and promoting human rights, broken down the shackles of colonialism and won independence successively, which culminated in the total collapse of the centuries-old evil colonial system. All this has created prerequisites and opened up broad vistas for the realization of basic human rights for people of all countries in the world. The United Nations and the international community have done a great deal of work in terms of eliminating colonialism, racism, apartheid, massive and gross violations of human rights as a result of foreign invasion and occupation, safeguarding the right of small and weak countries to self-determination and the right of developing countries to development, and helping people of all countries to obtain the basic human rights. All these represent a major development of the Universal Declaration of Human Rights. Moreover, the series of programmatic documents such as the Proclamation of Teheran and the Declaration on the Right to Development adopted successively by the United Nations have further enriched the contents of and defined the objectives and guiding principles for international activities in the field of human rights. In preparation for this Conference, Africa, Latin America, and Asia convened regional preparatory meetings which passed respectively the Tunis Declaration, the San José Declaration, and the Bangkok Declaration. These important instruments on human rights have identified some pressing issues of concern to the developing countries, which make up the overwhelming majority of the world population and put forward their practical and feasible principled propositions, thus further enriching and expanding the contents of human rights protection and promotion.

The issue of human rights has attracted universal attention in the international community as it bears on the basic rights and vital interests of the world's people. In recent years, the international situation has undergone drastic changes. The world has entered a historical juncture whereby the old pattern is giving way to a new one. The international community has before it difficulties and challenges on the one hand, and hopes and opportunities on the other. In the international human rights field, the pressing task facing the people of all countries is to sum up experience and set the correct direction and principles for the future course in light of the changing situation, with a view to effectively protecting and promoting basic human rights. This World Conference on Human Rights is an important conference linking the past and future. Its success will undoubtedly be of great significance to the realization of this objective.

We should also be soberly aware that the serious consequences of colonialism, racism, apartheid, foreign invasion and occupation are yet to be fully removed. People in countries still under foreign occupation or apartheid have not yet enjoyed basic human rights and freedom. Though the Cold War characterized by confrontation between the two military blocs has come to an end, the world today is far from tranquil as is evidenced by increasing factors of destabilization and emergence of new hot spots. People in some regions are still struggling for survival. Many developing countries find themselves in greater economic difficulties and impoverishment. Over one billion people in the world are still living below the poverty line, suffering from starvation, diseases, and shortages. These, no doubt, are the stumbling blocks in the way to the realization of universal human rights. Therefore, to remove these obstacles and carry out international cooperation in this connection should be given top priority by the international community in its efforts to promote the cause of human rights.

The concept of human rights is a product of historical development. It is closely associated with specific social, political, and economic conditions and the specific history, culture, and values of a particular country. Different historical development stages have different human rights requirements. Countries at different development stages or with different historical traditions and cultural backgrounds also have a different understanding and practice of human rights. Thus, one should not and cannot think of the human rights standard and model of certain countries as the only proper ones and demand all other countries to comply with them. It is neither realistic nor workable to make international economic assistance or even international economic cooperation conditional on them.

The concept of human rights is an integral one, including both individual and collective rights. Individual rights cover not only civil and political rights but also economic, social, and cultural rights. The various aspects of human rights are interdependent, equally important, indivisible, and indispensable. For the vast number of developing countries to respect and protect human rights is first and foremost to ensure the full realization of the rights to subsistence and development. The argument that human rights is the precondition for development is unfounded. When poverty and lack of adequate food and clothing are commonplace and people's basic needs are not guaranteed, priority should be given to economic development. Otherwise, human rights are completely out of the question. We believe that the major criteria for judging the human rights situation in a developing country should be whether its policies and measures help promote economic and social progress, help people meet their basic needs for food and clothing, and improve the quality of their life. The international community should take actions to help developing countries alleviate economic difficulties, promote their development, and free them from poverty and want.

The rights and obligations of a citizen are indivisible. While enjoying his legitimate rights and freedom, a citizen must fulfill his social responsibilities and obligations. There are no absolute individual rights and freedom, except those prescribed by and within the framework of law. Nobody shall place his own rights and interests above those of the state and society, nor should he be allowed to impair those of others and the general public. This is a universal principle of all civilized societies. Moreover, to maintain social stability and ensure the basic human rights to citizens do not contradict each other. The practice of the international community has proved once and again [that] only when there is justice, order, and stability in a country or society, can its development and the well-being as well as the basic human rights of all its citizens be guaranteed.

According to the UN Charter and the norms of international law, all countries, large or small, strong or weak, rich or poor, have the right to choose their own political system, road to development, and values. Other countries have no right to interfere. To wantonly accuse another country of abuse of human rights and impose the human rights criteria of one's own country or region on other countries or regions [is] tantamount to an infringement upon the sovereignty of other countries and interference in the latter's internal affairs, which could result in political instability and social unrest in other countries. As a people who used to suffer tremendously from aggression by big powers but now enjoys independence, the Chinese have come to realize fully that state sovereignty is the basis for the realization of citizens' human rights. If the sovereignty of a state is not safeguarded, the human rights of its citizens are out of the question, like a castle in the air. The view that the principle of noninterference in other's internal affairs is not applicable to [the human rights question] is, in essence, a form of power politics. It runs counter to the purposes and principles of the UN Charter and to the lofty cause of the protection of human rights.

China believes that the protection of human rights, like the promotion of development, requires international cooperation and a peaceful and stable international environment. For the purpose of strengthening international cooperation in the field of human rights and promoting activities in the protection of human rights in the whole international community, the Chinese delegation hereby puts forth the following principled proposals and wishes to discuss them with you.

1. The international community should give its primary attention to the massive gross violations of human rights resulting from foreign aggression and occupation and continue to support those people still under foreign invasion, colonial rule, or [the] apartheid system in their just struggle for national self-determination. It should also commit itself to the elimination of the massive gross violations of human rights ensuing from regional conflicts.

2. World peace and stability should be enhanced and a favorable international environment created for the attainment of the goals in human rights protection. To this end, countries should establish a new type of international relationship of mutual respect, equality, amicable coexistence, and mutually beneficial cooperation in accordance with the UN Charter and the norms of international law. All international disputes should be solved peacefully in a fair and reasonable manner and in the spirit of mutual accommodation and mutual understanding, and consultation on equal footing, instead of resorting to force or threat of force. No country should pursue hegemonism and power politics or engage in aggression, expansion, and interference. This is the way to ensure regional and global peace and stability and to prevent armed conflicts which may incur massive violations of human rights.

3. The right of developing countries to development should be respected and guaranteed. To create a good international economic environment for the initial economic development of developing countries, the international community should commit itself to the establishment of a fair and rational new international economic order. Developed countries, in particular, have the responsibility to help developing countries through practical measures in such areas as debt, capital, trade, assistance, and technology transfer, to overcome their economic difficulties and develop their economy. This is the way to gradually narrow the gap

between the North and the South, which may otherwise be widened, and finally to bring about common development and prosperity.

4. The right of each country to formulate its own policies on human rights protection in light of its own conditions should also be respected and guaranteed. Nobody should be allowed to use the human rights issue to exert political and economic pressures on other countries. The human rights issue can be discussed among countries. However, the discussions should be conducted in the spirit of mutual respect and on an equal footing.

It is the sole objective of the Chinese government to serve the Chinese people and work for their interests. Therefore, China has always attached importance and been committed to the guarantee and promotion of the basic human rights of its people. It is known to all that the old China was an extremely poor and backward semifeudal and semicolonial society where the Chinese people did not have any human rights to speak of as they were enslaved and oppressed by the imperialists and Chinese reactionary forces. This bitter past was not ended until the founding of the People's Republic. Since then, the Chinese people have, for the first time in history, taken their own destiny into their own hands, become masters of their own country, and enjoyed basic human rights. According to China's Constitution, all power in the People's Republic of China belongs to the people. The law guarantees that each and every Chinese citizen, regardless of gender, family background, ethnic status, occupation, property status, and religious belief, enjoys genuine democracy and freedom, civil and political rights as well as extensive economic, social, and cultural rights. China is a unitary multinational state. To strengthen national unity and safeguard the unification of the motherland accord with the common interests and aspiration of the Chinese people of all nationalities. To handle properly the ethnic question and the relations among different nationalities has all along been of vital importance to the stability, development, and equality among all nationalities of the country. The Chinese government, therefore, attaches great importance to the work in this regard. Equality and unity among all nationalities and regional national autonomy are China's basic principles and policies for handling matters concerning nationalities. As a result, people of all nationalities living in the same big family are now marching toward common prosperity. Since China began to implement the policy of reform and opening to the outside world, its economy has been developing vigorously and its democratic and legal system improving steadily. The nearly 1.2 billion Chinese populace of all nationalities, who are united as one, have seen their material and cultural well-being improved considerably. As their basic needs have been more or less met, they are briskly heading toward a fairly comfortable and affluent life. China has made steady progress in promoting and protecting human rights, which has been acknowledged and commended by all fair-minded people in the international community.

China respects and abides by the basic principles of the UN Charter and the Universal Declaration of Human Rights. It attaches importance to and has actively participated in international exchanges and coopera-tion in the field of human rights as well as UN activities in this field. China has acceded, one after another, to eight international conventions on human rights and is earnestly honoring the obligation it has thereby undertaken. It is ready to further strengthen exchanges and cooperation with other countries on human rights in the international arena and to contribute its part to the effective promotion and protection of human rights in the international community and to the achievement of the lofty ideal that people throughout the world will be able to fully enjoy the basic human rights.

Further Reading

The Bangkok Declaration is reprinted in Michael C. Davis, ed., *Human Rights and Chinese Values* (Hong Kong: Oxford University Press, 1995), pp. 205–9. Statements by representatives of other Asian nations, as well as of Asian nongovernmental or-ganizations, can be found in the same volume from which the present selection comes. For a detailed discussion of China's relationship with the UN human rights regime, see Ann Kent, *China, the United Nations, and Human Rights: The Limits of Compliance* (Philadelphia: University of Pennsylvania Press, 1999).

57
Developing Countries and Human Rights (1994)

Liu Nanlai

"Fazhanzhong guojia yu renquan" (Developing Countries and Human Rights), in Liu Nanlai et al., eds., *Renquan de pubianxing he teshuxing* [The Universality and Particularity of Human Rights] (Beijing: Shehui kexue wenxian chubanshe, 1996), pp. 115–30. The translation comes from from Peter R. Baehr, Fried van Hoof, Liu Nanlai, Tao Zhenghua, editors in chief; Jacqueline Smith, ed., *Human Rights: Chinese and Dutch Perspectives* (The Hague: Martinus Nijhoff, 1996), pp. 103–17, slightly modified.

Liu Nanlai (b. 1933) is a professor at the Institute of Law and deputy director of the Center for Human Rights Studies at the Chinese Academy of Social Sciences. He was one of the co-conveners of a conference held in Beijing in 1994 between Chinese and Dutch specialists in human rights issues; the goal of the conference was to take stock and assess human rights issues in light of the results of the 1993 Vienna World Conference on Human Rights (for the statement of the Chinese representative to that conference, see Text 56). Liu's article is a detailed and sophisticated account of the position of developing countries on human rights and of their struggle to realize such rights. Liu addresses the issue of the particularity and universality of human rights, and stresses the importance of cultural and historical factors in explaining differences between societies with respect to the understanding and implementation of human rights. But the main thrust of his argument is that different levels of economic development and the heritage of colonialism explain the differences between developing and developed (i.e., Western) countries. Liu does not disparage previous international human rights work and, unlike some official spokespersons, he does not see the UDHR as solely imbued with Western ideas. Instead, Liu goes to great lengths to defend the UDHR as a universal project, describing in great detail the contributions from various countries in the Third World. He even mentions the fact that a Chinese person served as a member of the drafting committee (see Text 33), albeit without mentioning the individual's GMD affiliation.

Introduction

After intense and sometimes fierce discussions and thorough consultations, on June 25, 1993, the second World Conference on Human Rights held in Vienna by the UN adopted by consensus the Vienna Declaration and Program of Action, which provides the international community with concrete tasks and clear direction for international cooperation in the field of human rights. It is well worth noting that while reiterating the universality of human rights, this important document explicitly points out that in international human rights activities "the significance of national and regional particularities and various historical, cultural, and religious backgrounds must be borne in mind."[1] Thus, a conclusion has been drawn with respect to a long-debated issue over the universality and particularity of human rights among countries all over the world. . . .

The population of the developing countries accounts for 70 percent and more of the total population of the world. Of the 180–odd member states of the United Nations, more than two-thirds are developing countries. It is self-evident that a human rights concept which has not embodied human rights ideas of the developing countries cannot be regarded as a universal human rights concept. Similarly, if full attention is not given to special situations and demands in the field of human rights in developing countries, one cannot claim to have acquired a real understanding of contemporary human rights issues, and shall not be able to find appropriate ways and means to realize the goal of protection and promotion of human rights and principles as contained in the UN Charter at a global level, either.

1. Developing Countries Are Striving for Human Rights

. . . People from developing countries, learning from their tragic experience, cherish a greater enthusiasm and initiative for the pursuit of human rights as compared with some developed countries that have oppressed and exploited them in history. They have paid a great deal more attention to human rights.

For the survival of the whole nation and for the right to be a human (*zuo ren de quanli*), peoples in Asia, Africa, and Latin America have waged innumerable and protracted armed struggles against foreign oppressors. In 1790, under the influence of the French Revolution, the colored people in the French colony of Haiti launched the first armed uprising against colonialists in Latin America. Using the French Declaration of Human Rights and Civil Rights, they raised the demand for equal rights with the whites. Soon after the uprising was put down, the black leader, Toussaint L'Ouverture, led another slave uprising that was even greater in strength and impetus. Singing their battle song "better to die than live as a slave," the blacks fought a life-or-death fight against Spanish, British, and French colonialists. In 1881, on the African continent, relying on the Islamic creed and under the slogan of "Everyone is equal before Allah," Muhammad Ahmad Mahdi of Sudan waged the largest and the longest Mahdi uprising in the history of Africa, and during the uprising, British governor-general Gordon, who had taken part in the suppression of the Movement of the Heavenly Kingdom of Peace [Taiping] (1850–1864) in China, was killed. On one occasion the British aggressors were driven out of Sudan. Other struggles and movements, such as the independent struggle led by Simón Bolívar in the northern areas of South America in the early nineteenth century, the Bab Uprising in Iran in the middle of the nineteenth century, the Movement of the Heavenly Kingdom of Peace in China, the National Revolutionary War led by Mustafa Kemal of Turkey in the twentieth century, the noncooperation movement led by Gandhi in India, and the armed uprising led by Sandino in Nicaragua, all bore the imprint of human rights to varying degrees. Although few of these struggles were successful, they served as a brilliant page in the history of fights for human rights waged by oppressed peoples.

The struggle for human rights waged by peoples and states in Asia, Africa, and Latin America entered into a new phase after World War II. The defeat of fascist Germany, Japan, and Italy, the decline of colonialist powers such as Britain and France, the upsurge of socialist movements and the attention paid by the United Nations to human rights during the course of the re-establishment of international order after the war, and moreover, a series of developments (for example, the principle of promotion of international cooperation in order to enhance the universal respect of human rights contained in the UN Charter was stipulated as a purpose of the UN), all strengthened the awareness of human rights in developing countries. While unfolding national liberation movements, they participated in working out international human rights standards in the UN and in activities to promote international cooperation in the field of human rights with full enthusiasm, bringing forward their own human rights demands. The developing countries' involvement and participation gave an impetus to a closer combination of international human rights activities of the UN with struggles for complete political, economic, and social liberation launched by oppressed nations and peoples. In their struggles, developing countries achieved considerable success.

As early as 1945 when the United Nations got together in San Francisco to prepare for the adoption of the UN Charter and laying the foundation for the UN, states from Asia, Africa, and Latin America showed a greater desire and enthusiasm for human rights than some of the developed countries. At that time, the Dumbarton Oaks Proposal put forward by the four major powers, China, the United States, Britain, and the Soviet Union, had only requested that the UN Charter make a general provision with respect to human rights, whereas representatives from Chile, Cuba, and Panama had advanced some more active proposals, requesting the UN to provide guarantees for some specific rights. Further, the representative of Panama called for an international human rights chapter in the Charter of the United Nations. However, these proposals have were not accepted mainly due to objections from Britain and the United States.

In 1947, the UN began to draft an international bill of human rights. After nearly twenty years, the UN did, by adopting the Universal Declaration of Human Rights, the International Covenant on Economic, Social, and Cultural Rights, and the International Covenant on Civil and Political Rights in succession, at last accomplish this arduous and significant task. Developing countries in Asia, Africa, and Latin America actively participated in the drafting of these three most important international human rights instruments, and contributed distinctively to the adoption of these documents.

The Universal Declaration of Human Rights was formulated as "a common standard of achievement for all peoples and all nations." It has been taken as the basis for all activities in the human rights area in the UN ever since its adoption and the international community has attached great importance to it. The significance of the Universal Declaration of Human Rights lies also in the fact that this international document is the first listing in detail of various human rights that should be protected by the international community. Among these human rights, there are both civil and political rights, and economic, social, and cultural rights. This means that the Declaration has overcome traditional Western human rights concepts, not only naming civil and political rights as human rights, but proclaiming that economic, social, and cultural rights are also human rights. This new development is of great importance, both to human rights theories and to human rights practice. Perhaps for the above-mentioned reason, many developing countries, including China, spoke highly of the Declaration. In 1988, the UN celebrated the fortieth-anniversary of the adoption of the Universal Declaration of Human Rights. At the meeting, the representative of India made a speech, saying that "the Universal Declaration of Human Rights marks the beginning of a new era in the history of mankind." The representative of Egypt called the Universal Declaration of Human Rights "the voice of the times." And the representative of Cuba remarked that "the adoption of the Declaration expresses the aspiration of a whole generation who had just been recovering from the nightmare of fascist warfare."

In the human rights literature, it is sometimes said that the drafting of the Universal Declaration of Human Rights took place under the influence of Western countries, and that the Declaration represented Western human rights ideas. This is a lopsided view which disregards the role played by developing countries, the former Soviet Union, and East European countries in the course of drafting the Declaration. Moreover, this view reflects a prejudice held by some scholars in the West, that only Western countries stress human rights, and that developing countries and socialist countries have paid no attention to human rights at all.

A lot of facts prove that developing countries and socialist countries actively participated in the drafting and discussion of the Declaration, and made a contribution to its adoption. For example, the UN Human Rights Commission appointed a three-member committee for the drafting of the Declaration. Among these three members, one was from China and one from Lebanon; later, the said committee was expanded to eight members. Besides the above-mentioned two representatives from developing countries, one member from Chile was added to the committee. They, and particularly Dr. Charles Malik, played a very important role in the drafting of the Declaration. There is also no doubt with regard to the influence of developing countries and socialist countries on the Declaration. As a matter of fact, the Universal Declaration of Human Rights, adopted on 10 December 1948 by the General Assembly of the UN, was the result of blends and clashes of various philosophies and human rights ideas. In recalling the course of drafting the Declaration, Dr. Charles Malik made the following remarks. He said: "The emergence of every clause of the Declaration, and every part of each clause, is a piece of work full of enthusiasm and activities. During our work, a great deal of ideas, interests, backgrounds, legal systems, and ideologies and beliefs played their respective parts." Even now, it is hard to say clearly from whom these clauses were brought forward.[2] The speech made by the representative of Egypt at the fortieth anniversary meeting of the adoption of the Universal Declaration of Human Rights also illustrated this characteristic. He said: "The Declaration has become an expression of coexistence between different values, cultures, ideologies, and principles in this world." Accordingly, the position that the Universal Declaration of Human Rights only represented Western human rights ideas is untenable. The erroneousness of that position shall be even more obvious if we note that some Western countries refused to accept economic, social, and cultural rights as human rights and opposed at the time the incorporation of these rights into the Declaration.

The pursuit of human rights and contributions made by the developing countries in the area of human rights is also prominently manifested in the recognition of collective rights, such as the right of self-determination and the right to development.

The idea of the right to self-determination is of long standing. One can find it in doctrines of natural rights of the seventeenth and eighteenth centuries, social contracts, the American Declaration of Independence, and Lenin's theories of nationalities. At the time of World War I, the right to self-determination had also been expounded as a political principle and a legal right. But the link between the right to self-determination and human rights and its definition as a collective right only emerged after World War II, with the upsurge of national liberation movements.

Early in the 1950s, decolonization spread all over the world. Countries in Asia, Africa, and Latin America, which had already gained their independence or were still striving for it, linked closely the enjoyment of human rights with the exercise of the right to self-determination, shaking off colonialism and establishing themselves as fully independent states. They demanded that the international community recognize the right to self-determination. Accordingly, the UN adopted a series of resolutions and declarations. The earliest UN document that reflected this demand was the resolution concerning the drafting of an international human rights covenant passed in February 1952. Said resolution required that the right to self-determination be included in the proposed international human rights covenant. . . . [Several] years later, the General Assembly of the United Nations adopted the International Covenant on Economic, Social, and Cultural Rights and the International Covenant on Civil and Political Rights, thus confirming in the form of international treaties that the right of self-determination is a fundamental human right with the status of a legal right. Using the same language, these two important international covenants explicitly stipulate: "All peoples have the right of self-determination. By virtue of that right they freely determine their political status and freely pursue their economic, social, and cultural development." The important position of the right of self-determination in the human rights system was thus fully established.

Ever since 1970, the world economy has been caught in grave economic crises. Economies in developing countries had a change for the worse and the disparity between the poor and the rich countries increased even further. As the old international economic order was established when most of the developing countries had not won their independence, the system hampered the development of developing countries and the realization of human rights proclaimed in the international bill of human rights. In that situation, a great number of developing countries demanded a change of the old international economic order, the establishment of a fair and reasonable and new international economic order, and recognition of the right to development, in order to create suitable conditions to guarantee the economic and social development of developing countries.

In 1970, Mr. Keba M'Baye, president of the Supreme Court of Senegal, delivered a speech at the International Human Rights Institute in Strasbourg. In his speech, the concept of the right to development was brought forward for the first time and claimed as a human right. Mr. M'Baye proved that all fundamental human rights and freedoms were closely linked with the right to survival and the right to an increasing improvement of the standard of living, that is, the right to development. Mr. M'Baye and representatives from other developing countries have repeatedly raised their claims for the establishment of a new international economic order and the recognition of the right to development in the framework of the UN, and their endeavors have initiated a series of discussions in UN agencies with regard to the above-mentioned issues. As a result, the United Nations adopted in succession a number of important documents, such as the Declaration on the Establishment of a New International Economic Order, the Charter of Economic Rights and Duties of All States, and the Declaration on the Right to Development. These documents established the idea of a fair and reasonable new international economic order as a goal for every member state in the UN, and demanded that all members of the international community should cooperate broadly on the basis of fairness, to help developing countries speed up their economic and social development. In accordance with the above-mentioned documents, the right to development was confirmed as an "inalienable human right," and "states have the duty to take steps, individually, and collectively . . . to facilitate the full realization of the right to development."

The vigorous activities conducted by developing countries in the field of human rights achieved remarkable successes. Human rights demands raised by the developing countries were paid attention to by states, and a better international environment was created, which enabled developing countries to overcome various difficulties and to improve their human rights conditions step by step. Moreover, the international human rights movement was enriched with new contents and dynamics. To a certain extent, the contributions made by developing countries have changed the situation that the major powers always had the final say.

The human rights movement now has advanced in a direction more favorable to the realization of ideals of human rights.

2. Human Rights Viewpoints

Over the long course of history, developing countries have formed their
own human rights perspectives, which differ distinctively from traditional human rights ideas held by Western countries, due to the developing countries' unique histories and cultural origins. The current political,
economic, and social statuses of developing countries also determine
their human rights claims and human rights policies, which again are
greatly different from those pursued by developed countries. These differences and dissimilarities constitute a series of characteristics. They
mainly manifest themselves through the following aspects.

The contents of human rights include both civil and political rights,
and economic, social, and cultural rights, and both individual rights and
collective rights. All these rights are interrelated and interdependent,
constituting an indivisible body of human rights.

According to classical human rights ideas of Western states, human
rights used to refer only to civil and political rights. They rejected economic, social, and cultural rights as human rights. Since the UN proclamation that economic, social, and cultural rights are human rights, some
Western states have changed their viewpoints. However, in practice, they
continue to stress the importance of civil and political rights and ignore
economic, social, and cultural rights. Developing countries, in comparison with Western states, invoke provisions in the Universal Declaration
of Human Rights and other international human rights instruments to
prove that, like civil and political rights, economic, social, and cultural
rights are an indivisible part of human rights that should be given equal
attention. Developing countries hold that the two sets of rights are interrelated and interdependent and [that] both sets of rights are necessary for
safeguarding personalities (*renge*). Just as personality is indivisible, human
rights are also indivisible. If one loses civil and political rights or economic, social, and cultural rights, one shall lose one's personality. Di-
recting [his remarks] at the one-sided attitude of stressing only civil and
political rights by some states, the representative of Zimbabwe pointed
out at the 14th General Assembly of the UN: "Having these rights [civil
and political rights] is far from enough. People must also enjoy economic and social rights: the right to health, to food and shelter, and most

importantly, to acquire minimum living conditions. Nobody should suffer from illiteracy and poverty. Human rights are one indivisible body, among them, all rights complement each other. The deprivation of any right shall lead to the weakening of the whole body of human rights."[3]. . .

Another view held by developing countries deals with the existence of collective rights, such as the right of self-determination and the right to development. Some Western states, starting from the classical idea that human rights cover only individual rights, refused to recognize the doctrine of collective rights. Whereas developing countries hold that every individual is part of a collective and his rights are accordingly closely linked with the collective to which he belongs, "the promotion and protection of all these rights should be undertaken in an integral and balanced manner."[4]

Developing countries hold that the people's right of self-determination is a "fundamental human right" and "the prerequisite and the guarantee for the enjoyment of other rights and fundamental freedoms by the people." They point out that when being subject to foreign domination and oppression, it is impossible for each person of the nation to enjoy human rights; only when acting as a collective to exercise the right of self-determination and after winning independence and establishing their own state, can a people's human rights be guaranteed. This is why the developing countries "insist on the link between commonly recognized human rights and the freedom, progress, and the right of self-determination of peoples in all states."[5]

While stressing the right of self-determination, developing countries also lay emphasis on the right to development of peoples of all states. Learning from their own experience, these states became fully aware that "underdevelopment is a main obstacle in the realization and enjoyment of human rights." Peoples living in poverty and backwardness are not in the position to talk about the enjoyment of human rights. Developing countries therefore realize that in order to guarantee and promote the realization of human rights, it is imperative to create conditions for each state to have an equal opportunity for development, in order to enable both the state and the individual to develop fully. Mr. José Figueres, the former president of Costa Rica, conducted a special study on the economic foundation of human rights. He came to a conclusion that "the fulfillment of human rights requires economic and social development." In view of the relationship between development and human rights, developing countries regard the right to development as an inalienable right and demand that the international community should recognize the right to development of peoples in all states, and to ensure the realization of that right, international cooperation should be strengthened. . . .

While enjoying rights and freedoms, individuals also bear obligations and duties to society and the state; and there should be a balance between the rights and duties of an individual.

In essence, the human rights perspective of Western states is individualism-oriented. It concentrates on personal values and rights and interests, but neglects the individual's duties toward society. The Western human rights perspective may be summarized in the following way, that is, an emphasis on the individual's human rights on the basis of a separation of rights from duties.

The human rights perspective maintained by developing countries is rooted in an emphasis on the interests of the community and the state. In a cultural tradition in which social harmony has been advocated, the individual is regarded as belonging to his community. The development of his personality depends upon the development of the community as a whole. Only in association with the society can one realize one's personality (*gexing*). Accordingly, the implementation of human rights and freedoms by individuals and obligations and duties borne by individuals to the community and the state are inseparable. When implementing rights and freedoms, one must also respect the rights of others and the interests of society. It is not permitted to infringe upon the interests of society and the state. The foreign minister of Indonesia expounded this viewpoint, upheld by developing countries, at the Vienna Conference on Human Rights as follows: "We in Indonesia, and perhaps throughout the developing world as well, do not and cannot maintain a purely individualistic approach toward human rights, for we cannot disregard the interests of our societies and nations." After citing Article 29 of the Universal Declaration of Human Rights, he continued: "Implementation of human rights implies the existence of a balanced relationship between individual human rights and the obligations of individuals toward their community. Without such a balance, the right of the community as a whole can be denied, which can lead to instability and even anarchy, especially in developing countries."[6]

The viewpoint maintained by the developing world that individual rights must be integrated with obligations to the community and the state manifests itself in the constitutions of many developing countries, and especially in the African Charter on Human and People's Rights. In Part I of said Charter, entitled "Rights and Obligations," there are not only provisions on individual rights and freedoms, but also people's rights and individual obligations toward the family, the state, and other legitimate communities and the international community. African human rights scholars extol these provisions of the Charter and regard them as a major contribution to the development of international human rights law.

Human rights have the nature of universality as well as of particularity; and in dealing with human rights issues, diversities in political, economic, social, and cultural dimensions must be taken into account.

The developing world considers that human rights are universal; however, their approach to the interpretation of the universality of human rights differs from that of Western developed states. Furthermore, there are different interpretations among the developing countries themselves. This shows that different cultures, religions, and legal ideas have exerted various influences on the understanding of human rights. Some developing countries have accepted the theory of natural rights and like most Western states, hold that human rights are inborn and inherent, and they use the theory to illustrate the universality of human rights. Some other developing countries base themselves mainly on the fact that human rights are stipulated in the Charter of the United Nations, the Universal Declaration on Human Rights, and other international human rights instruments and they have been universally accepted by the international community, to show the universal effect of human rights. Still, some Muslim nations in Asia and Africa explain the universality of human rights in accordance with Muslim creeds. They maintain that Allah has created human beings and entrusted them with the right to life. The universality of human rights lies in the truth that is granted by Allah, in disregard of race, sex, or any other attributes.

Based on their understanding of the universality of human rights, [states of] the developing world generally recognize a common standard of human rights at the international level; however, they also maintain that due to different histories, cultures, and traditions and different levels of development, the approaches and interpretations of human rights by states vary considerably. Human rights, therefore, also have a nature of particularity. Besides a common standard, there also exists a human rights standard embodying regional and national features. The Sudanese minister of justice gave a speech representing the above-mentioned approach at the Vienna Conference on Human Rights. He remarked: "Universality does not mean denial of clear cultural, religious, and national particularity. That is why some regional nationalities have adopted standards consistent with their practices and traditions." To further prove this point, he added: "The Universal Declaration of Human Rights has not prevented an American, European, African, or Arab declaration of human rights." Again at this conference, the foreign minister of Singapore reiterated the particularity of human rights. He cited examples that in the forty-five years since the adoption of the Universal Declaration of Human Rights, controversies over differing understandings of the meanings of articles contained in the Declaration have not only occurred between the West and the developing world, but also among Western states. Divergence of views exists on human rights issues and this fact cannot be just ignored. He said: "Universal recognition of the ideal of human rights can be harmful if universalism is used to deny or mask the reality of diversity."

Starting from the particularity of human rights, the developing world thus maintains that "Each state must promote the respect for fundamental human rights according to its own tradition,"[7] whereas international concerns over human rights must "duly take into account the tremendous political, economical, social, and cultural diversity of the world we live in,"[8] and "priority in the solution of human rights issues should be instituted in keeping with the historical and cultural characteristics and development stage of each region and country."[9]. . .

Notes

1. Paragraph I.5 of the Vienna Declaration and Program of Action.

2. See John Humphrey, *No Distant Millennium: International Law of Human Rights* (Paris: UNESCO, 1989), pp. 143–47.

3. Speech given by the representative of Pakistan at the fortieth anniversary of the adoption of the Universal Declaration of Human Rights by the United Nations.

4. Speech delivered by the foreign minister of Indonesia at the Vienna World Conference on Human Rights.

5. Speech given by the representative of Egypt at the 44th General Assembly of the UN.

6. Speech delivered by the foreign minister of Indonesia at the Vienna World Conference on Human Rights.

7. Remarks given by the representative of India at the 45th General Assembly of the UN.

8. Speech given by the head of the Indonesian delegation at the Bangkok conference in preparation for the Vienna World Conference on Human Rights.

9. Statement made by the head of the Korean delegation at the Vienna World Conference on Human Rights.

Further Reading

For further reading on the Vienna conference, and more generally on China's relation to the UN human rights regime, see suggestions for Text 56.

58
What Are Asian Values? (1998)

Liu Junning

"Shenme shi Yazhou jiazhiguan?" [What Are Asian Values?], *Ao Gang xinxi ribao* [Macao–Hong Kong News] (August 29–September 4, 1998), weekend edition.

In the early 1990s, "Asian values" became a hot topic in the international human rights debate. Several countries, with Singapore among the most prominent, accused the West of imposing its human rights standards on Asia without regard for Asia's specific culture and history. The proponents of Asian values argued that their countries had a different understanding of human rights due to their specific culture and history. While they did not completely reject universal human rights, their cultural relativism nevertheless represented a major challenge to an international consensus on human rights. References to culture and to national conditions (guoqing) have become more prominent in Chinese human rights discourse in the 1990s, but the Chinese government itself has placed much less emphasis on cultural arguments than have nations like Singapore. As a socialist country, China is more wont to argue that different economic systems and levels of economic development influence the understanding and realization of human rights. China's official position is to identify itself with the Third World as a whole, rather than with Asia alone. Examples of the relative balance between economic, cultural, and other arguments can be seen in Texts 56 and 57. Despite the relatively small importance of cultural arguments in official discourse, several Chinese intellectuals and dissidents have written explicit critiques of Asian values. Liu Junning (b. 1961) is one of those who strongly refutes the view that Asian people would have different views from Westerners on human rights and democracy. He believes that the Asian values advocated by Asian political leaders only serve to defend their hold on power and suppress people's genuine demands for human rights and democracy. Writing in 1998, Liu blames the leaders' particular concept of Asian values for both the recent Asian economic crisis and the attacks on ethnic Chinese in Indonesia in May of that year.

In April 1993, Indonesia, Malaysia, Burma, Singapore, China, and other East and Southeast Asian nations signed [the Bangkok Declaration]. According to the representative of Singapore, this declaration outlined the unique stance of the Asian nations toward the question of human rights. The signatories of the declaration assert that, because of Asian nations' belief in the uniqueness of Asian values and the special nature of their historical conditions, Asian people's understandings of democracy and human rights are radically different from those of Westerners.

When the outbreak of violence against ethnic Chinese in Indonesia took place with official collusion and cover-up, although the reasons were no doubt complex, responsibility certainly can be laid at the feet of so-called "Asian values."

Suharto and his successors are advocates of Asian values, according to which individual liberty is subordinate both to national needs and to the stability the leaders need for their unconditional rule. However, the sacrifice of individual freedoms and interests does not bring real stability, but instead gives rise to the factors that generate real instability. It guarantees that those who are oppressed will merely wait for their chance for revenge, which will lead to outbreaks of violence.

Some people try to use the Asian values argument to prove that the values of human rights, freedom, and democracy are inappropriate for Asian societies. More precisely, it is not that freedom and democracy are inappropriate for Asian societies but rather that they are inappropriate for dictators like Suharto. If ordinary Asians were to advocate Asian values, the unique virtues of Asian people, or their unique cultural traditions, this would perhaps not be unreasonable. But when rulers talk loudly about Asian values, especially when they claim that Asian values mean that the state is above the individual, or insist that Asian values should replace both the respect for individual freedoms and rights and the necessity of building democracy in Asia, then we know that they are harboring hidden intentions.

The nucleus of the Asian values argument is that stability and harmony are above individual rights and freedom. The rights of the state take absolute precedence over those of individuals; national stability is absolutely more important than the dignity of the individual person. Among Asian values, the most important are not the rights and freedoms of the individual but the stability of the state. But then why are such countries as Indonesia and Burma, champions of Asian values, simply unable to maintain political stability? Suharto and many other Asian rulers preserve their power through relying on familial and personal relationships. Such relationships can always initially provide more harmony. In this sense, emphasizing harmony is synonymous with emphasizing cronyism. Suharto's fall showed us that this kind of harmonious relationship will begin in harmony but end in betrayal. Asian values are no more than a secret code, difficult for Westerners to understand, for suppressing human rights in the name of native culture and economic development.

The supporters of the Asian values argument consider that the meaning of Asian values lie in their being beneficial for economic development. If Asian prosperity necessitates Asian values, then it can be said that the Chinese of Indonesia, Malaysia, and Vietnam are those most capable of realizing Asian values in the economic realm. So why do Indonesia's rulers and native people so mistreat the ethnic Chinese, realizers of Asian values? It is apparent that Suharto's public stance was not a whole hearted defense of Asian values, but rather a screen behind which to hide his dictatorial rule, with all its violations of human rights. In the sphere of economics, Asian values have produced some undesirable results, such as collusion between state officials and businessmen, influence peddling, corruption, manipulation of the markets, monopolies, and other deprivations of the people's interests. Corruption is the political cancer of Asia. The Asian values to which Asian political leaders refer are in fact the values of encouraging the malignant growth of corruption.

In East Asia, the countries that can hope to experience true stability are those with representative forms of government. The long-term stability enjoyed by such Western nations as the United States and Great Britain is due to the fact that their values and institutions are based on giving individual rights and freedoms higher priority than is given to stability and harmony. The reality is that the more the need for stability is allowed to repress everything else, including individual rights and freedoms, the harder it will be to achieve stability; by contrast, the more individual rights and freedoms are respected, the easier it will be to achieve stability.

According to the Asian values argument, special emphasis is put on the rights to subsistence (*shengcun quan*) and development. However, based on the experience of Indonesia's ethnic Chinese, these rights are not intended for individuals but rather for nations and governments.

Another important issue related to Asian values is the question of a country's internal affairs. Recently, a high Indonesian official criticized

412 PART VIII: THE 1990s

China for interfering in Indonesia's internal affairs with regard to the violence against ethnic Chinese Indonesians; he [also] said that Indonesia's Chinese have long been citizens of Indonesia, are no longer citizens of the People's Republic of China, and that the treatment of these ethnic Chinese Indonesians was an internal Indonesian affair which did not permit any criticisms from other nations. The Chinese government has also long considered that human rights are each nation's internal affair. However, in light of China's signing the International Covenant on Civil and Political Rights and its criticism of Indonesia for persecuting ethnic Chinese, it is no longer so easy for China to claim that human rights are purely an internal matter.

The invention of Asian values has provided those who would resist liberalism, democratic government, and human rights with the newest of ancient weapons, a weapon that has now been used to suppress internal critics and to incite fiercely anti-Western nationalism. In East Asian countries, multiculturalism—the product of advanced Western thought—provided the design principle for this weapon; with it, proponents of Asian values can grandly use the particularity (*teshuxing*) of their cultures to deny both the universalism (*pubianxing*) of values fundamental to human nature (such as freedom and human rights and their corresponding institutions) and the universal effectiveness of human rights. With the denial of the universal efficacy of human rights, a few people will pay the heavy price of losing their rights, freedoms, and dignity; among these unhappy people are the Chinese of Indonesia.

According to the views of some of East Asia's leaders, Asia's history and traditions preclude any need for democracy. Then why do so many people in so many Asian countries struggle and shed blood for democracy and human rights, and why are more and more Asian countries moving in the direction of democracy? From this point of view, it seems that the leaders of a few Asian countries have completely different values from Asian people, even to the extent of being fundamentally in conflict. Thus, Asian values seem more like the values of a few Asian leaders who do not like human rights and democracy, rather than the values of the people of Asia.

Further Reading

For some additional examples of Chinese skepticism of Asian values, see Xin Chunying, "Yazhou jiazhiguan yu renquan: Yizhang meiyou jieyu de duihua" [Asian

Values and Human Rights: A Dialogue Without Conclusion], *Gongfa,* no. 1 (1999), and Li Shenzhi, "Yazhou jiazhi yu quanqiu jiazhi" [Asian Values and Global Values], *Dongfang,* no. 4 (1995).

For the Asian NGOs' alternative Bangkok Declaration, see *Our Voice: Bangkok NGO Declaration on Human Rights.* Reports of the Asia Pacific NGO Conference on Human Rights and NGOs' Statements to the Asia Regional Meeting (Bangkok, 1993). For Western works on Asian values, see Joanne R. Bauer and Daniel A. Bell, eds., *The East Asian Challenge for Human Rights* (Cambridge: Cambridge University Press, 1999); Peter van Ness, ed., *Debating Human Rights: Critical Essays from the United States and Asia* (London: Routledge, 1999); and Michael Jacobsen and Ole Bruun, eds., *Human Rights and Asian Values: Contesting National Identities and Cultural Representations in Asia* (London: Curzon Press, 2000).

59
Declaration on Civil Rights and Freedoms (1998)

Ding Zilin, Lin Mu, Jiang Qisheng (spokesperson), Jiang Peikun (drafter), and Wei Xiaotao

The full text of the declaration (in both English and Chinese) can be found on the website of Human Rights in China: http://www.hrichina.org.

Since the early 1990s, many statements, open letters, and appeals demanding the release of political prisoners and respect for human rights have been drafted and circulated among Chinese citizens (see Text 53). In the beginning of 1994, a group of seven influential scientists, intellectuals, poets, and writers published "An Appeal for Human Rights," which called on the government to respect human rights. In 1995, the UN Year of Tolerance, forty-five Chinese citizens drafted "An Appeal for Tolerance." China's signing of the International Covenant on Economic, Social, and Cultural Rights in 1997 and the International Covenant on Civil and Political Rights in 1998 served to further inspire Chinese citizens to push the issue of human rights. In the autumn of 1998, some of those involved in the earlier appeals and statements then drafted two declarations, one dealing with civil and political rights, which we reprint here, and the other discussing social and economic justice. The drafter of these two declarations was Jiang Peikun, a professor of aesthetics at People's University, and the spokesperson was Jiang Qisheng, former Ph.D. candidate at People's University. (Jiang Qisheng was arrested in 1999 and, on December 26, 2000, was sentenced to four years in prison.) Jiang Peikun's wife, Ding Zilin, also signed the Declaration. Their son was among those killed in the suppression of the 1989 Democracy Movement. Ding, an assistant professor at People's University, has taken the lead in collecting information on those killed and seeking compensation for their relatives. The two remaining signatories were Lin Mu, the former Communist secretary for China's Northwestern University, and Wei

Xiaotao, an engineer and brother of Wei Jingsheng. Although we here reprint the Declaration on Civil Rights and Freedoms, it should be noted that many of the statements and appeals published by Chinese citizens during the 1990s take up economic, social, and environmental rights, addressing many of the social and economic problems with which workers and peasants (among others) are struggling.

At the close of this century, in which people seeking freedom have defeated the inhumanity of fascism and triumphed over various forms of dictatorship and slavery, the cause of freedom has achieved unprecedented progress. At the close of the 1980s and the beginning of the 1990s, the totalitarian system in Eastern Europe and the Soviet Union disintegrated. The end of the Cold War between East and West enabled even more people around the world to win their freedom. However, as the century ends, China is still essentially unfree, the largest such country in today's world, a fact that is a cause of profound distress to all Chinese people.

With the birth of the new century on the horizon, on behalf of ordinary Chinese citizens, intellectuals, workers, peasants, soldiers, students, the self-employed and private entrepreneurs, managers, officials and officers of parties, government, and the armed forces, and public servants at all levels, as well as all Chinese inside or outside the territory of China, we solemnly declare:

The China of the twenty-first century should be a free China; and the Chinese people of the twenty-first century should be free people.

The primary basis of our appeal is the recognition that human rights are innate, that everyone is born free. This freedom belongs to each of us, regardless of race, color, sex, language, religion, political or other views, nationality or class origin, wealth, birth, or other identity; it is inalienable, and non-negotiable; in exercising our own freedom and rights, each of us should respect and refrain from obstructing others in their equal enjoyment of such rights. These human rights are enshrined in the UN Universal Declaration of Human Rights and the two human rights covenants which elaborate it, namely the International Covenant on Economic, Social, and Cultural Rights and the International Covenant on Civil and Political Rights (along with its optional protocols), and have been acknowledged as the progressive norms of the human community.

Our appeal is also based on history's revelation that to every individual who is conscious of his or her own value, freedom is an end in itself. Such freedom not only serves as the foundation upon which a civilized modern society rests, it also provides an inexhaustible source of vitality. The level of civilization and quality of life of any country or nation should not merely be measured by whether or not it safeguards the survival of its people and provides them with an abundance of material goods, but also by whether or not every citizen enjoys the freedom to choose his or her own way of living, and the freedom to pursue self-realization in accordance with his or her individuality and aspirations. Any country that has continued until the present day in its autocratic traditions will never be able to ascend into the ranks of modern civilized nations before it recognizes and safeguards the freedoms and rights of its citizens.

Our appeal is further based on the fact that various forms of democracy have been officially accepted in Communist-ruled China, such as so-called "democratic centralism" (which in fact is nothing but dictatorship by the few or even by a single individual); the Cultural Revolution–style democracy advocated during that period by Mao Zedong; and Deng Xiaoping's reinterpretation of the system known as "socialist democracy with Chinese characteristics." All were labeled as forms of proletarian or socialist democracy. But the innate freedom of individuals has never actually been accorded official acknowledgment, nor has it been favored with the proletarian or socialist label. However, we believe that, from a human rights perspective, freedom is prior to democracy. Any so-called democracy that excludes freedom is just totalitarianism and dictatorship under another name. At the same time, we also believe that the ultimate objective of the modern democratic movement is the establishment of a political system that ensures the protection of the individual freedoms of citizens. If this movement becomes merely a battle for political power, or for a redistribution of power among various political factions, then there will still be no distinction between democracy and dictatorship.

Today, what we Chinese people are most lacking, and thus most urgently need to establish protections for, is precisely our individual civil freedoms.

For more than a century, we Chinese people have painstakingly struggled to make the nation wealthy and powerful and to liberate the Chinese race, and have made great sacrifices in the process. During this period, certain worthy Chinese people unremittingly fought for individual rights and freedoms, but they were unable to achieve their goal due to a lack of economic and social support.

In the first half of this century, we Chinese people expelled foreign aggressors and achieved national liberation. However, just at the moment when we could begin the fight for our own basic rights and freedoms, we were thrown into the grave calamity of civil war, paying a similarly heavy price for so-called class liberation. Once again, the liberation of Chinese people's individual freedoms was postponed.

In 1949, one side was victorious in the civil war, and when the trusting Chinese people hoped to realize the ideal of freedom, they again found a system forcibly imposed on them which was hostile to everything to do with humanitarian values, including human rights and freedoms. In subsequent years, the people's efforts to seek freedom and rights were repeatedly suppressed, and tens of millions of Chinese suffered persecution, even violent death. Finally, in 1989, the June Fourth Massacre, which shocked China and the world, took place on Chinese soil. In one night, the freedom that Chinese yearn for was drowned in a pool of blood.

The fact that Chinese people have painstakingly struggled for freedom and rights for over a century without achieving these goals is due not only to missed historical opportunities, but even more to pursuing paths that proved to be historical dead ends.

Shortly after the Chinese Communist Party came to power in mid-century, it implemented nationwide policies of land reform, establishment of agricultural cooperatives and socialist transformation of privately-owned industrial and commercial enterprises, which completely deprived citizens of the right to own property, one of the most basic human rights. Thus, twentieth-century China was put into a condition that had only existed in ancient times: "All under heaven is the land of the king; all the lords who rule in his domains are the king's subjects." In such circumstances, all Chinese people were alienated from their own means of ensuring their survival and placed in a relationship of subjugation, thus losing the possibility of realizing their economic freedom and their social, political, and cultural rights and freedoms.

At the same time, while legitimizing their power in the name of the so-called people's democratic dictatorship and the dictatorship of the proletariat, China's rulers sought and achieved a monopoly of power over all public goods. Such absolute power was in control of virtually every sphere of social life, including even the spiritual dimension. All relationships among people, even relationships based on humanity and morality, were replaced by a singular class relationship: all the kind, pure, and beautiful emotions in human society were ruthlessly expunged, while evil conduct such as hatred, cruelty, false accusations, betrayal, lies, and deception reached unprecedented proportions, justified as being in the interests of a certain class. People witnessed and suffered the most blatant desertion of humanity since the beginning of history, the most shameless trampling on the morality and values of humankind. Under such circumstances, the only choice people had was to turn their backs on freedom.

This is a disgrace to the entire twentieth century and to all of humanity.

Nevertheless, throughout the world, the path toward freedom for humankind had already been opened. An oppressive and self-isolated China could no longer hold off the challenge posed by world civilization. The desire of the Chinese people to leave their cage and face the world became increasingly uncontainable. During the past twenty years, group after group of courageous Chinese people have stood up to fight for freedom. Throughout the 1980s, calls for freedom and humanity were a crucial trend of the times, a trend denounced by autocratic preservers of the old ways as "peaceful evolution" from the West working in concert with "bourgeois liberalization." Nonetheless, such ideas welled up, washing away all kinds of things based in rigid dogmas and outmoded totalitarianism. At the end of the 1980s, this trend finally coalesced into a nationwide mass movement of demonstrations and protests demanding freedom and democracy, the 1989 Tiananmen Movement.

Although this movement of unprecedented scale ended in bloodshed, it marked a new awakening for the Chinese people, who realized that they had a fresh choice before them. At the same time, it also presages a future in which the dawn of freedom for humankind will illuminate the heart of every Chinese person and every inch of land under their feet.

The 1989 Tiananmen Movement expressed the will of the people, posing an unprecedented challenge to the legitimacy of the current system. However, in the face of this crisis of legitimacy, the ruling authorities did not have the fortitude to comply with the will of the people. Today, their most fundamental, important policies and acts continue to serve a fixed objective: to maintain the existing order by continuing to exert control to the greatest extent possible, suppressing the will of the people and preventing citizens from exercising their freedoms and rights.

Chinese people have a great capacity for patient endurance. As long as they can bear the existing order's violation of their rights and free-doms, they will just put up with it. They have endured the great suffer-ing caused by the June Fourth Massacre; they have endured deception and outright robbery at the hands of corrupt government officials acting with impunity in collusion with the evil forces of society; they have endured the authorities' suppression of any expression of dissatisfaction or resistance justified by the slogan "stability above all." However, great changes have occurred in China in the past nine years or so.

As consciousness of citizens' rights has grown, increasingly Chinese people are aware that they must fight to protect their own rights and interests. As the private economy has grown, so the number of higher-income residents has increased, and their social status has also risen. People in the intellectual, academic, media, and publishing circles, in-cluding some within the CCP, have begun to break through prohibitions on what can be discussed and have enlarged the boundaries of expres-sion more and more. A pluralistic, modern society that is relatively in-dependent of the existing system is beginning to take shape, and the dependence of the people upon state power has already weakened. Un-der such circumstances, if the authorities continue to impose repressive policies without instituting any reforms, they will become increasingly unpopular; if the authorities continue to cling obstinately to such a course, mistaking people's patience for acquiescence, people will reach the limit of endurance and will have every reason to resist those in power, to remove the shackles imposed upon them.

Now the time has arrived when we must expose the misgov-ernance that the ruling authorities recalcitrantly refuse to change, misgovernance that now and in the past has been the principal obstacle in our struggle for freedom and civil rights.

Up until today, the property rights of ordinary Chinese citizens have still not been accorded legal recognition. This fundamentally restricts citizens' rights to pursue freedom, to participate equally in social and economic activities, and to compete in the market, while it provides corrupt officials with opportunities to embezzle state assets and land, disrupting the operation of the market. Legal protection of citizens' right to own property is the foundation for citizens' enjoyment of all other rights and freedoms. In China today, however, the powerless who con-stitute the majority of society not only have no legal protection for their property, but are in fact deprived of the opportunity of acquiring or pos-sessing property.

Up until today, China's rulers continue to impose on all Chinese citizens a political party that cannot represent the interests and will of all the people. They enact legislation to put this political party above the government and all other political parties and organizations, and to subordinate the nation's armed forces to this political party. In today's world, people cannot accept such a method that ensures one specific party the top position without the assent of the citizens. If this situation continues, there is bound to be increasing conflict with the reality of pluralistic interests and values that have emerged in the process of China's modernization.

Up until today, China's rulers still have not relaxed their ideological control over citizens. They force citizens to maintain unity with the "center," allowing citizens to accept only one theory and one "ism," and prohibiting them from accepting any ideology or value system that has not received official endorsement, particularly the so-called "Western" value system. To this day, all mass media such as newspapers, radio, and television stations are kept under the control of a specified party's propaganda organs, thus forcing the media to act as the mouthpiece of this party and to perform the function of suppressing public opinion. They block the dissemination of information, conceal the facts, cover up what occurs in real life with elaborately fabricated lies and conceal the special privileges given to a particular party and other interest groups. But such obviously outdated and rigid ways of interfering with freedom of thought and of restricting citizens' freedom to seek, receive, and impart information are increasingly incompatible with the present information age.

Up until today, China's rulers still continue to exercise tight control over elections at all levels. They use the powers at their disposal to approve the nomination list of candidates in advance, to manipulate election procedures, to exert pressure on voters, and to restrict or ban altogether any methods that introduce competition into the electoral process, in order to ensure that those who cannot gain the support of the people but are loyal to the rulers are elected, thus maintaining their control over state power. Replacing free elections with such domineering tactics tramples openly on civil rights, [and] violates not only the principle of social justice, but also completely disregards the laws of social evolution on survival of the fittest.

Up until today, China's current legal system is in reality still a tool used by the ruling clique to maintain and safeguard its grip on power.

Because under the existing legislative and judicial system the power of the CCP is still higher than the power of citizens, while the individual authority of leaders surpasses the authority of the law, it is very difficult for ordinary citizens to protect their legitimate rights and interests effectively through the current legal process. Indeed, it is hardly possible to restrain the government's power, particularly its abuse of power, through such procedures. As to so-called "judicial fairness" and all citizens being equal before the law, these remain, in most cases, mere slogans not reflecting the reality. In recent years, the authorities have repeatedly promised they would put into practice the idea of "ruling the country according to law" and said they would "strengthen the legal system." But such endeavors cannot fundamentally alter the subordinate status of the existing legal system in the framework of state power.

Up until today, China's rulers continue to suppress such liberties and civil rights as the freedoms of expression, publication, assembly, association, procession, and demonstration. Using groundless charges such as "jeopardizing state security" and "conspiracy to subvert the government," the authorities arrest and put on trial those who attempt to exercise these rights and freedoms in accordance with the law, particularly the freedoms of expression and association. They employ completely inhumane methods to restrict the personal freedom of such people, even using forcible measures in violation of the law, such as arbitrary detention, residential surveillance, and "reeducation through labor." During the past ten years or so, the disadvantaged sectors of society, including workers and peasants who live by their labor, have been rapidly relegated to the margins of society, as their lawful rights and interests have been more severely violated than those of any other social group. Yet these ordinary working people are deprived of any right to resist, in particular the right to organize independent trade unions (or peasant associations). Whenever they are pushed so far that they express their resistance by exercising their rights and freedoms through such means as marches and demonstrations, the government authorities either fail to respond, make some perfunctory gesture, or resort to violent, ruthless repression. Over a long period of suppressing the fundamental freedom of citizens, China's ruling authorities have established an ugly record of human rights abuses, a record that has evoked consistent opposition from people inside China and widespread condemnation from the international community. However, the ruling authorities still refuse to bring about any substantive improvements.

Up until today, China's rulers have not halted their suppression of the freedoms of religion and belief. They ban unofficial religious organizations and religious activities, [and] use trumped-up charges to persecute religious dissidents and threaten and intimidate followers of independent churches. They have never ceased their destruction of religious figures and religious culture in areas inhabited by Tibetan people. With respect to the issue of religious belief, China's rulers ignore the multifaceted spiritual needs of the people and the significance of their transcendent pursuit of a spiritual life for the survival of humanity; in the name of so-called "materialism" and "science," they even deny religion a legitimate existence. The arbitrary attitude of China's rulers toward freedom of religion and belief demonstrates not only their ignorance, but also their hatred of the free spirit of humanity.

Up until today, China's rulers have not halted establishing prohibitions on and carrying out censorship of academic activities and artistic creation. They exercise strict bans on any academic and literary works that cover subjects officially considered to be taboo, and tightly control the activities of unofficial academic and art organizations. They take a laissez-faire attitude toward the crude, the mediocre, the evil, the vulgar, and the base, but adopt an attitude of intolerance toward serious creativity and individuality. They coerce scholars and artists into self-censorship, and induce people in academic and artistic circles to concern themselves only with their wallets, abandoning their sense of responsibility and conscience. This has not only reduced the pursuit of higher values among the people, but has also led to a widespread deterioration in the quality of national education and culture.

All these practices are in conflict with the principles enshrined in the Universal Declaration of Human Rights and the two covenants on human rights. For a long time, many people of insight inside and outside China have drawn the attention of China's ruling authorities to the serious violations of citizens' fundamental rights and freedoms that continue to occur, and have called on them to institute practical measures to correct the situation. But the authorities have either turned a deaf ear to these calls, or have resorted to vicious slander and vengeance against those who raised them.

In the light of the authorities' disregard of the will of the people, we hereby call on all Chinese citizens and those with understanding in all walks of life: as we move into the new century, China needs a new breakthrough. We call on everyone to contribute their utmost to achieving such a breakthrough. We hope that the process will be peaceful and orderly. We hope for citizens' extensive participation.

To this end, we ask every Chinese citizen to take note of the elements we have described which are blocking our achievement of freedom, and to realize that it is not only the obligation of the government, but also the responsibility of each and every citizen, to change the current situation.

Today, the situation inside and outside the country, whether the foreseeable evolution of the domestic situation or the likelihood of support from the international community, indicates that the century that is about to arrive will bring conditions favorable to the realization of freedom in China. We must not pass up any historical opportunity, or forgo any possible effort toward this end.

Therefore we reiterate that freedom is an innate right for each and every individual, and thus the individuals' struggle to achieve this right is inherently legitimate. This struggle should be considered sympathetically by all actors, including the government. We call on China's rulers to comply with the will of the people, acknowledge the legitimacy of the citizens' right to resist, and abandon the suppression of such resistance. We wish to see China's rulers confront, with a rational and sensible attitude, the fundamental transformation of the existing system, which will inevitably appear on the agenda as the next century begins.

China is a country with a long history and tradition. Bound by a firmly established system of imperial power and a hierarchical structure for several thousand years, we Chinese people have always had a relatively weak sense of individuality, individual rights, and freedoms. We have to acknowledge that this is not a virtue of our race, but a failing. This kind of weakness makes it difficult for a large proportion of Chinese people to break away from their traditional dependence and historical inertia; but without changing such traditional characteristics, China will continue to remain mired in the historical cycle of imperial autocracy. For this reason, our whole nation needs to conduct a self-examination, so as to fundamentally change the outdated concept of giving supremacy to the so-called interests of the nation and the collective while blurring the value of the individual into the whole, and to allow the independent personality of citizens to arise. With their new image, Chinese people shall make it known to the world that, as have other peoples in the world, we have sufficient courage and wisdom to part from our past and to face the future.

We firmly believe that the China of the future will be a China that is full of hope and that the Chinese people of the future will be a people who are rightfully proud.

September 22, 1998

Note: Opinions from many different groups of people have been incorporated into this Declaration, and we wish to express our sincere gratitude for their input. We continue to welcome suggestions and criticisms from all quarters.

Further Reading

For the sequel to the above declaration, the Declaration on Civil Rights and Social Justice, see http://www.hrichina.org. For a representative selection of the 1994–95 appeals, see "Letters from Citizens: China's Human Rights Movement," *China Rights Forum* (Summer 1995): 10–14.

60
Freedom of Speech Is the Foremost Human Right (1998)

Hu Ping

"Yanlun ziyou shi diyi renquan" [Freedom of Speech Is the Foremost Human Right], *Shijie zhoukan* (October 25, 1998).

Freedom of speech has been a highly valued right for many Chinese over the years. This holds true of people of widely different political persuasions, ranging from Li Dazhao (see Text 12), to Luo Longji (see Text 22), to Hu Ping in this article. Hu Ping published his first piece on freedom of speech during the Democracy Movement of 1978–79. Although this article was far-reaching and quite radical in its defense of the freedom of speech, Hu Ping did not then make use of the language of human rights when describing it, nor did he refer to international human rights documents. His language and approach reflected the political situation of the time and the theoretical framework within which most Chinese were still operating. In 1986, a revised version of this article was published in an official magazine where it drew a lot of attention and positive comments. In 1986 Hu Ping went to the United States to study, where he has lived since and edits Beijing Spring, *an influential Chinese-language magazine. Hu is an active and thoughtful contributor to the intellectual and political debate of Chinese in exile, and has published extensively, including both theoretical works and more political pieces. In this article Hu refutes the Chinese government's view on human rights point by point, strongly defending the idea that human rights are universal. He argues the case for the right to freedom of speech as the most important of human rights, both by using examples from Chinese history and by drawing on the views of non-Chinese scholars, such as Nobel laureate Amartya Sen.*

1. The Great Victory of the Human Rights Concept

On December 10, 1948, the United Nations General Assembly adopted the Universal Declaration of Human Rights (UDHR) in Paris. Of the 58 UN member-states at the time, 48 countries voted in favor, two countries—Honduras and Yemen—were not present at the voting, and 8 countries abstained: these were the Soviet Union, the Ukraine, Byelorussia, Poland, Czechoslovakia, Yugoslavia, Saudi Arabia, and South Africa.

In the beginning, the UDHR was merely a statement of intention which only later became substantiated and fixed in the form of international law. After a long period of unremitting struggle, the human rights concept has today won a great victory all over the world. Although there are certain governments that in reality do not respect human rights and do not wholeheartedly implement the relevant [legal] stipulations, there is no government that dares to openly oppose human rights. Even though critiques from international society against those [countries] violating human rights cannot always check or redress [the problems], there are nonetheless few governments that dare to remain completely indifferent to such critiques.

2. Distortion and Confusion of the Theory of Human Rights

The human rights concept has won a great victory. Today even those opposing human rights at least have to pay lip-service to it. As late as the mid-1980s, the CCP still took the position of completely rejecting the concept of human rights, dismissing it as a "bourgeois concept." Since then, the CCP's attitude toward human rights has gradually changed. During the past few years, the Chinese authorities have accepted the concept of human rights and agreed to sign the two UN covenants on human rights, namely the International Covenant on Economic, Social, and Cultural Rights and the International Covenant on Civil and Political Rights. However, this does not mean that the debate surrounding the concept of human rights has already subsided. At present, the basic strategy of those opposing human rights is to accept the expression "human rights" but twist its contents, so that they can resist the genuine demands of human rights.

The reason why those opposing human rights can distort its meaning is related to prevalent confusions concerning the theory of human rights itself.

Taking the UDHR as an example of this [confusion], the human rights enumerated in its thirty articles can be divided into two clear categories. Freedom of speech, association, and movement, for example, all belong to the category of "primordial" (*yuanshi xing*) rights. As long as the government only acknowledges their legal character and does not obstruct them, it is possible to exercise them. The rights in the [second] group, such as the right to education and basic social rights, are all a kind of "extended" (*kuozhanxing*) right. Their realization depends on the active intervention of the government.

Let us take Article 25, [Paragraph 1] of the Declaration as an example. [It reads:] "Everyone has the right to a standard of living adequate for the health and well-being of himself and of his family, including food, clothing, housing and medical care and necessary social services, and the right to security in the event of unemployment, sickness, disability, widowhood, old age, or other lack of livelihood in circumstances beyond his control." The question is, who will provide for all this?

In Article 22 of the Declaration, it is very clearly written that this needs to be done "through national effort and international cooperation and in accordance with the organization and resources of each State." From this it is evident that the rights belonging to this category are not something which are inherent (*guyou*) in the individual, but [that their realization] depends on the assistance of others and of the government. But the original meaning of the word "rights" [is] something inherent in the individual person, something that exists with which others cannot interfere. When discussing the meaning of freedom and the meaning of rights, [Albert] Einstein often quoted a passage from Schopenhauer: "Man can do what he wants to do but not necessarily obtain what he wants to obtain." Thus, only the first category of rights, that is, the primordial rights, are rights proper. The second category of rights, that is, extended rights, are strictly speaking not actually rights at all, but material benefits (*fuli*).

We are not, of course, arbitrarily opposed to the government providing necessary material benefits, but we do not approve of lumping together rights and material benefits. As for the phrase "everyone has the right [to work, to free choice of employment, to just and favorable conditions of work, and] to protection against unemployment" (Article 23), it clearly reveals the influence of the prevalent socialist tide at the time. This [right] is hardly possible in a free [market] economy. In the past, socialist countries bragged that they could protect people against unemployment, taking this as proof of their superiority to capitalist [countries]. But today they no longer engage in this kind of bragging.

It should be pointed out that to talk about material benefits as rights is not a development of the concept of rights but rather an abuse of it; an abuse that can only result in a devaluation [of rights]. Just as Milan Kundera in his novel *Immortality* has written: "But because people in the West are not threatened by concentration camps and are free to say and write what they want, the more the fight for human rights gains in popularity, the more it loses any concrete content, becoming a kind of universal stance of everyone toward everything, a kind of energy that turns all human desires into rights. The world has become man's [*sic*] rights and everything in it has become a right; the desire for love, the right to love; the desire for rest, the right to rest; the desire for friendship, the right to friendship; the desire to exceed the speed limit, the right to exceed the speed limit; the desire for happiness, the right to happiness; the desire to publish books, the right to publish books; the desire to shout loudly on the streets in the middle of the night, the right to shout loudly on the streets in the middle of the night."

According to such a diluted and general concept of human rights, no country would be able to fully realize human rights, not even in the future. If the human rights concept becomes so boundless, its strength will not increase, but instead erode.

3. A Rebuttal to Opposition to Human Rights

Even though at present the theory of human rights itself leaves much to be desired, we can for the moment put this question aside. In order to refute the theories opposing human rights that are popular today, we do not need to go into such minute details.

Today, the most frequently used methods to oppose human rights are without doubt the following: (1) in the name of cultural relativism (*wenhua xiangdui zhuyi*), reject the universality of the concept of human rights; (2) in the name of the right to subsistence (*shengcun quan*) and the right to development, reject and defer freedom of speech and other similar rights; and (3) in the name of stability, suppress individual rights. The common foundation of these three points is their emphasis on so-called national conditions (*guoqing*). They also use another shameless tactic: "Our human rights situation has some problems but your human rights situation is not perfect either; no one is more brilliant than anyone else, so no one can pick on anyone else." Here follows a point-by-point rebuttal of these views.

Regarding Cultural Relativism

To reject human rights in the name of cultural relativism is a new tactic of the opponents of human rights which has appeared in the past few years. A fish is swimming in the water and one person says that the fish is very happy. Another person retorts: "You are not a fish, how do you know that the fish is happy?" This is an old form of relativism.[1] On the surface it seems quite difficult to refute. But what if I were to say that if you were to fish that living fish up from the water and kill it, then the fish would certainly be very unhappy? This proposition nobody would dare to refute. (Nobody would retort: You are not a fish, how do you know that the fish is unhappy about being brought to death?) Otherwise, you would be defending any and all crimes.

Pol Pot killed two million Cambodians. He can completely deny guilt because he could retort to you: You are not a Cambodian, how can you know that Cambodians are not happy about being massacred? He could in addition reply to the world that Cambodians have different ways of expressing happiness and sorrow from others. When they face massacre they cry and call out loudly; this does not mean that they are unhappy but as a matter of fact signifies that they are particularly happy and satisfied.

The logic behind the universality of human rights is very simple. It can perhaps be summarized in this self-evident proposition: no country's people want a government that is domineering and does not allow critique and opposition; no country's people desire to be imprisoned or massacred because they have expressed critical views of the government; no country's people are happy with being deprived of the opportunity for public defense in the face of arrest and interrogation.

On the Right to Subsistence and Freedom of Speech

The CCP argues that, since the levels of economic development in China and the United States are different, "the two countries' roads and methods of realizing human rights and basic freedoms will also differ." "China emphasizes that one first of all needs to pay attention to the right to subsistence and the right to development, and at the same time energetically strengthen democracy and the construction of the legal system in order to protect people's economic, social, cultural, civil, and political rights."

These statements are not logical because whether a country realizes human rights and basic freedoms or not does not depend on its level of economic development. The common saying that "freedom is invaluable" expresses it well. This saying has two meanings. One is that freedom is of unparalleled value: "freedom is priceless."[2] The other is that you don't need to spend money for freedom. . . : "freedom is costless" or "freedom is free." Of course, there is another saying according to which freedom is expensive since in order to oppose tyranny and win freedom you have to pay a high price. But this price is something that the tyrants force upon us; this [latter] saying therefore does not stand in opposition to the one according to which "freedom is costless."

Let us take freedom of speech as an example. How shall we realize the freedom of speech? Abolish the practice of punishing people because of their speech. When somebody expresses a different political opinion, all that is needed is for the government simply not to arrest him and suppress it. When we demand freedom of speech, we are not asking the government to do anything, just asking it to refrain from doing something. This is not something that requires spending money and effort but, rather, saves money and effort. How can one say that this is something that only rich countries can accomplish, and poor countries cannot?

The reality is quite the opposite. Everybody knows that, in order to suppress opposition, autocrats have supported who knows how many thugs and spent who knows how much money. To developing countries such as China this is a great and meaningless waste of manpower and resources. Shouldn't it satisfy both sides to turn swords into ploughs?

There is an additional layer of meaning hidden in the rejection of the rights to freedom and democracy in the name of the rights to subsistence and development: this is the view that freedom and democracy are harmful to subsistence and jeopardize development. The assumption seems to be that with freedom and democracy, countries will fall into chaos and people will fight without end, and so will not be able to devote themselves to developing the economy. This is a complete fallacy!

As everyone knows, during the years 1959–61 China experienced a severe famine unprecedented in humankind's history. The conservative estimate of the number of people who died from starvation is 40 million people. (This figure is taken from an officially published book put out by the People's Press in 1996, *History Will Not Hesitate Again*.) The basic reason behind this disastrous famine was not, however, a mistaken economic policy.

The famous economist and Harvard professor Amartya Sen has proved that: "An important fact in the history of famines is that a major famine has never occurred in a country with a democratic government and a free press. Famines have taken place in old monarchies, in contemporary authoritarian societies, in primitive tribal [societies], in technological-bureaucratic dictatorships, in colonies controlled by imperialist rulers, and in newly independent dictatorships and one-party dictatorships. But in those countries which are independent, which regularly hold elections, where there are opposition parties which offer critical views, where the press is allowed to report freely and can call into question the correctness of government policy, and where there doesn't exist censorship of books and the media, there has never been a famine."[3]

In the final analysis, as Li Zhisui[4] has said, when Mao Zedong launched the Great Leap Forward he didn't deliberately want the Chinese people to starve to death. For a long period of time, not even Mao himself knew how bad the situation had become. But since the CCP's centralized rule, led by Mao, was so ruthless and the freedom of speech had been so completely denied, there was in the end no one who dared to speak the truth, not even within the circle of the ruling elite, except for Mao. In the end, even Mao himself, who had suppressed the truth and encouraged lies, was deceived by those excellent lies. In this way the mistaken economic policy slowly became impossible to correct; one mistake was added to another, so that it all ended up in a tragedy of unparalleled proportions.

During the time of Emperor Hui of the Jin dynasty, some areas were stricken by famine. But when the ministers reported to the emperor that people were starving to death because they had no rice to eat, the emperor asked: "Why don't they eat meat instead?" When the Great Leap

Forward only had been running for a couple of months, it became obvious that the production of grain had dropped significantly and many people did not have enough to eat. But in newspapers and at meetings [people] were still striving to surpass one another, claiming that the grain yield would be 10,000 *jin* or 100,000 *jin* per *mu*; [everyone asserted] that there would be a bumper harvest. The result was that our Great Helmsman and his comrades in arms in Zhongnanhai earnestly discussed how to cope: "The [output] of grain is too huge! We will never be able to eat it all, neither can we store it all; what shall we do?"

At that time, people on the verge of starvation were not allowed to call out that they were starving. Many people who publicly did this were labeled counterrevolutionaries. It was not permitted to mention that the many millions of people who died had died from starvation. Many officials who reported to higher levels that people were dying from starvation were labeled rightist opportunists. Today when one mentions freedom of speech some people believe that this is just something of special value to intellectuals, especially those intellectuals who are not content with their lot. The tragic example of the three-year-long famine is the most forceful rebuttal of such a view.

The facts prove that for each one of us freedom of speech is the right that protects all other rights. It is the most important protection and the most elementary. If during those years the Chinese people had enjoyed elementary individual rights, foremost of which is freedom of speech, and those on the verge of starvation had been able to call out aloud, to criticize and engage in resistance, would 40 million of our compatriots still have starved to death?

It is quite true that not all places without freedom of speech have experienced major famines, but all places which have had major famines have lacked any freedom of speech. On this point, no one in the world has learned that lesson to the same tragic degree as the Chinese people of today; it is engraved in our bones and hearts. To reject freedom of speech in the name of the right to subsistence resulted in 600 million people living for three years on the verge of starvation, and more than 40 million people losing their lives.

Regarding Stability and Individual Rights

The Chinese authorities time and again profess that, based on the lessons of China's turbulent history, stability must be given priority. Stability must prevail over everything else and therefore individual rights have to be sacrificed. This opinion has been voiced so many times that even [President] Clinton has come to accept it as somewhat true. At the round-table meeting in Shanghai [in 1998], Clinton said: "China's history has caused it to be very sensitive about turmoil, and therefore it has had difficulties tolerating individual rights." The facts actually show otherwise. The turmoil in China during the past half-century has not been due to the existence of individual rights, but to a lack of individual rights. In contemporary China, it's not that people have sacrificed their individual rights in order to avoid social turmoil, but rather that the sacrifice of individual rights has caused social turmoil.

The most striking example is the Cultural Revolution. Even the Chinese authorities acknowledge that the Cultural Revolution was "ten years of turmoil." As everybody knows, the Cultural Revolution began with the order from Mao Zedong to criticize Wu Han's play "Hai Rui Is Dismissed from Office." This is a typical case of someone being punished because of his speech. The death of Liu Shaoqi and his unknown place of burial shows that not even the chairman of the country had the least bit of human rights. During the Cultural Revolution, the victims and their family members who were implicated numbered more than 100 million people. In the final analysis, this was not created by the existence of individual rights.

It is exactly as the saying has it: "It takes more than one day for the river to freeze three *chi* deep." The seeds of the chaos of the Cultural Revolution were planted deeply already in the early days after CCP's founding of the country. From 1949 to 1966, the CCP began by suppressing a handful of people and depriving them of their fundamental human rights, and gradually escalated this [policy until it developed into the policy of] "sweeping away all monsters and demons" and [establishing] "a complete dictatorship."[5] It has been said that when the CCP ordered him to be criticized in 1955, Hu Feng predicted that: "Beginning with the critique of Hu Feng, the Chinese literary scene is bound to sink into the Middle Ages." This prediction came true in merely ten years; but in fact those who faced this danger went well beyond the "insignificant" literary scene.

In the name of the 100 million people who suffered from the ten years of chaos, who dares to argue that chaos in contemporary China has been caused by individual rights and not the opposite? All the talk and action which in the name of stability continues to suppress individual rights is the utmost betrayal of our people's tragic history.

When it comes to the claim that "individual rights must not harm the interest of the group," this is quite superfluous because the boundaries of rights originally signify that limits are drawn between the individual and the collective. When Yan Fu translated John S. Mill's *On Liberty*, he translated it as "On the boundaries between the rights of the group and those of the individual" in order to prove this point.

The reason we affirm freedom of speech is because its use is indirect and not direct. Speech does not create dangers for other individuals or the group (except in cases of instigation and slander), so that others or the group have no reason to engage in force against it. The so-called "freedom of speech must not violate the law" also belongs to the category of nonsense. The First Amendment to the American Constitution clearly stipulates that the Congress cannot adopt any laws that restrict the freedom of speech. From this can be gathered that the question is not that freedom of speech cannot violate the law, but that the law cannot violate the freedom of speech.

Regarding National Conditions

In order to resist human rights, the CCP always uses "national conditions" as an excuse. But what is China's real national condition? This can of course not be based upon the authorities' own views but must be based upon the Chinese people's personal experiences.

I remember that in the 1960s, the CCP energetically launched the so-called campaign to "recall sufferings and cherish happiness." Old workers and poor peasants were requested to lecture us young people about "their sufferings in the old society and happiness in the new society." These people were originally carefully chosen by the Party because they were the ones who had "suffered the most and whose hate toward the old society was the fiercest." The Party had already instructed them regarding the content of their talks. But even so, they couldn't help but often make a slip of the tongue when talking, and without being careful mention the years 1961–62: ". . . and talking about suffering, 1961 and 1962, during those two years we really suffered!"

From this it is evident that to the great majority of the Chinese people, the suffering created by the old society cannot be compared to Mao Zedong's "three red banners" [of the General Line, the Great Leap Forward, and the People's Communes].[6] In addition, if one were to ask today's Chinese when was the greatest chaos they have lived through, the majority would definitely answer that it was the Cultural Revolution. Were we not talking about national conditions? Well, this is the national condition!

The Dividing Line Between Respecting Human Rights and Despising Them Must Not Be Obscured

Jiang Zemin has said that: "There is no country which has a perfect human rights situation." The real meaning of this is that our human rights situation has problems but others have problems too, so everyone has problems, and at most it is like one who retreats fifty paces mocking the one who retreats a hundred.

This statement is not correct. Does the fact that there are no perfect people in the world and that everybody makes mistakes imply that there are no differences between good and evil people in the world? It is evident that there is a clear demarcation between good and evil. In the same way it is obvious that there is a clear distinction between respecting human rights and despising them. When people's property is stolen by thieves and innocent people killed by thugs, and the government's protection is not satisfactory and the solutions to the cases are not pursued with determination, this is one thing. But when the government itself confiscates property and kills innocent people, this is quite a different matter.

It is impossible for a country to protect people's lives and property without anything going wrong. In this sense you can say that there is no country which has a perfect human rights record, regardless of the good faith and ability of the government. However, the government only needs the most rudimentary good faith for it not to engage in any kinds of criminal activities, such as violating and trampling upon human rights. In this sense, the differences between a government that respects human rights and one that despises them become instantly obvious; they are as different as the waters of the Jing River and the Wei River.

4. Why Say That Freedom of Speech Is the Foremost Human Right?

Others have already published many penetrating thoughts regarding the great importance of freedom of speech, and I myself have also written a few articles on the topic. Below I will make some additional remarks.

Although the theory that "the first among human rights is the right to subsistence" is a recent invention of the CCP, it nonetheless did not deny during the great famine that in order to live, people first of all need food to eat; but even so the great tragedy of several million people dying of starvation still occurred. From this it is evident that affirming the priority of people's need to eat in order to subsist is actually not important, because it is of no [concrete] help. You can declare that man's foremost need is to eat, but that does not mean that it is the foremost human right. It needs to be understood that "rights" are not the same as "needs."

To be sure, freedom of speech cannot be eaten, but when you meet with natural and man-made disasters, and especially when due to the government's mistaken policy you have no food to eat, if you cannot then raise a call of warning to make society aware of it, and receive the masses' support in order to make the government correct its mistakes, you will not be able to change your own plight.

Lin Yutang has said that freedom of speech is the right to squeal when hurt.[7] People of old said "when there are injustices, there will be outcries." When people encounter injustices, regardless of what kind, the most important thing is "to cry out." Aristotle a long time ago said that among the animals, only man has the ability to speak. Sound can express joys and sorrows. Ordinary animals have an ability to make sounds and on basis of this they can communicate sad and happy sounds between themselves. But in order to express whether something is beneficial or harmful, fair or unjust, we need the spoken language.

The difference between humankind and other animals is that we have the ability to understand the differences between good and evil, justice and injustice, and in addition can use language to communicate this between ourselves. In this way, humankind can support goodness and oppose evil, support truth and oppose falsehood, support justice and oppose injustice. Language is that important. Whether people in a society can communicate by language freely and completely, directly relates to the moral quality of that society.

The first magic weapon of autocracies and dictatorships at all times and in all lands has been to cut off people's free communication: that is, to suppress the freedom of speech. This is a powerful negative argument that the freedom of speech is the foremost human right. All people who are concerned about human rights questions must first of all resolutely fight for the freedom of speech.

Notes

1. Hu Ping is here referring to a famous story from *Zhuangzi*. See Burton Watson, trans., *Chuang Tzu: Basic Writings* (New York: Columbia University Press, 1964), p. 110.
2. English in original.
3. Among Sen's recent books on the topic Hu Ping discusses, see *Development as Freedom* (New York: Knopf, 1999).
4. Li Zhisui was one of Mao Zedong's physicians, who in 1994 became famous for his book *The Private Life of Chairman Mao: The Memoirs of Mao's Personal Physician Dr. Li Zhisui* (New York: Random House, 1994).
5. The editorial of the *People's Daily* on June 1, 1966, carried an article entitled "Sweep Away All Monsters and Demons." This term referred to all those "specialists," "scholars," "authorities," and others who had had positions in the ideological and cultural fields but now came under attack.
6. The so-called Three Red Banners movement ran from 1958 to 1961. In 1958, the Eighth Party Congress adopted Mao's General Line, which was to "Go all out, aim high, and achieve greater, faster, better, and more economical results in building socialism." The Party Congress also affirmed the ongoing Great Leap Forward as well as the process of communalization.
7. Lin Yutang actually quotes Bernard Shaw here. See Lin Yutang, "On Freedom of Speech," *China Critic* 6:10, 9 (March 1933).

Further Reading

For Hu Ping's first article on freedom of speech, see He Bian (Hu Ping), "Lun yanlun ziyou" [Freedom of Speech], *Wo tu* (April 2, 1979), reprinted in *Dalu dixia kanwu huibian* [A Collection of Underground Publications Circulated on the Chinese Mainland] (Taipei: Zhonggong yanjiu zazhi she bianyin, 1982), vol. 12, pp. 67–115.

For English-language materials on the debate on human rights among Chinese dissidents, see the magazine *China Rights Forum* put out by Human Rights in China, a human rights NGO based in New York. And for Chinese-language materials, see the magazine *Beijing zhi chun* [Beijing Spring].

61

Moving in the Right Direction: China's Irreversible Progress Toward Democracy and Human Rights (1999)

Liu Qing

Liu Qing, "Moving in the Right Direction: China's Irreversible Progress Toward Democracy and Human Rights," *China Rights Forum* (Fall 1999): 16–19, 47.

Liu Qing (b. 1946) belongs to the 1978–79 generation of Chinese dissidents. He was one of the editors of the moderate magazine April Fifth Forum *during the Democracy Wall Movement. When Wei Jingsheng was arrested in March 1979, many fellow dissidents who had earlier been quite critical of his views spoke out in his defense. Liu Qing managed to retrieve the transcript of Wei's trial and published it in his magazine, and because of this Liu himself was arrested. While serving a three-year term of re-education through labor, Liu's prison memoir was smuggled out and published in Hong Kong. This angered the authorities and Liu was put on trial and sentenced to a further eight years for counterrevolutionary propaganda and incitement. Like Wei, Liu thus spent the fateful year 1989 in prison, only being released in December of that year. Since he did not have a valid residence permit for Beijing, he was then briefly detained in 1990. In 1992 Liu left China for New York, where he became engaged in the organization Human Rights in China, set up in 1989, and now serves as its chairman. Liu has since then continued to devote himself to the struggle for human rights and plays an active role in the dissident community in exile. Despite the many setbacks in human rights work over the years and the continuing repression in the PRC, Liu takes an optimistic outlook and remains convinced that the struggle for human rights and democracy will eventually bear fruit. In the text reprinted here, Liu describes and analyzes the Chinese citizens' struggle for human rights since 1979.*

I am convinced that China has embarked on an irreversible course toward democracy and human rights. This unshakable conviction is based on four observations.

First, China already has in place a core group of people who resist repression and persecution in their efforts to pursue democracy and human rights, namely the people commonly known as dissidents or democracy movement activists. The struggle for democracy and human rights has been going on since the Democracy Wall Movement of 1979. During these twenty years, the CCP has relentlessly repressed these efforts. The suppression of the Democracy Wall Movement in 1979–81, the Campaign Against Spiritual Pollution in 1983, the political rectification under the guise of anti-crime campaigns in 1983, the suppression of the student movement in 1986, and the 1989 Beijing Massacre and subsequent crackdown are all demonstrations of how the CCP has crushed such movements with an iron fist one after another.

In the ten years since 1989, the nationwide strategy of arrests and repression has continued unabated, and has even intensified with large-scale arrests and convictions in the past half-year. Yet these efforts at suppression have failed to eliminate the dissidents. Rather, the number of people openly joining the resistance has greatly expanded, spreading from just a handful of cities like Beijing to a majority of provinces and towns throughout the entire country. This fact shows that the Chinese democracy movement has gained an indomitable strength and that a core of people committed to the realization of democracy and human rights has been formed, and it also reveals the demand for democracy and human rights in Chinese society. Although this core group admittedly is very small relative to a population of 1.3 billion, according to the Chinese saying, "A battalion of steel turns out a continuous flow of soldiers"—in other words, the existence of this core group provides a firm basis for future expansion. If suitable circumstances arise in China for democracy and human rights, one can imagine how the movement will flourish on this foundation.

Second, as more and more people are realizing, the national crisis that is growing daily in severity and that may well lead to social unrest can be avoided only by steering a course toward democracy and human rights. The ruling elite in Beijing has drawn one lesson from June Fourth: that maintaining their rule requires the eradication of all dissent. Yet ten years of repression have failed to eliminate the deep dissatisfaction in society, and the problems have grown increasingly serious. These include corruption, injustice, urban unemployment, pockets of rural unrest, unfairness in the economic system, the growing gap between rich and poor, problems in economic reform, and the plundering of state capital, as well as the authorities' disregard for human rights such as freedom of religion and freedom of thought.

All these are potentially explosive, as became clear when disciples of the *qigong* group, Falun Gong, recently organized a sit-in outside the leadership compound in Zhongnanhai to petition for redress of their grievances. The severity of China's problems was also demonstrated by the extreme nature of the nationalistic response to the NATO bombing of the Chinese embassy in Belgrade and the political storm caused by Taiwan president Lee Teng-hui's characterization of cross-strait relations as "state-to-state." These reactions exposed the deep insecurity in China's authoritarian government. Furthermore, these [latter] two incidents meant that international human rights scrutiny has been deemphasized in favor of repairing relations with China and dealing with security concerns. The Chinese authorities took advantage of the international situation and demonstrated their desperate desire for control at home by stepping up the persecution of dissidents. After the severe sentences imposed on Zhang Shanguang, Wang Youcai, Xu Wenli, and Qin Yongmin late last year, repression intensified this July and August resulting in prison sentences of ten years or more for Liu Xianbin, She Wanbao, Yue Tianxiang, and others.

Even official theorists acknowledge that China has reached another moment where the possibility of instability is high. Clearly, dictatorial repression has proven ineffective, since corruption and all the other problems listed above are the very results of this autocratic system. Solutions to these social problems can be found only with a democratic system in which the people are able to supervise government and enjoy freedom of expression and the right to elect the officials and government of their choice.

Third, the struggle for democracy and human rights in China is part of a global trend and therefore elicits more sympathetic attention from the international community. With the collapse of autocratic regimes in Eastern Europe and the Soviet Union, and the end of the Cold War, the value of democracy and human rights has become universally recognized. After the dissolution of the Soviet Union, China's poor human rights record has come under the international community's spotlight. This interest arose in part because the international community directly witnessed the bloodbath of June Fourth, and in part because China, as a superpower, has put up the fiercest resistance to democracy and human rights.

The international support for the Chinese democracy and human rights movement has been an important cause, aside from the struggle of the Chinese people themselves, for the positive changes in human rights that China has experienced in the past ten years. Although many democratic countries in the international community have been inconsistent in applying pressure on China regarding its human rights record, or have grown increasingly reluctant to apply such pressure for reasons of economic, political, or other benefits, these countries will most likely sustain their pressure out of a concern for their own safety and advantage, and out of a general respect for humanity. Moreover, once China shows a favorable attitude toward democracy and human rights, it will be able to count on all the more support from the international community.

Finally, and perhaps most importantly, democracy and human rights accord with human nature. Human beings by their nature strive for dignity and rights, and only democracy and human rights can guarantee that they will achieve these. This is not to say that democracy and human rights are all-powerful or that they are flawless. The countries that now practice democracy and respect human rights certainly can be criticized on many points. But compared to other political structures and value systems, democracy and human rights remain without doubt the best possible choice in the present world. Due to rapid progress in science, technology, and information, the Chinese people will be able to appreciate that the cause of democracy and human rights is based on justice and rationality, and therefore it will be possible to gain the popular support necessary to realize this system that can guarantee their dignity and their rights.

Although the future of democracy and human rights in China is bright, there are plenty of barriers at present. For various reasons, the Chinese struggle for democracy and human rights has just reached a stage of confusion. Since the June Fourth Massacre, the Communist authorities have pursued a course of severe political repression combined with significant relaxation of restrictions in areas such as the economy and daily life, and even to some extent in the realm of thought and ideology. As the political pressure on individuals diminished and life gained richness in both substance and structure, political resentment has also gradually lessened. As the phenomenon of political cleansing and terror faded at the end of 1992, control on the Chinese economy was relaxed to allow space for greater marketization, and international economic sanctions were reduced or lifted. The Chinese economy began to expand at a feverish pace, creating unprecedented opportunities for people to profit from commerce. Since many had long dreamt of such an opportunity, the general interest shifted toward money.

Moreover, after the people's fury over the June Fourth Massacre had abated, the barbarous cruelty of the despots and the crushing defeat of the democracy movement inspired in the people feelings of frustration, hopelessness, and powerlessness. And after the shock of June Fourth, the Communist authorities came increasingly to regard dissidents as dangerous enemies who were a challenge to their power, and they never ceased to suppress dissidents with an iron hand. Meanwhile, under the pressure of international criticism of its human rights record, the Chinese government has succeeded in coming up with policies that have allowed it to persecute dissidents while deflecting international attention. These circumstances have stirred up the people's doubts about the possibility of realizing the ideals of democracy and human rights, and as a result, people's concern about politics has diminished or turned cold.

After 1995, the international community modified its position of concern about the deficiencies in China's human rights record, partly due to practical circumstances and needs. Countries all over the world gradually relaxed the economic and political sanctions they had imposed on China, to the point of suspending moral condemnation and diplomatic pressure, as they jockeyed for a piece of the huge Chinese market. From an economic and political perspective, cooperation with a large country like China is a practical necessity for many countries. Now that the 1989 Beijing Massacre is long past and many years of diplomatic pressure on China have failed to yield the desired results, the support of the international community for the Chinese democracy and human rights movement has declined. Although this decrease in international concern is not the reason for the present confusion in the Chinese democracy and human rights movement, it obviously is not a situation that is helpful to the movement in regaining its momentum in the near future.

The problems faced by the dissidents who strive for democracy and human rights are also an important reason for the movement's present state of distraction. In the past year or two, critical voices have arisen on all sides, including in the media, condemning specific members of the Chinese democracy movement, especially dissidents in exile. The Internet, where one can post whatever one wants, has simply become rampant with people who use aliases or borrow names to make personal attacks on the democracy movement and its members, freely employing insults, slander, and rumor-mongering. There can be no doubt that the CCP is directly or indirectly involved in this and that the wanton vilification of dissidents can be effective in the eradication of the democracy movement. This suspicion is certainly not a baseless illusion borne of mere animosity, since insults, slander, and rumor-mongering have always occupied an important place in the repertoire of political combat methods of the CCP. Moreover, hidden forces and ulterior motives clearly play a role in the background of the present attacks, struggles, and general chaos. But apart from these malevolent elements, the dissidents also suffer from their own problems.

Here I refer to the unprecedented disorder and chaos into which the people's movement has sunk at the present time. Irresponsibility, impetuous and thoughtless behavior, self-glorification, jealousy and attacks inspired by malice toward other people or other organizations, groundless rumor-mongering and slander, and incessant fights and confrontations—these have all reached rather serious proportions. There is also a very small number of people who, under the banner of the democracy movement, shamelessly and selfishly seek private gain and in doing so do not even refrain from breaking the law, thereby tarnishing the image of the democracy movement in the eyes of all and diminishing the moral and ideological appeal of the movement. Ideological and moral strength are of utmost importance in the struggle of the democracy and human rights movement, and without such strength the movement will fail to gain widespread support. To remedy this situation, the people's movement will require the promotion of a specific culture. Every social movement starts in chaos, yet in order to grow, a movement has to develop a culture of its own and put an end to the chaos. Without a culture of its own, a social movement cannot become mature or powerful.

The culture of the democracy movement should include rules, ethics, and procedures. The rules of action should be clear and concrete; they should be obeyed and they should be regarded as law. However, at present, the culture of the Chinese democracy movement is lax. Not only does it consist of many organizations of varying sizes, but it also includes a large number of scattered individuals, so that it is impossible to implement a uniform system of discipline and rules. Therefore, we shall have to rely on the gradual development of a few influential organizations whose basic rules of action will come to represent the significant mainstream and thereby come to serve as a set of rules that applies to everyone. It is only an organization with good rules that can become strong and successful and gain the approval of an expanding following. Although the formulation of such rules certainly poses a challenge, it is by no means impossible. But rules by themselves do not suffice. A culture of greater scope and higher standards is based upon corresponding ethics. The ethics of the CCP serves only the Party's advantage and needs, and the ethics of pre-Communist society has been practically destroyed.

Whether a society or an organization, a group of people can function effectively only when it has developed a new set of ethics and moral principles that safeguards public opinion and that guarantees in the people's minds the realization of their collective ambition.

Ever since the Democracy Wall, the democracy movement has engaged in concrete actions to promote its struggle for democracy and human rights. But from an analysis of the present situation, it appears that this modus operandi has fulfilled its historical mission and that a new way of working is required.

In the past, small organizations managed to influence public opinion, creating a significant social impact and exerting pressure for democracy and human rights solely through such channels as producing magazines. But now this approach no longer achieves the same effect as it did in the past. The people barely respond to such efforts. There are four reasons for this. First, the economic reforms and the changes in daily life have eliminated the intense political pressure and feelings of fear for the majority of people. Second, the democracy and human rights movement has become an abstract ideology and political movement. The general population, which no longer suffers immediate oppression or fear, is unable to feel the urgent need for ideological or political activity to seek democracy and human rights, and does not know how to contribute. Third, in the present struggle for democracy and human rights, such goals as true economic, social, and cultural rights, justice, and freedom of religious belief cannot be fully or concretely realized. Fourth, while allowing greater economic and personal freedom, the CCP has pursued a barbarous repression of the democracy and human rights movement, even more ruthless than that before 1989.

Democracy and human rights in China is a matter that concerns the Chinese people as a whole, and only the support and participation of the majority will give the movement continuous and resolute strength. A modus operandi for the future should therefore be concerned with the majority and should inspire a sense of purpose, enthusiasm, and a desire to participate. All of China's current severe problems—corruption, injustice, urban unemployment, pockets of rural unrest, unfairness in the economic system, the growing gap between rich and poor, problems in economic reform, and the plundering of state capital—in fact relate to concrete matters of democracy and human rights. From now on, the struggle for democracy and human rights should therefore be a struggle for the resolution of these concrete problems. If we are able to devise ways of working that can effectively strive for practical solutions to the concrete problems of democracy and human rights, and at the same time produce a set of rules and ethics for the democracy movement, then the cause of Chinese democracy and human rights will enter a new period of vitality. Thus we may very well realize these ideals for which China has striven for so long.

Further Reading

For Liu Qing's prison diary, see "Prison Memoirs," *Chinese Sociology and Anthropology* 15:1–3 (Fall/Winter 1982–83). For additional writings by Liu Qing during the 1990s, see various issues of *China Rights Forum*.

62
Taiwan Urgently Needs a National Human Rights Commission (2000)

League for the Promotion of a National
Human Rights Commission

Guojia renquan weiyuanhui tuidong lianmeng [League for the Promotion of a National Human Rights Commission], "Taiwan jixu yige guojia renquan weiyuanhui: Guojia renquan weiyuanhui tuidong lianmeng zhengqiu lianshu shuotie" [Taiwan Urgently Needs a National Human Rights Commission: A Joint Petition from the League for the Promotion of a National Human Rights Commission], accessed at http://www.tahr.org.tw/committee/2000.02.16.htm (October 2000).

After the GMD had in 1979 supported the establishment of a human rights organization (see the Introduction to Text 45), the political opposition also decided to set up its own organization. In 1984, the Taiwan Association for Human Rights, led by pro-independence activists, was established. This organization at first encountered considerable difficulties from governmental authorities, and was officially registered only in 1995. Nonetheless, after martial law was lifted in 1987, political organizing and human rights activism flourished, helping to push Taiwan toward democracy. By the 1990s, the GMD government began to acknowledge past human rights violations, leading it to establish a human rights monument on Green Island, where political prisoners had been imprisoned, on December 10, 1999, and to apologize to all those who had suffered during the White Terror. New laws have also been passed that allow for compensation to these victims. However, concern about continuing human rights violations, coupled with the fact that since it lost its seat in the

UN to the PRC in 1971, Taiwan has stood outside the UN human rights system, have led people in Taiwan to continue their struggle for human rights. After years of discussions, twenty-two NGOs formed a coalition in December of 1999 to take advantage of the upcoming presidential election and push the issue of human rights. They advocate the establishment of a National Human Rights Commission, the draft proposal for which we translate here.

Since the end of martial law in 1987, as the constitutional protection of various human rights has continued to "thaw," the human rights situation in Taiwan has in fact seen considerable improvement. Political prisoners and blacklists have already by and large disappeared. Freedoms of thought, belief, speech, assembly, association, and so on, along with the political rights to vote and to participate in elections, now rest on relatively firm foundations. The first steps have even been taken on certain social rights (like environmental protection). When compared to the dictatorial and autocratic system of the past, this is genuine, objective progress. But as time passes and society develops, an increasing number of people feel that this kind of self-satisfaction in fact has only a [limited,] historical significance. Viewed from a broader, more reliable perspective, Taiwan's human rights situation and prospects paint a different picture.

First of all, the scope of human rights far exceeds the rights mentioned above. If we take the current approximately two hundred international human rights treaties as a standard, we will see that the scope of human rights is virtually equivalent to all of human social life. Our first steps toward understanding human rights have thus had too narrow a scope. This is true of the civil and political rights that are relatively familiar to our countrymen; [as for] the economic, social, and cultural rights which cannot be neglected if civil and political rights are to have any concrete meaning—they are rarely even spoken of, much less have they [truly] entered our consciousness.

Second, even those human rights that are relatively well protected are not necessarily [completely] consolidated. For instance, the political rights of voting and participating in elections can be seriously distorted by the power of money, which renders meaningless the citizen's equal "participation in public affairs" and "receipt of public services" (International Covenant on Civil and Political Rights, Article 25). Another [example is that] since when an application [for a public assembly] is turned down, there are no timely and effective mechanisms with which to appeal, whether people are able to enjoy their rights of assembly and demonstration is completely dependent on the arbitrary decisions of police organs. The unchecked spread of [secret] monitoring is yet another example. Other rights described above as "relatively firm" have similar problems.

Third, when the Republic of China withdrew from the United Nations in 1971, it simultaneously withdrew from the international human rights system that revolves around the UN, yet the large-scale [implementation through] international treaties of human rights standards—especially in the areas of institutionalization and internationalization—really began in the [subsequent] period. Our past dictatorial, autocratic system already meant that we lacked [soil] in which a human rights culture and tradition would take root and grow; long-term international isolation has still more meant that Taiwan lacks the international participation, exchange, stimulus, and pressure without which human rights cannot develop.

Fourth, one of the results of this historical and international situation is that Taiwan lacks many fundamental conditions [necessary] for the further development of human rights. The improvement and progress of human rights depends on the mutual action of two important factors: human rights consciousness taking root, and the establishment of protective institutions. However, in Taiwan knowledge and information concerning human rights is extremely lacking: the largest library in the country contains less than two hundred Chinese documents (without taking into account their quality) on human rights; our higher education system is almost completely lacking in human rights education. The chapter on human rights in our constitution is still limited to the prewar level, and the government lacks a single official responsible for human rights, to say nothing of a bureau for human rights policies and affairs.

In the current conditions, if we want Taiwan's human rights situation to improve to a higher level—to say nothing of wanting it to improve in direct proportion to [the improvement] in the numerous [areas in which] Taiwan has relatively excellent conditions—it is obvious that we have to begin (even if it is very tardy) efforts at fundamental construction. Establishing a National Human Rights Commission is an essential first step.

Starting in 1964, the UN began to pay attention to the question of carrying out the institutionalization that [should] follow the setting down of international human right standards in treaties. Among the four levels [of implementation]—international, regional, nongovernmental (the UN emphasized popular participation from the very beginning; see Article

71 of the UN Charter), and individual state, the most important is obviously the individual state. The UN began in 1978 to more urgently encourage each state to use constitutional or legislative means to establish national human rights commissions [or similar organs]. After the UN General Assembly in 1992 established standards to ensure the independence and effectiveness of national human rights commissions (also known as the Paris Principles), the widespread [appearance of] global and regional organizations and activities [aimed at] promoting [such commissions] further encouraged the rising tide of individual state establishment [of these commissions]. Even in the Asian region, which was filled with [talk of] "Asian values" for a time, [commissions] have already been established in Australia, Philippines, New Zealand, India, Indonesia, Thailand, and Sri Lanka, and South Korea and Japan are in the planning stages.

Although a National Human Rights Commission will only supplement the inadequacies of existing legislative, executive, judicial, and control organs, the necessity of its establishment—especially with respect to Taiwan, which long ago dropped out of the international human rights system—can be seen from its most commonly discussed functions and powers:

1. Investigate human rights cases (especially concerning discrimination) of alleged criminals, and undertake mediation, arbitration, and adjudication. When necessary, it can also assist individuals or groups who have been harmed, or act on behalf of organizations to undertake lawsuits.
2. In accordance with constitutional and international human rights standards, investigate and research domestic existing and draft legislation, and make suggestions for legislative and constitutional revisions, as well as for draft legislation.
3. Plan for national human rights policies, including [participation in] international human rights policies, and aid other governmental organs in establishing procedures and policies that accord with human rights standards.
4. Plan and promote human rights education both in and out of school, including preparatory and continuing education for public servants and professionals like judges, lawyers, police, journalists, and social workers. It should also establish a human rights information center and establish and promote human rights research.

5. Issue national human rights reports both annually and on special human rights topics, and make suggestions for improvement or resolution of human rights problems it has unearthed.

With only a little thought, all can understand that these various points are the fundamental functions needed to promote human rights that our country still lacks, and they can help to resolve the four problematic bottlenecks to improving and protecting human rights that our country faces, as discussed above. Implementing these functions can also begin to raise our country's human rights standards and improve our protective mechanisms toward the level of civilized, international society.

The necessity of establishing a national human rights commission has already been made clear, but there are still two problems that we face.

First, although the UN advocates the establishment of national human rights commissions that suit the political, economic, and cultural conditions of each country, especially in the Declaration and Program of Action from the 1993 Vienna World Human Rights Conference, the UN itself passed the Paris Principles, and in the last twenty years of countries' establishing such commissions, considerable experience has accumulated. If our country is to establish one, we should avoid diverging from certain fundamental principles, so as to keep ourselves from incurring the ridicule of international experts.

1. The legal position, composition, organization, and financing of the National Human Rights Commission should be such as to protect its ability to operate independently and effectively.
2. To ensure its independence, the National Human Rights Commission should be independent of the five governmental branches, as is done in the Philippines. A second-best alternative would be to model it on the Academia Sinica, and put it organizationally under the president's office, but allow it to work independently, without receiving any direction, supervision, or interference from the president.
3. Commissioners should have expertise and experience in the promotion and protection of human rights, and should represent the diversity of civil society, including nongovernmental, professional, and academic organizations.
4. The president and the legislature should each appoint a certain

number of commissioners; their term of office, procedure for appointment and dismissal, active special powers, and passive immunities should all be protected by a formal legal document.

5. The commission must be able to independently and effectively employ people and use other resources; its budget cannot be reduced by the Executive Yuan, though it can be amended during legislative deliberations.

6. The commission should have the right to conduct independent investigations and review materials, and also to subpoena witnesses.

7. After the commission has submitted investigative reports and opinions concerning specially designated human rights matters to the appropriate governmental organs, each such governmental organ must, within a legally specified time limit, produce a report in response.

8. After its establishment, the commission should undertake a comprehensive review of domestic human rights problems, particularly with regard to the human rights environment of weak versus powerful social groups.

9. A minority of states have also established offices for adjudicating human rights issues, either within or in addition to their national human rights commissions. We can also consider this, as a way of reducing the burden on regular courts.

In addition to according with international standards, a second question is: if we are to establish a National Human Rights Commission, what process should we follow?

Since we have already been separated from the international human rights system for a long time, this case is similar to many other new international developments: the great majority of our citizens are unfamiliar with national institutions like a National Human Rights Commission. In addition, not only have many nations already established such commissions, but both the UN and international people's movements have also established standards for such commissions (the former being the Paris Principles, and the [Amnesty International] Principles being an example of the latter). Therefore, when we establish our commission, we must try extremely hard not to drive with our eyes closed and find ourselves in a ditch. We recommend:

1. The public, democratic discussions that have begun in the media, the presidential campaign, and even within the government (for example, in the Control Yuan), should continue.
2. Civil society (including the media) should play its proper role in a democratic society. In addition to [conducting] comparative research into various countries' national human rights commissions and preparing draft laws, it can also convene international conferences, inviting both current and retired foreign commissioners to participate, give us the benefit of their personal experiences, and exchange ideas, in order to ensure that even if our commissioners will not stand out above those [in other nations], at least they will be as good as those in other nations.
3. As for those political parties and governmental offices that have promised to establish a National Human Rights Commission, they ought to proceed with an equally serious attitude to establish special working groups and lay out concrete preparations, legislative plans, and timetables.

Human rights, rule of law, and democracy: we must have them all. Among the three of them, without doubt human rights is the one with the weakest foundation in our country, which has seriously influenced the quality and development of our democracy and rule of law. But human rights is the common moral standard of world society in the twentieth century: it is not just an abstract moral standard, but is a moral standard that had been agreed to in treaties and institutionalized at levels ranging from international, to regional, to nongovernmental, to individual states. Because of this, for our country, the establishment of a National Human Rights Commission simultaneously has important and wide-ranging domestic and international significance. We call on our nation's citizens to join together in seriousness and common concern, and hasten the birth of a National Human Rights Commission.

Further Reading

For other materials on the work to set up a National Human Rights Commission, see http://www.tahr.org.tw.

63

Address by President Chen Shuibian on the Occasion of Establishing the President's Advisory Group on Human Rights (2000)

Chen Shuibian

"Zongtong chuxi 'Zongtong fu renquan zixun xiaozu chengli dahui' zhici" [Address by President Chen Shuibian on the Occasion of Establishing the President's Advisory Group on Human Rights], accessed at: *http://www.oop.gov.tw/1 news/ index.html* (October 24, 2000).

In March 2000, the candidate of the Democratic Progressive Party, Chen Shuibian, won the presidential election in Taiwan. This signified the first transfer of power from the GMD to the political opposition. Chen, a lawyer by profession, has taken a strong interest in human rights issues. In his inaugural address, Chen expressed his commitment to strengthening the human rights regime on the island. He pledged to work for the adoption of the International Bill of Human Rights as domestic law in Taiwan and to support the establishment of an independent National Human Rights Commission; he also extended an invitation to human rights organizations such as Amnesty International to help in the work to protect human rights. This concern for human rights led his office to set up a President's Advisory Group on Human Rights in October of 2000. The group, which is headed by Vice-President Annette Lu, consists of twenty-one persons who have backgrounds in human rights work, including the writer Bo Yang, a former political prisoner, and Professor Mab Huang (see Text 38). The advisory group is divided into six subgroups; their tasks include advising the president on human rights, reviewing existing legislation, and investigating human rights abuses. In addition, the group will work toward establishing a National Human Rights Commission and will generally promote human rights education and human rights awareness at all levels of society.

I feel very honored to chair this meeting today on the occasion of the establishment of the President's Human Rights Advisory Group. First of all, I want to thank our convener, Vice-President Lu, and the members of the Advisory Group, all of whom with sincerity and respect have devoted themselves to studying human rights issues and human rights policies. Let me once again convey my [deepest] respect and gratitude to them all.

When we look back at the whole of [the twentieth] century—from the period of governmental domination, to the period when the idea of people's rights (*minquan*) first was raised, to the period of human rights protection—this value of ours, human rights, is like a mother who has been tormented but remains firm and persistent, and for this we must express our highest respect to all those pioneers who have suffered because of their pursuit of democracy and human rights. As Bo Yang has said: "Past mistakes and evil acts can be understood, tolerated, and forgiven, but should not be forgotten." Those who forget [previous mistakes and evil acts] are likely to repeat their past wrongdoings. Therefore we must explore, record, and reflect, in order to continue to move forward.

Human rights form the core and basis of a constitutional country, and each governmental department is established with the purpose of promoting and protecting people's rights. Therefore we believe that the work of the government is human rights work; each and every government official should be a human rights worker. At the very least we should solemnly face the three dimensions of the human rights issues. This is related to the human rights policy which I raised in my inaugural presidential address on May 20, 2000, and which I will here discuss.

The first dimension concerns human rights consciousness and education. Due to the past authoritarian political system, we are quite deficient in human rights consciousness and human rights education, to say nothing of [progressing toward] the establishment of a human rights research institute. However, it is only when one is first clearly aware of one's own rights that one will fight for their protection and furthermore will not violate other people's rights. Therefore, the fostering of human rights consciousness demands our immediate attention. This includes human rights education at various levels of the school [system], and education and on-the-job training for public functionaries and professionals.

The second dimension concerns human rights standards. The section on people's rights and duties in the second chapter of our constitution has recently been interpreted in a meeting of our Supreme Court, such that the simple articles have been broadened to include space for quite a few human rights. We now need to pay attention to Article 22 of the constitution, which reserves for the people those rights that have not been explicitly stipulated in the constitution. This involves [the question of] international human rights standards. To a great extent, the human rights standard was [laid down and took the form] of international treaties after World War II. Our country has signed or ratified at least eleven different international human rights conventions. We should therefore introduce international human rights standards in order to enrich the second chapter of our constitution, and in particular Article 22, in order to elevate our human rights standards and guideposts. We must not let our current setback in international relations, which for a time has separated us from the UN human rights system, lead us to stand outside the human rights global village.

The third dimension is the mechanism for the promotion and protection of human rights. When we have increased our human rights consciousness through human rights education, and measured up to the international human rights standard, we still will need concrete mechanisms to promote and protect human rights. The purpose of a constitutional state is the promotion and protection of people's rights and welfare. The ordinary legislative, executive, and judicial branches cannot violate this purpose. However, human rights cover a very broad range [of issues] and have many different dimensions, as both the experiences of advanced countries and the recommendations of the UN show. We therefore also need an institution that will be [specially] responsible for human rights work.

On the basis of the above three [dimensions], in my May 20 inaugural speech I raised three policies: the first is to take the most basic international human rights standard, the International Bill of Human Rights, and make it into a domestic law as the Human Rights Bill of the Republic of China; the second is to establish an independent National Human Rights Commission, something which the UN has long advocated; and the third is to invite outstanding international human rights organizations (such as the International Commission of Jurists and Amnesty International) to discuss and assist us in order to push forward human rights in accordance with international standards. I am very happy and grateful to note that among the six subgroups of the advisory group there are three that will specifically focus on research and advisory work on these three policies. Of course, we also earnestly need the assistance of the members of the three other subgroups on other human rights issues.

I am also very happy that [work on establishing] a National Human Rights Commission, to which I have given a high priority, has already entered the phase of [public discussion]. The nongovernmental League for the Promotion of a National Human Rights Commission and members of the Legislative Assembly have both put forward draft bills, and the Executive Yuan is going over these different drafts. During the current [parliamentary] session, the Organic Law of the National Human Rights Commission will be put on the agenda of the Legislative Assembly and discussed. As the president of the Republic of China I am very happy to see this promotion from many different corners and the strong unity of efforts.

My past professional experience as a lawyer has made me aware that human rights protection cannot solely rely on law: the human rights attainments of those in charge of enforcing the law cannot be overlooked. No matter how perfect legal regulations are, they leave room for law enforcement officers to act on their discretion. How this discretion is exercised hinges on law enforcement officers' human rights consciousness and standards. Due to the importance of this I sincerely suggest that Taiwan as soon as possible set up a human rights research center.

In 1930, Jiang Weishui and the Taiwan People's Party that he led began an international and domestic human rights struggle against the Japanese colonial power. During the period of dictatorship, Professor Zhang Foquan's book *Freedom and Human Rights*, which for a period was banned (this was the only human rights work at the time), continued to enlighten several generations of democracy activists. The purpose of recalling these two sages is to remind ourselves that we are duty-bound to continue and develop the human rights tradition, both with respect to Taiwan's own domestic tradition and to that of the international community.

Human rights, rule of law, and democracy are the three pillars of a modern country, none of which we can do without. And protection of human rights is the measurement of whether democracy and rule of law have any real legitimacy. At the end of the twentieth century, under the ferment of humanitarian and democratic ideas, we have completed the task of the peaceful transfer of political power. I sincerely hope that with our joint efforts we can quickly realize our aspirations and make the Republic of China into a country [blessed with] perfect democracy, rule of law, and human rights, so that our mothers will no longer have to shed anguished tears.

Once again I want to thank everyone and wish you good health and all the best!

Further Reading

For Chen Shuibian's inaugural speech, "Taiwan Stands Up: Toward the Dawn of a Rising Era," see http://www.taipeitimes.com/news/2000/05/21. See also the previous text.

Glossary and Index